TO MY CHILDREN
AND THEIR CHILDREN'S CHILDREN

**Afoot & Afield Denver, Boulder, Fort Collins, and Rocky Mountain National Park**

2nd edition 2015

Copyright © 2015 by Alan Apt and Kay Turnbaugh

Cover photos çopyright © 2015 Alan Apt
Interior photos, except where noted, by Alan Apt
Maps and cover design: Scott McGrew
Book design: Andreas Schuller; adapted by Annie Long
Library of Congress Cataloging-in-Publication Data

Apt, Alan, 1948-

  Afoot & afield Denver/Boulder & Colorado's Front Range : a comprehensive hiking guide / by Alan Apt and Kay Turnbaugh. — Second edition.

    pages cm

  ISBN 978-0-89997-755-3 — ISBN 0-89997-755-3

  1. Hiking—Colorado—Denver Metropolitan Area—Guidebooks. 2. Hiking—Colorado—Boulder Region—Guidebooks. 3. Hiking—Colorado—Colorado Springs Region—Guidebooks. 4. Hiking—Colorado—Guidebooks. 5. Colorado—Guidebooks. I. Turnbaugh, Kay. II. Title. III. Title: Afoot and afield Denver/Boulder and Colorado's Front Range.

  GV199.42.C62D436 2015

  796.5109788'83—dc23

                    2015008842

Manufactured in the United States of America

Published by:    🌲 Wilderness Press
                 An imprint of Keen Communications, LLC
                 PO Box 43673
                 Birmingham, AL 35243
                 800-443-7227, fax 205-326-1012
                 info@wildernesspress.com
                 wildernesspress.com

Visit our website for a complete listing of our books and for ordering information.

Distributed by Publishers Group West

*Cover photos, clockwise from top*: Niwot Ridge (see page 145); South Arapaho Trail (see page 162); Sawhill Ponds (see page 98)
*Frontispiece:* Striking rock face from Fowler Trail (see page 101)

**SAFETY NOTICE:** Although Wilderness Press and the author have made every attempt to ensure that the information in this book is accurate at press time, they are not responsible for any loss, damage, injury, or inconvenience that may occur to anyone while using this book. You are responsible for your own safety and health while in the wilderness. The fact that a trail is described in this book does not mean that it will be safe for you. Be aware that trail conditions can change from day to day. Always check local conditions and know your own limitations.

Both near and far mountain ranges are part of the view from the top of South Arapaho Peak.

# Afoot & Afield
2nd edition

# Denver, Boulder, Fort Collins, and Rocky Mountain National Park

## 184 Spectacular Outings in the Colorado Rockies

Alan Apt

with Kay Turnbaugh

 WILDERNESS PRESS .

The trail across Mummy Pass opens up to soaring views of not-so-distant peaks.

Notchtop Mountain rises above Odessa Lake in Rocky Mountain National Park.

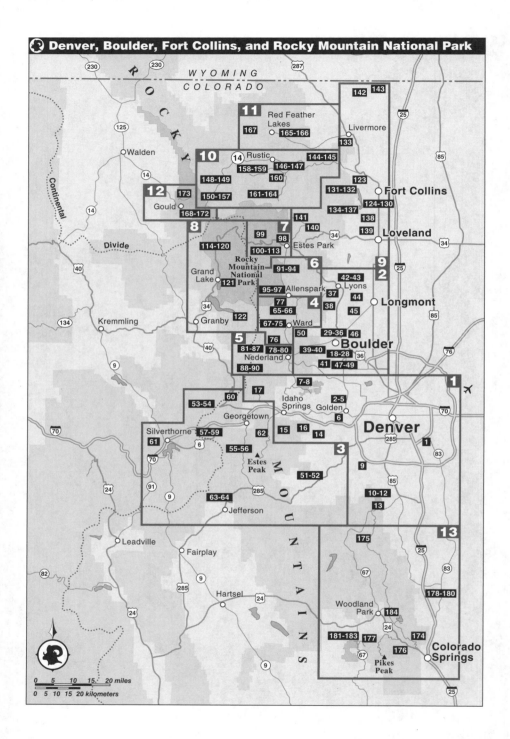

WYOMING
COLORADO

R O C K Y

230   230   287

142   143

125   25

11   Red Feather
Lakes
167   165-166   Livermore   85

Walden   10   14 Rustic   144-145   133

14   158-159   146-147
148-149   160   123
12   173   161-164   131-132   Fort Collins
Gould   150-157   124-130
168-172   134-137   Loveland
8   141   138
7   140   139
99   98   34
114-120   100-113   Estes Park   9
Rocky   91-94   6   2
Mountain   42-43
National   95-97   Lyons   44
Grand   Park   37   Longmont
Lake   121   Allenspark   38   45
34   77   Ward   46
122   65-66   4   29-36
Granby   67-75   50   Boulder
5   76   39-40   18-28   36
81-87   78-80   Nederland   41   47-49
88-90

Continental
Divide
40

Kremmling   134

9

7-8
60   17
53-54   Idaho   2-5
Springs   Golden
Georgetown   15   16   14   Denver
57-59   62
Silverthorne   61   6   285   1
55-56   3   83
Estes   51-52   9
Peak   85
63-64   10-12
Jefferson   13

Leadville   1   70   76

Fairplay   13
82   175   25
9   67   83
285   Hartsel   178-180
24   Woodland
Park   184
M   181-183   177   24   174
O   67   176   Colorado
U   Pikes   Springs
N   Peak
T
A
I
N
S   9

0   5   10   15   20 miles
0   5   10   15  20 kilometers

iv

# Contents

## CHAPTER 3: Denver Area: Mountains. . . . . . . . . . . . . . . . . . . . . .106

### 1–2 Hours From Denver

## CHAPTER 10: Poudre Canyon & Cameron Pass Areas . . . . . . . . . . .286

### *1 Hour or Less From Fort Collins*

### *1.5–3 Hours From Denver-Boulder*

### *1–2 Hours From Fort Collins*

## CHAPTER 11: Red Feather Lakes Area . . . . . . . . . . . . . . . . . .328

### *1 Hour From Fort Collins*

### *2 Hours or More From Denver-Boulder*

# Preface

The Rocky Mountains bisect Colorado almost exactly in half, with plains on the east side and mountains on the west. The urban corridor that also bisects the state sits in the lap of these majestic mountains between their eastern flanks and the plains, an area called the Front Range. Fortunately, there are millions of acres of public lands to explore that have been set aside thanks to taxpayer dollars generously contributed by cities, counties, and the state of Colorado. Add to this the legacy of public lands set aside by the federal government for all to use, and we who live and recreate in the Front Range mountains enjoy millions of acres of priceless places to roam and hopefully pass on to future generations. These are mountains that are well loved and well used. The first edition of this book described 170 trails, enough to keep the average hiker on the trail for decades, and yet it was just a taste of what this area has to offer.

Why write a second edition? The new edition offers much more than the first edition:

- **184 trails,** many of them new
- **70-plus hikes within 1 hour of Denver or Boulder**
- **36 trips to peak summits** (20 mountain summits and 16 foothills summits)
- **94 options for families with children**

- **34 hikes in Rocky Mountain National Park**
- **49 trips to lakes**
- **74 trails good for mountain biking**
- **108 options suitable for winter sports**

Much has changed because of the fires and floods of the past five years. New open-space areas and trails have become available; others have been rerouted or closed, or usage policies have changed. There were a few corrections too. My new coauthor, Kay Turnbaugh, and I have carefully revised the trails from the first edition. We have also added a substantial number of trails to the book that are closer to the Front Range cities, especially Denver, Boulder, and Fort Collins.

The trails have been carefully chosen for ease of access and variety. They range from easy family strolls to challenging summits. If you visit 10 trails per year, you will have almost 20 years of trails to explore and enjoy.

Wherever you live in the Front Range, you are always close to a trailhead that offers an escape from the challenges of yard work or crowded highways. Anyone who wants to revel in the nearby wonderlands of the Colorado Rocky Mountain environment will find something to explore in this book. You don't have to limit your possibilities to hiking—run, bike, kayak, swim, but get out there and enjoy the hills and vales of paradise. This is heaven, and you don't have to wait.

# Acknowledgments

I'd like to thank the many terrific people who accompanied me on these hikes over the years or offered advice: my family—Amy Johnston, Kate Apt, Laura Apt, Ryan Apt, and Jeremiah and Lylah Johnston—and my friends: Gina Apt; Alan Bernhard; Bill Black; Debra Beasly; David Bye; Dan Bowers; Larry and Margie Caswell; Joel Claypool; Nancy DuTeau; Jeff and Catherine Eighmy; Lars and Becky Eisen; Lenny and Susan Epstein; Phil and Joanie Friedman; John Gascoyne; John and Ann Hunt; Alan (former hiking partner) and Linda Stark; Rodney Ley; Ward Luthi; Jim and Shereen Miller; Robin Nielsen; Brendt, Nick, and Paul Orndorff; Joe Piesman; Mike Roggy; Sharon Roggy; Dian Sparling; Jay Stagnone; Jim Welch; and Jerry White. I especially want to thank Nancy Martin, who accompanied me on countless occasions over the last three years.

I also thank John Gascoyne for the excellent job he did producing draft maps for the book.

John Bartholow and Joe Grim provided a wide variety of excellent photos for the book, and I thank them for their valuable contributions. Thanks also to Jeff Eighmy and Alan Stark for photos.

Thanks to Jennifer Ackerfield, at the Colorado State University Herbarium, for her excellent reference on mountain climate zones.

I also want to thank Kay Turnbaugh; her help on this edition was invaluable. It would not have happened without her.

Thanks to the highly competent staff at Wilderness Press: Molly Merkle, who offered great advice and shepherded the book at the press; Amber Kaye Henderson, for doing a marvelous and thorough job during the production process; and Tanya Sylvan, for doing an excellent job on the marketing front. On the publishing front, this book certainly wouldn't have happened without the help of Alan Stark and his virtual literary agency.

Thanks to the many friendly and helpful employees and volunteers of Colorado State Parks, Rocky Mountain National Park, the U.S. Forest Service, the city of Fort Collins, Boulder County, El Paso County, and Larimer County, including Larry Frederick, Diana Barney, Maribeth Higgins, Becky Kelly, Jeff Maugans, Vicki McClure, Dick Putney, and Kristi Wumkres, just to mention a few.

# Introducing the Front Range Area

The recreational options in Colorado are virtually limitless because of the varied terrain and spectacular geology. Ancient uplift created the lofty peaks of the Front Range, including countless mountains over 12,000 feet and Colorado's 54 fourteeners. Glaciers carved the magnificent high mountain valleys and cirques from uplifted highlands and mountains. Rivers carved canyons that tumble down from the rolling 12,000-foot highlands. The rugged backdrop of the Colorado Rockies Front Range starts at the Colorado-Wyoming border and spills south of Colorado Springs. The present mountain range of the Rockies was born nearly 55 million years ago, with the final uplift happening as recently as 10 million to 20 million years ago. Some of the rocks in Rocky Mountain National Park are almost 1 billion years old; 1,750 million, to be more precise. There is evidence of volcanoes, ancient seabeds, and more than one ice age, the last of which ended only 10,000 years ago. The dinosaurs were but a minor event in the geologic drama.

The high mountains contrast sharply with the unexpected gently rolling high plains where Colorado's Front Range cities are located and that seem to stretch forever to the Colorado borders with Nebraska and Kansas. Most visitors are surprised to find the cities residing on the flats. The unexpected gift of the Rockies is their superb foothills zone, where the transition from plains to mountains occurs. In most other states, these foothills would be considered a major mountain range. They could rival the Appalachian Mountains, which are much lower in elevation, though broader. That is to say, the foothills aren't really hills; they are a set of delightful "mountains" unto themselves, as well as gracious and impressive gateways to the true monarchs of the state. The foothills also offer a refreshing landscape—soaring cliffs, scenic canyons, enchanting flora and fauna, and sculpted rock formations of their own, making it easy to stay closer to home and yet escape the urban. The foothills are also easier to enjoy because of their lower elevations.

The foothills zone is familiar to anyone living along the Front Range of Colorado, and some of the lofty "hills" climb up to 9,000 feet. This zone is generally dominated by shrubs such as mountain mahogany, skunk brush, and wild plum, though species composition is highly diverse, and ponderosa and lodgepole pine forests are common. In the north to central portions of the state, these species dominate. Farther south, fragrant juniper becomes more common. This vegetation type is commonly called piñon-juniper woodland. Great expanses of this vegetation type are found throughout southern Colorado. High in the foothills region, forest vegetation becomes more important, and that is where ponderosa and lodgepole pine, and even a spruce and nonnative Russian olive, appear.

The subalpine zone is what many people envision as Colorado vegetation. This zone starts at about 9,000 feet in elevation and covers a vast region in the center of the state. Though it is generally considered a single zone, plant species vary widely. The magical quaking aspen stands occur near the lower boundary of the subalpine. They are typically thought of as being transitional and not long-lived, giving rise to spruce-fir forest after about 75–100 years. Higher in elevation, lodgepole pine replaces aspen as the primary tree species. The most common type of vegetation is the spruce-fir forest. This forest type is present at all altitudes in the subalpine zone and can grow under most conditions. Though not as common as other vegetation types, subalpine wetlands provide important biodiversity as well as habitat for elk and moose. Also interesting are the broad, flat, high-elevation "parks," such as North and South Park between the mountain ranges. These beautiful parks are framed by towering mountain ranges and frequently have short-grass prairie vegetation, contrasting with the spruce-fir forest.

The alpine zone in Colorado begins at about 11,400 feet. Around 11,000-plus feet is what is known as the treeline, the point at which large trees cannot grow. Characterized by long, cold winters and a short growing season, it is challenging for flora, fauna, and humankind. The plants that have adapted to these harsh conditions frequently take on novel growth forms. The contorted growth of the stunted krummholz species is a striking example of one such adaptation. A krummholz, or krumholtz, formation (from German *krumm* meaning "twisted" and *holz* meaning "wood") is a feature of subarctic and subalpine treeline landscapes with low-growing, twisted, dwarf pine trees. Tundra vegetation is frequently dominated by islands of dwarf krummholz trees, expansive stands of shrubs, and a field layer of grasses, shrubs, and cushion plants.

Hiking the trails in this book will give you a chance to experience the varied geology, geography, and stunning beauty of this landscape firsthand.

*Fox kits in the Indian Peaks Wilderness*

# Comfort, Safety, & Etiquette

**M**ost of the adventures in this book do not require special equipment. All you need is a good pair of walking shoes, a willing pair of legs, and a small sense of daring and adventure. The weather in Colorado is, however, always interesting, because it can and does change rapidly and unpredictably. Early fall or late spring blizzards are especially sneaky, as are thunderstorms and weather fronts that can sneak up on you at any time of the day. I have experienced 40- to 50-degree temperature swings, with sun and heat being replaced by wind and freezing hail in a matter of minutes, compliments of a thunderhead mushrooming into the stratosphere, fueled by water from as far away as the Gulf of Mexico and the fires of the sun. It is always wise to be prepared for the unexpected if you are going to wander far. When the weather is in doubt, head back to your car or cabin. Lightning, freezing downpours, and whiteouts have been deadly for many recreationists.

## Surviving in Style: Clothing & Equipment

High fashion standards have not made an impact in the world of hiking, unless you're in the vicinity of Vail or Aspen, where you will likely encounter uniformed tourists who feel that the right clothing labels or styles are essential. Wear what you find comfortable, but be prepared for any kind of weather. If you are dressed appropriately, dramatic temperature drops, unseasonable snow, and high winds can be entertaining. Bundle up and amble down the trail cozy and smug in spite of Mother Nature's

tricks; don't go high and far in only a T-shirt and shorts because hypothermia can be deadly. The first symptom of hypothermia is uncontrollable shivering followed by a loss of coordination and slurred speech (see page 9 for more information). People have died from it in air temperatures in the 40s and 50s—getting caught in a downpour or falling into a lake or stream and then being unable to get warm and dry or even simply dressing inadequately and experiencing dropping temperatures, strong wind, snow, or rain. Taking along extra clothing is very important.

When you pack, imagine hot, sunny, morning weather followed by an afternoon of cold, driving wind and 3 inches of hail. Dress in layers, and avoid cotton altogether if you can; opt instead for moisture-wicking clothing—nylon or synthetic fabrics. Though wool doesn't wick, it'll keep you warmer than cotton would. Carrying a day pack, or at least a fanny pack, is essential. You'll be chilly when you start if it is early, but as you walk you'll warm up nicely. You'll need the pack for peeling off your layers so you don't overheat. If you allow yourself to overheat and sweat, you will be chilled to the bone when you stop, especially if it is fall or spring. When you stop for lunch, you'll cool off quickly and want to put some layers back on. Cotton is not recommended because when it gets wet or damp it does not dry out easily, nor does it insulate you against the cold.

On your average day, long-sleeved and short-sleeved shirts made of polypropylene, or synthetic composite, are recommended. Then a backup of wool sweaters or fleece with a water- and windproof jacket will work. I suggest an outer layer that is breathable and waterproof. Start off dressed so that you feel a little chilly, and keep a warmer layer in your pack for when you stop for lunch or a snack break. You'll warm up quickly. If jeans are your only option, be sure to pack a waterproof poncho or pants to put over them in case it rains or snows. I prefer pants with zip-off legs for maximum flexibility.

Headgear is especially important; you will lose most of your body heat through your head if it isn't covered with a good wool or polypropylene hat. A hat or cap that shields you from the strong, high-altitude sun is essential. Sunglasses are a must to avoid damaging sun and radiation. Goggles will also be important for an enjoyable experience in hail, snow, or high wind. Mittens are generally warmer than gloves, but whichever you bring should be waterproof, if possible. If you don't have waterproof mittens or gloves, bring an extra pair in case they get soaked. An extra pair of dry socks is a good idea too.

## Boots

A good pair of well-designed walking or running shoes or waterproof boots will make your trip much more enjoyable. Lightweight, low-cut summer hiking boots or running shoes that are somewhat waterproof can work well if you're planning a very short trek close to your car. Surviving a thunderous downpour in comfort will require more. I highly recommend that you use high-top, waterproof boots and polypropylene (synthetic composite) or composite wool socks if you're going very high or very far. Getting caught in a cold rain and hailstorm with soaking wet feet far from civilization can be bone chilling. A pair of short gaiters is also a good idea to keep the rocks, stickers, mud, and early- or late-season snow out of your boots and away from your Achilles tendons that are supposed to carry you a long, pain-free, happy-go-lucky way.

Every pound on your feet, however, is equivalent to two on your back, so footgear weight is a consideration. Light- to mid-weight boot options are almost unlimited; many are lightweight like running shoes with their technology and cushioning and the additional protection of high-tech fibers, including waterproof fabric such as Gore-Tex. With a good coating of snow sealant or other waterproofing treatments, leather boots—though old technology and somewhat heavier—can be as waterproof or more so than synthetic boots. It is wise to waterproof all boots according to the manufacturer's recommendations before going on an all-day or multiday trip because you'll likely be rained on. The disadvantage of some lightweight boots and shoes is that they offer less support for heavy backpacks and protection from the elements. Try to imagine how your footgear will feel after an all-day hike when you are bounding downhill on a rocky trail with weary feet and legs.

## I've Got Blisters on Me Feet!

Blisters can ruin the day for you and your friends and family, cutting short an excursion. Regardless of the boots or shoes you decide to wear, break them in for a couple of weeks, at a minimum, before you wear them on a long day hike or a backpacking trip. The leather or fabric adjusts and conforms to your toes, heels, and ankles as you wear them the first few times. Wearing them at home or on short jaunts around town will also tell you if they fit comfortably—something you cannot determine in a store.

Cover potential hot spots on your heels, toes, or ankles with Moleskin, duct tape, or adhesive bandages, especially if you are wearing new boots. It is always a good idea to apply Moleskin or duct tape to your heels before you begin hiking to prevent blistering. When you feel a hot spot, don't wait until it becomes a blister to cover it up. Stop immediately and attend to it to avoid injury that could ruin your trek.

Avoid cotton socks to keep from getting cold feet if your socks get soaked. Polypropylene and wool are much better insulators. Polypropylene socks also wick sweat to some degree. The primary advantage of cotton is it can keep your feet cooler, but thin synthetic socks can do that as well.

When you hike, get into a good rhythm not unlike cross-country skiing or skating. Establishing a steady rhythm is much more enjoyable and easier on the body than lots of sprints and stops and starts.

If, after all of the above, you still get a blister, it is medically advisable to break it. Then clean and disinfect it, and cover it with an adhesive bandage, duct tape, or Moleskin until it heals.

## The Advantages of Trekking Poles

Many avid hikers do not use trekking poles, but I find them very useful, particularly when I go off-trail or on a steep slope. When traversing downhill, I especially like the extra stability and power of using cross-country ski poles or a pair of the modern, shock-absorbent trekking poles. Some people see poles as an unnecessary appendage. The choice is yours. If you have cross-country ski poles, they work fine for hiking as long as they aren't too long. They are really only necessary when you are planning to climb or descend very steep slopes. Even then, you can survive without them, though you may be much more likely to do a face-plant.

I enjoy using poles when descending because they take pounds of pressure off your knees. That is a major asset of poles for hiking, particularly if you have had knee, hip, or ankle problems or if you are carrying a heavy backpack. Using poles also gets more of your body involved and provides an upper body workout that can burn more fat if that's a secondary goal.

Don't use poles that are too long, though, or you will stress your elbows. Your arms should be bent at 90 degrees when you use the poles. If someone in your party thinks your use of poles is humorous, have them walk in front of you and motivate them with a few carefully placed, supportive prods.

## Food & Water

Take plenty of food and drink. Also take water, at least 2 liters if you plan a multi-hour walk; assume a rate of 1 liter or quart per hour on very hot days when exercising strenuously. Bring easy-to-access snacks such as energy bars or trail mix. You'll burn lots of energy and calories hiking uphill; some people estimate that a hiker can burn up to 800 calories per hour. Eating something with a little fat in it will also help keep you warm. Because of the extreme conditions they experience, Arctic explorers often eat large quantities of butter, lard, or blubber, but you would probably prefer chocolate. Bring extra food in case of an

*Colorado Mountain Club hikers on the Mule Deer Trail (see page 35)*

emergency, and ask your companions to bring enough for themselves as well.

Much has been made of the new high-protein diets and foods for exercise. Though eating something that contains protein along with carbohydrates will work well, carbohydrates are still the key ingredients for energy. You don't have to overeat, however, because excess calories from either carbohydrates or protein will simply be stored as fat. Exercising aerobically for longer than 40 minutes will cause your body to use fat stores as energy. If you don't want to deplete your glycogen (the fuel your muscles use) supply and want to stay as fresh as possible, have a small snack about once an hour or add a sports drink mixture or fruit juice to your water. Also try to exercise at an aerobic pace (a pace at which you are not out of breath), so you won't accumulate lactic acid, which will give you sore muscles. Always include some extra high-calorie food for emergencies.

As mentioned, drink plenty of water, but don't drink directly from mountain streams and lakes. Though crystal clear and inviting, the bodies of water are not creature-free. The coldness of mountain water does not purify it; a parasite called giardia actually thrives in cold water. If you want to drink from streams and lakes, then take along a water filter or purification system or water-purifying tablets. Without tablets or a filtering system, water must be boiled for 10 minutes to kill giardia. Drinking tainted water can cause all of the following symptoms: diarrhea, nausea, cramping, fever, foul belching or gas, chills, and weight loss (contracting giardia is not a good diet strategy). These symptoms might not manifest themselves until a week or two after you drink the tainted water. To prevent them, take along lots of water from home or the right equipment, and know how to use it.

## Here Comes the Sun

The harmful effects of the sun are magnified at high altitudes, so cover up and avoid direct sunlight between the hours of 10 a.m. and 2 p.m. Even on a cloudy day, you can end up with a terrible sunburn. Use a sunscreen with a sun protection factor, or SPF, of at least 15, and be sure to reapply it frequently. Sunburns can set the stage for skin cancer, and this is coming from a former sun worshipper. Your friendly dermatologist will tell you that there is no such thing as a healthy tan. Excess sun also adversely affects the immune system.

## Things That Bite

An assortment of wild beasts can be found in the Colorado woods. The least trustworthy is usually on two legs, but the most likely to affect you are insects. Most of the animals that live in the forest would prefer not to encounter you at close quarters, nor would they find you as appetizing as their normal gourmet fare. They are wild animals, not tame, so keep your distance. The exceptions are mosquitoes and ticks, who want very badly to dine on your blood. Mosquitoes can carry West Nile virus, a nasty bug that can cause flulike symptoms, partial paralysis, and even death. Ticks can carry Rocky Mountain spotted fever, a multiweek experience that is not enjoyable. You can avoid ticks by using repellents, wearing long-sleeved shirts and pants, and checking your warm and fuzzy body parts frequently during and after your hike.

Insect repellent works well for mosquitoes—the higher the DEET content the better. A new alternative to repellents containing DEET is products containing picaridin, which doesn't dissolve plastic, as DEET does, and smells better. Lemon of eucalyptus is more fragrant than picaridin and DEET but is not quite as effective or as long lasting.

Some people feel that DEET has a negative impact on skin, but there is no scientific evidence to support this when products containing it are used within the manufacturer's guidelines. It's prudent to select the lowest concentration effective for the amount of time spent outdoors and apply it just once a day—it isn't water soluble and lasts up to 8 hours. Don't use products that combine DEET with sunscreen because you will likely need to reapply them for effective sun protection. Apply DEET on clothing when possible and sparingly on exposed skin; do not use under clothing. Don't use it on the areas around the eyes and mouth, on cuts or wounds, or on the hands of young children. Wash treated skin with soap and water and treated clothing after returning indoors. Avoid spraying in enclosed areas, and don't use it near food.

Larger carnivorous residents of the forests such as mountain lions, bears, and bobcats will generally avoid people if given the choice. They would much rather have normal, tastier diets of squirrels and other rodents. Mountain lions rarely attack or approach people, but if one does approach you for a lunch or dinner date, stand tall, open your jacket so you appear larger, yell convincingly that you are big and bad, and don't run. Keep your children and pets close by because mountain lions see them as potential snacks.

Snakes, and rattlesnakes in particular, have been given a bad reputation. You don't want to spend time with one, nor do they want to spend time with you. They will try to avoid you, and they are slow movers. Just try to encourage one to move off-trail; it doesn't happen quickly. Unless you are in literal striking distance, you are in no danger. Their sizzling rattle doesn't mean they want to chew on you; they are simply warning you to back off. If the snake is in vegetation, throw some small rocks or sticks at it and make some noise, and it will slither away. If you are bitten, your life is only at risk if you have a severe allergic reaction. Stay calm, slowly walk to your car, and have someone drive you to a hospital. Dogs and small children are at more risk from snake bites, though unlikely to die; you should seek immediate medical care for them. Rattlesnakes are rare at higher elevations but common in foothills areas.

## Safety Measures & Checklist

Do not hike alone; go with a companion, and let others know where you will be going and when you will be coming back. Watch for trail markers and be very aware of your surroundings. Extra clothing is essential, not optional. Extra food and water is also necessary because cold temperatures and exercise will increase your caloric needs. Staying warm by dressing in layers of warm synthetic or wool clothing is the best way to prevent hypothermia. Wear sunblock and protect your eyes with ultraviolet-rated sunglasses. UV radiation is much more intense at higher elevations, and snow and water reflect the rays, making it even more intense. Avoid severe sunburns and snow blindness by being prepared. Use extreme caution whenever crossing streams—they are almost always stronger and deeper than they appear. Consult this clothing and equipment checklist before heading out on a trip:

- Wind- and waterproof outer coat or shell
- Extra fleece or wool clothing, polypropylene long underwear, and extra socks
- Warm hat, face mask, or balaclava
- Warm, waterproof mittens or gloves
- Space blanket, tarp, or garbage bags big enough to crawl into
- Hand- and foot-warmer gel packets if you get cold easily
- UV-rated sunglasses and goggles, and a ski mask
- Prescription glasses or extra contacts
- Sunscreen (SPF 15 or higher)
- Extra food and water and water purification tablets
- First-aid kit
- Knife
- Waterproof matches, lighter, and candle
- Map and compass or GPS unit
- Headlamp or flashlight with spare batteries
- Ice ax and ski or trekking poles
- Insect repellent
- Mirror for signaling or a whistle
- Cell phone (Sometimes there is coverage, but frequently there is not.)
- Camera (for evidence of the fun you had!)

## Effects of Altitude

If you live in Colorado and are accustomed to exerting yourself in the high country, then you have nothing to fear. If you or your companions, however, rarely venture above 5,000 feet, then recognize your potential limitations at higher elevations. Keep in mind that altitude's effects are unpredictable, especially for those who are visiting from sea level. If you have visitors who have just arrived from a lower elevation, give them at least two days to acclimate before venturing above 5,000 feet. If you live at 5,000 feet, you need less time to adjust to higher altitudes. Taking 250 milligrams of the prescription medication acetazolamide (Diamox) twice daily for two days before going to higher elevations and for the first two days you are at altitude will also help. Don't take it if you don't need it, and as always, check the possible side effects before taking any medication.

Above 8,000 feet, plan easy adventures until you determine how well everyone acclimates. Physical conditioning can ease the impact but doesn't prevent altitude sickness. It is risky to drink a lot of alcoholic beverages the evening before or during a high-country adventure. Alcohol's impact is enhanced at altitude; plus, the dehydration and oxygen deprivation alcohol consumption will cause is likely to give you a headache. Alcohol will slow your metabolism and make you feel colder on a chilly day, not warmer. Wait until you're back at camp or lower elevations to enjoy your favorite alcoholic beverages.

Drinking a lot of water before and during high-altitude exercise is a good preventive measure, though not foolproof. Your body needs as much as 8 quarts of water per day if the weather is hot and your exertion strenuous. You will need a minimum of 2 quarts or liters per person for an all-day excursion to avoid headaches. Take along some headache remedies, such as aspirin, and nausea medication (some people feel that Tums have ingredients that can prevent the effects of altitude) just in case. One benefit of aspirin, if your stomach tolerates it, is thinner blood, which can carry more oxygen to your brain and help you avoid an altitude headache. Whatever you choose, take it with food to avoid stomach upset. Altitude and elevation gain definitely slow you down. Assume at least 1 hour per mile or per 1,000 feet of elevation gain if you aren't well conditioned.

The most common symptoms of altitude sickness, which can last a couple days, are severe headaches, nausea, loss of appetite, insomnia or poor sleep with strange dreams, lethargy, and a warm, flushed face. Resting, hiking at lower elevations, eating lightly, and drinking more liquids can help. Avoid taking barbiturates because they can aggravate the illness.

The most serious illness caused by altitude is high-altitude pulmonary edema (HAPE), which occurs when fluid collects in the lungs. Symptoms include difficulty breathing, a severe headache with incoherence, staggering, and a persistent hacking cough. If you or anyone in your party experiences these symptoms, they should be taken to a lower altitude immediately and see a physician as soon as possible. High-altitude cerebral edema (HACE), which occurs when your brain swells because fluid collects in it, is very serious; the symptoms include severe headache, delirium, and loss of consciousness. This is a rare condition but does occur.

When traveling to higher altitudes, some people, most often women, experience swelling of the face, hands, and feet, with a weight gain of as much as 12 pounds. It is uncomfortable but harmless and will subside after returning to lower elevations. Though the cause is unknown, the condition can be treated with a low-salt diet and diuretics.

Nosebleeds are more common at higher elevations because of the very dry air. Staying hydrated and avoiding getting a cold (good luck) are the best ways to avoid them. The most effective way to stop a nosebleed is to gently pinch the nose shut for 5 minutes.

## Weather & Road Conditions

High mountain weather can and does change rapidly and severely. Some of the most violent weather occurs after clear blue-sky mornings with no hint of rain or thunderstorms. Be prepared for the unexpected. Dramatic temperature swings are common year-round. In the early 20th century, Colorado miners were known to say of the weather, "There are only two seasons in the mountains: winter and the Fourth of July." Mountain weather can produce 90°F temperatures and snow or hail in the same place on the same day. It's wise to plan to be on your way down by 11 a.m. or noon at the latest; most thunderstorms occur by midday, though they can happen earlier.

Colorado has one of the highest numbers of reported lightning strike deaths in the United States, second only to Florida. The climate tends to produce highly volatile weather at high altitudes; we scrape much closer to the jet stream than most of the country. This doesn't mean you have to be afraid to venture up next to the clouds on our soaring summits; many people at lower elevations are struck while mowing the grass, playing golf, or playing softball. (No, drinking beer doesn't have anything to do with attracting lightning.) It does mean that you should get below treeline as quickly as you can when you hear the roll of thunder or see dark clouds forming near your route. Watch for gathering cumulus clouds and the characteristic anvil shape that signals the dramatic uplift of moisture into the stratosphere and its impending return journey to the ground you are walking on, accompanied by the thunderbolts of Zeus. As mentioned, it also means you should get an early start on your hike if you want to avoid thunderstorms so that you can have a leisurely stroll back to the trailhead. Assume a thunderstorm will occur on the trail by noon on most summer days, especially warm ones, and plan accordingly. The warmer the temperature, the more likely there is enough energy for a thunderstorm. I generally like to turn around by 11:30 a.m. during thunderstorm season, which is June–August.

It is always a good idea to check road or trail conditions after major storms in the spring or fall, especially mountain passes, to make sure they are still open. To get statewide road condition reports, call 877-315-7623 or visit **coloradodot.info.** Call 303-275-5360 or 303-371-1080 for Denver/Boulder weather and snow conditions, 303-639-1111 for Denver road conditions, and 719-520-0020 for Colorado Springs roads.

## Symptoms of Hypothermia

Hypothermia, which occurs when your body's core temperature drops below 98.6°F, is a serious and sometimes fatal condition that can severely impair the brain and muscles. If someone dresses inadequately or falls into a lake or stream, stop immediately and take steps to get them dry and warm. Preventing hypothermia is much wiser than waiting until the situation becomes life threatening. Some symptoms of this condition include: uncontrollable shivering, slurred or slow speech, fuzzy thinking, poor memory, incoherence, lack of coordination causing stumbling or vertigo, and extreme fatigue or sleepiness. If you observe any of these symptoms, take immediate action to warm the individual. Stop and use your emergency supplies to make a fire and provide warm liquids, or wrap the individual in additional warm clothing and see if you can get them to move around enough to warm them up.

## Trail Etiquette

"THIS LAND IS YOUR LAND, THIS LAND IS MY LAND . . . "          —Woody Guthrie

Wilderness is the poetry of the physical world—untrammeled, pristine, and invaluable. There are few places on our small planet that have not been paved, plowed, built upon, sold off, or developed. Public wilderness is a limited and vanishing commodity; roads and all that they bring are not. Please let your elected officials know that you value wilderness for hiking, camping, fishing, hunting, and other low-impact pursuits and want it to be around and freely available for future generations of family and friends.

Public land is not owned by the government. It is land that we, the public, own that the government protects and keeps for us. This ownership comes with the opportunity for "re-creation" of the body and soul and the responsibility of care and maintenance. Many of the areas described in this book are wilderness areas and require extra precautions and work to prevent the deterioration of the wilderness experience. We should all try to apply the Leave No Trace philosophy to the use of all public lands so that we can all enjoy them without the negative impacts that heavy use can exact. The National Outdoor Leadership School (also known as NOLS) developed these basic principles:

- Avoid building a fire; bring a lightweight stove and extra clothing for cooking and warmth. Enjoy a candle instead of a fire. Where fires are permitted, use them only for emergencies and don't scar large rocks, overhangs, or trees. Use only down or dead wood and do not snap branches off of live trees. Minimize campfire impacts.
- Pack out whatever you pack in. Don't burn trash; pack it out. If you see unburned trash, pack it out.
- Dismantle structures and cover latrine pits.
- Get as far off the trail as possible when you have to urinate. Use toilet paper or wipes sparingly, and pack them out or bury them at least 9–12 inches deep. Dispose of human waste at least 200 feet from the trail or water sources. Use bare ground for burial or pack out human waste. Use backcountry toilets whenever they are available.
- Know the risks and regulations of the area you are visiting. Visit the backcountry in small groups. Try to avoid popular areas in times of high use.

- Be considerate of others. Be respectful of wildlife—don't get too close, and control your pets.
- Wear clothing and use equipment that is natural hued unless it is hunting season, though bright colors would make it easier to find you if you get lost.
- Repackage food into reusable containers that won't leak.
- Do not remove trees, plants, rocks, or historical artifacts; they belong to everyone.
- Stay at least 200 feet from wildlife forage or watering areas. Camp at least 200 feet from the trail, water sources, and muddy areas. Save the water, trail, and vegetation from damage.
- Stay on trails unless you are hunting or fishing or have a unique destination that requires it. Shortcuts cause erosion and resource damage.

## Friends of the Forest

You can help maintain our forests and have a great time by volunteering with the U.S. Forest Service or the National Park Service, as well as city and county open lands agencies. Check at your local Forest Service office or Rocky Mountain National Park for opportunities. The Fort Collins/Roosevelt/Arapaho U.S. Forest Service office sponsors a summer group called the Poudre Wilderness Rangers and a winter group called the Nordic Rangers. There are also the Diamond Peaks Mountain Bike and Ski Patrols. A variety of nonprofit organizations offer hiking and other outdoor activities, as well as volunteer opportunities, such as the Rocky Mountain Nature Association, Colorado Mountain Club, Sierra Club, and more. For contact information and their locations, see the appendix of organizations. Please consider contributing to or joining organizations that make a difference in preserving and enhancing outdoor recreation and the environment.

# Using This Book

This book includes everything from mountain climbs to easy strolls and wheelchair-accessible trails. Frequently, long, demanding hikes include a short segment at the beginning that can be easy and enjoyable for the less ambitious. So don't immediately rule out a hike if it includes climbing a mountain; the first mile or so could be quite easy and scenic.

A safe estimate for travel time is 1 hour per mile, or slower when going uphill at higher altitudes, unless you are exceptionally fit and acclimated. Add time for every 1,000 feet to be gained. If you are very fit and acclimated, your pace could be 20–30 minutes per mile. If the trail is fairly level and you live at 5,000 feet or above and exercise regularly, then you can safely estimate 30 minutes per mile. Of course, the more you stop, the longer it will take you to hike the trail; fitness and experience levels and trail and weather conditions all have a significant impact on the amount of time it takes a particular person to negotiate a particular trail. Conditions vary, and your hiking time could double or even triple if you become caught in a severe storm that includes heavy rain, hail, or lightning. If

*Hikers on the Montgomery Pass Trail (see page 311)*

novices are along, it is wise to have reasonable ambitions and monitor for potential blisters or fading energy levels. Use your watch to judge time out and back. Be conservative—you don't want to end up far from your car or cabin in the dark.

Conditions can vary dramatically and unpredictably. Trails that are normally relatively easy to negotiate can become challenging in major rainstorms or late spring or early fall snow squalls, but conditions can vary greatly at any time of the year. Spring conditions can make a short jaunt exhausting because of wet, snowy, or slippery trails. One of my recent late fall hiking trips had some of the most variable conditions I have seen—all on the same trail. The south-facing slopes were bare, while the north-facing slopes were frozen and slick. And the part of the loop I faced last required the most work to avoid landing on my posterior. Needless to say it made for an interesting day that required twice the expenditure of energy I had expected.

## Your First Adventure

Be conservative your first time out and emphasize enjoyment, not goals. Don't be like my friend "the Bear," who always lives on the edge and pushes himself or his friends beyond reasonable limits. He usually ignores weather forecasts, gets a late start, and insists on going off-trail and straight uphill at a rapid pace. In fact, I've even seen him go charging off into the wilderness late in the day only to become engulfed by thunderstorms well above treeline. Don't be a "Bear." Pick a short, easy round-trip that will be an enjoyable half-day jaunt. That will give you a chance to see how your body will react on any given day. Have a good time and don't expect too much of anyone, including yourself.

## Great for Kids

Within some trail descriptions, you'll notice "Great for Kids" boxes; these designate

trails or trail segments that are appropriate for more relaxed family outings and children of all ages. They are often part of a longer, more challenging hike, but I have highlighted the portion that works best for a laid-back stroll so that families may find a suitable hike. These trail sections include opportunities for scenery, picnics, and a bit of exercise without major effort.

## Capsulized Summaries

Each trip entry includes a capsule summary, highlights, directions to the starting point, and the full description of the trail itself. The capsule summary at the beginning includes distance, difficulty rating, elevation information, trail uses, governing agency, recommended maps, location of nearby facilities, and any special notes.

DISTANCE

All distances listed have been cross-checked with multiple source maps, many of which are contradictory, so the mileage is a very close estimate. The mileages given are round-trip.

DIFFICULTY

All trips include a difficulty rating. Many trips have a range because you can always opt for traveling only a portion of the trail and thereby turn a moderate or challenging trail into an easy one. Many of the trails offer multiple options because even a short out-and-back trip has a nice outdoor experience with pleasing scenery. Your primary goal is to do what is enjoyable to you at the optimal pace for you and your companions.

The difficulty ratings in this book are generally on par with those given by the U.S. Forest Service. It is assumed that people using this book are reasonably fit and physically active or have been medically cleared for physical activity at altitudes above 5,000 feet. If you have been leading a sedentary lifestyle and decide to start hiking, check in with a health care professional to make sure you're ready for strenuous activity.

**EASY**  Most of these trails are appropriate for beginners who have never hiked. The number of steep sections and the overall elevation gains are limited. To truly enjoy one of these treks, you should be physically active and exercising at least two times per week for at least 20 minutes per session. The ratings assume that you have determined that you are able to handle the elevated heart rate and lack of oxygen at higher elevations. It also assumes you won't attempt the entire route but will cover what you can while still having fun and will turn around before you are exhausted. Decide how long you want to be out before you go. Then time your outbound trip and estimate how long it will take to return to the trailhead to avoid exceeding your comfort range. The physically active young will generally, but not always, have a negligible advantage over an equally active "mature" adult.

**MODERATE**  These trails include several steep sections and require a longer, more sustained effort. You will enjoy trails rated as moderate if you have a somewhat higher level of fitness. This doesn't mean you have to be a serious athlete. It just means that you are physically active and exercise 20–40 minutes at least three times per week. You can, of course, choose to challenge yourself if you aren't currently at the "enjoyable" fitness level.

**CHALLENGING/DIFFICULT**  Trails rated as challenging assume a high level of fitness to successfully enjoy them, and the experience to survive under the possibility of rapidly changing weather conditions. These trails will have many steep sections, which require sustained climbing. You should be challenging yourself with almost daily exercise if you want to enjoy this kind of all-day, strenuous trek to the mountaintops. You should also have good route-finding skills and bring and know how to use a topographic map and compass and even perhaps a GPS unit.

ELEVATION

This is the elevation gain to reach the high point or summit on a particular trip. It does not include possible elevation gains to get back to the trailhead. A rolling trail will require uphill climbs on the return, which are not included in this figure. In cases where it is relevant, the starting elevation is listed as well so that you know what general elevation range a particular hike covers.

TRAIL USE

While all of the trails are suitable for hiking, some are also good for backpacking, camping, fishing, horseback riding, motorized recreation, mountain biking, paddling, road biking, rock climbing, or running, all of which I generally note. I point out which trails are accessible for wheelchair users and whether a trip is great for families hiking with kids or has an option that is appropriate for such groups, which is covered in a sidebar in the actual trip description.

Dogs are allowed in all national forests and Bureau of Land Management areas and most state, county, and city parks and open spaces. Within the summary information for the individual trails, I mention whether they are allowed. They usually have to be leashed to protect them from the wildlife and the wildlife from them. They are not allowed on trails in national parks, like Rocky Mountain National Park. Though dogs are allowed on many trails, it is often easier to leave them at home. If you do bring them, carry plastic bags to clean up after them if they leave waste on the trail. Be sure to control your pets at all times. Some dogs are too friendly or aggressive, and many people are intimidated by dogs, especially when they're barking or growling.

AGENCY

The name of the governing local, state, or national agency that you can contact for information is included; their contact information is listed in the appendixes.

## MAPS

Maps by Latitude 40° or in the National Geographic Trails Illustrated series covering Colorado are generally the recommended maps. If you are mountaineering, you should purchase the appropriate U.S. Geological Survey topographical map for the area you will be visiting.

## FACILITIES

Any nearby facilities, such as restrooms or restaurants, are pointed out here, whether they're at a trailhead or perhaps a nearby visitor center.

## NOTES

This section covers regulations for areas where dogs are prohibited or restricted, fees, or other special information that you'll want to know before you go to the trailhead.

## HIGHLIGHTS

This is a brief overview of the trail and the main sights you will encounter.

## DIRECTIONS

The driving directions provided are generally from the closest city or town. In some cases, driving times or distances from larger metropolitan areas are provided.

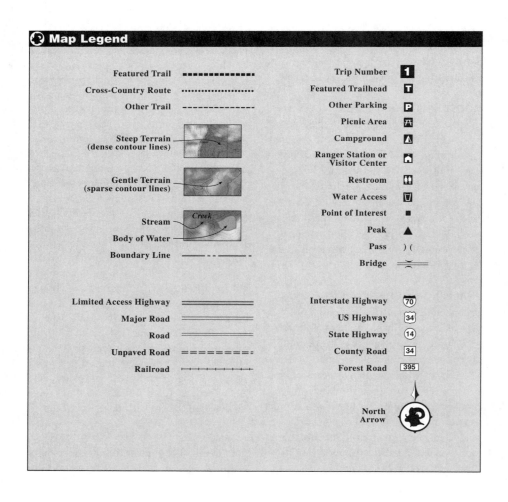

# OVERVIEW OF HIKES

| HIKE NUMBER | HIKE NAME | DISTANCE (miles) | DIFFICULTY | ELEVATION GAIN (feet) | DOGS ALLOWED | GREAT FOR KIDS | MOUNTAIN BIKING | HORSEBACK RIDING | TRAIL CONFIGURATION |
|---|---|---|---|---|---|---|---|---|---|
| **CHAPTER 1: DENVER AREA: PLAINS & FOOTHILLS** *Less Than 1 Hour From Denver* | | | | | | | | | |
| 1 | Cherry Creek State Park | Over 28 | Easy | 300 | dog | kids | biking | horseback | out-and-back or loop |
| 2 | White Ranch: Belcher Hill Trail | 8 | Moderate–Challenging | 1,700 | dog | | biking | horseback | out-and-back |
| 3 | White Ranch: West Access Trails | Up to 10 | Moderate | 1,500 | dog | | biking | horseback | out-and-back |
| 4 | North Table Mountain | 3.2 or 7.4 | Moderate | 480 | dog | | biking | horseback | out-and-back or loop |
| 5 | Mount Galbraith | 4.2 | Moderate | 1,100 | dog | | | | loop |
| 6 | Lookout Mountain: Beaver Brook Trail | Up to 9.9 | Moderate | 1,700 | dog | | biking | | out-and-back |
| 7 | Coyote & Mule Deer Trails | 8 | Easy | 600 | dog | | biking | | loop |
| 8 | Raccoon Trail | 2.5 | Easy–Moderate | 500 | dog | | biking | | loop |
| 9 | South Valley Park: Coyote Song Trail | Up to 3.2 | Easy | 300 | dog | | biking | | balloon |
| 10 | Fountain Valley Trail | 2.2 | Easy | 200 | dog | | | | balloon |
| 11 | Carpenter Peak | 2.2–6.4 | Easy–Moderate | 900 | | kids | | | out-and-back |
| 12 | Willow Creek & South Rim Trails | 1.4 or 4.4 | Easy–Moderate | 300 | | kids | | | loop |
| 13 | Ringtail Trail | 12.2–16 | Moderate–Challenging | 1,500 | | | biking | horseback | out-and-back |
| 14 | Elk Meadow Park: Meadow View Trail | 4.4 or 6 | Easy | 600 | dog | | biking | | loop or out-and-back |
| 15 | Chief Mountain | 4.5 | Moderate | 900 | dog | kids | | | out-and-back |
| 16 | Beaver Brook Watershed Trail | 5.2 | Easy | 300 | dog | | biking | horseback | out-and-back |
| 17 | St. Mary's Glacier & James Peak | 2–8 | Moderate–Challenging | 270–3,250 | dog | | | | out-and-back |
| **CHAPTER 2: BOULDER AREA: PLAINS & FOOTHILLS** *Less Than 1 Hour From Boulder* | | | | | | | | | |
| 18 | Mesa Trail: Northern Segment | Up to 14 | Moderate | 800–1,000 | dog | | | | out-and-back |
| 19 | Mesa Trail: Southern Segment | Up to 13.5 | Moderate | 900 | dog | | | | out-and-back |
| 20 | Royal Arch Trail | 3.3 | Moderate | 800 | dog | | | | out-and-back |
| 21 | Gregory Canyon: Crown Rock & Flagstaff Mountain Summit | 2–5.4 | Moderate | 400–1,100 | dog | | | | out-and-back |
| 22 | Range View & Ute Trails | 1.6 | Easy | 200 | dog | kids | biking | | loop |
| 23 | Tenderfoot Trail | 2.5 | Moderate | 400 | dog | kids | | | loop |
| 24 | Green Mountain Summit: West | 2.8 | Easy–Moderate | 650 | dog | kids | | | out-and-back |
| 25 | Marshall Mesa East: Marshall Valley, Community Ditch, & Cowdrey Draw Trails | 4 | Easy | 300 | dog | kids | biking | | out-and-back |

Neg. = Negligible elevation gain    Ω = loop    O = balloon    8 = figure eight    ➚ = out-and-back    ➚ = point to point

**CHAPTER 2: BOULDER AREA: PLAINS & FOOTHILLS**  *Less Than 1 Hour From Boulder (cont'd)*

| HIKE NUMBER | HIKE NAME | DISTANCE (miles) | DIFFICULTY | ELEVATION GAIN (feet) | DOGS ALLOWED | GREAT FOR KIDS | MOUNTAIN BIKING | HORSEBACK RIDING | TRAIL CONFIGURATION |
|---|---|---|---|---|---|---|---|---|---|
| 26 | Marshall Mesa West: Marshall Valley, Community Ditch, Greenbelt Plateau, Flatirons Vista, & Spring Brook Trails | 13.4 | Moderate–Difficult | 700 | 🐕 | 👪 | ⬤ | 🐎 | Loop |
| 27 | Doudy Draw Trail | Up to 6.2 | Easy | 300 | 🐕 | | ⬤ | 🐎 | Out-and-back |
| 28 | South Boulder Creek Trail | Up to 8 | Easy | | 🐕 | | ⬤ | | Out-and-back |
| 29 | Cobalt, Sage, & Eagle Loop | 5.4 | Easy | 100 | 🐕 | 👪 | ⬤ | | Loop |
| 30 | Left Hand Reservoir | 6–11.4 | Easy–Moderate | 200 | 🐕 | | ⬤ | | Out-and-back |
| 31 | Foothills Trail: Hogback Ridge Loop | 2.3 | Moderate | 300 | 🐕 | | ⬤ | | Loop |
| 32 | Foothills Trail: Wonderland Lake Loop | Up to 7.9 | Easy | Neg. | 🐕 | | ⬤ | | Figure 8 |
| 33 | Anne U. White Trail | 3 | Easy | 200 | 🐕 | 👪 | | 🐎 | Out-and-back |
| 34 | Gunbarrel Farm: White Rocks Trail | 9.4 | Easy–Moderate | 340 | 🐕 | 👪 | ⬤ | | Out-and-back |
| 35 | Red Rocks Trail & Mount Sanitas | 1.5 or 3.3 | Easy or Moderate | 200 or 1,345 | 🐕 | 👪 | ⬤ | | Loop |
| 36 | Betasso Preserve | 3.3–6.5 | Moderate–Difficult (hike); Easy–Moderate (mtn. bike) | 200 | 🐕 | | ⬤ | 🐎 | Loop |
| 37 | Hall Ranch | 9.4–13.4 | Moderate | 1,220 | | 👪 | ⬤ | | Loop |
| 38 | Heil Valley Ranch | 8 | Easy–Moderate | 600 | | 👪 | ⬤ | | Loop |
| 39 | Walker Ranch: Meyers Homestead Trail | 5.2 | Easy | 750 | 🐕 | | ⬤ | 🐎 | Out-and-back |
| 40 | Walker Ranch | Up to 7.6 | Moderate (hike); Challenging (mtn. bike) | 1,500 | 🐕 | | ⬤ | 🐎 | Loop |
| 41 | Eldorado Canyon Trail | Up to 9 | Moderate–Challenging | 1,000 | 🐕 | 👪 | | 🐎 | Out-and-back |
| 42 | Rabbit Mountain: Little Thompson Overlook Trail | 3 | Easy–Moderate | 500 | 🐕 | 👪 | ⬤ | 🐎 | Out-and-back |
| 43 | Rabbit Mountain: Eagle Wind Trail | 4.3 | Easy–Moderate | 380 | 🐕 | | ⬤ | 🐎 | Loop |
| 44 | Pella Crossing | Up to 3 | Easy | Neg. | 🐕 | 👪 | ⬤ | 🐎 | Figure 8 |
| 45 | Lagerman Reservoir | 1.6 | Easy | Neg. | 🐕 | 👪 | ⬤ | | Loop |
| 46 | Walden & Sawhill Ponds | 2.6 | Easy | Neg. | 🐕 | | ⬤ | | Loop |
| 47 | Streamside Trail | 0.6 | Easy | Neg. | 🐕 | 👪 | ⬤ | | Out-and-back |
| 48 | Fowler Trail | 1.4–4 | Easy | 100 | 🐕 | | | | Out-and-back |
| 49 | Rattlesnake Gulch Trail | 2.8–3.6 | Moderate | 800–1,200 | 🐕 | | ⬤ | | Loop |
| 50 | Switzerland Trail | 3–5 | Easy | 300 | 🐕 | | ⬤ | | Out-and-back |

| HIKE NUMBER | HIKE NAME | DISTANCE (miles) | DIFFICULTY | ELEVATION GAIN (feet) | DOGS ALLOWED | GREAT FOR KIDS | MOUNTAIN BIKING | HORSEBACK RIDING | TRAIL CONFIGURATION |
|---|---|---|---|---|---|---|---|---|---|
| **CHAPTER 3: DENVER AREA: MOUNTAINS** *1–2 Hours From Denver* | | | | | | | | | |
| 51 | Davis Ponds Loop | 2.2 | Easy | 100 | 🐕 | 🧑 | | | loop |
| 52 | Staunton Ranch Trail | 6.6 | Easy–Moderate | 500 | 🐕 | | ⊕ | 🐎 | out-and-back |
| 53 | Butler Gulch | Up to 5 | Moderate | 1,200 | 🐕 | | ⊕ | | out-and-back |
| 54 | Jones Pass | Up to 8 | Easy–Challenging | 2,600 | 🐕 | | ⊕ | | out-and-back |
| 55 | Guanella Pass: Silver Dollar Lake Trail | Up to 3 | Easy | 1,000 | 🐕 | 🧑 | ⊕ | | out-and-back |
| 56 | Mount Bierstadt | 6 | Difficult | 2,930 | 🐕 | 🧑 | | | out-and-back |
| 57 | Loveland Pass Ridgetop | 2 | Moderate | 1,110 | 🐕 | 🧑 | | | out-and-back |
| 58 | Grizzly Peak | 5 | Moderate | 1,635 | 🐕 | | | | out-and-back |
| 59 | Mount Sniktau | 4 | Moderate | 1,635 | 🐕 | 🧑 | | | out-and-back |
| 60 | Eastside Trail: Continental Divide Trail | 4 | Moderate | 1,000 | 🐕 | | | 🐎 | out-and-back |
| 61 | Lily Pad Lake | 3 | Easy | 200 | 🐕 | 🧑 | | | out-and-back |
| 62 | Echo Lake & Chicago Lakes Trails | 0.8–9 | Easy–Moderate | 50–1,500 | 🐕 | 🧑 | | | out-and-back |
| 63 | Colorado Trail: West Branch | Up to 11.4 | Easy–Moderate | 800 | 🐕 | 🧑 | ⊕ | | out-and-back |
| 64 | Colorado Trail: East Branch | Up to 14.4 | Easy–Moderate | 800 | 🐕 | | ⊕ | | out-and-back |
| **CHAPTER 4: BOULDER AREA: INDIAN PEAKS** *1 Hour or Less From Boulder* | | | | | | | | | |
| 65 | Middle Saint Vrain | Up to 9 | Easy | 1,000 | 🐕 | 🧑 | ⊕ | | point to point |
| 66 | Coney Flats Trail & Beaver Reservoir | Up to 7.5 | Easy–Moderate | 600 | | | ⊕ | | balloon |
| 67 | Sourdough Trail: Red Rock Trailhead to Beaver Reservoir | Up to 15 | Easy–Moderate | 860 | 🐕 | | ⊕ | | point to point |
| 68 | Sourdough Trail: Red Rock Trailhead to Rainbow Lakes | 11 | Moderate | 900 | 🐕 | | ⊕ | | point to point |
| 69 | Red Rock Lake | 100 yards | Easy | Neg. | | 🧑 | | | out-and-back |
| 70 | Mitchell Lake & Blue Lake Trail | 1–4.8 | Easy–Moderate | 400–1,000 | | 🧑 | | | out-and-back |
| 71 | Long Lake & Jean Lunning Trails | 0.6–1.5 | Easy | 100 | | 🧑 | | | out-and-back or loop |
| 72 | Lake Isabelle | 3 | Easy | 300 | | | | | out-and-back |
| 73 | Pawnee Pass & Peak | 9.8–11 | Moderate–Challenging | 2,500 –2,445 | | | | | out-and-back |
| 74 | Mount Audubon | 7 | Moderate–Difficult | 2,730 | 🐕 | | | | out-and-back |
| 75 | Niwot Ridge | 8 | Moderate | 1,750 or 2,750 | 🐕 | | ⊕ | | out-and-back |
| 76 | Rainbow Lakes & Arapaho Glacier Overlook Trails | 2–12 | Easy–Moderate | 300–1,100 | | 🧑 | | | out-and-back |
| 77 | Saint Vrain Mountain & Meadow Mountain | 8 | Moderate | 3,190 or 2,660 | | | | | point to point |

Neg. = Negligible elevation gain   = loop   = balloon  **8** = figure eight   = out-and-back   = point to point

| HIKE NUMBER | HIKE NAME | DISTANCE (miles) | DIFFICULTY | ELEVATION GAIN (feet) | DOGS ALLOWED | GREAT FOR KIDS | MOUNTAIN BIKING | HORSEBACK RIDING | TRAIL CONFIGURATION |
|---|---|---|---|---|---|---|---|---|---|
| **CHAPTER 5: NEDERLAND AREA** *35 Minutes From Boulder* | *1–2 Hours From Denver* | | | | | | | | |
| 78 | Caribou Ranch Open Space | 3.1 | Easy | 200 | | ✓ | | 🐎 | loop |
| 79 | Mud Lake Open Space | 2.6 | Easy | 200 | 🐕 | ✓ | ⚙ | 🐎 | figure-8 |
| 80 | West Magnolia Trails | Up to 8 | Easy | 400 | 🐕 | | ⚙ | 🐎 | loop |
| 81 | Arapaho Pass | Up to 25.5 | Easy–Difficult | 1,090 | 🐕 | | | | out-and-back |
| 82 | South Arapaho Peak | 8 | Difficult | 3,250 | 🐕 | | | | out-and-back |
| 83 | Diamond Lake | 5 | Moderate | 850 | 🐕 | | | | out-and-back |
| 84 | Lost Lake | 5.2 | Easy–Moderate | 700 | 🐕 | ✓ | | | out-and-back |
| 85 | Woodland Lake Trail | 10 | Moderate | 300 | 🐕 | | | | out-and-back |
| 86 | Devil's Thumb Lake Trail | 13 | Difficult | 2,200 | 🐕 | | | | out-and-back |
| 87 | King, Betty, & Bob Lakes Trail | Up to 13 | Difficult | Up to 2,895 | 🐕 | | | | out-and-back |
| 88 | Rogers Pass Lake/Heart Lake | 8.2 | Moderate–Challenging | 2,100 | 🐕 | | | | out-and-back |
| 89 | Forest Lakes | Up to 7 | Moderate | Up to 1,620 | 🐕 | | | | out-and-back |
| 90 | Crater Lakes | 6 | Moderate | 2,000 | 🐕 | | | | out-and-back |
| **CHAPTER 6: ROCKY MOUNTAIN NATIONAL PARK: SOUTH** *1 Hour From Denver-Boulder-Fort Collins* | | | | | | | | | |
| 91 | Lily Lake & Ridge | 1 | Easy | 200 | | ✓ | | | loop |
| 92 | Estes Cone | 6.4 | Moderate | 1,500 | | | | | out-and-back |
| 93 | Chasm Lake | 8.4 | Moderate | 2,300 | | | | | out-and-back |
| 94 | Twin Sisters Peaks | 7.5 | Moderate | Up to 2,320 | | | | | out-and-back |
| 95 | Copeland Falls | 2.6 | Easy | 195 | | ✓ | | | out-and-back |
| 96 | Allenspark & Finch Lake Trails to Wild Basin | Up to 13.4 | Easy–Moderate | 950 | | | | | out-and-back |
| 97 | Calypso Cascades, Ouzel Falls, & Ouzel Lake | 3.6–13 | Easy–Moderate | 880–2,500 | | ✓ | | | out-and-back |
| **CHAPTER 7: ROCKY MOUNTAIN NATIONAL PARK: EAST** *1–2 Hours From Denver-Boulder-Fort Collins* | | | | | | | | | |
| 98 | McGregor Ranch | Up to 10 | Easy–Moderate | 1,130 | | ✓ | | | loop or out-and-back |
| 99 | Horseshoe Park | 2 | Easy | 100 | | ✓ | | | loop |
| 100 | Deer Mountain | 2–6 | Easy–Moderate | 1,075 | | ✓ | | | out-and-back |
| 101 | Cub Lake | Up to 4.6 | Easy | 550 | | | | | out-and-back |
| 102 | Fern Lake | Up to 7.6 | Moderate | 1,380 | | ✓ | | | out-and-back |
| 103 | Mill Creek Basin | Up to 6.4 | Easy–Moderate | 1,000 | | | | | out-and-back or |
| 104 | Glacier Basin & Sprague Lake | Up to 3 | Easy | 200 | | ✓ | | | loop |
| 105 | Around Bear Lake | 1 | Easy | Neg. | | ✓ | | | loop |

# OVERVIEW OF HIKES

| HIKE NUMBER | HIKE NAME | DISTANCE (miles) | DIFFICULTY | ELEVATION GAIN (feet) | DOGS ALLOWED | GREAT FOR KIDS | MOUNTAIN BIKING | HORSEBACK RIDING | TRAIL CONFIGURATION |
|---|---|---|---|---|---|---|---|---|---|
| **CHAPTER 7: ROCKY MOUNTAIN NATIONAL PARK: EAST** *1–2 Hours From Denver-Boulder-Fort Collins (cont'd)* | | | | | | | | | |
| 106 | Nymph, Dream, & Emerald Lakes | 3.6 | Easy | 605 | | ♀♂ | | | ↗ |
| 107 | Flattop Mountain & Hallet Peak | Up to 10 | Moderate–Challenging | 2,850 | | ♀♂ | | | ↗ |
| 108 | Odessa Lake | 8.2 | Moderate | 1,205 | | | | | ↗ |
| 109 | Bierstadt Lake | 2.8 | Easy | 565 | | ♀♂ | | | ↗ |
| 110 | Alberta Falls | 1 | Easy | 100 | | ♀♂ | | | ↗ |
| 111 | The Loch | 5.4 | Moderate | 940 | | | | | ↗ |
| 112 | Jewel & Black Lakes | 10 | Moderate | 1,400 | | | | | ↗ |
| 113 | North Longs Peak Trail | Up to 13.6 | Moderate; varies | 2,840 | | | | | ↗ |
| **CHAPTER 8: ROCKY MOUNTAIN NATIONAL PARK: WEST** *2–3 Hours From Denver-Boulder-Fort Collins* | | | | | | | | | |
| 114 | Ute Trail | Up to 8 | Easy–Challenging | 300–3,000 | | ♀♂ | | | ↗ or ↗ |
| 115 | Toll Memorial Trail | 1 | Easy | 260 | | ♀♂ | | | ↗ |
| 116 | Mount Ida | 11.5 | Moderate | 2,110 | | | | | ↗ |
| 117 | Colorado River Trail to Little Yellowstone Canyon | 7.4–10 | Easy–Moderate | 350–990 | | ♀♂ | | | ↗ |
| 118 | Baker Gulch to Mount Nimbus & Mount Status | 7.4–12.8 | Moderate–Challenging | 2,305–3,755 | | | | | ↗ |
| 119 | Holzwarth Trout Lodge | 1 | Easy | Neg. | | ♀♂ | | | ↗ |
| 120 | Coyote Valley Trail | 1 | Easy | Neg. | | ♀♂ | | | ↗ |
| 121 | East Inlet & Thunder Lake Trails | 0.3–11 | Easy–Challenging | 80–3,600 | | ♀♂ | | | ↗ |
| 122 | Monarch Lake to Brainard Lake | 0.7–15 | Easy–Challenging | Up to 4,000 | | ♀♂ | | | ↗ or ↗ |
| **CHAPTER 9: FORT COLLINS AREA** *30 Minutes–1 Hour From Fort Collins* \| *1–2 Hours From Denver-Boulder* | | | | | | | | | |
| 123 | Poudre River Trail | 16.8 | Easy | Neg. | 🐕 | | ⚙ | 🏇 | ↗ |
| 124 | Spring Creek Trail | Up to 13.1 | Easy | 200 | 🐕 | ♀♂ | ⚙ | | ↗ |
| 125 | Cathy Fromme Prairie Natural Area | 4.6 | Easy | 100 | 🐕 | ♀♂ | ⚙ | | ↗ |
| 126 | Foothills Trail: Pineridge Natural Area | Up to 5 | Easy | Neg. | 🐕 | ♀♂ | ⚙ | | ↗ |
| 127 | Foothills Trail: Maxwell Natural Area | Up to 4 | Easy–Moderate | 300 | 🐕 | | ⚙ | | ↗ |
| 128 | Foothills Trail: Centennial Drive | 4.4–8 | Moderate | 200 or 600 | 🐕 | ♀♂ | ⚙ | | ↗ |
| 129 | Foothills Trail: Reservoir Ridge Natural Area | 5 | Easy | 300 | 🐕 | | ⚙ | 🏇 | ◯ |
| 130 | Reservoir Road/Centennial Drive | Up to 8 | Challenging | 600 | 🐕 | | ⚙ | | ◯ |
| 131 | Arthur's Rock Trail | 3.4 | Moderate | 1,280 | 🐕 | ♀♂ | | | ◯ or ↗ |

Neg. = Negligible elevation gain    = loop   ◯ = balloon   8 = figure eight    = out-and-back   ↗ = point to point

| Hike Number | Hike Name | Distance (miles) | Difficulty | Elevation Gain (feet) | Dogs Allowed | Great for Kids | Mountain Biking | Horseback Riding | Trail Configuration |
|---|---|---|---|---|---|---|---|---|---|
| **CHAPTER 9: FORT COLLINS AREA** — *30 Minutes–1 Hour From Fort Collins* \| *1–2 Hours From Denver-Boulder (cont'd)* | | | | | | | | | |
| 132 | East & West Valley Trails | 7 | Easy | 300 | 🐾 | | ⊕ | | loop |
| 133 | Eagle's Nest Open Space | Up to 5 | Easy | 200 | 🐾 | 👤 | | | figure-8 |
| 134 | Bobcat Ridge Natural Area: Ginny Trail | Up to 6 | Moderate (hike); Challenging (mtn. bike) | 1,500 | | 👤 | ⊕ | | loop or out-and-back |
| 135 | Bobcat Ridge Natural Area: Valley Loop Trail | Up to 4.5 | Easy | 200 | | 👤 | ⊕ | 🐴 | loop |
| 136 | Horsetooth Rock Trail | 7 | Moderate | 1,500 | 🐾 | 👤 | ⊕ | | out-and-back |
| 137 | Horsetooth Falls & Connecting to Lory State Park | 2–9 | Easy–Moderate | 300–600 | 🐾 | 👤 | ⊕ | | out-and-back or out-and-back |
| 138 | Coyote Ridge Trail | 3–7 | Moderate | 500 | 🐾 | 👤 | ⊕ | 🐴 | out-and-back |
| 139 | Devil's Backbone, Blue Sky, & Coyote Ridge Trails | Up to 16 | Easy–Moderate | 400 | 🐾 | 👤 | ⊕ | | out-and-back |
| 140 | Crosier Mountain Trail | Up to 10 | Moderate | 2,800 | 🐾 | | | 🐴 | out-and-back |
| 141 | North Fork Trail | Up to 14.8 | Easy–Challenging | 1,800 | 🐾 | | | | out-and-back |
| 142 | Red Mountain Open Space: Bent Rock Trail | 2 | Easy | 200 | | 👤 | | | loop |
| 143 | Soapstone Prairie Natural Area: Towhee–Overlook Trail | 3 | Easy–Moderate | 300 | | 👤 | | | loop |
| **CHAPTER 10: POUDRE CANYON & CAMERON PASS AREAS** — *1 Hour or Less From Fort Collins* \| *1.5–3 Hours From Denver-Boulder* | | | | | | | | | |
| 144 | Grey Rock | 7 | Moderate | 2,000 | 🐾 | 👤 | | | loop |
| 145 | Hewlett Gulch | 6 | Easy | 570 | 🐾 | | ⊕ | 🐴 | out-and-back |
| 146 | Mount McConnel | 4+ | Easy–Moderate | 1,240 | 🐾 | | | | loop |
| 147 | Lower Dadd Gulch | 7 | Easy–Moderate | 1,800 | 🐾 | | ⊕ | 🐴 | out-and-back |
| 148 | The Big South | 6–16 | Easy–Moderate | 960 | 🐾 | | | | out-and-back |
| ***1–2 Hours From Fort Collins*** | | | | | | | | | |
| 149 | Green Ridge Trail | 200 yards to 4.5 | Easy | 495 | 🐾 | 👤 | ⊕ | | out-and-back |
| 150 | Sawmill Creek Trail to Clark Peak | 3–10 | Moderate–Challenging | 3,500 | 🐾 | | | | out-and-back |
| 151 | Blue Lake Trail to Clark Peak | 2.5–12.4 | Easy–Challenging | 1,300–3,450 | 🐾 | 👤 | | | out-and-back |
| 152 | Trap Park Trail to Iron Mountain | 4.5–5.6 | Moderate–Challenging | 1,300–2,745 | 🐾 | 👤 | | | out-and-back |
| 153 | Zimmerman Lake Trail | 2.2–3 | Easy | 475 | 🐾 | 👤 | | | loop or out-and-back |
| 154 | Meadows Trail | 10 | Moderate | 1,295 | 🐾 | 👤 | | | out-and-back |
| 155 | Montgomery Pass | 3.5 | Moderate+ | 1,000 | 🐾 | | | | out-and-back |
| 156 | Diamond Peaks | 4 | Moderate+ | 1,505 | 🐾 | | | | out-and-back or out-and-back |
| 157 | Cameron Connection | 3 | Easy | 200 | 🐾 | | | | out-and-back |
| 158 | Brown's Lake | 8 | Moderate | 1,500 | 🐾 | 👤 | | | out-and-back |

# OVERVIEW OF HIKES

| HIKE NUMBER | HIKE NAME | DISTANCE (miles) | DIFFICULTY | ELEVATION GAIN (feet) | DOGS ALLOWED | GREAT FOR KIDS | MOUNTAIN BIKING | HORSEBACK RIDING | TRAIL CONFIGURATION |
|---|---|---|---|---|---|---|---|---|---|
| **CHAPTER 10: POUDRE CANYON & CAMERON PASS AREA** *1–2 Hours From Fort Collins (cont'd)* | | | | | | | | | |
| 159 | Mineral Springs Gulch to Prospect Mountain | 4 | Easy | 500 | 🐾 | 🚶 | | | ↗ |
| 160 | Fish Creek & Little Beaver Creek Trails | 4–10 | Easy–Moderate | 600 | 🐾 | 🚶 | | 🐴 | ↗ |
| 161 | Stormy Peaks Trail | Up to 10 | Easy–Challenging | 3,120 | 🐾 | 🚶 | | | ↗ |
| 162 | Emmaline Lake Trail | Up to 10 | Easy–Moderate+ | 2,100 | 🐾 | 🚶 | ⊛ | | ↗ |
| 163 | Mummy Pass Trail | Up to 14 | Moderate+ | 2,500 | 🐾 | 🚶 | ⊛ | | ↗ |
| 164 | Signal Mountain Trail | Up to 10 | Moderate+ | 2,700 | 🐾 | | | | ↗ |
| **CHAPTER 11: RED FEATHER LAKES AREA** *1 Hour From Fort Collins* \| *2 Hours or More From Denver-Boulder* | | | | | | | | | |
| 165 | Mount Margaret Trail | 7–8 | Easy | 255 | 🐾 | | ⊛ | 🐴 | 8 |
| 166 | Dowdy Lake Trail | 1.5 | Easy | Neg. | 🐾 | 🚶 | | | Ω |
| 167 | North Lone Pine Trails to Mount Baldy Overlook | 5–12 | Moderate | 400 | 🐾 | | | | ↗ |
| **CHAPTER 12: COLORADO STATE FOREST** *2 Hours or More From Fort Collins* \|<br>*3.5–4 Hours From Denver-Boulder* | | | | | | | | | |
| 168 | Michigan Ditch Trail to Thunder Pass Trail | 2–12 | Easy or Difficult | 100 or 1,060 | 🐾 | 🚶 | ⊛ | | ↗ or ↗ |
| 169 | Lake Agnes Trail | 1.6 | Easy | 500 | 🐾 | 🚶 | | | O |
| 170 | Seven Utes Mountain Trail | 2–8 | Moderate | 2,000 | 🐾 | 🚶 | | | ↗ |
| 171 | Mount Mahler Trail | 10 | Moderate–Challenging | 3,000 | 🐾 | | | | ↗ |
| 172 | Ranger Lakes Trail | Up to 10 | Moderate+ | 610 | 🐾 | | ⊛ | | ↗ |
| 173 | Grass Creek Yurt Trail | 5.3–10 | Easy–Moderate | 400 | 🐾 | | ⊛ | | Ω or ↗ |
| **CHAPTER 13: COLORADO SPRINGS AREA** *1 Hour or Less From Colorado Springs* \|<br>*2 Hours or More From Denver* | | | | | | | | | |
| 174 | Garden of the Gods | Up to 5 | Easy | 300 | 🐾 | 🚶 | ⊛ | | Ω |
| 175 | Devil's Head Lookout | 1.5 | Moderate | 940 | 🐾 | | | | ↗ |
| 176 | Pikes Peak | 10.7–21.4 | Challenging | 3,400–7,500 | 🐾 | | | | ↗ or ↗ |
| 177 | The Crags | 1–3.5 | Easy–Moderate | 800 | 🐾 | 🚶 | | | ↗ or Ω |
| 178 | What in a Name Trail | 0.25 | Easy | Neg. | | 🚶 | | | ↗ |
| 179 | West Loop | 2 | Easy | 100–200 | 🐾 | 🚶 | | | Ω |
| 180 | North Loop | 2.3 | Easy | Neg. | 🐾 | 🚶 | | | Ω |
| 181 | Peak View, Elk Meadow, & Livery Loop | 4 | Moderate | 400 | 🐾 | 🚶 | | | Ω |
| 182 | Homestead Trail | 2.5 | Easy–Moderate | 300 | 🐾 | | | | Ω |
| 183 | Revenuer's Ridge | 2.3 | Easy | 100 | 🐾 | 🚶 | | | ↗ |
| 184 | Rainbow Gulch Trail to Rampart Reservoir | 3–11 | Easy | 200 | 🐾 | 🚶 | ⊛ | | ↗ or Ω |

Neg. = Negligible elevation gain   Ω = loop   O = balloon   8 = figure eight   ↗ = out-and-back   ↗ = point to point

*Chief Mountain Trail (see page 48)*

# chapter 1

# Denver Area: Plains & Foothills

## LESS THAN 1 HOUR FROM DENVER

**D**enver's urban renewal has made it one of the better US cities in which to live. What many nonresidents don't know is how rich and varied the nearby natural resources and wonders are. Because of space constraints, I am covering only a tiny slice of the many trails, parks, and open spaces that abound in the Denver metropolitan area. You don't have to suffer the traffic on I-70 to enjoy spectacular scenery or escape from urbanity on your bike or with your hiking boots. The following natural wonders are short and easy commutes you can enjoy without a deadline. The hiking, biking, and horseback riding are exceptional, with options ranging from easy strolls to heart-pumping challenges but always with time to stop, listen, relax, breathe deeply, and recreate.

## Cherry Creek State Park

So close to Denver, this popular state park is a rewarding escape from the next-door urban landscape. Play next to the reservoir, hike trails, or watch wildlife—this park has something for everyone.

## Jefferson County Parks

Jefferson County continues to expand its parks and trails and now has 28 parks and 227 miles of trails. Seven of those trails that offer a taste of the backcountry right on the city's doorstep are described here. They may be close to the city, but when you visit you can see wildflowers, wildlife, creeks, mountain vistas, and panoramic bird's-eye views of the plains and cities.

## White Ranch Park

Part of Jefferson County Open Space, this inspirational place is a former ranch that is draped on the side of 8,000-foot-high foothills mountains and offers pretty meadows, a pristine canyon, rock formations, and buttes. These mountains are the equal of many stretches of mountain ranges like the Appalachian Mountains but are mere foothills to the Rockies. The park is almost 4,400 acres and was the home of nomadic Ute and Arapaho Indians until settler James Bond set up a ranch on the property in 1865. The Whites purchased it in 1913 and maintained a ranch on it until 1969, when it was purchased as open space.

There are 18 miles of trails to hike, bike, or horse around on. Either start all of your hikes uphill from the northeast access point at 6,300 feet, or drive 10 miles up to the west access at 7,700 feet and begin your hikes going downhill and finishing uphill. The open space includes two camping options: Sawmill Hikers Camp and Sourdough Springs Equestrian Camp.

## Golden Gate Canyon State Park

Though for many years this state park was not well developed for recreation, it has finally been expanded into a hidden treasure that is easily accessible from the Denver, Boulder, and Golden areas. The park offers mellow trails for hiking and biking, abundant wildflowers, spectacular vistas of the Front Range, and almost every type of tree seen in the mountains of Colorado.

## Roxborough State Park

A geological spectacle, Roxborough State Park is one of the Front Range's most dramatic displays of monumental rocks and is part of the same 300-million-year-old Fountain Formation visible in Boulder's Flatirons and the Garden of the Gods in Colorado Springs. A wide variety of Earth's geologic history is displayed within Roxborough's relatively small confines, including 280-million-year-old, light-colored Lyons sandstone; 260-million-year-old Morrison rocks colored by ancient blue-green algae; and 1-billion-year-old granite on Carpenter Peak. The Dakota hogback sandstone, deposited a mere 100 million years ago, when Colorado was covered by a sea that stretched from the Arctic to the Gulf of Mexico, is also a highlight. It is a patch of serenity near a growing swell of suburban development and foothills subdivisions. Trails range from easy to moderate, and an informative visitor center is open year-round. Bikes and horses are not allowed on the trails inside the park. (Also check out nearby Douglas County and Pike National Forest trails that connect with the park.)

## Indian Creek Trailhead & Campground: Pike National Forest

South of Roxborough State Park, this little-known and little-used area has lots of recreational trail assets. This trailhead offers two major options for hiking, biking, or horseback riding: the Indian Creek Trail north to the Elk Valley Trail and the Ringtail Trail north to the Swallowtail and Sharptail Trails.

## 1  Cherry Creek State Park

| | |
|---|---|
| **Distance** | More than 28 miles of trails, with many easy adventures |
| **Difficulty** | Easy |
| **Elevation Gain** | 300' (starting at 5,600') |
| **Trail Use** | Hiking, biking, horseback riding, great for kids, leashed dogs OK on some trails |
| **Agency** | Cherry Creek State Park |
| **Map(s)** | *Cherry Creek State Park* |
| **Facilities** | Restrooms throughout |
| **Note(s)** | State park pass required, daily or annual. The park gets crowded on summer weekends, so arrive early or visit on weekdays if you want to avoid the masses. |

**HIGHLIGHTS** This popular state park that is very close to Denver offers a wide variety of trails you can use to escape from urbanity while enjoying water views with a Rocky Mountain backdrop. You can hike or pedal next to the 850-acre, scenic reservoir or enjoy trails that feature streams, wetlands, waterfowl, and other wildlife. There are 22 trails, and only two are more than 2 miles long, making the park ideal for family outings. There is a swim beach, so you can take a dip and cool off on warm days. The Smoky Hill and Cherry Creek Trails are next to the reservoir. The Pipeline, Wetland, and North and South Connector Trails are more secluded. A dog park allows off-leash dogs.

**DIRECTIONS** Go 1 mile south of I-225 on Parker Road at Lehigh to 4201 S. Parker Road. You can take Light Rail from downtown Denver to the park.

Rather than describing one trail, I am going to give overviews of several options.

If you like hiking or biking with water views, then the separate, paved Smoky Hill and Cherry Creek Trails are good options. Both trails are wheelchair accessible. Each trail will provide you with an easy 3.2- to 4-mile out-and-back next to the water, with lots of picnic options. Leashed pets are allowed on both trails. The Cherry Creek Trail continues for a total of 4.75 miles and

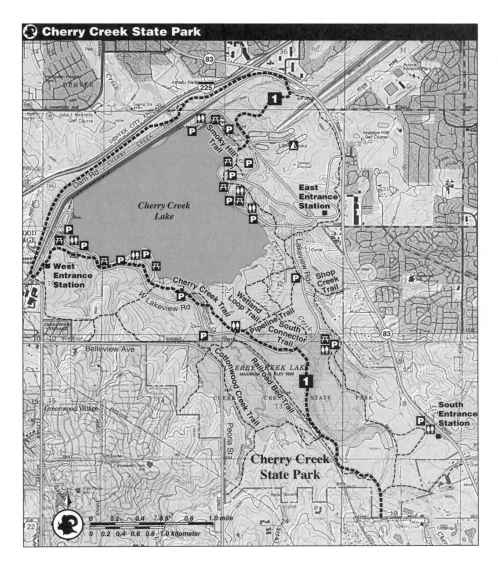

is part of a regional trail system that you can take all the way to Franktown, near Castle Rock. So you can use it for a more ambitious bike or hike. You can access the Cherry Creek Trail from Cherry Creek Crossing or the Cottonwood Creek Trailhead. You can access the Smoky Hill Trail from Dixon Grove, the swim beach, or its own parking lot.

The Wetland Loop Trail is a good choice for ambling through a wetland with wildlife. The South Connector Trail goes north along

Cherry Creek to the Pipeline Trail and the Wetland Loop, while the North Connector and Pipeline Trails offer direct connections to the loop. Each of these trails is around 0.5 mile, while the Wetland Loop is 1.22 miles, giving you just over 2 miles round-trip. Pets are not allowed on these unpaved trails. You can access the trails from the Cottonwood Creek or Shop Creek Trailheads.

If you want a short singletrack trail for mountain biking, try the Railroad Bed

Trail. It is a little more than 2 miles long, and you can reach it from the Cottonwood Creek Trailhead. The Cottonwood Creek Trail runs next to a pretty, restored riparian area with good wildlife habitat. Leashed pets are allowed on both trails.

## 2 White Ranch: Belcher Hill Trail

JEFFERSON COUNTY PARKS

| | |
|---|---|
| **Distance** | 8 miles, out-and-back |
| **Difficulty** | Moderate (hiking), challenging (mountain biking) |
| **Elevation Gain** | 1,700' (starting at 6,300') |
| **Trail Use** | Hiking, mountain biking, horseback riding, leashed dogs OK |
| **Agency** | White Ranch Park, Jefferson County Parks |
| **Map(s)** | Jefferson County Parks *White Ranch Park*; Trails Illustrated *Boulder & Golden* |
| **Facilities** | Restrooms, backcountry camping |

**HIGHLIGHTS** This most challenging and rocky of the ranch trails offers a great workout and excellent views of the buttes, mountains, plains, and canyon. It starts in a suburban setting that is distracting for the first couple of miles but then opens up to the magic panorama of these high foothills. You can access easier trails along the way (Whippletree, Longhorn, Maverick, and Sawmill) and make the trek much easier and shorter if you wish. It is popular with very fit mountain bikers and is as wide as the former ranch road it once was.

**DIRECTIONS** The trailhead is 1.7 miles north of Golden on CO 93. Turn west on 56th Avenue, and go 1 mile; then turn right onto Pine Ridge Road. Look for the parking lot on the right (north) side of the road. This is a much closer access point for the open space, and you'll see several estates on the way.

Travel north from the parking lot and go downhill, passing through two gates. The trail then goes uphill gradually through lots of rocks on a sandy creek bottom. It climbs onto the hillside, crosses the stream on a bridge, and continues uphill more steeply. The trail then begins to switchback, and when you reach the 1-mile mark you see the easier Whippletree Trail on the right (north) side. The Whippletree Trail climbs up through a major drainage of mixed forest with butte views and becomes the Longhorn Trail, traveling through meadows as it climbs. That trail combination doesn't climb as high or as steeply as the Belcher Hill Trail, and you won't get away from views of suburbia as quickly. It merges with the Belcher Hill Trail, where you can continue to climb or descend to the trailhead on the Belcher Hill Trail if you prefer a short loop instead of a long out-and-back trip.

The Belcher Hill Trail switchbacks up the mountainside and travels southwest toward the canyon. At 6,700 feet you see Golden's characteristic tabletop mountains and downtown Denver in the distance. Around the 2-mile mark, at 6,900 feet, you get sweeping views of high foothills that are reminiscent of foothills in similar hill country in Montana and California. The Longhorn Trail branches right around 7,200 feet, and you have an extensive canyon view with striking rock formations on your left. The trail has fewer steep sections as it climbs up to 7,400 feet and levels out as the Mustang Trail takes off downhill to the southwest into canyon country. You can of course explore the canyon views on the Mustang Trail and then return to the Belcher Hill Trail, avoiding another 600 feet of climbing. There is a bench available for a rest or snack break.

In 100 yards you see the short Round Up Loop Trail that travels about 0.1 mile out for a northerly view; it rejoins the Belcher Hill Trail in short order. Another 100 yards takes you to the Maverick Trail, another easier

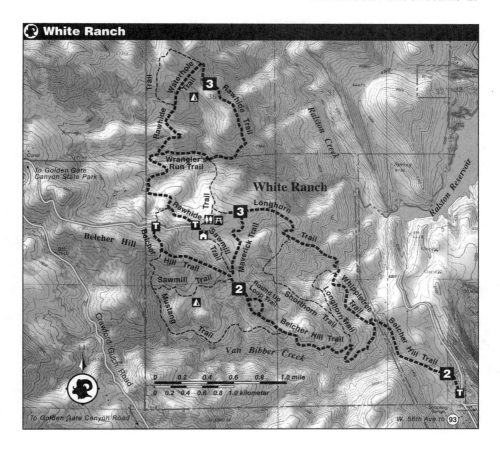

but scenic option that goes downhill to the broad meadows of the Longhorn Trail. In 50 yards or so, you reach an intersection with the Sawmill Trail and the route back to the Sawmill Hiker campsites (left). Take Sawmill right (north) for a short, easy trek downhill to the westside parking area. The Belcher Hill Trail gets much steeper again as it climbs quickly up to 7,800 feet, levels temporarily, and then climbs to around 8,000 feet. The final panorama of views is well worth the effort, with 8,000- to 9,000-foot foothills all around and even distant 14,000-foot Pikes Peak to the southeast.

### 3   White Ranch: West Access Trails

JEFFERSON COUNTY PARKS

|  |  |
|---|---|
| **Distance** | Up to 10 miles, out-and-back |
| **Difficulty** | Moderate |
| **Elevation Gain** | 1,500' (starting at 7,700') |
| **Trail Use** | Hiking, mountain biking, horseback riding, leashed dogs OK |
| **Agency** | White Ranch Park, Jefferson County Parks |
| **Map(s)** | Jefferson County Parks *White Ranch Park*; Trails Illustrated *Boulder & Golden* |
| **Facilities** | Restrooms, backcountry camping for hikers or equestrians |

**HIGHLIGHTS** The western access to White Ranch is peaceful and bucolic. Soft, rounded hills, stately foothills, and the buttes in the distance make this a rural rather than suburban entry point. There are two picnic tables 100 yards from the parking lot, and many of the trail options are mellow. This trailhead is 1,400 feet higher than the eastern access, so you can more easily limit your level of exertion without sacrificing scenic density if you so desire.

**DIRECTIONS** Take CO 93 north from Golden approximately 1 mile to Golden Gate Canyon Road. Travel west approximately 4.1 miles to Crawford Gulch Road (County Road 57). Turn right onto Crawford Gulch Road and follow the signs to White Ranch Park.

## Longhorn Trail

This trail gently descends for the first 0.5 mile and then gradually steepens for 3 miles with meadow and butte views. Descend as far as you like and climb back up, or take the Whippletree or Belcher Hill Trail all the way down if you set up a car shuttle.

## Maverick Trail

For superb views of the canyon, take this roller-coaster, 2.2-mile trail down from the western access, and then climb back up (up to 530 feet of gain/loss), or access the Maverick Trail off the Belcher Hill Trail on your way up.

## Sawmill Trail

This relatively mellow 1.6-mile trail with up to 700 feet of gain/loss is the primary route to the campground or the Belcher Hill Trail from the west side. You can just walk the first 0.5 mile up and back to the Belcher Hill Trail if you want a short and easy adventure.

## Rawhide Trail

The most interesting and challenging of the west side trails, the Rawhide Trail lunges and climbs and rolls over hills and gorgeous dales and meadows (up to 1,400 feet of gain/loss).

*View to the north from the top of the White Ranch West Access Trails*

## 4   North Table Mountain

JEFFERSON COUNTY PARKS

see map on p. 30

| | |
|---|---|
| **Distance** | Varies; 3.2 miles out-and-back to quarry; 7.4 miles full outer loop |
| **Difficulty** | Moderate |
| **Elevation Gain** | 480' (starting at 6,030') |
| **Trail Use** | Hiking, mountain biking, climbing, horseback riding, leashed dogs OK |
| **Agency** | North Table Mountain Park, Jefferson County Parks |
| **Map(s)** | Jefferson County Parks *North Table Mountain Park* |
| **Facilities** | Restroom at trailhead |
| **Note(s)** | Rattlesnakes are common. Dogs can also be bitten, a good reason to keep them leashed. You can download the "Snakebite Prevention and First Aid Guide" from the Jefferson County Parks site. |

**HIGHLIGHTS** North Table Mountain is a mesa formed by Paleocene basaltic lava flows about 60 million years ago. The more popular North Table Mountain and South Table Mountain, also a mesa, are separated by Clear Creek Canyon. Jefferson County Open Space has constructed a trail system to explore the mesa with expansive views of Golden and Denver from its top. North Table Mountain Park encompasses 1,998 acres, and a couple of areas are closed to the public, one of them a sensitive lichen area. Other seasonal closures protect cliff-nesting birds, mule deer, and other fragile or unique vegetation. The numerous mountain bikers we encountered were friendly and courteous, not at all a negative impact on the hiking experience. These trails are good for spring or fall days. Shade is scarce; on summer days it's best to hike or bike early or late in the day to avoid the worst of the heat. Don't forget your sunscreen, and take plenty of water.

**DIRECTIONS** From CO 6 in Golden, take CO 93 north for 2.1 miles. The trailhead is at 4758 CO 93, just north of Pine Ridge Road.

For a taste of the outer loop, a canyon trail, and mesa-top views, try this approximately 6.5-mile section of the outer loop. Pick up a map at the trailhead signs, and head south out of the parking lot. The North Table Loop is wide and roadlike as it climbs straight up to the mesa top. Stop if you need to catch your breath; this is a great place to watch golden eagles and red-tailed hawks cavorting around the cliff tops. At the top, you'll pass the Sea Cliff climbing area trail and an old quarry. You could stop here for a snack and head back down for a 3.2-mile workout.

For a longer trip, stay on the North Table Loop; don't take the left to Tilting Mesa. The sounds of the highway drop away, and the trail narrows. After a slight downhill, you get good views of Lookout Mountain and Golden. At the next couple of intersections, stay on North Table Loop. You descend a bit and follow alongside a pretty spring on the rocky trail, where you also see yucca and cottonwoods. Views of the Coors facility with downtown Denver in the distance start to appear. After a couple of brief, narrow, rock-stair sections, you get more views of the city and cliffs. You are paralleling the road below, and the trail rolls up and down to where you can see the trail that comes up Cottonwood Canyon from the neighborhood far below and continues up to the mesa top. Don't take the neighborhood access, but continue left on the big switchbacks that take you gradually away from the city noise. At the intersection with Cottonwood Canyon Trail, we went left, toward the quieter interior and away from the city views. To the right is North Table Loop, which you can take for a longer trip around the perimeter of the mesa.

Continue uphill for about a mile on Cottonwood Canyon Trail. Watch for deer and views of the peaks to the west. The switchbacks get steeper as you approach the top. When you reach it, you will cross under transmission lines and enormous towers.

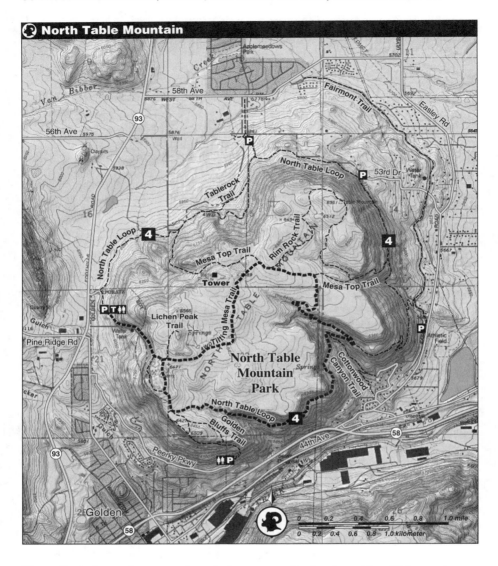

North Table Mountain

North Table Mountain Park

The trail gets less rocky, a smooth path that meanders through the tall grasses. At the intersection with Mesa Top Trail, turn left onto Mesa Top Trail. At the next intersection with Rim Rock Trail, continue left. At the next intersection take a left (south) onto Tilting Mesa Trail. Turning right and staying on Mesa Top Trail will also take you to the parking lot. If you take this route, you should turn left on North Table Loop and follow it to the trailhead. If you choose to take the Tilting Mesa Trail, it becomes a doubletrack,

great for chatting with a hiking partner or giving mountain bikers room to pass. You pass a photogenic pond, complete with cattails, ducks, and shorebirds. The trail bends around to head west, and you pass black lava rock and see the quarry again. Don't take Lichen Peak Trail (unless you want to take a hiker-only side trip up to the park's highest point, Lichen Peak), and at the intersection with North Table Loop, go right and descend steeply to the parking lot on the roadlike trail where you started your adventure.

*Cliffs on top of North Table Mountain*

## 5   **Mount Galbraith**

JEFFERSON COUNTY PARKS

see map on p. 32

| | |
|---|---|
| **Distance** | 4.2 miles, balloon |
| **Difficulty** | Moderate |
| **Elevation Gain** | 1,100' (starting at 5,700') |
| **Trail Use** | Hiking, leashed dogs OK |
| **Agency** | Mount Galbraith Park, Jefferson County Parks |
| **Map(s)** | Jefferson County Parks *Mount Galbraith Park* |
| **Facilities** | Restroom at trailhead |
| **Note(s)** | Rattlesnakes are common. Dogs can also be bitten, a good reason to keep them leashed. You can download the "Snakebite Prevention and First Aid Guide" from the Jefferson County Parks site. |

**HIGHLIGHTS** The 812 acres in Mount Galbraith Park comprise the first hiker-only Open Space Park in Jefferson County. Close to Golden, the trail steeply ascends and then loops around 7,260-foot Mount Galbraith, offering expansive views of city and peaks and often sightings of bighorn sheep, elk, and red-tailed hawks.

**DIRECTIONS** From CO 93 just north of Golden, take CO 46, Golden Gate Canyon, 1.5 miles west to the small parking area and trailhead on the left.

You can pick up a map at the parking lot. Cross a small footbridge and start the uphill trek alongside a small burbling creek. The Cedar Gulch Trail skirts the side of Mount Galbraith for 1.3 miles to the intersection with the 1.6-mile loop trail. As you climb, you can see and hear traffic on CO 46 and see houses across the valley, but the traffic noise gradually fades away the higher you get. Coming up the

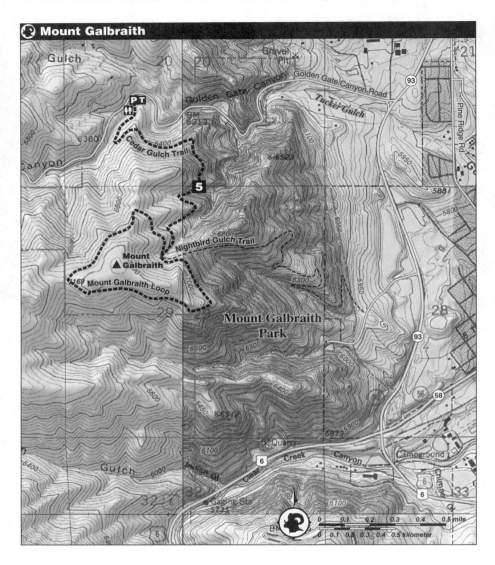

trail, you'll see the backs of the signs at the intersection. Take the Mount Galbraith Loop trail; the Nightbird Gulch Trail is a neighborhood access. I went left up a few rock stairs to hike the loop clockwise. As you continue to climb, you start to get views of the Coors plant in Golden, with the brown cloud and Denver skyline in the distance. Eventually, the trail begins to level out and you can see Lookout Mountain with the Lariat Loop Road winding up

its side, Golden below you, and Denver in the distance. A little farther along the trail, you can hear the cars and spot Tunnel 1 below you on US 6.

You round a corner and start heading west toward the views of the distant peaks, and the narrow trail, flanked by sage, cacti, and miner's candles, gets rockier. At times the trail can be a little difficult to find, and the top is one of those places. At the first big rocks, take a sharp downhill turn to the left down a few rock steps. There are arrows on the trees to mark the way. As you descend, you pass through a grove of burned black trees and woodpeckers drumming them in their search for insects. This side of the mountain is cooler, and there is some shade here and there. The trail wanders around trees and through tight rock passages and clings to the side of the steep valley wall, offering views of houses and roads across the valley. As you curve around the mountain, you once again get views of Golden and Coors far below. Take care to stay on the main trail. When in doubt, keep in mind that often the trail is a series of rock stairs that aren't always obvious from above. The trail smooths out as you exit the trees. At the intersection, take the hairpin left turn and connect once again with the Cedar Gulch Trail.

*Distant peaks and closer foothills from the Mount Galbraith loop*

## 6  Lookout Mountain: Beaver Brook Trail
### JEFFERSON COUNTY PARKS

see map on p. 34

| | |
|---|---|
| **Distance** | Up to 9.9 miles, out-and-back |
| **Difficulty** | Moderate |
| **Elevation Gain** | 1,700' if you turn around halfway (starting at 7,300') |
| **Trail Use** | Hiking only on Beaver Brook Trail, mountain biking on first 1.2 miles, leashed dogs OK |
| **Agency** | Lookout Mountain Nature Center and Preserve, Jefferson County Parks |
| **Map(s)** | Jefferson County Parks *Lookout Mountain Nature Center*; Sky Terrain *Golden Evergreen Trail* |
| **Facilities** | Restrooms in Nature Center |

**HIGHLIGHTS** Carved into the south rim of Clear Creek Canyon, the Beaver Brook Trail connects Windy Saddle on Lookout Mountain to Genesee Park. Though it's easily accessible from Golden or Denver, the trail has a backcountry feel. It's a good choice in spring when the high country has not yet melted, and in the summer months it can be a cooler alternative to much of the hiking close to Denver. It has views, wildflowers, creek crossings, and rock scrambling.

**DIRECTIONS** From US 6 in Golden, turn west on 19th Street. Follow it up through the large rock towers, and it turns into Lookout Mountain/Lariat Loop Road. Turn off on Colorow Road and follow it to the parking lot for the Lookout Mountain Nature Center and Boettcher Mansion. From I-70 W, take Exit 256 and turn right. From I-70 E, take Exit 254 and turn left. Then follow the brown signs.

This historic trail has several access points, including the one described here. The trail starts across Colorow Road from the parking lot. The first mile is an elongated downhill switchback on the Lookout Mountain Trail. Take the downhill turn when the trail continues to the Buffalo Bill Museum and Grave. You may encounter mountain

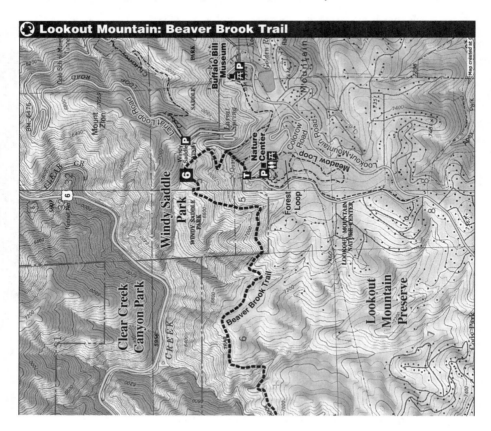

Lookout Mountain: Beaver Brook Trail

bikers on this section of the trail, but only hikers are allowed on the Beaver Brook Trail. You get an occasional glimpse of cars and bicyclists below you on the Lookout Mountain Road and several good views of Golden. At just over a mile, the trail splits. The right turn goes to the Windy Gap parking lot on the Lookout Mountain Road. The left fork turns west onto the Beaver Brook Trail. Usually, this turn is marked, but sometimes the only sign is the one for no bikes, no horses, and no fires. The trail itself is marked with signs that say B/B and note the mileage.

This trail is not for you if you don't like exposure. It's carved into the side of the canyon, far above Clear Creek, and in places you will have to scramble hand-over-hand over rocks. Look for painted white rectangles on the rock faces for guidance. The acoustics of the canyon walls can bring sounds from the river and road far below

you: the occasional calls of one kayaker to another, the infrequent car horn. Cars on the road are the size of gnats flying next to the slender silver ribbon of river in the dark canyon bottom, with the distant mountains rising regally over the canyon walls.

At just over 1.4 miles, you cross the first of two large boulder fields. Again, watch for white rectangles painted on the sides of the rocks to guide you across. Small creek crossings create little lush oases, good spots to stop for a snack or lunch. Go as far as you like; all the way to Genesee Park is about 8.65 miles. If you go all the way to Genesee, you will climb 800 feet in the last 1.5 miles. When deciding where to turn around, remember that once you leave the Beaver Brook Trail and head back uphill to the Nature Center parking lot, you leave the shade of the forest. The last mile uphill to the parking lot can be hot.

*The trail disappears into the rocks at the 1-mile sign on the Beaver Brook Trail.*

Colorado Mountain Club volunteers built the Beaver Brook Trail in 1917–1919 to connect Genesee Park to Lookout Mountain Park. Hikers used to take the trolley from Denver to Golden and then travel by train to the Beaver Brook station in Clear Creek Canyon to access the trail.

### GREAT FOR KIDS

Two short hikes from the Nature Center are perfect for families with young children. Bring a picnic lunch to eat under massive ponderosa pines, and keep an eye out for wildlife because it's a good bet you'll see some. Start your hike with a visit to the Discovery Corner in the Nature Center, which features exhibits where children can handle and explore natural objects, play with wildlife puppets, and read a book in the giant bird's nest. The 0.6-mile Forest Loop Trail and the 0.8-mile Meadow Loop Trail wind through the forest and meadows south of the Nature Center over gently rolling terrain. No dogs allowed.

## 7    Coyote & Mule Deer Trails

GOLDEN GATE CANYON STATE PARK

see map on p. 36

| | |
|---|---|
| **Distance** | 8 miles, loop |
| **Difficulty** | Easy |
| **Elevation Gain** | 600' (starting at 8,860') |
| **Trail Use** | Hiking, mountain biking, fishing, leashed dogs OK |
| **Agency** | Golden Gate Canyon State Park |
| **Map(s)** | *Golden Gate Canyon State Park*; Trails Illustrated *Boulder & Golden* |
| **Facilities** | Campgrounds, picnic areas, and restrooms at trailhead and along trail |
| **Note(s)** | Park fee required. |

**HIGHLIGHTS** Though for many years this state park was not well developed for recreation, it has finally been expanded into a hidden treasure easily accessible from the Denver, Boulder, and Golden areas. The park offers mellow trails for hiking and biking, abundant wildflowers in spring, spectacular vistas of the Front Range, and a broad range of almost every type of tree seen in the mountains of Colorado. The rampant aspen make it a superb place to visit in the fall. This route in particular is an excellent spring wildflower loop.

**DIRECTIONS** From Boulder take CO 119 up Boulder Canyon and then south toward Rollinsville. About 5 miles from Rollinsville, turn left on Gap Road. Turn right on Mountain Base Road to Bootleg Bottom Trailhead. Or go 8.5 miles south on CO 119 from Rollinsville, and turn left onto CO 46. It's another 5 miles to the park. Turn left on Mountain Base Road and continue to Bootleg Bottom Trailhead.

Or, from Boulder or Golden, take CO 93 to CO 46, Golden Gate Canyon. It's 13 miles to the visitor center. Stay on CO 46 (left) and continue to Mountain Base Road, which is closed in winter. Take Mountain Base Road to Bootleg Bottom Trailhead.

Or take I-70 west to Exit 265 for CO 58. Take CO 58 west to CO 93, which turns into CO 6 at the stoplight. Follow CO 6 west to CO 119. Go north on CO 119 through Blackhawk approximately 11 miles to Gap Road. (Or you could turn at CO 46 and follow directions from Rollinsville above.) Turn right on Gap Road toward Aspen Meadow campground. From Denver, this route is approximately 27 miles one way. The Panorama Point overlook, 1.5 miles from the campground, is worth a stop. Look for the Bootleg Bottom Trailhead, where you park.

Downhill from the parking area is a restroom; it will be a long time before you see another. The Coyote Trail goes gradually downhill from the parking area between the picnic tables, traversing the side of a small, heavily forested hill that would be a mountain in many other states with expansive views of slanting meadows and lofty foothills rolling off into the horizon. The downhill lasts approximately 0.1 mile and, in the spring, you immediately see geraniums, white bedstraw, and sulfur

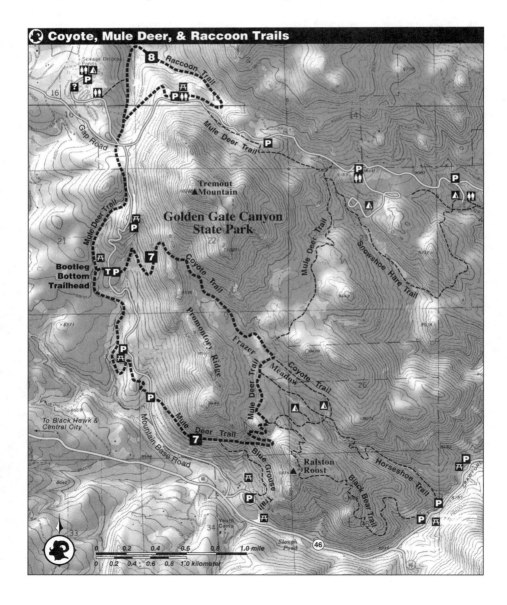

flowers among the aspen and ponderosa pine trees. The trail turns sharply left and crosses a meadow with great views before it climbs gradually and then more steeply uphill. If your timing is right, you will see wild roses, cow parsnip, black-eyed Susans, and blanket flowers. The trail then travels uphill steeply for 0.25 mile, and you see remains of a bootleggers' cabin from the 1920s, when alcohol was illegal in the United States during Prohibition.

The trail turns right and then switchbacks broadly uphill. Look for cinquefoil flowers and subalpine zone Douglas fir trees. As you walk you also see lodgepole and limber pine and Engelmann and blue spruce trees. The views open up as you reach some rock outcrops that are a good spot for a snack or water break. You can see part of the Front Range, with James Peak (13,296 feet) in the distance, as well as Grays and Torreys Peaks and even Mount Evans. Far to the right side are Arapaho and Audubon peaks. Look carefully and you might see chiming bluebells, shooting stars, cow parsnip, and wallflowers, as well as lots of aspens.

The trail climbs to the west from the rocks, descends steeply, and then mellows into gorgeous meadows. The Frazer backcountry campground and a covered shelter for picnics are on your left. Turn around to see the striking rock outcrop of Promontory Ridge (9,442 feet) behind you. This can be used as a turnaround point if you want a shorter out-and-back hike. Ahead are signs for more backcountry campsites (Rim and Greenfield Meadow) and the intersection with Mule Deer Trail. Turn right onto Mule Deer (southwest and south) and continue the loop. Where you see signs for the Frazer, Black Bear, and Blue Grouse Trails, turn sharply to the right. Eventually, the trail goes uphill for 0.25 mile as it turns west. After some short, steep switchbacks, it rolls for another 0.25 mile, veering from west to north.

On the way, you see an intersection for the Blue Grouse Trail that goes left downhill to Kriley Pond. If you want to detour for fishing or soaking your feet, a car shuttle would make your trip easier. You will see Mountain Base Road below as the trail turns north, opens up, goes gradually down a very long hill, and then crosses the road. You then have a steady uphill on the Mule Deer Trail and can enjoy a different view of Promontory Ridge as you pass restrooms and picnic areas along the way. Watch for the sign for the Coyote Trailhead on the right to go back to the starting point at Bootleg Bottom.

## 8 Raccoon Trail

GOLDEN GATE CANYON STATE PARK

see map on p. 36

| | |
|---|---|
| **Distance** | 2.5 miles, loop |
| **Difficulty** | Easy–moderate |
| **Elevation** | 500' (starting at 9,120') |
| **Trail Use** | Hiking, mountain biking, snowshoeing, leashed dogs OK |
| **Agency** | Golden Gate Canyon State Park |
| **Map(s)** | *Golden Gate Canyon State Park*; Latitude 40° *Colorado Front Range Recreation Topo Map*; Sky Terrain *Golden Evergreen* |
| **Facilities** | Pit toilets at the trailhead |
| **Note(s)** | Park fee required. |

**HIGHLIGHTS** This beautiful family trail is very popular. Enjoy a grand overlook of the Continental Divide and the Indian Peaks Range at the start. The trail goes downhill from the overlook, with great peak views all along the way if you go counterclockwise. You will have an uphill to get back, unless you start at the campground. This description starts from the overlook.

**DIRECTIONS**  From Boulder, you have two alternatives:
1.  Take Canyon Boulevard/CO 119 west 16 miles to Nederland. Go left (south) through the round-about, on to Peak to Peak CO 119 south for 10 miles to Gap Road (County Road 2), 5 miles south of Rollinsville. There is a large brown state park sign, as well as other park signage. You can access the trail from either Reverend's Ridge Campground or the overlook. For the overlook, continue uphill past the campground turnoff for another 1.5 miles; it will be on your left. There is a parking area with pit toilets.
2.  Take CO 93 south to Golden Gate Canyon Road, just north of Golden; turn right; and go 13 miles to the visitor center. Ask for directions if it is open. Or continue on CO 46 for 4 miles to turn right (north) onto CO 119. In approximately 4 miles, turn right onto Gap Road (CR 2). You can access the trail from either Reverend's Ridge Campground or the overlook. For the overlook, continue uphill past the campground turnoff for another 1.5 miles; it will be on your left. There is a parking area with pit toilets.

From Denver or Golden, take CO 93 north from Golden to Golden Gate Canyon Road. Turn left, and go 13 miles to the visitor center. Ask for directions if it is open. Or continue 4 miles on CO 46, and then turn right (north) onto CO 119. In approximately 4 miles, turn right onto Gap Road (CR 2). You can access the trail from either Reverend's Ridge Campground or the overlook. For the overlook, continue uphill past the campground turnoff for another mile, and it will be on your left.

Enjoy the photogenic view from the deck at the overlook before you start. From the overlook parking area you have two choices for this loop; northeast (clockwise) or south (counterclockwise). In both cases you will be going downhill at the start and uphill at the end. If you want the initial downhill to be more gradual, go clockwise, but your uphill will be steeper. If you don't mind the steep downhill and want more immediate views, go counterclockwise. The clockwise trail is to the right of the deck and turns southwest through switchbacks. You will have some peak views as the trail rolls gently through the mixed forest to an intersection in about 0.7 mile. If you go left/straight, you will be on the Mule Deer Trail to Bootleg Bottom (1.2 miles). Turn right (west-northwest), and continue downhill in a pretty glade. The campground trail will be on your left. In 100 yards take a sharp right (south) turn to stay on the Raccoon Trail. You will see a private cabin on your right. Savor the stately aspens and crags soaring above. After the aspen grove, the trail climbs 200 feet quickly, regaining part of the 500-foot descent. The trail levels and

*Views of snowcapped peaks above the aspen-studded Raccoon Trail*

then climbs steeply again. Look behind you for the peak views and catch your breath. After another 0.5 mile take a sharp right (southeast) through aspen trees. The trail winds and descends, then goes left uphill, reaching the park road, and then parallels it back to the overlook. Take the side trail on

the right, and enjoy more spectacular views for the last 0.25 mile.

The counterclockwise trail starts on the right side of the restrooms and goes east along the road before going left into the trees. You will have good peak views as you descend.

---

**9**   **South Valley Park: Coyote Song Trail**

JEFFERSON COUNTY PARKS

see map on p. 40

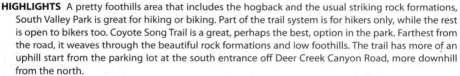

| | |
|---:|:---|
| **Distance** | Up to 3.2 miles, balloon |
| **Difficulty** | Easy |
| **Elevation Gain** | 300' (starting at 5,800') |
| **Trail Use** | Hiking, mountain biking, leashed dogs OK |
| **Agency** | South Valley Park, Jefferson County Parks |
| **Map(s)** | Jefferson County Parks *South Valley Park* |
| **Facilities** | Restrooms and picnic area at South Valley Road entrance |

**HIGHLIGHTS**  A pretty foothills area that includes the hogback and the usual striking rock formations, South Valley Park is great for hiking or biking. Part of the trail system is for hikers only, while the rest is open to bikers too. Coyote Song Trail is a great, perhaps the best, option in the park. Farthest from the road, it weaves through the beautiful rock formations and low foothills. The trail has more of an uphill start from the parking lot at the south entrance off Deer Creek Canyon Road, more downhill from the north.

**DIRECTIONS**  Take CO 470 south to the Ken Caryl exit, and turn west. Turn left onto South Valley Road to the park's north parking area. Or, from the South Wadsworth and CO 470 intersection, take Deer Creek Canyon Road west to the south parking area.

If you want a mellower start, go to the north lot, though the hill you immediately encounter at the south entrance isn't terribly steep. From the south entrance you climb the short hill through a pretty, small canyon with inspiring rock walls. You crest the primary part of the hill after a little more than 0.25 mile; a small rock formation on the west side of the trail can be used for a rest break.

At the 0.4-mile mark you come to an intersection with the Swallow Trail. If you are on foot, you can go downhill to the left

(west) and take the Swallow Trail as your outbound loop, which is closed to bikes. The Swallow Trail is closer to relatively quiet South Valley Road. If you want to stay farther from the road, go straight and stay on the Coyote Song Trail. You go very gradually uphill and into the more intimate surroundings of the rock and foothills. It is 0.9 mile to the restrooms, picnic area, and water (summer only). The trails continue up to the north parking area, where they rejoin.

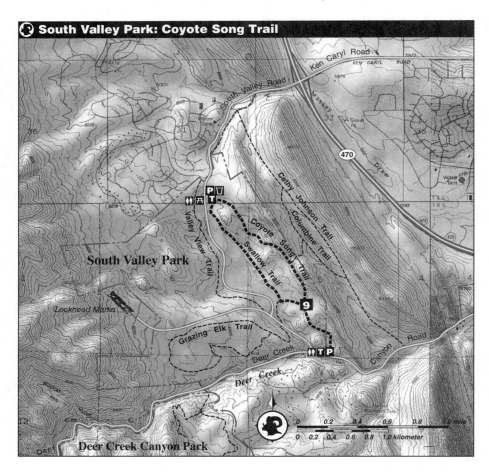

**South Valley Park: Coyote Song Trail**

---

## 10  Fountain Valley Trail

ROXBOROUGH STATE PARK

see
map on
p. 43

| | |
|---|---|
| **Distance** | 2.2 miles, balloon |
| **Difficulty** | Easy |
| **Elevation Gain** | 200' (starting at 6,200') |
| **Trail Use** | Hiking |
| **Agency** | Roxborough State Park |
| **Map(s)** | *Roxborough State Park* |
| **Facilities** | Restrooms at visitor center |
| **Note(s)** | Pets are not permitted anywhere in the park. |

**HIGHLIGHTS**  Roxborough State Park is a red rock wonder that shouldn't be missed. This trail gets the award for highest scenic density and beauty for the smallest amount of physical effort.

**DIRECTIONS**  Take CO 470 to Wadsworth Boulevard (CO 121) and go south to Waterton Road. Turn left (east) on Waterton Road and drive 1.5 miles to Rampart Range Road. Turn right (south) and drive 2.5 miles to where the road narrows at the Golf Club. Turn left onto the Roxborough Park Road and then take an immediate right onto the park road. It is approximately 1.4 miles to the visitor center. This loop trail originates at the visitor center.

The trail goes uphill north from the visitor center, with a short detour for the Lyon Overlook on the west side. Though a nice overlook with two benches, it is marred by a subdivision to the west. The views to the north and south, up valley, are still worth the side trip. Descend the gradually sloping trail to the loop intersection. I suggest going clockwise to the left (west) on the trail for the best views of the dazzling leaning towers; an out-and-back venture on only the west side of the loop was more enjoyable to me than the less scenic east side. As you round the turn, you get a 180-degree view of the rock garden with soaring fingers, parapets, and fins. The trail wanders through scrub oak and comes to a magnificent view of the rock formations, with willows in the foreground and a bench for meditating on the last 300 million years and humankind's recent appearance.

At 0.6 mile the trail flattens, the wet meadow widens, and the giant flakes of sandstone stand as sentinels. You can round the end of the loop and follow the trail as it turns northeast into a pretty arroyo. Here I suggest turning around and retracing your steps on the west side of the loop, rather than completing the loop, so you can enjoy the inspirational rocks from a different perspective.

*Leashed dogs are allowed on the Coyote Song Trail.*

**11 Carpenter Peak**

ROXBOROUGH STATE PARK

see map on p. 43

| | |
|---|---|
| **Distance** | 2.2–6.4 miles, out-and-back |
| **Difficulty** | Easy–moderate |
| **Elevation Gain** | 900' (starting at 6,200') |
| **Trail Use** | Hiking, option for kids |
| **Agency** | Roxborough State Park |
| **Map(s)** | *Roxborough State Park* |
| **Facilities** | Restrooms at visitor center |
| **Note(s)** | Pets are not permitted anywhere in the park. |

**HIGHLIGHTS** Roxborough State Park is a red rock wonder that shouldn't be missed. You can enjoy a short and easy route by hiking the Carpenter Peak Trail over to County Road 5. The road route isn't mentioned in park literature, but it is one of the most scenic and easy (2.2 miles) out-and-back treks. You can savor intimate views of the dark red "sculptures" while strolling along the road. You have to cross the road to access the Carpenter Peak Trail. If you're ambitious, continue on to the summit of Carpenter Peak.

You don't have to go all the way to enjoy golden eagle views of the park from the Carpenter Peak Trail. The views of the park on your return from the Carpenter Peak summit are better than the outbound views, which are somewhat marred by an intrusive subdivision. The main visual benefit of summiting is seeing Waterton Canyon and the distant snowcapped peaks near the Continental Divide.

**DIRECTIONS**  Take CO 470 to Wadsworth Boulevard (CO 121) and go south to Waterton Road. Turn left (east) on Waterton Road and drive 1.5 miles to Rampart Range Road. Turn right (south) and drive 2.5 miles to where the road narrows at the Golf Club. Turn left onto the Roxborough Park Road, and then take an immediate right onto the park road. It is approximately 1.4 miles to the visitor center. This trail originates at the visitor center, across from the roundabout.

The first 0.5 mile of the trail is a flat meander to the south-southwest with views of the green-hued Lykin/Morrison Formation rocks that frame the Willow Creek Loop Trail. It's easy to picture them as part of the landscape in the sea that once blanketed the area. At the 0.5-mile mark, the Willow Creek Trail splits off to the left (southeast). Bear right for Carpenter Peak Trail or straight for the South Rim Trail. In another 0.1 mile bear right when you see the South Rim Trail

on the left. Go uphill past the pretty meadow to see the colorful rocks towering next to CR 5 and some scattered cabins. If you want to savor the rocks, go left (south) along the road for 1.1 miles to the gate.

If you want to enjoy them from an eagle's height, continue straight ahead on the Carpenter Peak Trail, which then bends to the right and into switchbacks. You'll see a sign that says the summit is 2.6 miles away, which means that the road is the 0.8-mile

*Rock formations on the Fountain Valley Trail at Roxborough State Park*

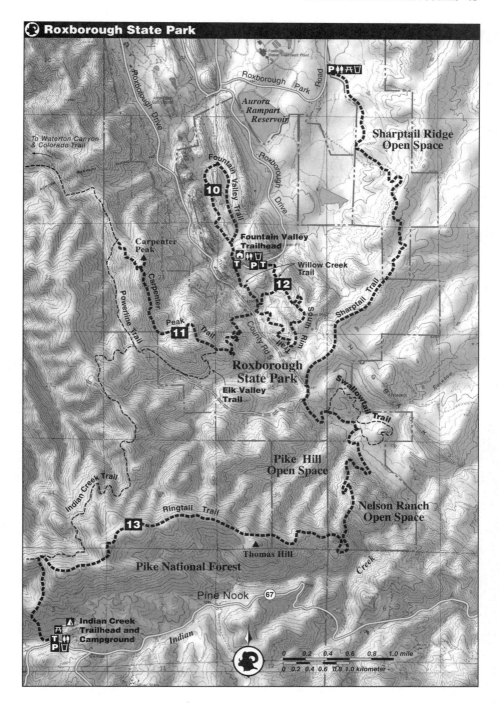

# Roxborough State Park

To Waterton Canyon & Colorado Trail

Foothills Water Treatment Plant

Roxborough Park Road

Aurora Rampart Reservoir

Roxborough Drive

**Sharptail Ridge Open Space**

Roxborough Drive

**10**

Fountain Valley Trail

Carpenter Peak

**Fountain Valley Trailhead**

Willow Creek Trail

Carpenter Peak Trail

**12**

Powerline Trail

South Rim Trail

Sharptail Trail

Peak Trail

**11**

County Rd 5

**Roxborough State Park**

**Elk Valley Trail**

Swallowtail Trail

**Pike Hill Open Space**

Indian Creek Trail

**Nelson Ranch Open Space**

Ringtail Trail

**13**

Thomas Hill

Creek

**Pike National Forest**

Pine Nook (67)

Indian

**Indian Creek Trailhead and Campground**

0   0.2   0.4   0.6   0.8   1.0 mile

0   0.2  0.4  0.6  0.8  1.0 kilometer

mark. You still have about 900 feet of gain for the peak. The switchback sweeps steeply up to the southwest; you reach a bench in about 0.1 mile, where you might consider taking a water break or stretching. The bench has a commanding view at around 6,400 feet that is worth the effort.

After climbing to almost 6,600 feet over the next 0.25 mile, you finally have more shade and another bench. The trail levels for a bit and then climbs under tree cover to an intersection with the Elk Valley Trail, which climbs and then goes down to the Indian Creek Trailhead and Campground at 6,800 feet. The next 0.5 mile is a very gradual uphill with cooling shade, nice on a warm day. You emerge from the trees onto a ridge walk with some peaks peeking through in the distance to the north. The trail tops out on a ridge, with another bench at around 7,100 feet, about the same elevation as Carpenter Peak.

Unless you are a peak bagger and want the workout or want to see the Continental Divide peaks, you can just as easily turn around after reaching this ridgetop bench and be satisfied. After a snack and water break at the bench, follow the trail downhill into a gulch, dropping about 100 feet. You enjoy a relatively mellow trail with lots of shade for the next 0.3 mile, where you reach the intersection of Waterton Canyon and the possible connection to the eastern end of

*Rock formations in Roxborough State Park*

the Colorado Trail 4.4 miles away; you are 3 miles from the Waterton Canyon Trail.

The summit is another 0.25 mile; from there, at 7,140 feet, you can see distant snowcapped peaks and the canyon. The best part of this hike is the return, where you get a view of the ancient Rox rocks that will soothe your soul.

### GREAT FOR KIDS

If you have small children or breathless friends, combining a trip to the first bench with County Road 5 could be an easy round-trip.

 **12**  ## Willow Creek & South Rim Trails

ROXBOROUGH STATE PARK

see map on p. 43

| | |
|---|---|
| **Distance** | Willow Creek Trail: 1.4 miles, loop; South Rim Trail: 4.4 miles, loop |
| **Difficulty** | Easy–moderate |
| **Elevation Gain** | 300' (starting at 6,200') |
| **Trail Use** | Hiking, great for kids |
| **Agency** | Roxborough State Park |
| **Map(s)** | *Roxborough State Park* |
| **Facilities** | Restrooms at visitor center |
| **Note(s)** | Pets are not permitted anywhere in the park. |

*Rock arch window at Roxborough State Park*

**HIGHLIGHTS** Roxborough State Park is a great red rock display. The Willow Creek Trail is essentially a connector trail to the South Rim Trail but can be used as a pleasant, almost flat loop alone if you prefer. It provides good views of some of the rock formations. More ambitious and interesting, the South Rim Trail features a sweeping switchback that climbs 300 feet to an overlook with a bench. You'll more intimately experience the 260-million-year-old Morrison Era rocks, with their character-istic blue-green algae tinge.

**DIRECTIONS** Take CO 470 to Wadsworth Boulevard (CO 121) and go south to Waterton Road. Turn left (east) on Waterton Road and drive 1.5 miles to Rampart Range Road. Turn right (south) and drive 2.5 miles to where the road narrows at the Golf Club. Turn left onto the Roxborough Park Road, and then take an immediate right onto the park road. It is approximately 1.4 miles to the visitor center. This loop trail originates at the visitor center.

**B**oth trails originate across from the visitor center. Walk west and then south, and watch for the signs on the left that take you southeast. You then cross a meadow and see the trail continuing to the top of the rock outcrop to the south-east. The view from the top is worth the gently climbing switchbacks. There are great views all the way, with a bench at the top for the weary. From there you get a 360-degree view of the park and especially the plains to the east, but some of the rock formations are obscured by the ridge to the west.

**13** **Ringtail Trail**
PIKE NATIONAL FOREST

see map on p. 43

| | |
|---|---|
| **Distance** | 12.2–16 miles, out-and-back |
| **Difficulty** | Moderate–challenging, depending on distance |
| **Elevation Gain** | 1,500' (starting at 7,000') |
| **Trail Use** | Hiking, mountain biking, horseback riding |
| **Agency** | Pikes Peak Ranger District, Pike National Forest |

|  |  |
|---|---|
| **Map(s)** | *Pike National Forest*; Douglas County *Sharptail Ridge Map* |
| **Facilities** | Restrooms and campground |
| **Note(s)** | Pets are not permitted anywhere in the park. |

**HIGHLIGHTS**  Adjacent to Roxborough State Park and well worth a visit, this rolling trail is better for biking than hiking and offers everything from sagebrush to foothills views.

**DIRECTIONS**  Indian Creek Trailhead and Campground is 10 miles west of Sedalia on CO 67. To reach Sedalia, drive south from CO 470 on CO 85, or take I-25 about 30 miles south of Denver to Castle Rock and then CO 67 to Sedalia.

This trail climbs up and over Thomas Hill and then travels down into a major drainage and back up the other side to the Swallowtail Trail. You'll experience forest, plains, and rock formations and get a significant workout.

Bikes are not allowed in Roxborough State Park, so this is a way to enjoy the area with a bike. If you have two cars, you could do a shuttle. The conflicting reports on the actual length of this adventure range from 12.2 to 16 miles round-trip. Head off for an out-and-back trek of your chosen length, and turn around in time to beat the sunset.

**Other Trails to Explore**

Great for hiking or horseback riding, the Sharptail Trail, adjacent to Roxborough State Park in Douglas County, is 4.4 miles of rolling prairie that travels to the southern boundary of the park and County Road 5, which exits the park there. It rolls over hill and through dale, climbing 700 feet gradually over the ridgeline that continues beyond the park. From there the trail intersects with the Swallowtail and Ringtail Trails that travel south through the Nelson Ranch Open Space 6 more miles to the Indian Creek Trailhead and Campground.

Approximately 7 miles one way, Indian Creek Trail connects to Elk Valley Trail in Roxborough State Park. The trail itself has rugged, rolling terrain and is great for mountain biking (though bikes are prohibited in Roxborough) and horseback riding.

**14**  **Elk Meadow Park: Meadow View Trail**

JEFFERSON COUNTY PARKS

|  |  |
|---|---|
| **Distance** | 6 miles, out-and-back; 4.4 miles, loop |
| **Difficulty** | Easy |
| **Elevation Gain** | 600' (starting at 7,600') |
| **Trail Use** | Hiking, biking, leashed dogs OK |
| **Agency** | Elk Meadow Park, Jefferson County Parks |
| **Map(s)** | Jefferson County Parks *Elk Meadow Park* |
| **Facilities** | Pit toilets at Lewis Ridge Road trailheads; a dog park at the Stagecoach Boulevard entrance where dogs can be off leash |
| **Note(s)** | Some of the trails are sun exposed and better used early when it is cool. The upper trails toward Bergen Peak are shaded. |

**HIGHLIGHTS**  The Elk Meadows are magnificent examples of mountain meadows with wildflowers, wildlife, and well-maintained trails for easy mountain bike rides and gentle hikes. If you want a more strenuous outing, you can summit Bergen Peak or take the trails that venture onto the ponderosa pine–covered slopes. This is an especially good place for beginner mountain bikers who want fun, nontechnical rides on rolling terrain.

# ⊙ Elk Meadow Park: Meadow View Trail

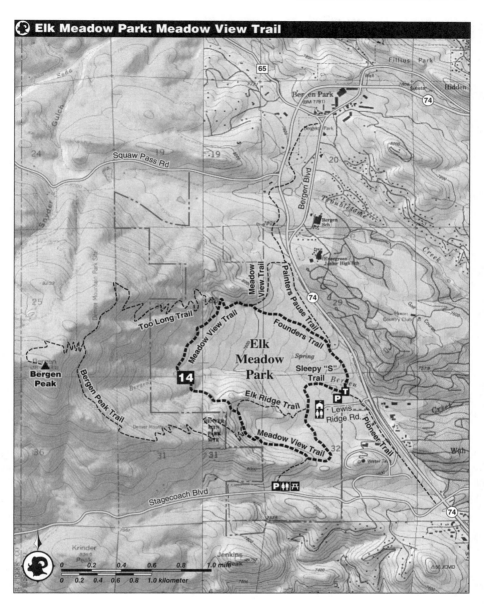

**DIRECTIONS** From downtown Denver, take Sixth Avenue to I-70 west and Exit 252, CO 74 south, toward Evergreen and Bergen Park. Just after passing CO 103, look for the ELK MEADOW PARK sign on the right. Turn right on Lewis Ridge Road for parking lots. There is also trail access and parking from Stagecoach Boulevard.

From the Lewis Ridge parking lot, go left (west) on the Sleepy "S" Trail. It goes gradually uphill with meadow and Bergen Peak views. At the intersection with the Elk Ridge Trail, bear left (south) for a gentler route. (If you want a shortcut on a steeper uphill, take the Elk Ridge Trail.) After 0.6 mile turn right on the Meadow View Trail as it climbs gradually toward trees to an intersection with the Elk Ridge Trail. Bear left at the intersection and stay on the Meadow View Trail as it passes 8,000 feet. Pat yourself on the back for climbing 400 feet and enjoy the thick tree cover and shade on hot summer days. Elk are common on this trail in the winter months. When you reach the intersection with the Too Long trail, you will be at the 3-mile mark and will break out of the trees. Now you can choose to take Meadow View downhill to where it ends at the Painter's Pause Trail, or take the Founders Trail as a shortcut for a 4.4-mile outing back to the trailhead. Both will take you to the Painter's trail next to the Evergreen Parkway. If you want to avoid biking or hiking next to the highway, simply reverse course and enjoy a 6-mile out-and-back.

## 15 Chief Mountain

### ARAPAHO NATIONAL FOREST

| | |
|---|---|
| **Distance** | 4.5 miles, out-and-back |
| **Difficulty** | Moderate |
| **Elevation Gain** | 900' (starting at 10,800') |
| **Trail Use** | Hiking, snowshoeing, skiing, great for kids, leashed dogs OK |
| **Agency** | Clear Creek Ranger District, Arapaho National Forest |
| **Map(s)** | Latitude 40° *Colorado Front Range Trails* |
| **Facilities** | None |

**HIGHLIGHT** This is one of the best panoramic Front Range hikes near Denver. A short climb gets you rather quickly above treeline and onto tundra, where you will enjoy an expansive 360-degree view of Mount Evans, Mount Goliath, Rogers Peak, and Roslin Peak to the west; Griffith, Saxon, and Alps Mountains to the west and north; and the foothills and plains to the east. The elevation makes it a good route for winter sports on calm days.

**DIRECTIONS** There are two alternatives:
1. Take I-70 to Idaho Springs Exit 240, Mount Evans. Take CO 103 south to mile marker 18. Drive another 0.7 mile and park on the north side of the road. The marked trail is on the south side of the highway but difficult to see from a moving car. If you reach Old Squaw Pass Road, you have gone too far.
2. Take I-70 to Exit 252 and go south on CO 74, the Evergreen Parkway, to Bergen Park. Look for Mount Evans signage, and turn right onto CO 103/Squaw Pass Road. Drive 11 miles, and after you see the Echo members-only ski hill, look for a wide spot on the road on the right and park. The trail is on the left (south) side of the road.

The trail climbs west quickly away from the road and veers southeast. In 0.25 mile you will intersect the Old Squaw Pass Road. Cross it and look for the continuing trail on the other side, marked with a large sign that says CHIEF MOUNTAIN 2. The trail travels southeast, breaks out of the thick trees, and goes south. After 0.25 mile the trail goes northwest and you can locate it with tree blazes.

The trail begins to switchback as the trees thin, and you enjoy an ever-increasing mountain panorama to the northwest. As you reach some low rock formations, the trail turns sharply southwest and climbs toward the summit that is west-northwest.

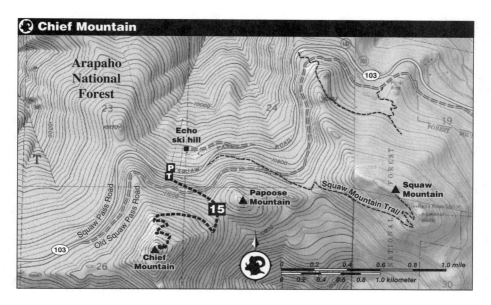

You will pass larger rock formations on the final switchbacks and then have a short rock scramble to the small summit, with an impressive view of the Mount Evans massif and road to the west, and Squaw Mountain to the east. Squaw Mountain can be climbed from the Old Squaw Pass Road that the Chief Mountain Trail crosses. When you go down, turn east and go approximately 1 mile, until you reach the Squaw Mountain Trail; then take the trail south and east to the summit.

## 16 Beaver Brook Watershed Trail
ARAPAHO NATIONAL FOREST

see map on p. 50

| | |
|---|---|
| **Distance** | 5.2 miles, out-and-back |
| **Difficulty** | Easy |
| **Elevation Gain** | 300' (starting at 8,500') |
| **Trail Use** | Hiking, biking, horseback riding, snowshoeing, skiing, leashed dogs OK |
| **Agency** | Clear Creek Ranger District, Arapaho National Forest |
| **Map(s)** | *Arapaho and Roosevelt National Forests North Half* |
| **Facilities** | None |

**HIGHLIGHTS** This recently acquired parcel includes a couple of reservoirs and lots of beautiful, rolling terrain interspersed with high mountain meadows just waiting to be explored. It isn't well known so you won't see a lot of people. It is easy doubletrack mountain biking, or hiking on closed roads. You can extend your ride or hike by going north or west from Lewis Gulch or the Beaver Brook Reservoir. There are many doubletrack dirt roads to choose from.

**DIRECTIONS** From Denver, take I-70 W, and then go south on the Evergreen Parkway (CO 74) to Squaw Pass Road (CO 103). Go right (west) on CO 103 to Old Squaw Pass Road (County Road 170) and turn right (north); the gate and trailhead are on the left (west) side immediately after you turn. From Idaho Springs, drive 10 miles on CO 103, and look for the parking area on the curve. The trailhead is unnamed at the west end. The west end is across from Witter Gulch Road (CR 475).

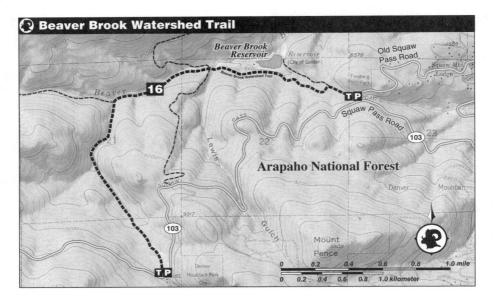

From the east end of the trail, the trail descends from the gate and reaches a fork in 0.5 mile; bear left. You will enter trees as the trail then curves past a pretty meadow. It turns southwest and rolls over a small ridge with views of Beaver Brook Reservoir. It descends as it passes meadows that adjoin the reservoir. It climbs another small ridge and travels west and south away from the reservoir. It then descends into Lewis Gulch. When you intersect the road in Lewis Gulch, you have gone around 1.2 miles. Bear left or straight, unless you want to extend your hike or ride beyond 5 miles. If you do, take a soft right and climb north out of the gulch toward North Beaver Brook Road. Go out and back as far as you wish through open meadows. Going straight or left (west), the road will edge meadows on your right and trees on your left. Turn left (south) at the next intersection to go back to Squaw Pass Road (CO 103). When the trail crosses a large meadow, bear left. You will go back into trees and in 0.25 mile cross another meadow. After another 0.3 mile you will reach the last large meadow that will take you to the west end trailhead.

*High mountain meadows are a highlight of the Beaver Brook Watershed Trail.*

## 17 St. Mary's Glacier & James Peak

ARAPAHO NATIONAL FOREST

| | |
|---|---|
| **Distance** | Top of glacier: 2 miles; James Peak summit: 8 miles; out-and-back |
| **Difficulty** | Top of glacier: Moderate; James Peak summit: Challenging |
| **Elevation Gain** | Top of glacier: 270'; James Peak summit: 3,250' (starting at 10,000') |
| **Trail Use** | Hiking, snowshoeing, skiing, leashed dogs OK |
| **Agency** | Clear Creek Ranger District, Arapaho National Forest |
| **Map(s)** | Trails Illustrated *Winter Park, Central City, and Rollins Pass* |
| **Facilities** | Restrooms at trailhead |

**HIGHLIGHTS** This very climbable permanent snowfield, or glacier, with a spectacular setting is an easy drive from Denver. When it shrinks in the summer, trails go around it. If you have an ice ax and know how to use it for self-arrest, you can have fun glissading on the snowfield. Don't attempt it otherwise because it is easy to career out of control onto the rocks and remove valuable brain cells or body parts.

**DIRECTIONS** Take I-70 west from Denver, past Idaho Springs, to the Fall River Road/St. Mary's Glacier exit onto County Road 275. Follow the signs approximately 8 miles to the glacier parking area. (It is essentially a dead-end road, so you can't miss it.) On a clear day you can see the glacier from the road.

You have a lot of recreational options when visiting St. Mary's Glacier. Many people enjoy the climb from the lake to the top of the glacier, and you can enjoy the nonstop round-trip views of the Front Range and call it a day.

When you reach the area near the summit of the glacier, you see an impressive panorama of James Peak and its Front Range neighbor, Bancroft Peak. Some hikers find this sight an irresistible invitation and decide on an extended adventure to

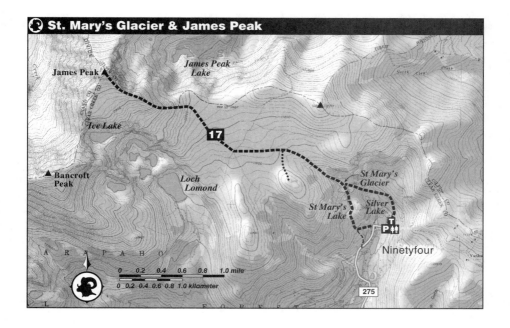

**St. Mary's Glacier & James Peak**

the summit of James Peak. The distance to the summit of James is 4 miles one way.

From the parking lot follow the drainage toward the lake, approximately a 1-mile trek. Once you reach the lake, circle it to the right (east). When you reach the edge of the lake, continue to the east side and climb upslope to the saddle. By the end of June the east edge of the snowfield shrinks and the snow-free corridor widens, making snowshoe and crampon-free travel possible. The climb to the saddle is a moderate, fairly steep challenge that requires catching your breath more than once. Take your time and switchback as much as possible, enjoying the ever-expanding view as you climb. From the saddle either finish your hike to the top of the glacier to the west or bear east toward James Peak.

Continuing northeast toward James Peak is an easy climb in clement weather. The route to the peak is obvious because it is well traveled. If you cannot see James Peak because of weather, reconsider unless you are an experienced mountaineer. The route is a gradual uphill until you reach the foot of the peak; then it climbs steeply, and you'll have to employ some route-finding skills. The best route follows the right or northeast slope. Stay just below the top of the ridge, and you can angle your way to the summit. Don't trek too far to the northeast, or you will climb a false summit and end up on cliffs. Enjoy the views!

*Snowshoers on St. Mary's Glacier*

*Foothills views on a sparkling day on Marshall Mesa*

# chapter 2

# Boulder Area: Plains & Foothills

## LESS THAN 1 HOUR FROM BOULDER

Few places on Earth offer as many recreational opportunities as the city and county of Boulder. Community leaders and voters in the 1960s and 1970s wisely passed tax initiatives to set aside a superb, almost endless variety of public open spaces. The city and county have done an excellent job of managing and protecting these special places from overuse and user conflicts. They can be used for hiking, biking, running, strolling, horseback riding, picnicking, or even just napping. Uses are often separated; making hikers, bikers, horseback riders, and dog lovers happy. You can enjoy foothills, prairies, canyons, arroyos, lakes, and riparian areas; urban and rural settings; rock outcrops for climbing and scrambling; or expansive ranches. A leash law for dogs is strictly enforced, and dogs are prohibited on some trails and welcomed on others.

(Please bring a plastic bag along for cleaning up after your pet, and don't leave the bag on the side of the trail—there is no poop fairy that comes along to pick them up, and the sight of them changes the experience for other trail users.) There are hungry mountain lions in the hills, so keep a close eye on your children and keep your dog leashed to prevent them from becoming snack food.

### Eldorado Canyon State Park

This world-class rock climbing mecca and delightful state park south of Boulder has more than death-defying rock climbing routes. It has an expansive picnic area, a visitor center, a bookstore, a hot springs pool nearby, a wide variety of trails for children of all ages, and one of the most amazing settings along the Front Range only minutes from Boulder.

 **18**  **Mesa Trail: Northern Segment**
CITY OF BOULDER OPEN SPACE & MOUNTAIN PARKS

see map on p. 56

| | |
|---|---|
| **Distance** | Up to 14 miles, out-and-back |
| **Difficulty** | Moderate |
| **Elevation Gain** | 800'–1,000', depending on route taken (starting at 5,700') |
| **Trail Use** | Hiking, running, leashed dogs OK |
| **Agency** | City of Boulder Open Space & Mountain Parks |
| **Map(s)** | City of Boulder Open Space & Mountain Parks *Chautauqua Area*; Latitude 40° *Boulder-Nederland Trails* |
| **Facilities** | Ranger station and restrooms |

**HIGHLIGHTS** Hiking nirvana in Boulder cannot be attained without a jaunt on the well-known and venerable Mesa Trail—one of the original foothills trail networks and open space parks that inspired the creation of so many other pieces of paradise in Boulder County. This rolling trail climbs high onto the side of Green Mountain and travels below the landmark Flatiron rock formations all the way south to Eldorado Springs Road. It features great vistas to the west and east as it roller-coasters

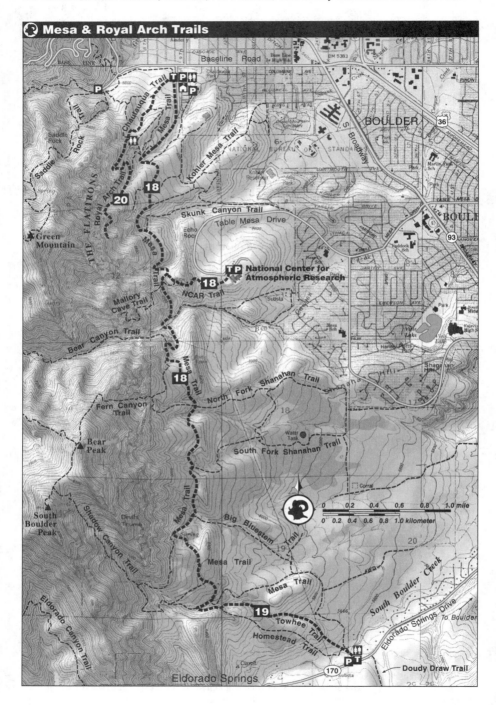

ever southward. You can also access the trail from several places along the way; consult a map. Aside from Chautauqua, one of my favorite starting points is at the south end off of the Eldorado Springs Road. The trail climbs up to spectacular views of the Flatirons in about 1 mile. A variety of loop trail options make for delightful outings of varying difficulty.

**DIRECTIONS** A good starting point, but challenging for parking (I recommend that you carpool or take the bus), is Chautauqua Park. It is straight uphill from the famous Hill district near the university and on the way up Flagstaff Mountain. Take Ninth Street south from downtown until it dead-ends into Baseline Road, or take Baseline Road west from Broadway to Chautauqua Park. There is a parking lot at the trailhead and street parking around the park.

The trail begins west of the circular park drive, past the ranger cottage, through the gate to the fire road. It goes uphill either to the south or more directly west to the foot of the Flatirons. It is at the east edge of the beautiful meadow that sprawls across the hillside at the foreground of the Flatirons and is graced with wildflowers in the spring. I recommend that you bear left to travel south and then west, unless you plan to climb one of the Flatirons or want to take the loop trails that circle the Flatirons. You can clamber around on the Flatirons without ropes for grins, but don't go very high without technical climbing gear.

Because the southern route is a roller coaster, you will have some uphill sections on the way back; they are moderate if you do an out-and-back trip. As the trail travels south, you find it goes up, down, and sideways in almost every direction. For an out-and-back route of approximately 3 miles, go to the area behind the National Center for Atmospheric Research (NCAR) and then turn around. You pass lots of options for picnics or snack and water breaks along the way. It is generally a good winter hiking option unless there has been a recent Front Range snowstorm.

Going south from Chautauqua, bear right (west) and go uphill at the first intersection at the end of the buildings, at around 0.4 mile. The trail traverses at first gradually and then more steeply uphill for approximately 0.5 mile. When it enters the trees, it levels temporarily. You can go either uphill to the right (north) or roller-coaster up and downhill along and in the enchanting foothills ecosystem to the south. I recommend the southerly route unless you want a shorter, challenging uphill workout on the loops to the north. So go left (south) at the next trail intersection, and travel more gradually uphill for 0.5 mile to a loop trail. Bear left (straight) unless you want to explore the steeper 0.5-mile loop that offers some pretty views to the west and is worth the detour. You can see the other end of the loop trail in a little more than 0.25 mile if you skip it. The trail then zigzags and offers the option of traveling east 1.5 miles downhill to Table Mesa Drive, just north of NCAR. The trail then travels downhill for more than 0.5 mile, goes uphill briefly, and then meets an intersecting trail that heads east, switchbacking downhill to a point just north of NCAR.

The trail splits at the next intersection in 0.25 mile, offering either a steep uphill or downhill section. This is a good turnaround point unless you want to take a plunge through Bear Canyon. You can cross the canyon and make this a major adventure by climbing Bear Peak.

## 19  Mesa Trail: Southern Segment

CITY OF BOULDER OPEN SPACE & MOUNTAIN PARKS

see map on p. 56

| | |
|---|---|
| **Distance** | Up to 13.5 miles, out-and-back |
| **Difficulty** | Moderate |
| **Elevation Gain** | 900' (starting at 5,700') |
| **Trail Use** | Hiking, leashed dogs OK |
| **Agency** | City of Boulder Open Space & Mountain Parks |
| **Map(s)** | City of Boulder Open Space & Mountain Parks *South Mesa/South Boulder Creek West*; Latitude 40° *Boulder-Nederland Trails* |
| **Facilities** | Restrooms at trailhead |
| **Note(s)** | Park visitors whose cars are not registered in Boulder County need a daily or annual permit to park. Permits are available at the self-serve station. |

**HIGHLIGHTS** You can access the Mesa Trail from the south end and travel north to see some of the most spectacular views of the Flatirons rock formations. It is a winding, somewhat steep trail initially but then mellows and rolls along.

**DIRECTIONS** Take Broadway in Boulder south toward Golden, turn right on Eldorado Springs Drive, and look for the South Mesa Trailhead on the north side of the road, across from Doudy Draw.

From the parking lot, cross the creek, pick one of the intersecting loop trails (Towhee or Homestead), and then bear west and north, going straight uphill. All of the trails merge as you climb, and then you are on the Mesa Trail, which is well signed. Go as far as you wish and then reverse course, or set up a car shuttle.

The Mesa Trail connects to the Towhee, Homestead, and Big Bluestem Trails. A very scenic round-trip can be had by going to the National Center for Atmospheric Research (NCAR) from the south and back. It is 13.5 miles round-trip to Chautauqua Park.

## 20  Royal Arch Trail

CITY OF BOULDER OPEN SPACE & MOUNTAIN PARKS

see map on p. 56

| | |
|---|---|
| **Distance** | 3.3 miles, out-and-back |
| **Difficulty** | Moderate |
| **Trail Use** | Hiking, climbing access, leashed dogs OK |
| **Elevation Gain** | 800' (starting at 5,710') |
| **Agency** | City of Boulder Open Space & Mountain Parks |
| **Map(s)** | City of Boulder Open Space & Mountain Parks *NCAR*; Latitude 40° *Boulder-Nederland Trails* |
| **Facilities** | Restrooms at Chautauqua Ranger Cottage, on east side of front porch, and at top of Bluebell Road; picnic facilities at Bluebell Shelter |

**HIGHLIGHTS** One of the somewhat challenging options along the Mesa Trail is an interesting trail in its own right because you end up at a small arch with striking views, especially to the north, and you have unique glimpses of the Flatirons along the way. It has the feel of a high mountain hike, even though it is close to town. The challenging part is the fairly steep rock-garden trail that makes you feel like you're on a short Himalayan trek with all of the twists, turns, and ups and downs, without the altitude or length. If you go at a slow pace, the challenge becomes a fun, moderate clamber rather than a heart-thumping workout.

**DIRECTIONS** A good starting point, but challenging for parking (I recommend that you carpool or take the bus), is Chautauqua Park. It is straight uphill from the famous Hill district near the university and on the way up Flagstaff Mountain. Take Ninth Street south from downtown until it dead-ends into Baseline Road, or take Baseline Road west from Broadway to Chautauqua Park. There is a parking lot at the trailhead and street parking around the park.

You have two options at the trailhead: Take the gravel road uphill due south from the ranger station and travel next to Chautauqua if you want fast access. If you want a much more scenic but less direct approach that requires an extra 0.1 mile, go uphill toward the Flatirons and angle southwest, and then watch for the intersection of the Bluebell Shelter Trail on the left (east) side of the trail. Backtrack downhill past the shelter to the Royal Arch Trail. If you're on the road, bear right at the first intersection and continue uphill to near the Bluebell Shelter, where you will bear left (south) onto the actual Royal Arch Trail. There are restrooms trailside near the shelter. The trail travels uphill, narrows, and passes a group of picnic tables in the trees. You can picnic either at Bluebell Shelter or under the trees.

Past the shelter, the trail crosses two streams on footbridges and gets steeper as you climb through a major rockslide. To the west you see the interesting Flatirons mountainside that makes you feel like you're in a national forest miles from nowhere. The trail then rolls a little but generally climbs steeply uphill, often on stone steps, as it winds through the thick tree cover that is a bonus on hot days. After 1.25 miles you encounter steep switchbacks that take you to the top of a small ridge. You then get to travel steeply downhill for 0.1 mile, climbing over rocks, and, yes, you climb uphill on the way back. You have another 0.1 mile push uphill to get to the arch, but the view is well worth the finale.

## 21   Gregory Canyon: Crown Rock & Flagstaff Mountain Summit

*see map on p. 60*

CITY OF BOULDER OPEN SPACE & MOUNTAIN PARKS

|  |  |
|---|---|
| **Distance** | Realization Point: 4.4 miles; Flagstaff Summit: 5.4 miles; Crown Rock: 2 miles; out-and-back |
| **Difficulty** | Moderate |
| **Elevation Gain** | Realization Point: 900'; Crown Rock: 400'; Flagstaff Summit: 1,100' (starting at 5,600') |
| **Trail Use** | Hiking, leashed dogs OK |
| **Agency** | City of Boulder Open Space & Mountain Parks |
| **Map(s)** | City of Boulder Open Space & Mountain Parks *Chautauqua Area*; Latitude 40° *Boulder-Nederland Trails* |
| **Facilities** | Restrooms at Chautauqua, Crown Rock, and Flagstaff Summit Trailheads |

**HIGHLIGHTS** This is an amazingly scenic hike that can be used for a before- or after-work sojourn on a less traveled and car-free trek to Flagstaff Mountain's summit. If you want a very short anaerobic shot, take the side trail to Crown Rock garden at a higher rate of speed. It is still a nice side trail with views at a slower pace.

**DIRECTIONS** In Boulder take Baseline Road west to Chautauqua Park, across from Eighth Street, and take the trailhead farthest to the north from the parking area. Or continue past the park, and park on or near Sixth Street. Walk west from Sixth Street and take the first unmarked trail you see on the left. You will see a BOULDER MOUNTAIN PARK sign. Turn west on the main Gregory Canyon Trail. Flood damage closed access to the trailhead on Gregory Canyon Road in 2013; it is due to reopen in early 2016. Until then, you can park on Flagstaff Road and hike to the trailhead.

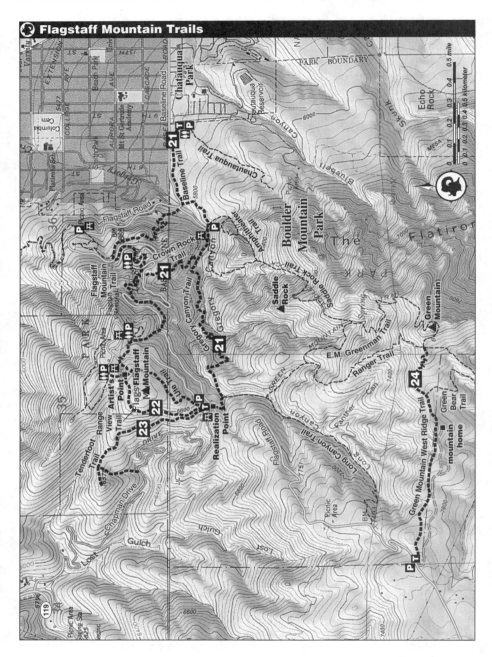

**Flagstaff Mountain Trails**

ike west 0.5 mile on the Baseline Trail and you will see a sign for the Chautauqua Trail; go straight. You will enter thick tree cover and then descend toward the creek on wooden steps. Unless there is heavy spring runoff, you can step across the stream. You will see signs for the Amphitheater and Saddle Rock Trail on the left; bear right uphill. The Saddle Rock Trail was damaged in the 2013 flood, so a stepladder

*A view of the Flatirons from the Crown Rock Trailhead*

section was put in place. In about 0.6 mile you will see the Crown Rock Trail on the right. If you don't have time for the summit, go right onto it. Bear right at all forks. You will be walking over some very rocky sections. It doesn't take long for it to open up to dramatic views to the south, highlighted by a miniature Flatiron-shaped rock formation. You will see a sign for Flagstaff Mountain Road and Crown Point Rock as you climb the final stretch. The rock garden is 400 feet higher than your starting point.

The Gregory Canyon Trail goes up past the Crown Rock Trail and climbs steadily, eventually getting steeper as it reaches a ridgetop with great views. The trail then descends into a saddle, flattens, and climbs gradually to Flagstaff Road and Realization Point. If you want to summit Flagstaff Mountain, cross the road and take the Range View Trail 0.6 mile to the summit and enjoy the views. When you reach Artist's Point, you can take the trails around the west edge of the parking lot to the summit or go straight across the parking lot. For variety, you can take the Flagstaff Mountain Trail on the return to the Crown Rock Trail, but you will cross Flagstaff Road twice on the way. It intersects the Ute Trail.

## 22   **Range View & Ute Trails**
### CITY OF BOULDER OPEN SPACE & MOUNTAIN PARKS

see map on p. 60

|  |  |
|---|---|
| **Distance** | 1.6 miles, loop |
| **Difficulty** | Easy |
| **Elevation Gain** | 200' (starting at 6,785') |
| **Trail Use** | Hiking, biking (see notes), great for kids, wheelchair-accessible on part of Ute Trail, leashed dogs OK |
| **Agency** | City of Boulder Open Space & Mountain Parks |
| **Map(s)** | City of Boulder Open Space & Mountain Parks *Flagstaff Road*; Latitude 40° *Boulder-Nederland Trails* |
| **Facilities** | No restrooms at the Realization Point trailhead, but some are located 0.5 mile up the road at Artist's Point. |

| Note(s) | Bikes are allowed only on the Chapman Road segment and are prohibited on the Tenderfoot segment. Parking is very limited. There is a $5 fee unless you are a Boulder County resident. |
|---|---|

**HIGHLIGHTS** These scenic Flagstaff mountaintop trails are short, scenic alternatives to the crowds on the Mesa Trail, and you will enjoy great Continental Divide and Front Range views. You can start at either the Realization Point or Artist's Point parking lots. The Ute Trail includes the Sensory Nature Trail for children.

**DIRECTIONS** From Boulder go west up Baseline Road, and it will turn into Flagstaff Mountain Road after passing Chautauqua Park. Drive 3.4 miles to Realization Point or 3.9 miles to Artist's Point.

The Range View Trail is the west side of the loop, and the Ute Trail is the east side of the loop. You can go uphill first from the Realization Point trailhead or start downhill from Artist's Point. Starting at Realization Point, where you get one of those, "Wow, I really am in the Rocky Mountains!" moments, go downhill past the picnic tables and take the Range View Trail, which is signed and goes right. You will go downhill and then climb back uphill with great views of the Front Range and Continental Divide all along the way.

The wheelchair-accessible segment of this trail was built by Volunteers for Outdoor Colorado and is an out-and-back that starts at the Artist's Point end of the trails.

When you reach the intersection with the Ute Trail, you can go left through the Sensory Nature Trail toward the restrooms and picnic areas. This is great for children. You can also continue along the left edge of the parking area 0.25 mile to Artist's Point and enjoy that overlook. Another uphill 0.5 mile will take you over to the Flagstaff Mountain summits. Those excursions will add around a round-trip mile to your outing. You can shortcut across the parking lot to the restrooms and then to the Ute Trail. Go straight instead of back through the Sensory Trail. Bear left at the overlook sign, unless you want to see another view. Enjoy the shady downhill back to Realization Point.

### GREAT FOR KIDS

The Sensory Nature Trail starts behind the restrooms near Artist's Point. Its braille signs talk about the area and help visitors learn to use senses other than just sight to learn about the environment. Try tying a bandanna over your eyes and going through the exercises on the signs.

 **23** **Tenderfoot Trail**

CITY OF BOULDER OPEN SPACE & MOUNTAIN PARKS

see map on p. 60

| | |
|---|---|
| **Distance** | 2.5 miles, loop |
| **Difficulty** | Moderate |
| **Elevation Gain** | 400' (starting at 6,785') |
| **Trail Use** | Hiking, great for kids, leashed dogs OK |
| **Agency** | City of Boulder Open Space & Mountain Parks |
| **Map(s)** | City of Boulder Open Space & Mountain Parks *Flagstaff Road*; Latitude 40° *Boulder-Nederland Trails* |
| **Facilities** | No restrooms at the Realization Point trailhead, but some are located 0.5 mile up the road at Artist's Point. |
| **Note(s)** | Bikes are allowed only on the Chapman Road segment and are prohibited on the Tenderfoot segment. Parking is very limited. There is a $5 fee unless you are a Boulder County resident. |

**HIGHLIGHTS** This trail atop Flagstaff Mountain is a scenic alternative to the crowds on the Mesa Trail.

*Looking at the Betasso Water Plant and the distant peaks from the top of Flagstaff Mountain*

It starts at Realization Point and goes down around 400 feet, with a scenic overlook along the way. It starts under cover of ponderosa, juniper, and Douglas fir and then becomes a very sunny trail, so better to do this trail early in the summer. It can be coupled with the Range View and Ute Trails for a tour de Flagstaff trio.

**DIRECTIONS** From Boulder go west up Baseline Road and it will turn into Flagstaff Mountain Road after passing Chautauqua Park. Drive 3.4 miles to Realization Point.

From Realization Point, go counterclockwise and downhill past the picnic tables and you will see a sign pointing the way. Follow switchbacks downhill through a thick ponderosa pine/Douglas fir forest. The trees thin and the trail tracks through pretty high mountain meadows with wallflower, larkspur, and penstemon wildflowers. You will come to an intersection around the 1-mile mark; the post marker says OVERLOOK STRAIGHT, TENDERFOOT TRAIL LEFT. Detour 100 yards to the overlook, and climb up stairs to enjoy the view. From the overlook you will see some of the Front Range, Sugarloaf Mountain, and the backside of Boulder Mountain Parks. Go back to the trail split and go downhill, and in approximately 0.5 mile the trail T's into the Chapman Drive Road. Turn left and follow it uphill past the cattle guard. The road climbs gradually first south and then east to the starting point.

## 24   Green Mountain Summit: West
### CITY OF BOULDER OPEN SPACE & MOUNTAIN PARKS

see map on p. 60

|  |  |
|---|---|
| **Distance** | 2.8 miles, out-and-back |
| **Difficulty** | Easy–moderate |
| **Elevation Gain** | 650' (starting at 7,500') |
| **Trail Use** | Hiking, option for kids, leashed dogs OK |
| **Agency** | City of Boulder Open Space & Mountain Parks |
| **Map(s)** | Latitude 40° *Boulder-Nederland Trails* |
| **Facilities** | None |

**HIGHLIGHTS** This highly scenic, short, rolling trail offers views of foothills and plains, as well as an expansive vista of the Indian Peaks and Longs Peak from the summit of Green Mountain. You can stop anywhere short of the summit, enjoy the pretty meadows, and have a short family hike. There are two steep sections, especially the final rock-stepped 0.25 mile.

**DIRECTIONS** Drive 4.5 miles from Boulder (Chautauqua Park) up Flagstaff Mountain. Look for a wide spot in the road across from a sign that says LEAVING BOULDER PARKS. Park on the right; the trailhead is on the left (east) side of the road.

*Snow lingers on the peaks visible from the Green Mountain West Ridge Trail.*

The trail travels gradually downhill and enters the conifer forest. In 0.5 mile you will see views to the north of the foothills, Boulder, and the plains. The trail rolls back uphill and through rocks, and you will see a mountain home and Bear Peak to the south. It tops out and then plunges over rocks in a short, steep section. The trail rolls back up through a few more rocks, and you will have an open view of Green Mountain to the east and Bear Peak to the south. You will then see a sign for the Green Mountain Ridge Trail. In 200 feet you will come to an intersection; the Green Bear Trail goes right (south) toward Bear Canyon and Bear Peak. Go straight for the West Ridge/Green Mountain Summit (east-southeast). You will climb through steep switchbacks to an intersection with the Ranger Trail that goes left (north) toward Gregory Canyon. This is a good turnaround point if you have small children along because the final section is very steep rock steps. It is around another 100 yards to the summit.

## 25  Marshall Mesa East: Marshall Valley, Community Ditch, & Cowdrey Draw Trails

### CITY OF BOULDER OPEN SPACE & MOUNTAIN PARKS

| | |
|---|---|
| **Distance** | 4 miles, out-and-back |
| **Difficulty** | Easy |
| **Elevation Gain** | 300' (starting at 5,560') |
| **Trail Use** | Hiking, mountain biking, option for kids, leashed dogs OK |
| **Agency** | City of Boulder Open Space & Mountain Parks |
| **Map(s)** | City of Boulder Open Space & Mountain Parks *Marshall Mesa/Greenbelt Plateau*; Latitude 40° *Boulder-Nederland Trails* |
| **Facilities** | Picnic tables and pit toilets at trailhead |
| **Note(s)** | Park visitors whose cars are not registered in Boulder County need a daily or annual permit to park. Permits are available at the self-serve station. |

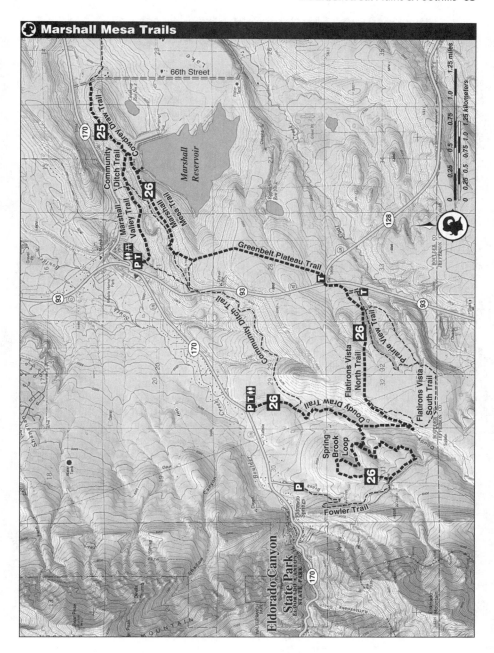

**Marshall Mesa Trails**

**HIGHLIGHTS** This is a relatively short, easy stroll or ride through pretty, rolling grasslands and hills, with an amazing backdrop of the Flatirons foothills on the way back, with snowcapped peaks in the distance. It is a short route for a family hike, or an easy mountain bike outing.

**DIRECTIONS** Take CO 93 to the Marshall Road intersection south of Boulder. Trailhead parking is on the east side of the intersection.

*The Marshall Mesa Trail rolls through meadows with the iconic Flatirons in the background.*

From the parking area, go southeast and look for signs for the Marshall Valley and Community Ditch Trails. Stay to the left to avoid a rock garden. Bear left and follow the hilly terrain as the trail descends into the drainage. The trail rolls over some large, flat rocks that are fun for kids and that require a little navigating for beginning mountain bikers. The trail climbs more steeply to a footbridge.

After the footbridge, you will see stairs going uphill to the Marshall Mesa Trail. This option is for hikers, not bikers; take it if you want to climb 200 feet and see the small reservoir. Continue to the left as the trail climbs more steeply to the intersection with the Community Ditch Trail. You will be on the Community Ditch Trail for a short distance to an intersection with the Cowdrey Draw Trail. The Cowdrey Draw Trail rolls east over hill and dale and gradually descends to 66th Street. Turn around here for a 4-mile round-trip outing. If you are more ambitious, you can continue east on the 1.5-mile Mayhoffer Singletree Trail.

**26**  **Marshall Mesa West: Marshall Valley, Community Ditch, Greenbelt Plateau, Flatirons Vista, & Spring Brook Trails**

see map on p. 65

CITY OF BOULDER OPEN SPACE & MOUNTAIN PARKS

| | |
|---|---|
| **Distance** | 13.4 miles, loop |
| **Difficulty** | Moderate–difficult |
| **Elevation Gain** | 700' (starting at 5,560') |
| **Trail Use** | Hiking, mountain biking, horseback riding on most trails, option for kids, leashed dogs OK |
| **Agency** | City of Boulder Open Space & Mountain Parks |
| **Map(s)** | City of Boulder Open Space & Mountain Parks *Marshall Mesa/Greenbelt Plateau*; Latitude 40° *Boulder-Nederland Trails* |

**Facilities**     Picnic tables and pit toilets at trailhead

**Note(s)**     Park visitors whose cars are not registered in Boulder County need a daily or annual permit to park. Permits are available at the self-serve station.

**HIGHLIGHTS**   This outing is most easily accomplished on a mountain bike but could also be hiked. It features some of the most stunning views of the Flatirons and Fountain-era rock formations on the western leg of the loop. As soon as you turn west, you will have panoramic views and varying scenery, including magnificent meadows. You can shorten the route by reversing course at any point and still have a satisfying day.

**DIRECTIONS**   Take CO 93 south from Boulder to the Marshall Road intersection. Trailhead parking is on the east side of the intersection.

From the parking area go southeast and look for signs for the Marshall Valley and Community Ditch Trails; stay to the left to avoid a rock garden. Bear left and traverse the hilly terrain as the trail descends into the drainage. The trail rolls over some large, flat rocks that are fun for kids, and it requires a little navigating for beginning mountain bikers. The trail climbs more steeply to a footbridge. After the footbridge you will see stairs going uphill to the Marshall Mesa Trail. This option is for hikers, not bikers; take it if you want to climb 200 feet and see the small reservoir.

Continue to the left as the trail climbs more steeply, and you will cross a section of steep rocks that might have you walk your bike. Climb gradually to the intersection with the Community Ditch Trail. You will be on the Ditch Trail for a short distance to an intersection with the Cowdrey Draw Trail. Turn right (west) uphill at the intersection with the main section of the Community Ditch Trail, which climbs gradually and then flattens next to the irrigation ditch. The views of the Flatirons are spectacular and you can see snowcapped peaks behind the foothills.

In another 200 feet is an intersection; detour briefly to the left if you want to see the private Marshall Reservoir. Continue on the almost flat trail to the west, and look for a footbridge on the left in 0.6 mile. Go across the bridge and uphill to reach the Greenbelt Plateau Trail that features pretty meadows with seasonal color schemes: bright wildflowers in the spring, golds and rusts in the autumn. After switchbacks you

will be next to the extensive Habitat Conservation Area. In an eighth of a mile you reach an intersection. Right (west) goes to the western half of the Community Ditch Trail via an underpass beneath CO 93. Continue straight (south) on the Greenbelt Plateau Trail as it gradually climbs. You will have climbed around 300 feet to this point. If you are with children or feeling satisfied, this can be your turnaround spot.

As you climb, the trail turns into a doubletrack road; close all gates behind you. You can see Marshall Reservoir to the northeast, and when you crest the hill, you will see the experimental wind turbines to the southeast. CO 93 is visible to the west. After a total of 1.2 miles on the Greenbelt Plateau Trail, you will reach its trailhead. You can reverse course for a 7-mile round-trip or continue to the southwest for the Flatirons Vista Trail, which lives up to its moniker. Use the crosswalk to safely cross CO 93, and go through the gate and head southwest on the Flatirons Vista Trail as it climbs gradually. Take the Vista North Trail option and bear right (west) as you climb a steep hill. When you crest the hill, you will have sweeping views of the Flatirons and the Indian Peaks behind the foothills.

In 1.5 miles you will reach the intersection with the Doudy Draw Trail. You can either complete the rest of the Vista Trail loop on your left for a total of 3.3 miles from the start at CO 93 and return to go for an over-10-mile outing, or venture onto the Doudy Draw Trail. You have climbed a total of 500 feet when you reach this intersection. Doudy Draw has much more technical mountain biking, with some sections requiring advanced skills or walking your bike because of the rocks. It is still pleasant to hike it and dodge the short rocky sections. The draw is very comely, with interesting high plains and foothills vegetation. The trail travels south before a hairpin turns you north and the trail plunges into the draw. This is the steepest section, and it mellows after a stream crossing. After climbing a short, gradual hill, you will reach the Spring Brook Loop intersection. This is where you can decide to either have a mellow ride back by going straight and then right (east) on the Community Ditch Trail or add more elevation and challenge on the Spring Brook Loop; both options are intermediate mountain biking trails or easy hiking. The Community Ditch Trail is an easy single- to doubletrack option with few rocks. Spring Brook Loop features more climbing, nice descents, and a few rocks, but nothing technical. You can also go straight at the Community Ditch intersection and end up at the Doudy Draw Trailhead.

Spring Brook offers a fun south loop option, or take the north section, which goes to a road that descends to CO 170/Eldorado Springs Road. If you take the south loop first, you will climb into ponderosa, welcome on a hot day, and encounter a lot of manageable rocks. If you want to complete the loop, bear left at the first intersection; right gives you an escape route onto the smooth gravel and then paved roads back to CO 170. It is marked as the Fowler Trail (which is in Eldorado Canyon State Park), but it isn't the same trail. If you bear left and stay on the Spring Brook south option, you will do some climbing through intermittent rocks and then have a nice descent sans rocks. At the next intersection after the descent, go right to exit through Doudy Draw, or go straight/left to complete the south loop. After completing it, repeat the first section of the north loop, and then bear right to exit down the smooth roads for an easy and fun descent to CO 170. At CO 170 turn right and take the paved road back to the Marshall Valley Trailhead.

## 27 Doudy Draw Trail

CITY OF BOULDER OPEN SPACE & MOUNTAIN PARKS

| | |
|---|---|
| **Distance** | Up to 6.2 miles, out-and-back |
| **Difficulty** | Easy |
| **Elevation Gain** | 300' (starting at 5,700') |
| **Trail Use** | Hiking, mountain biking, horseback riding, leashed dogs OK |
| **Agency** | City of Boulder Open Space & Mountain Parks |
| **Map(s)** | City of Boulder Open Space & Mountain Parks *South Mesa/South Boulder Creek West*; Latitude 40° *Boulder-Nederland Trails* |
| **Facilities** | Restrooms at trailhead |
| **Note(s)** | Park visitors whose cars are not registered in Boulder County need a daily or annual permit to park. Permits are available at the self-serve station. |

**HIGHLIGHTS** This short, very scenic, and easy trail is wheelchair accessible to a picnic area. It features spectacular views once you climb out of the draw.

**DIRECTIONS** Take Broadway in Boulder south toward Golden, turn right on Eldorado Springs Drive, and look for the trailhead on the south side of the road, across from the South Mesa Trailhead.

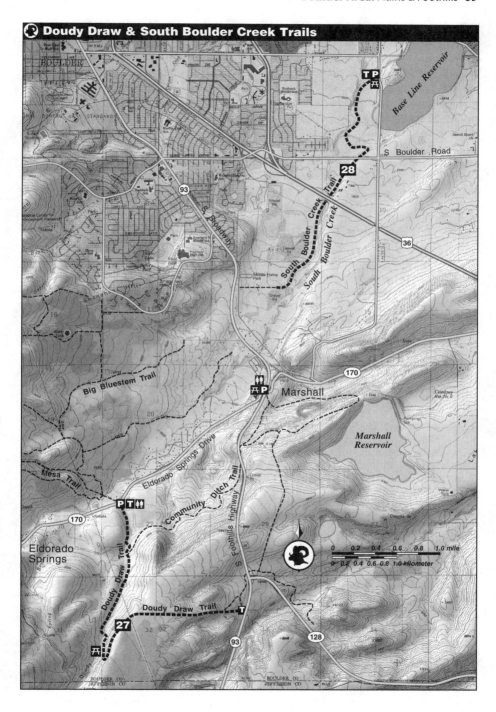

## Doudy Draw & South Boulder Creek Trails

The trail starts out flat for the first 0.5 mile and then climbs gradually to a picnic area, where the paved trail ends. You will see the Community Ditch Trail on the left; continue straight south, crossing a creek on a footbridge. The gravel trail climbs more steeply toward the top of a small mesa area that tops out at around 6,100 feet. The views are enhanced with every step, especially to the north, as the dramatic Flatirons come into view.

Once on the mesa you will be in a pretty ponderosa pine forest and will have views to the west of Eldorado Canyon and the soaring foothills. You can even see some snowcapped peaks if you're lucky. The trail continues north for 1 mile from the picnic area and then descends from the ridge, turning first north and then east as it goes the final 1.6 miles to the parking area on CO 93. It rolls and then descends a little more steeply to the parking lot.

## 28  South Boulder Creek Trail
### CITY OF BOULDER OPEN SPACE & MOUNTAIN PARKS

see map on p. 69

| | |
|---|---|
| **Distance** | Up to 8 miles, out-and-back |
| **Difficulty** | Easy |
| **Elevation Gain** | Negligible (starting at 5,430') |
| **Trail Use** | Hiking, biking, running, leashed dogs OK but not south of South Boulder Road to Marshall Road |
| **Agency** | City of Boulder Open Space & Mountain Parks |
| **Map(s)** | City of Boulder Open Space & Mountain Parks *South Mesa/South Boulder Creek West*; Latitude 40° *Boulder-Nederland Trails* |
| **Facilities** | One picnic table |
| **Note(s)** | Dogs are not allowed beyond the gate. |

**HIGHLIGHTS** This gently rolling trail has great views of the foothills and Flatirons and meanders through a pretty riparian area that is close to Boulder. It features woods, wetlands, and more than 30 varieties of wildflowers.

**DIRECTIONS** Take Baseline Road east of the Foothills Parkway to Cherryvale Road. Take Cherryvale south less than 0.5 mile to the turnoff for the Bobolink parking area on the right (west) side of the road.

Note: Flood damage destroyed the bridge on this trail in 2013. Until repairs are completed, the trail is open only on either side of the bridge.

Because it's crowded on weekends, try to visit during the week when possible. Bikers must stay on a paved path, while hikers and runners have a soft path option closer to the creek. The trails intertwine at times along the way, but it isn't possible for a biker and runner to stay together. You enjoy a short-grass prairie and creekside trees at the outset, the latter offering some shade late in the day. The trail loops east and then south before crossing under South Boulder Road via a tunnel. After you emerge from the tunnel, either go west, parallel to the road, for another 0.3 mile to a dead end or go through the gate on the south side of the road. This is a dog-free (as in no dogs allowed) extension that continues for another 1.8 miles to US 36 and then a dead end at the CO 93 intersection.

Once you pass South Boulder Road, you enjoy a very peaceful section of the trail, as it meanders as much as the creek and plays tag with some lofty, old cottonwoods. You also have nonstop foothills and Flatirons views.

*Foothills view from the South Boulder Creek Trail*

## 29 Cobalt, Sage, & Eagle Loop
### CITY OF BOULDER OPEN SPACE & MOUNTAIN PARKS

see map on p. 72

| | |
|---|---|
| **Distance** | 5.4 miles, loop |
| **Difficulty** | Easy |
| **Elevation Gain** | 100' (starting at 5,200') |
| **Trail Use** | Hiking, mountain biking, running, horseback riding, option for kids, leashed dogs OK |
| **Agency** | City of Boulder Open Space & Mountain Parks |
| **Map(s)** | City of Boulder Open Space & Mountain Parks *Boulder Valley Ranch/Lefthand/Eagle*; Latitude 40° *Boulder-Nederland Trails* |
| **Facilities** | Restrooms at trailhead |

**HIGHLIGHTS** The initial section of trail offers a mellow option that travels downhill due east and then northeast from the parking lot. It rolls fairly gently in any direction you choose to take, except south, which is uphill. It is a wide, well-maintained trail popular with hikers, bikers, and people using wheelchairs. You will enjoy superb views of the foothills, Boulder Reservoir, and even the Flatirons.

**DIRECTIONS** Take North Broadway in Boulder to US 36/CO 7; turn south and go 1 mile to Longhorn Road. Turn right (east) and go approximately 0.75 mile to parking. You will see signs for Boulder Ranch Open Space.

The trailhead at Longhorn Road offers three options: the Sage–Eagle Loop Trail, the network of hilly trails to the south accessed from the uphill Cobalt Trail, or the Left Hand Reservoir/North Rim Loop Trail. The Sage–Eagle Loop Trail is the mellowest, goes straight east out of the parking lot (Cobalt goes uphill right [south]), and offers a gently rolling trail and pretty scenery as it travels east and northeast before turning west and

then southwest back to the parking area. The first section features Boulder Reservoir views and is downhill for 1.3 miles, bottoming out next to a pretty pond that reflects the foothills on still days. The next section is a gradual uphill and tops out at the trail intersection of the Eagle Loop and Sage Trails. Go right (east), and you will go around a mile to the Eagle Loop Trailhead parking lot. Go left (north), and you will take the Sage Trail as it bends west and

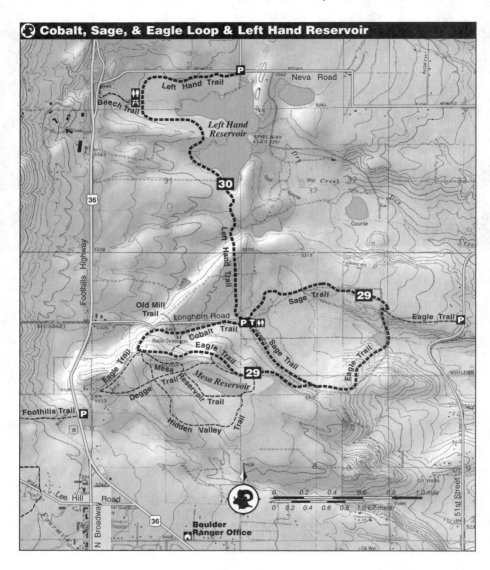

then south back to the Longhorn Road parking lot over gently rolling hills.

If you want a more challenging adventure, bear southeast and south out of the parking lot and choose either the Cobalt, Hidden Valley, or Mesa Reservoir Trails to climb up to the top of the ridge on the south side of the trail. It is a start that will get your blood pumping quickly, so make sure you warm up sufficiently before charging uphill. This route is only for intermediate mountain bikers; take no chances on the steep downhill.

Once you mount the ridge, after an approximately 0.25-mile climb, you have a good view of the reservoir in the distance to the east and the foothills to the west. The Hidden Valley and Mesa Reservoir Trails go downhill after mounting the ridge and are nice roller-coaster loops that will take you back to the east edge of the Sage Trail.

**GREAT FOR KIDS**

The first 1.5 miles of the Sage–Eagle Loop Trail is a very easy downhill and uphill return out-and-back, with the exception of the first drop, which is a steep hill that might require you to walk your bike. You see awesomely tall cottonwoods and end up at a pretty pond that reflects the foothills on calm days. This section is suitable as a short and easy mountain bike jaunt or a mellow hike.

## 30 Left Hand Reservoir
### CITY OF BOULDER OPEN SPACE & MOUNTAIN PARKS

| | |
|---|---|
| **Distance** | 6–11.4 miles, out-and-back |
| **Difficulty** | Easy–moderate |
| **Elevation Gain** | 200' (starting at 5,200') |
| **Trail Use** | Hiking, mountain biking, running, horseback riding, leashed dogs OK |
| **Agency** | City of Boulder Open Space & Mountain Parks |
| **Map(s)** | City of Boulder Open Space & Mountain Parks *Boulder Valley Ranch/ Lefthand/Eagle*; Latitude 40° *Boulder-Nederland Trails* |
| **Facilities** | Restrooms at trailhead; picnic area and restrooms at north end of trail |

**HIGHLIGHTS** This rolling trek to Left Hand Reservoir is somewhat more suitable for mountain biking or running than it is for hiking. It has foothills views, open fields, and a small, sparkling reservoir.

**DIRECTIONS** Take North Broadway in Boulder to US 36/CO 7; turn south and go 1 mile to Longhorn Road. Turn right (east) and go approximately 0.75 mile to parking. You will see signs for Boulder Ranch Open Space.

This trail starts north across the gravel road from the parking lot. Pass through the gate, and take a sharp left (west) turn to start. The trail goes up an easy uphill and then is a real roller coaster for the 2.9 miles to the parking area on Neva Road. There is one very steep downhill, about 1 mile north of the trailhead, that isn't advisable for kids or beginning mountain bikers. There is a covered picnic area with restrooms at the north end of the trail in the Beech Open Space area. When you reach the north parking lots for Beech Open Space and private Left Hand Reservoir, your best bet is to simply turn around for an out-and-back trek. Trying to complete the loop by going east on Neva Road and then through the Lake Valley golf community is not worth the trouble.

If you start at the Eagle Loop/Cobalt Trailhead, you can add 5.8 miles to your venture with the Eagle Loop/Cobalt round-trip. Take this route to the west side of Mesa Reservoir, and then return by the same route for 6 miles total. Completing the Sage–Eagle Loop will bring your total miles to 11.4.

## 31 Foothills Trail: Hogback Ridge Loop
### CITY OF BOULDER OPEN SPACE & MOUNTAIN PARKS

see map on p. 74

| | |
|---|---|
| **Distance** | 2.3 miles, balloon |
| **Difficulty** | Moderate |
| **Elevation Gain** | 300' (starting at 5,900') |
| **Trail Use** | Hiking, mountain biking (technical), leashed dogs OK |
| **Agency** | City of Boulder Open Space & Mountain Parks |
| **Map(s)** | City of Boulder Open Space & Mountain Parks *Foothills Area*; Latitude 40° *Boulder-Nederland Trails* |
| **Facilities** | None |

**HIGHLIGHTS** This steep trail includes great views and is a close-to-town alternative for a short hill workout. Most of the trail is subject to traffic noise, but the top of the rocky ridge is tree covered, fairly serene, and opens onto a beautiful meadow that attracts deer.

**DIRECTIONS** In Boulder, go to the intersection of North Broadway and US 36, travel 0.1 mile north, and immediately turn right (east) onto a gravel road. Follow it north to the parking area 0.25 mile on the left (west). The other access point is from a parking lot on Lee Hill Drive. Take Lee Hill Drive west from North Broadway 0.25 mile to a parking lot on the south side of the road. If you prefer to access the trail from Lee Hill Drive, cross the road to the north; the trail edges a subdivision before turning west and then north 0.6 mile to the loop.

This trail goes west under US 36 and gradually uphill for the first 0.5 mile. As it begins to climb, you will see a FOOTHILLS TRAIL sign pointing uphill to the south. An unmarked trail that travels uphill to the north is bike-free but travels within earshot of the highway. A better option is to turn left (south) on the actual Foothills Trail and take it 50 yards to a second intersection on the right side of the trail with the Hogback Ridge Trail. If you prefer to access the trail from Lee Hill Drive, cross the road to the north; the trail edges a subdivision before turning west and then north 0.6 mile to the loop.

When you reach the loop intersection, either go west and steeply uphill over widely spaced steps or turn north and go uphill more gradually—your choice depends on how you like to encounter steep sections, on the outbound uphill or on the return downhill. If you want to get your heart in gear as soon as possible, go left, or clockwise, to head straight uphill and see the meadow sooner. If you prefer a mellower warm-up, go north and gradually switchback up to the ridge. The view from the top is somewhat better going counterclockwise. Either way, you experience a fair amount of traffic noise unless you are hiking very early in the day.

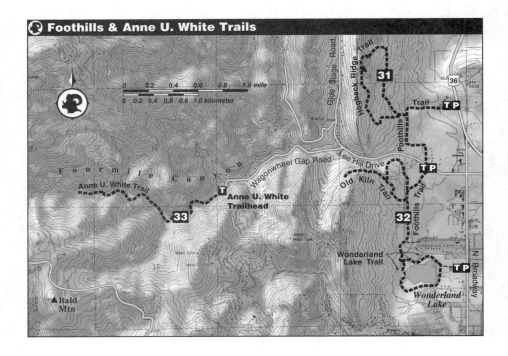

**32**    **Foothills Trail: Wonderland Lake Loop**
CITY OF BOULDER OPEN SPACE & MOUNTAIN PARKS

| | |
|---|---|
| **Distance** | Up to 6.6 miles (add 1.3 miles for Old Kiln Loop), figure eight |
| **Difficulty** | Easy |
| **Elevation Gain** | Negligible (starting at 5,200') |
| **Trail Use** | Hiking, biking, running, leashed dogs OK |
| **Agency** | City of Boulder Open Space & Mountain Parks |
| **Map(s)** | City of Boulder Open Space & Mountain Parks *Foothills Area*; Latitude 40° *Boulder-Nederland Trails* |
| **Facilities** | None |

**HIGHLIGHTS**  This delightful close-in trail, part of which is paved and accessible to sport chairs, can be used for hiking and running. You benefit from the beauty of the Boulder foothills and have the option of circumnavigating Wonderland Lake.

**DIRECTIONS**  There are many entry points along North Broadway and neighborhood streets and parks. The primary parking lot can be accessed by turning west from North Broadway onto Lee Hill Drive. Drive 0.25 mile; the lot is on the south side of the road for the Four Mile Creek trailhead.

The trail goes south out of the parking lot and rolls gently to Wonderland Lake with lots of side-trail options. If you want a flat route, go straight south. The first option you reach after 0.4 mile on the west side is the fairly steep Old Kiln Trail that goes up into the foothills. This 1.3-mile option climbs quickly with nice views, as the trail tracks north and then west, paralleling Lee Hill Drive, before going south and reaching a gate and sign that says PRIVATE ROAD. You then reach a 0.4-mile out-and-back that climbs and rolls to moderately challenge your heart, lungs, and joints. Another winding, hilly 0.3 mile takes you back to the Foothills Trail.

Traveling south on the Foothills Trail is straightforward. In 0.5 mile you can take the paved Wonderland Lake Trail. You can continue south on the main trail, with views of foothills, for as long as you wish before turning around. It is a gently rolling trail, making it ideal for easy jogging or walking. It can become icy in the winter after snowfalls and thaw–freeze cycles. The foothills shade the trail in late afternoon, so it does occasionally stay frozen in midwinter. Be sure to use appropriate footwear.

**33**    **Anne U. White Trail**
BOULDER COUNTY OPEN SPACE

| | |
|---|---|
| **Distance** | 3 miles, out-and-back |
| **Difficulty** | Easy |
| **Elevation Gain** | 200' (starting at 5,500') |
| **Trail Use** | Hiking, horseback riding, great for kids, leashed dogs OK |
| **Agency** | Boulder County Open Space |
| **Map(s)** | Boulder County Open Space *Anne U. White Trail*; Latitude 40° *Boulder-Nederland Trails* |
| **Facilities** | None |
| **Note(s)** | Bikes are prohibited. Parking is very limited. Trail was heavily damaged in 2013 flood; before you go, check to make sure it has reopened. |

**HIGHLIGHTS**  Proximity to Boulder and a pleasant arroyo environment make this a Boulder favorite for casual hikers and dog lovers. It features a delightful riparian area and rock gardens. Torrential rains and flooding closed this trail in 2013. The trail will be rebuilt, and as of press time, the planned reopening was tentatively scheduled for late 2015.

**DIRECTIONS**  Take Lee Hill Drive west from North Broadway in Boulder. Bear left just before Lee Hill Drive turns sharply north onto Wagonwheel Gap Road. Turn left on Pinto Road to the small parking area.

After the flood of 2013, this trail had to be rebuilt and may not completely match this description. After the first 0.3 mile the trail jogs across a stream bed and travels north while going uphill. It passes a small meadow and then climbs some rock steps, where you see a bench for snack or water breaks. It then rolls as it meanders through the creek bed and opens up onto a rock garden at 0.5 mile. You'll pass another small meadow at 0.7 mile. The trail steepens around the 1-mile mark as it climbs into a pretty tree canopy.

Turn sharply left when you reach a steep, rocky section; you'll see two tree stumps on the left as markers. The path rolls more steeply uphill, levels out, and abruptly ends at private property, blocking access to the Bureau of Land Management property ahead.

## 34   Gunbarrel Farm: White Rocks Trails
CITY OF BOULDER OPEN SPACE & MOUNTAIN PARKS

| | |
|---|---|
| **Distance** | 9.4 miles, out-and-back |
| **Difficulty** | Easy–moderate |
| **Elevation Gain** | 340' (starting at 5,100') |
| **Trail Use** | Hiking, biking, options for kids, leashed dogs OK |
| **Agency** | City of Boulder Open Space & Mountain Parks |
| **Map(s)** | City of Boulder Open Space & Mountain Parks *White Rocks*; Latitude 40° *Boulder-Nederland Trails* |
| **Facilities** | None |

**HIGHLIGHTS**  These surprisingly scenic trails in east Boulder are great options for hiking or intermediate mountain biking. There is a magnificent 180-degree view of the Indian Peaks and Meeker-Longs Peaks, as well as the Flatirons, from the top of Gunbarrel Hill. The rolling meadows, riparian areas, wetlands, hills and dales offer great visual variety and abundant birds. It is best to visit these sun-drenched trails in the fall or spring, or early morning, because there is no shade.

**DIRECTIONS**  You can have a long out-and-back (9.4 miles) with maximal views by using the Teller Farm North trailhead on the south side of Valmont, 0.6 mile west of 95th Street. You will have to cross Boulder Creek on the way north, not easily done at high spring runoff time because there is no bridge. If you want a shorter adventure or want to avoid the creek crossing, start at the White Rocks Trailhead near Phillips Road and 95th. Take Valmont east to 95th Street, and then go just north of Phillips Road; the trailhead will be on the west side of the road. Of course, you can start at the Teller trailhead and simply turn around whenever you wish. If it is spring runoff time for Boulder Creek, start at the White Rocks Trailhead and do out-and-back adventures on both trail segments.

From the Teller Farm trailhead go west 0.2 mile on the gravel path on the south side of Valmont, and look for the trail on the north side of the road when the path ends. It starts off flat through farm fields, jogs east after 0.25 mile, continues north 0.5 mile, travels west 0.25 mile, and then parallels a wetland and sparkling pond north 0.5 mile to the Boulder Creek crossing. After the creek crossing, the trail goes another 0.25 mile and then starts to roll over and climb a series of hills. There are nice views to the west as you climb. The trail steadily climbs, turns east for 0.25 mile, and then turns north and crosses a private road before intersecting the trail coming from the White Rocks Trailhead. Turn left (west) for the final climb to the top of

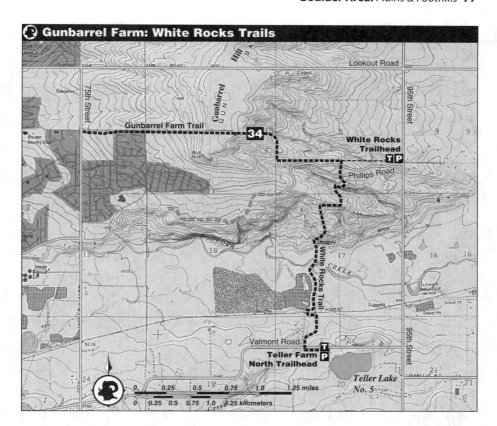

Gunbarrel Hill. The view is well worth the climb. Descend to 75th Street if you want to ride or hike the full distance.

The shorter option from the White Rocks Trailhead will take you west on a very gradual climb 0.5 mile to the intersection with the trail from the Teller trailhead.

You will be on top of a hill looking down at scenic meadows and hills. Another 1.7 miles of steeper climbing will take you to the top of Gunbarrel Hill and the great view. Return by the same route, and sample the trail to the south if you want a descent and climb back up.

***GREAT FOR KIDS***

The first sections of this trail from Teller Farm trailhead to the creek would be a short (2 miles round-trip), easy family option either on foot or on bikes in a beautiful riparian lowland with lots of vegetation. The creek has tricky rocks and logs for the crossing—easy for adults, not easy for little kids unless they get their feet wet, so this is a good spot to turn around.

---

**35**   ## Red Rocks Trail & Mount Sanitas
CITY OF BOULDER OPEN SPACE & MOUNTAIN PARKS

see map on p. 78

| | |
|---|---|
| **Distance** | Red Rocks: 1.5 miles, loop; Mount Sanitas: 3.3 miles, loop |
| **Difficulty** | Easy (Red Rocks), moderate (Mount Sanitas) |
| **Elevation Gain** | Red Rocks: 200' (starting at 5,430'); Mount Sanitas: 1,345' (starting at 5,520') |
| **Trail Use** | Hiking, mountain biking, great for kids (Red Rocks), leashed dogs OK |

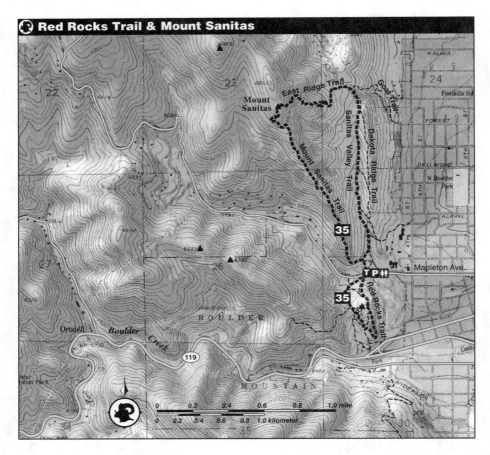

**Red Rocks Trail & Mount Sanitas**

| | |
|---|---|
| **Agency** | City of Boulder Open Space & Mountain Parks |
| **Map(s)** | City of Boulder Open Space & Mountain Parks *Centennial/Sanitas Area* and *Centennial/Red Rocks Area*; Latitude 40° *Boulder-Nederland Trails* |
| **Facilities** | Restrooms at trailhead |

**HIGHLIGHTS** Enjoy a little touch of Utah in this red rock garden. These are actually separate trails and can be experienced separately. Combining them gives you a longer, more satisfying workout, but hiking them individually can also be great fun.

**DIRECTIONS** The Red Rocks Trailhead and parking lot are at the west end of Pearl Street in Boulder, where it ends and merges into Canyon Boulevard. Mount Sanitas has its own trailhead off the west end of Mapleton Avenue.

This description assumes a starting point of Red Rocks Trailhead and hiking north. If you start there and loop Mount Sanitas, you will walk about 4 miles. If you take one of the side loops, you can hike a total of 6 miles.

### Red Rocks

If you just want a short family outing,

exploring this area is a treat. When you leave the parking lot, you'll see the bike route to Pearl Street or west to Eben Fine Park. If you walk the bike trail, watch out for high-speed bikers. The next trail is the short out-and-back Settler's Quarry. As you travel straight up the dirt path, you see the Red Rocks Trail. The whole loop is approximately 1.2 miles. Left takes you

*Outstanding formations on the Red Rocks Trail*

up into the drainage next to the first set of pretty sandstone sculptures. Right takes you up the switchbacks and to a sweeping view of Boulder. Go straight to mount the small ridge, where you'll have good views to the west and can scramble onto the rocks for photos or relaxation.

The more dramatic rocks are yet to come. Go through a short shady section that opens up to even more pleasing views of the next set of red rocks. The right trail intersects with the rest of the loop as you travel uphill to the saddle and finish the first 0.3 mile; you have a great view of Mount Sanitas and the wide trail that will take you there, as well as photo opportunities of the impressive rock monument. You can clamber onto the rocks for quiet contemplation before returning or continue down the trail to the north another 0.3 mile, through the trees to cross Mapleton/Sunshine Canyon Road, and discover the Mount Sanitas Trailhead.

## Mount Sanitas

This wide, well-groomed trail can be used for moderate hikes, though the top requires some minor rocky trail scrambling. If you don't want to combine this trail with Red Rocks, start at the trailhead on Mapleton and go up the easier Sanitas Valley Trail on the right (east) side of the valley. It is a more moderate grade in the beginning and gives you time to warm up for the steeper trails near the top. The downside of going counterclockwise is that you will have some steep downhills on the return. If you prefer to start steep and finish mellow, then go clockwise up the steeper Mount Sanitas Trail that travels straight uphill 1.4 miles to the summit, gaining more than 1,300 feet in the process. Take your time and enjoy the interesting rock formations and ponderosa pines along the way.

At around the 0.7-mile mark you are on a spectacular ridge with great views to the west. You then descend via the steep

East Ridge Trail for 0.9 mile to the mellow Sanitas Valley Trail. If you go up Valley Trail, you climb up the steep, breathtaking East Ridge Trail as you push for the summit of Mount Sanitas. From the top you'll have a canyon view to the west and the twinkling lights of Boulder spreading out into the plains below if you visit at twilight (or sunrise).

## 36  Betasso Preserve
### BOULDER COUNTY OPEN SPACE

| | |
|---|---|
| **Distance** | Canyon Loop: 3.3 miles; 6.5 miles if you do both loops |
| **Difficulty** | Moderate–difficult (hiking), easy–moderate (mountain biking) |
| **Elevation Gain** | 200' (starting at 6,400') |
| **Trail Use** | Hiking, mountain biking, horseback riding, leashed dogs OK |
| **Agency** | Betasso Preserve, Boulder County Open Space |
| **Map(s)** | Boulder County Open Space *Betasso Preserve*; Latitude 40° *Boulder-Nederland Trails* |
| **Facilities** | Restrooms, picnic tables, and grills near trailhead |
| **Note(s)** | Mountain bikes are not permitted on Wednesdays and Saturdays on Canyon Loop and Benjamin Loop Trails, and they are not permitted on Bummers Rock Trail or Blanchard Trail. Bikes are required to travel the posted direction on trails; the direction changes about every two weeks. |

**HIGHLIGHTS**  Betasso was Boulder County's first Open Space purchase in 1976. Before it became open space, it was a homestead and then a ranch owned by the Betasso family, who were originally hardrock miners. The preserve features scenic vistas, wildflowers, stands of ponderosa pine, and diverse terrain close to Boulder, and it's a great place to watch sunset colors over Boulder. Bikers can ride to Betasso from the west end of the Boulder bike path and up the steep and difficult Betasso Link Trail. There is also a steep link to the Benjamin Loop from Fourmile Canyon.

**DIRECTIONS**  Take Canyon Boulevard, CO 119, west out of Boulder for 6 miles to Sugarloaf Road. Turn right and go 0.9 mile to Betasso Road. Turn right (east) and follow the signs to the East Trailhead. Park in one of the three lots.

*Rolling meadows in Betasso Preserve*

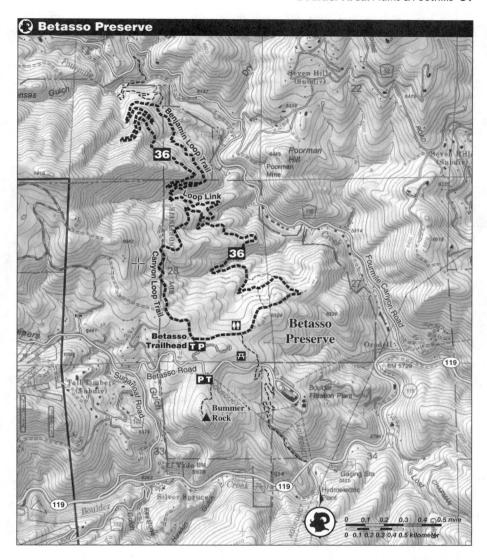

## Canyon Loop Trail

Both hikers and bikers should pay attention to the assigned direction for bikes on this loop, bikers because they are required to go that direction and hikers because you want to go in the opposite direction so you can see bikes as they approach you. Better yet, try to hike on Wednesdays or Saturdays, when Betasso is closed to bikes. This trail gets a lot of traffic, so be prepared to share. Whichever direction you go, you start on a downhill through the forest. You'll cross a seasonal stream and meander through meadows dotted with wildflowers. Watch for cabin ruins and old farm machinery left over from days when this was a working ranch. If you take a counterclockwise direction on the loop, in less than a mile you'll reach an overlook where you can see both Boulder Canyon and Boulder, with great views of the University of Colorado. Twisty turns and undulating terrain make this a fun loop for bikers to do over and over.

### Benjamin Loop

If you want more adventure, take the 0.75-mile Loop Link to the Benjamin Loop, which is also one-way for bikers. Built by volunteers, this 2.4-mile trail cruises through thick forest and in places is cut into the side of rock faces. It's steeper and narrower than Canyon Loop and more of a challenge for mountain bikers. It can also be particularly challenging for novice equestrians. If you're hiking, keep a sharp eye out for other users. Bikers should use caution when passing other users on the narrow trail.

## 37  Hall Ranch

### BOULDER COUNTY OPEN SPACE

| | |
|---|---|
| **Distance** | 9.4 miles for the Nighthawk, Bitterbrush, and Antelope Loop; add 4 miles for the Button Rock extension; loop |
| **Difficulty** | Moderate |
| **Elevation Gain** | 1,220' (starting at 5,500') |
| **Trail Use** | Hiking, mountain biking, running, option for kids |
| **Agency** | Hall Ranch, Boulder County Open Space |
| **Map(s)** | Boulder County Open Space *Hall Ranch*; Latitude 40° *Boulder County Trails* |
| **Facilities** | Restrooms at trailhead |
| **Note(s)** | Dogs are not allowed due to wildlife concerns. |

**HIGHLIGHTS**  This gem of the Boulder County Open Space Program features a beautiful loop trail popular with hikers, mountain bikers, and runners and features a great view of Longs Peak at its highest point. It is also very busy on weekends, so an early start or a weekday visit is advisable. The trail is nestled in the foothills just west of the charming town of Lyons.

**DIRECTIONS**  Lyons is north of Boulder, west of Longmont and south of the Loveland/Fort Collins area. From Lyons take CO 7 about 1 mile up the Saint Vrain Canyon. Hall Ranch will be on the right (north) side of the road. From Denver take I-25 to CO 66 to Lyons.

From the parking lot, start the loop hike on the Nighthawk Trail to the west and go clockwise if you are hiking. Bicyclists are only allowed to start to the north and travel counterclockwise. If you are on foot and want to avoid bikes altogether, go west and hike out and back rather than completing the entire loop. I describe this hike as a clockwise loop starting from the west side of the parking lot and joining the biking trail at the high point to return to the parking area.

From the parking lot go west as the trail rolls gently through tall yellow grass and crosses a service road. It goes uphill, steepening and getting rocky. The soaring cliffs offer some great sights behind you before you round the corner. The trail then travels north and west for 1 mile. When you come to the mile marker, you enjoy great foothills and vista views; that's what you will be climbing.

The trail turns south and gradually descends, losing almost 100 feet; a quarry and CO 7 are briefly visible from the trail. After you switchback down to the trickle of water, the trail turns right (north), regaining the lost altitude gradually as it climbs 100 feet up over the next 0.25 mile and away from the road and quarry noise. It then turns northwest through a beautiful meadow, where you see a fire marker and then the second mile marker at around 5,900 feet. The trail climbs 200 feet in the next 0.5 mile as it offers views of a small canyon that it parallels. At around 6,100 feet and 2.5 miles, the trail levels with superb 180-degree views.

The trail steepens for the next 0.5 mile and tracks to the southwest, becoming more

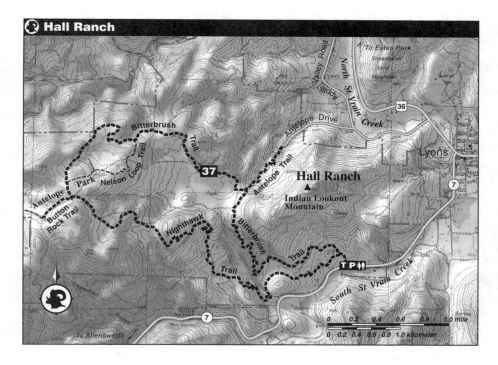

narrow and rocky as it traverses the foothills terrain. It levels and morphs into long, easy, but uphill switchbacks that top out at almost 6,400 feet at around 3.2 miles. Enjoy the sunny, flat spot, or descend 50 feet into some trees and shade, as the trail tracks north, climbing across a pretty meadow and then letting you enjoy a mountain view as it heads east. Another 0.25 mile brings you to around 6,500 feet. The trail continues to climb, mostly in the open. You come to a trail intersection at around 4 miles; next to a lone shade tree, bear left. After crossing another meadow, the trail enters a stand of lodgepole pines and passes a stone retaining wall. The long, gentle climb of almost 0.5 mile brings you to the high point of 6,700 feet, approximately 4.5 miles from the beginning of the trail—the highlight of the hike and a great place for lunch because you enjoy a spectacular view of Longs Peak and a panorama of the entire Rocky Mountain National Park massif. You also see signage that says you can add another 4.5

miles for the Button Rock Trail, which travels west from this intersection. You also see a trail that goes right for the old ranch road; your route continues straight and takes you near a long-abandoned hotel complex.

Now the descent begins in earnest and you're sharing the trail with mountain bikers. In approximately 0.1 mile you intersect the Nelson Loop Trail, a pleasant detour that can add another 2.2 miles to your day if you circle the entire loop. If you continue to the left, you get some better views as you trek 1.1 miles around the Nelson Loop Trail and eventually intersect the Bitterbrush Trail. From there you are approximately 4 miles from the trailhead. The trail descends rapidly across some classic mountain meadows with views of rocky cliffs, turning north to south at 6,440 feet. It then crosses a drainage and stream, and you see a trail marker. You are enjoying nonstop views of the hogback, foothills, and Saint Vrain Canyon while sharing the trail with frequent mountain bikers.

If you don't mind sharing the trail with bikers round-trip, this final segment of the Antelope Trail is also a nice, 8-mile counterclockwise out-and-back trip. The trail switchbacks in trees, crosses under a power line, and then levels for a wonderful panorama of meadows and foothills, and a prairie dog colony at 6,200 feet. The trail descends to a drainage and then climbs gently to a bench that offers a view of the hogback and a place for contemplation just off-trail from the legion of polite bikers. You are now 2.25 miles from the Antelope Trailhead, a side trail and alternate entrance to the area. The trail climbs briefly for 0.25 mile before descending to the 8-mile mark and great views of Heil Ranch across the canyon. The next 2 miles are a steep, rocky 600-foot descent, and then the trail levels as you enjoy hogback-view heaven. The trail turns south, rolls over a drainage through pinyon pine trees, and provides an easy stroll to the trailhead with great views all around.

## GREAT FOR KIDS

With its great views, the mile marker is a good turnaround for an easy 2-mile jaunt with small children. The 2.5-mile point is also a good place for families with small children to turn around for a 5-mile round-trip with superb scenery.

---

## 38  Heil Valley Ranch
### BOULDER COUNTY OPEN SPACE

| | |
|---|---|
| **Distance** | 8-mile loop, plus a potential side loop |
| **Difficulty** | Easy–moderate |
| **Elevation Gain** | 600' (starting at 6,000') |
| **Trail Use** | Hiking, mountain biking, option for kids |
| **Agency** | Heil Valley Ranch, Boulder County Open Space |
| **Map(s)** | Boulder County Open Space *Heil Valley Ranch*; Latitude 40° *Boulder County Trails* |
| **Facilities** | Restrooms and a tree-shaded picnic area |
| **Note(s)** | Dogs are not allowed due to wildlife concerns. |

**HIGHLIGHTS**  Another gem in the Boulder Open Space collection of precious jewels, just south of the Hall Ranch Trail. Though shorter and less challenging than the Hall Ranch loop, this trip offers a variety of scenery, including snowcapped peaks, wildlife, and the unique geology of fault and fracture foothills zone with the sedimentary rock of the hogback and the lichen-covered boulders of the hills. You also enjoy views of Hall Ranch and Saint Vrain Canyon on the northern corner of the loop. Heavy use and erosion have made this more challenging for mountain biking. The much rockier trails now require intermediate to advanced mountain biking skills.

**DIRECTIONS**  The trail is approximately 1 mile west of US 36, between Boulder and Lyons. It is on the north side of Left Hand Canyon Drive.

Upon leaving the parking area, you immediately come to the Lichen Loop Trail on the right (east) side of the road. The main route, the Wapiti Trail, continues straight (north) 2.5 miles to the intersection with the Ponderosa Loop Trail, which is another 2.6 miles round-trip. Approximately 0.5 mile from the parking lot, you come to the second intersection with the Lichen Loop Trail. You could walk the portion just the other side of the fence out or back for variety. Continuing on the Wapiti Trail, when you encounter a closed segment turn left (west) on the Wapiti Trail as it goes more steeply uphill. As you cross over the meadow, you have a great view of the hogback to the south. The next mile becomes rockier under good tree cover, pleasant on hot or windy days. There's a trail marker at 1 mile, and then you pass an old, low wall at approximately the 2-mile mark. The trail then turns left (west), climbs, levels in 0.25 mile, and

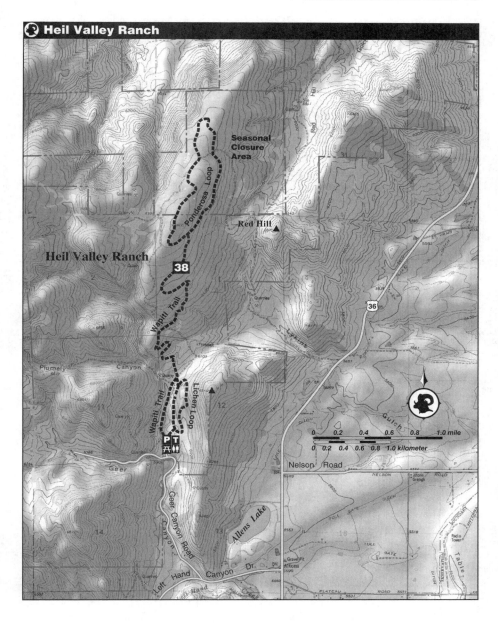

then climbs steeply through thick lodgepole pine trees to 6,600 feet, 700 feet higher than the trailhead, at the 2.5-mile mark, where you will reach the Ponderosa Loop Trail.

Your choice on the loop: Going counterclockwise (left) means you'll have a steeper hike on the way out, while going right (clockwise) means your hike on the way out will be more gradual, but the return trip to the Wapiti Trail will be steep. Either way, you have to watch out for bikes; I would rather have bikes bombing down steep sections coming at me head-on so that I can see them instead of approaching me from behind. If, however, you don't want to hike the whole loop, and do want to see

*Hogbacks and foothills peaks from Heil Valley Ranch*

great views, then go right (northeast)—in another 1.5 miles you can enjoy the overlook and turn around.

Going counterclockwise (southwest, then west) the trail switchbacks broadly and then more narrowly as it climbs through the forest. It tops the hill at around 6,750 feet, 150 feet higher than the beginning of the loop. It then levels and travels north. You have a view of snowcapped peaks off-trail on the left (west) side of the trail through lighter tree cover. The trail then descends through an open meadow with great views of Left Hand Reservoir and the plains to the east. The trail then enters ponderosa pines to confirm its name. In another 0.1 mile, you have good views of Longs Peak, the Indian Peaks, and Hall Ranch. The trail descends gently to an overlook at 6,500 feet. (This previously mentioned overlook can be reached more quickly if you travel counterclockwise, to the right when you first reach the loop.) From the overlook the trail descends gradually to the beginning of the loop.

### GREAT FOR KIDS

For an easy family-with-small-children hike, take the 1-mile Lichen Loop Trail. It climbs around 120 feet to the top of a small hill with superb views of the geology of the foothills and hogback.

### CHIEF NIWOT

The Arapaho Indians were the primary tribe in the 1800s when European settlers arrived in the area that would eventually become Boulder. Chief Niwot (*Niwot* is Arapaho for "left hand") was born in the 1820s and tried to live peacefully with whites in the Boulder Valley as an honorable, intelligent leader. Many Boulder County streets, towns, reservoirs, and canyons are named after him.

In the late 1850s settlers broke the Fort Laramie Treaty that Niwot had negotiated in 1851, taking the Arapahos' land and decimating the buffalo herds on which they depended for food. The tribe was devastated by disease and hunger and moved to the Great Plains to escape the white man's wrath. It was there, near Sand Creek, that Colonel John Chivington and 550 troops massacred 163 unarmed Arapahos, primarily women and old men. There is a new monument about this at the site.

## 39   **Walker Ranch: Meyers Homestead Trail**
BOULDER COUNTY OPEN SPACE

see map on p. 88

| | |
|---|---|
| **Distance** | 5.2 miles, out-and-back |
| **Difficulty** | Easy |
| **Elevation Gain** | 750' (starting at 7,500') |
| **Trail Use** | Hiking, biking, horseback riding, leashed dogs OK |
| **Agency** | Walker Ranch, Boulder County Open Space |
| **Map(s)** | Boulder County Open Space *Walker Ranch*; Latitude 40° *Boulder-Nederland Trails* |
| **Facilities** | Picnic area and restrooms at trailhead |

**HIGHLIGHTS** This is a truly mellow family trail that climbs gradually to a sweeping overview of Boulder Canyon, with the Indian Peaks in the distance. You will immediately enjoy grassy, rolling meadows, wildflowers, and stately stands of aspen and pine. Any round-trip distance on this trail is worthwhile. It is generally an easy doubletrack mountain biking trail, with only a few steep climbs. It commemorates homesteaders Walker and Meyers, who settled here in the 1800s.

**DIRECTIONS** From the Chautauqua Park intersection on Baseline Road in Boulder, drive 6.8 miles on Flagstaff Road to the trailhead that is on the right (west) side of the road.

The trail is to the right (north) of the Walker Ranch loop trail. It goes gradually downhill at the outset with views of the Walker Ranch rock formations to the southwest. It is a wide, soft dirt, doubletrack trail. After 0.25 mile there is a bench, and you will see signs about the Meyers and Walker homesteads, and a historic building across a meadow. The trail continues downhill to around the 0.5-mile mark and then starts its gradual uphill climb. As it climbs, you will enter the classic mixed forest of aspen and conifers with some stately ponderosa pines. At around 1.2 miles the rolling trail steepens and goes through a short rocky section. There is some erosion that narrows the trail to singletrack. After it travels under a power line it levels briefly before resuming its climb. At 1.5 miles, steep switchbacks climb next to a comely stand of aspens. The last mile is the steepest section, and you are rewarded with a bench that overlooks Boulder Canyon and the Indian Peaks.

*One of the remaining buildings from the Meyers Homestead on Walker Ranch*

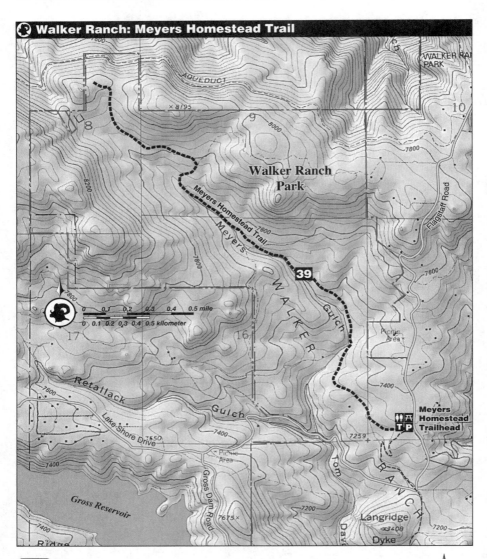

**Walker Ranch: Meyers Homestead Trail**

## 40  Walker Ranch

BOULDER COUNTY OPEN SPACE

see map on p. 89

| | |
|---|---|
| **Distance** | Up to 7.6 miles, loop |
| **Difficulty** | Moderate (hiking), challenging (mountain biking) |
| **Elevation Gain** | 1,500' (starting at 7,300') |
| **Trail Use** | Hiking, mountain biking, horseback riding, leashed dogs OK |
| **Agency** | Walker Ranch, Boulder County Open Space |
| **Map(s)** | Boulder County Open Space *Walker Ranch*; Latitude 40° *Boulder-Nederland Trails* |
| **Facilities** | Restrooms and picnic area at trailheads |
| **Note(s)** | Equestrians are discouraged from using the eastern leg due to extremely steep staircase conditions. |

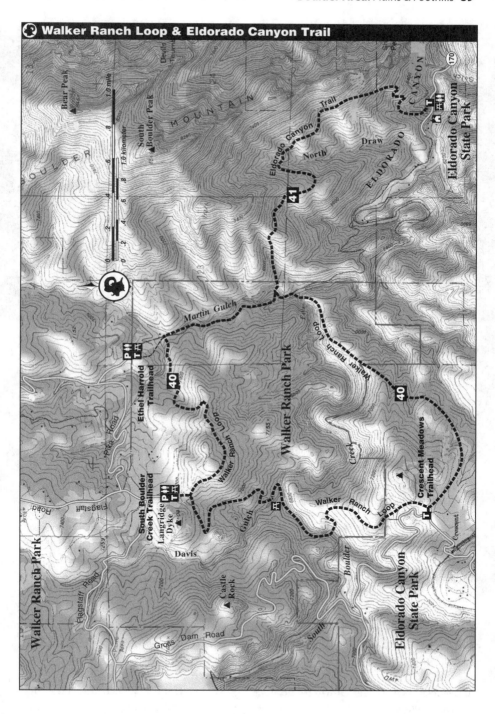

**Walker Ranch Loop & Eldorado Canyon Trail**

*Hillsides scorched by fire in 2000 are coming back to life on Walker Ranch.*

**HIGHLIGHTS**  This beautiful, rugged foothills area features high ridges and a beautiful canyon with sparkling Boulder Creek running through it. The ranch is almost 3,778 acres—more than 1,000 acres were scorched in the Eldorado fire in 2000, but the vegetation was generally reinvigorated by it. It features the mountain version of sparkling Boulder Creek, old ranch homestead buildings, and a dazzling display of wildflowers, ponderosa pines, and wildlife. The ranch is a premier mountain biking area and a superb hiking environment. If you're a hiker who wants to avoid bikers, visit during the week or be prepared to dodge lots of biking enthusiasts. If you're a biker, be prepared for some challenging, technical terrain.

Experiencing the entire loop is a delightful challenge at a fast pace on foot. You can enjoy out-and-back hikes down to the creekside canyon from either the South Boulder Creek (or nearby Ethel Harrold Trailhead) or Crescent Meadows Trailhead. Or you can hike all the way over from Eldorado Canyon State Park and use a car shuttle or enjoy a bike-free out-and-back adventure.

**DIRECTIONS**  The most popular trailhead is South Boulder Creek, accessed from Boulder by taking Baseline Road west to Flagstaff Mountain Road and going up and over Flagstaff Mountain. If the parking lot is full, you can just as easily use the nearby Ethel Harrold Trailhead and Picnic Area. Getting down to the creek is less scenic but 1.75 miles shorter than the South Boulder Creek Trailhead.

The Crescent Meadows Trailhead is closer to Denver and Golden and is 8 miles from CO 93. Take CO 72 west and watch for signs for Gross Dam Road, which takes you near the trailhead.

## Crescent Meadows Access

You can, of course, use this access point to hike or bike the entire 7.6-mile loop. Or you have two choices for shorter out-and-back hikes to get down to Boulder Creek Canyon. If you go north-northwest (left), it takes only 1.5 miles to reach the pretty canyon, but the trail parallels the road a short time. You also have views of the often snowcapped peaks of the Continental Divide. It is a steep, short plunge to the creek.

If you want a longer trek (2.5 miles to the canyon), then go right (northeast) across the beautiful meadow that gives the trailhead its name. It is a more gradual descent, with long, sweeping switchbacks and almost constant views of the rock formations that top Eldorado Canyon and the plains to the east. The last 0.25 mile to the creek is very steep steps with views of the arroyo on the way down.

## South Boulder Creek Trailhead

From this trailhead I recommend starting off to the right (southwest) toward the South Boulder Creek Picnic Area. This is the shorter trek down to the creek. If you decide that all you want to do is hike to the creek, this is definitely the way to go. If you want to hike or bike the entire loop, this is also the less steep, wider trail to start on for the descent into the canyon. You will have an uphill on the way back regardless of the way you go. This description goes counterclockwise (southwest or right) on the loop and starts toward South Boulder Creek Picnic Area 1.6 miles ahead—a good goal for families.

The trail immediately goes downhill with a view of two large, striking rock formations. In 0.25 mile there is an overlook of the dramatic valley that uplift and the creek have created. The wide, well-maintained trail descends gradually through the burn area and the thinned forest, where there is already much new growth. You lose about 600 feet in a little less than 1 mile. The soothing sounds of the stream are loud and clear here and at the 1-mile mark as the trail climbs gently before its final descent to the shaded picnic tables at around 6,500 feet. There is a sculpted wall of rock on the other side of the jostling water. Because the riparian area was untouched by the fire, the trees are stately. Once you are streamside, the wonderful arroyo opens up as you hike or bike next to the cascading water. You pass small waterfalls and then cross the stream on a footbridge.

The trail turns sharply northeast as it passes a bench. It is time to regain elevation as you climb 200 feet in the first 0.25 mile on the more narrow and rocky trail. Disregard a side trail to an unremarkable overlook unless you want a snack break. At the 2-mile mark you are back up to 7,150 feet and have an impressive view across the canyon of the entire trail and the distant parking lot high above.

The trail levels and then turns left (north-northeast) toward the Crescent Meadows Trailhead. You are climbing 100 feet every 0.25 mile in this steep trail section, back up to 7,200 feet quickly. You then parallel the Gross Mountain Reservoir Road for 0.25 mile and see the dam face. At the Crescent Meadows Trailhead take a sharp left (northeast) and cross the gorgeous meadow as the trail descends 150 feet to the 3-mile marker. You enjoy sweeping views all the way to the top of Eldorado Canyon and the plains beyond. When I scouted this trail, I reached the 4-mile marker at 6,800 feet about 2 hours from the start of the hike.

The trail switchbacks down more steeply to an option for a less technical mountain biking route that's also easier for hikers. At around 4.5 miles, you begin to hear the sounds of the stream again as you negotiate very steep steps that wind around 0.25 mile to the creek. Enjoy the panorama of the rock garden arroyo on the way down to the cool waters.

When you reach the water, you have to look carefully ahead to see the trail going northwest uphill. You can hear the small waterfalls producing a good roar. Watch for water ouzels as you cross the bridge and prepare to climb 900 feet back up to the parking lot. The trail roller-coasters through the valley and then screams straight uphill past an old mill site. Watch for the sharp left turn to stay on the South Boulder Creek Trail in 0.5 mile. If you don't turn, you will end up at the Ethel Harrold Trailhead. At 6,800 feet, after gaining 300 feet from the creek, you roll through Columbine Gulch drainage until it tops out on a ridgeline. From there you have a commanding view as you make the final climb to the ridgetop at 7,282 feet, where you're looking again at the scorched earth as you enjoy the panoramic ridge walk (with one short uphill section) back to the parking lot.

*GREAT FOR KIDS*

The 0.75-mile mark is a fine turnaround point for small children or the altitude-challenged. Walker Ranch's great views make for a satisfying, brief trip.

---

 ## Eldorado Canyon Trail
### ELDORADO CANYON STATE PARK

see map on p. 89

| | |
|---|---|
| **Distance** | Up to 9 miles, out-and-back |
| **Difficulty** | Moderate–challenging |
| **Elevation Gain** | 1,000' (starting at 6,000') |
| **Trail Use** | Hiking, horseback riding, option for kids, leashed dogs OK |
| **Agency** | Eldorado Canyon State Park |
| **Map(s)** | *Eldorado Canyon State Park*; Latitude 40° *Boulder-Nederland Trails* |
| **Facilities** | Restrooms, visitor center, picnic area, and hot springs pool |
| **Note(s)** | Park fee required. |

**HIGHLIGHTS**  See the panorama of 1.7 billion years of geologic history that has become some of the most renowned rock climbing terrain in North America, with countless climbers dangling from vertical cliffs on hundreds of challenging routes—all in the first mile you travel through the park on the trail. The state park is a fee area but is worth the price of admission. One of the best Front Range trails for scenery in one of the most accessible areas takes hikers along the top of a spectacular canyon with views of the Indian Peaks and the occasional Amtrak or coal train chugging along on the Moffat Road railroad tracks that were high above. Soak in the Eldorado Springs pool after your adventure. A hike of any length is rewarding. Allow most of a day for the 9-mile round-trip.

**DIRECTIONS**  From Boulder, take CO 93 south. Turn right on CO 170 and continue to the park entrance west of Eldorado Springs, about 8 miles southwest of Boulder. From Denver, take I-25 north to US 36 (west toward Boulder). Exit at Louisville-Superior and turn left (south) at the light. Take the first right (west) onto CO 170, and follow it 7.4 miles to Eldorado Canyon State Park. Continue to the visitor center.

Parking is limited and challenging on weekends, so carpool and arrive early. A large picnic area with a lot of tables surrounds the visitor center. The trail begins east of the center, crosses the road to the north, and then stairsteps quickly uphill. You experience steep switchbacks that climb around 300 feet in the first 0.5 mile and offer good photo opportunities. Enjoy the cluster of trees; most of the trail is open to the sun and can become warm if you get an early start. Around 0.75 mile the trail mellows, with spectacular 180-degree views, including often-snowcapped Indian Peaks, in the distance.

The trail temporarily descends and turns northwest, heading around a rockfall area and downed tree at around the 1-mile mark. It then climbs through a steep switchback to around 6,700 feet with even better peak views. At 1.5 miles it mellows into a ridge walk with sweeping views. It then descends gradually through ferns and poison ivy before roller-coastering a bit.

After hiking for about an hour and a half, you reach the point where the trail makes a short climb to the next ridge before plunging 500 feet down to the creek. It is a rewarding round-trip but pushes the hike into the more difficult range for most people because you'll have to climb back out and then descend what you just climbed.

**42** ## Rabbit Mountain: Little Thompson Overlook Trail

BOULDER COUNTY OPEN SPACE

| | |
|---|---|
| **Distance** | 3 miles, out-and-back |
| **Difficulty** | Easy–moderate |
| **Elevation Gain** | 500' (starting at 5,490') |
| **Trail Use** | Hiking, mountain biking, horseback riding, great for kids, leashed dogs OK |
| **Agency** | Rabbit Mountain, Boulder County Open Space |
| **Map(s)** | Boulder County Open Space *Rabbit Mountain*; Latitude 40° *Boulder County Trails* |
| **Facilities** | Restrooms and picnic tables at trailhead |
| **Note(s)** | Nearby Indian Mesa Trail is a great mountain biking option. |

**HIGHLIGHTS** This area was tropical lowland covered by rivers, swamps, and lagoons 140 million years ago. Dinosaurs and other reptiles wandered through the lush vegetation. In more recent history, American Indians lived in this area for at least 5,000 years. Eventually, battles were lost and treaties were signed and broken, and the Arapaho and Cheyenne were permanently removed from their lands by 1867; today their descendants live on reservations in Wyoming and Oklahoma.

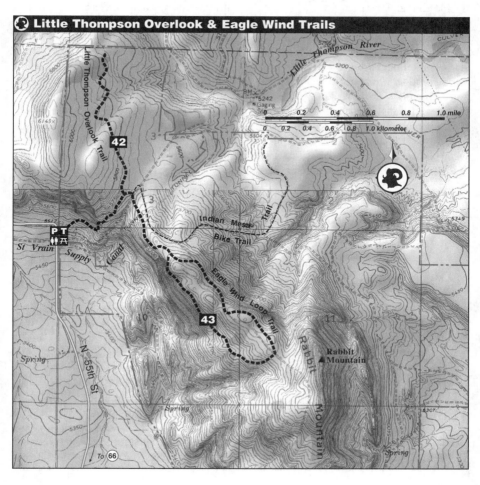

Little Thompson Overlook & Eagle Wind Trails

Rabbit Mountain offers a variety of family-friendly trails that feature sweeping views of the plains, foothills, mountains, and hogback. There is some shade, but most of the ponderosa pine trees are scattered and not large; these trails are better on cool days, or in the spring and fall or even winter, unless you start early and avoid the midday heat. Rolling Little Thompson Trail has a perch for a hogback and foothills view. If you'd like a moderate day, combine this trail with the Eagle Wind Trail.

**DIRECTIONS**  From Boulder, take US 36 north toward Lyons. At the intersection with CO 66, turn right. In 1 mile turn left on 53rd Street at the sign for Rabbit Mountain. Look for the parking lot in about 2 miles.

From the parking lot, you have two options. If you are hiking, bear northeast and go up the hiking trail that switchbacks gently up the south-facing slope. If you're biking, hop on your bike, bear right, go due east on the road, and then turn left (north) in about 0.25 mile. After you turn left (north), you'll be going uphill on a trail that is more like a service or access road and is wide enough for cars.

If you are hiking, you immediately have changing hogback views to the northwest as you are going up. The steepest section is at the beginning, so don't be discouraged as the trail moderates after the first 0.25 mile. You can enjoy early season wildflowers, cactus, and trailside rocks that kids might like to perch on. After the switchbacks, the trail travels north-northeast, and you will see a biking route on the right (east) side of the trail. The trail climbs more gradually over the next 0.25 mile before reaching a level spot and a trail intersection. At this point you can bear left (northwest) to stay on the overlook trail, which is signed, or go downhill, cross the road, and take the Eagle Wind Trail loop (trail 43). Though it is tempting to stop here, wait until you reach the overlook, so you can savor the view.

The Little Thompson Trail climbs a little more and then descends for approximately 0.25 mile, with pretty views of the dramatic rock formations to the north. You also have a view of the northeast slope of Rabbit Mountain as you traverse down and then up across the mountainside. The trail gets somewhat steeper and is surrounded by a variety of shrubs that are taller as you reach the overlook. There is a bench for a snack break or other rock options if you want to rock scramble and escape your fellow travelers.

## 43  Rabbit Mountain: Eagle Wind Trail
### BOULDER COUNTY OPEN SPACE

see map on p. 93

|  |  |
|---|---|
| **Distance** | 4.3 miles, balloon |
| **Difficulty** | Easy–moderate |
| **Elevation Gain** | 380' (starting at 5,490') |
| **Trail Use** | Hiking, mountain biking, horseback riding, leashed dogs OK |
| **Agency** | Rabbit Mountain, Boulder County Open Space |
| **Map(s)** | Boulder County Open Space *Rabbit Mountain*; Latitude 40° *Boulder County Trails* |
| **Facilities** | Restrooms and picnic tables at trailhead |
| **Note(s)** | The nearby Indian Mesa Trail is a great mountain biking option. |

**HIGHLIGHTS**  The Rabbit Mountain area was tropical lowland covered by rivers, swamps, and lagoons 140 million years ago. Dinosaurs and other reptiles wandered through the lush vegetation. In more recent history, American Indians lived in this area for at least 5,000 years. Eventually, battles were lost and treaties were signed and broken, and the Arapaho and Cheyenne were permanently removed from their lands by 1867; today their descendants live on reservations in Wyoming and Oklahoma.

Rabbit Mountain offers a variety of family-friendly trails that feature sweeping views of the plains, foothills, mountains, and hogback. There is some shade, but most of the ponderosa pine trees are scattered and not large; these trails are better on cool days or in the spring and fall unless you start early and avoid the midday heat. A pleasant, rolling jaunt with great views, the Eagle Wind Trail overlooks the plains and steep slopes of Rabbit Mountain from an easy loop. If you'd like a moderate day, combine this trail with the Little Thompson Overlook Trail.

**DIRECTIONS** From Boulder, take US 36 north toward Lyons. At the intersection with CO 66, turn right. In 1 mile turn left on 53rd Street (which becomes 55th Street) at the sign for RABBIT MOUNTAIN. Look for the parking lot in about 2 miles.

From the parking lot, you have two options. If you want to take the trail to the Eagle Wind loop, bear northeast and go up the trail that switchbacks gently up the south-facing slope. If you'd rather follow the dirt road, bear right, go due east on the road, and then turn north in about 0.25 mile. After you turn north, you'll be going uphill on a trail that is more like a service or access road and is wide enough for two cars.

If you are hiking the trail, you immediately have changing hogback views to the northwest as you are going up. The steepest section is at the beginning, so don't be discouraged as the trail moderates after the first 0.25 mile. You can enjoy early season wildflowers, cactus, and trailside rocks that kids might like to perch on. After the switchbacks, the trail travels north-northeast, and you see the biking route on the right (east) side of the trail. The trail climbs more gradually over the next 0.25 mile before reaching a level spot and a trail intersection. At this point you can bear left (northwest) to stay on the overlook trail, which is signed, or go downhill, cross the road, and take the Eagle Wind Trail loop.

If you've chosen the dirt road from the parking lot to reach the turnoff for the Eagle Wind Trail loop, look for the trail on the right (east) side of the road after you crest the hill. The loop begins in a saddle between the two humps that form Rabbit Mountain and traverses the easternmost broad ridge of Rabbit Mountain.

The loop starts uphill from the dirt road, and you have views of the distant Flatirons

*Shade can be sparse on the Eagle Wind Trail.*

and foothills north of Boulder, to the south, through the occasional trees that border the trail. The first 0.25 mile from the road is uphill; then the trail climbs more gradually and levels as it reaches the top. You pass several social (informal) trails on the right (south), but the actual trail is well marked—so stay on it to prevent erosion. Once you reach the actual loop trail intersection, if you go right (counterclockwise) around the loop, you will emerge from the trees and shrubs to the aforementioned views to the

south and the panorama of the Continental Divide that opens up to the west. The trail descends gradually with impressive arroyo views as it narrows and gets rockier. Sweeping views of the plains greet you as you roll around to the east side of the mountain.

You have a slight climb on the way back either way because a section of the east end of the trail is lower than the west side, but not significantly so. The views and effort are equal regardless of the direction you choose and well worth the price of admission.

## 44  Pella Crossing

### BOULDER COUNTY OPEN SPACE

| | |
|---|---|
| **Distance** | Up to 3 miles total (1.9 miles on Braly Trails, 1 mile on Marlatt Trails, 0.5 mile on trail connecting them), figure eight |
| **Difficulty** | Easy |
| **Elevation Gain** | Negligible (starting at approximately 5,000') |
| **Trail Use** | Hiking, mountain biking, running, horseback riding, fishing (catch-and-release bass, belly boat), great for kids, leashed dogs OK |
| **Agency** | Pella Crossing, Boulder County Open Space |
| **Map(s)** | Boulder County Open Space *Pella Crossing*; Latitude 40° *Boulder County Trails* |
| **Facilities** | Restrooms, picnic tables, and a group shelter at trailhead |
| **Note(s)** | These trails were damaged by the flood of 2013 and rebuilt. Before you go, check to make sure they have reopened. |

**HIGHLIGHTS**  This delightful collection of peaceful, small lakes is circled by wide, flat, short trails ideal for easygoing strolls near Boulder. Circumnavigate Sunset and Webster Ponds or Heron Lake on the Braly Trails on the eastern side of the park, or the smaller Poplar, Dragonfly, and Clearwater Ponds on the Marlatt Trails on the western side of the park—or perhaps connect the two for a longer outing. Both feature waterfowl, dragonflies, deer, foxes, and butterflies. Longs Peak peers over the top of the west side, while the distant foothills highlight the views of the east side ponds and almost reflect in the still waters. Belly-boat fishing is allowed.

**DIRECTIONS**  From the informal village of Hygiene, which is north of Boulder, west of Longmont, and east of Lyons, turn south onto North 75th Street. Pella Crossing is 0.5 mile south of town. The parking area is on the east side of road.

These lakes and ponds are reclaimed gravel pits that Boulder County purchased in 1995 and restored; the county did a beautiful job, making this a delightful natural area. The whole area is a great place for family strolls and mellow picnics. If you only have time to circle one lake, I suggest the largest one, Heron Lake. It has a few tiny islands that birds enjoy, as well as trees and views.

For the Braly Trails, go right (east) from the parking area between Sunset and

Webster Ponds 0.25 mile to a trail intersection. Go left (north) between Sunset Pond and Heron Lake another 0.25 mile; then turn right (southeast) and enjoy the 0.5-mile jaunt along the northern edge of Heron Lake. Circle the lake back to Webster and Sunset Ponds, where you can circumnavigate either of them. Circle all three and you have completed an almost 2-mile loop.

From the northwest edge of Sunset Pond, you can extend your excursion and walk

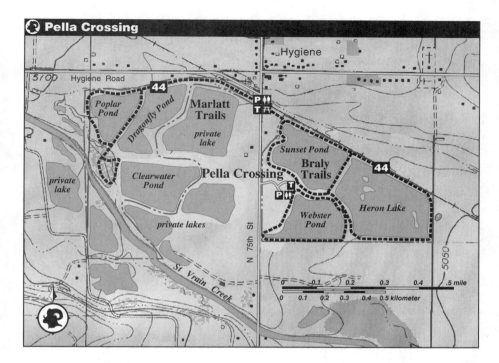

**Pella Crossing**

0.3 mile over to the Marlatt Trails on a connector trail. You get a farm-framed view of Longs Peak as your reward. You'll add another mile to your trek if you walk around this group of pretty ponds (Poplar, Dragonfly, and Clearwater).

**45**    **Lagerman Reservoir**

BOULDER COUNTY OPEN SPACE

see
map on
p. 98

| | |
|---|---|
| **Distance** | 1.6 miles, loop |
| **Difficulty** | Easy |
| **Elevation Gain** | Negligible (starting at 5,200') |
| **Trail Use** | Hiking, mountain biking, fishing, great for kids, leashed dogs OK |
| **Agency** | Lagerman Reservoir, Boulder County Open Space |
| **Map(s)** | Boulder County Open Space *Lagerman Reservoir*; Latitude 40° *Boulder-Nederland Trails* |
| **Facilities** | Restrooms, picnic table, and a group shelter at trailhead |
| **Note(s)** | From April 1 to August 31, the western end of the reservoir is closed for nesting birds. |

**HIGHLIGHTS** This easy, flat loop trail is great for families with small children or anyone wanting some quiet contemplation of the Flatirons/foothills views.

**DIRECTIONS** Take North 75th Street north from CO 119 between Boulder and Longmont, and turn left on Pike Road, which is called Clover Basin Road on the other side of 75th. Drive 0.5 mile west on Pike Road to the entrance on the left (south) side.

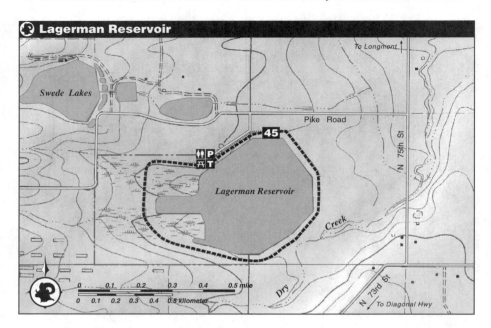

Lagerman Reservoir

Circle the reservoir clockwise to get the best foothills views. A thicket of beautiful sunflowers decorates the north shoreline in season. You will have a good, though distant, view of the Flatirons from the reservoir. This is a good place to bring small children for an easy nature adventure. The trail is virtually flat, and you will likely see ducks and geese. The picnic area and restrooms make it easy for a picnic, too. Tie together routes with adjacent gravel roads for easy mountain biking.

## 46  Walden & Sawhill Ponds
BOULDER COUNTY OPEN SPACE

| | |
|---|---|
| **Distance** | 2.6 miles, loop |
| **Difficulty** | Easy |
| **Elevation Gain** | Negligible (starting at 5,200') |
| **Trail Use** | Hiking, mountain biking (bikes prohibited on the boardwalk), fishing, bird-watching, leashed dogs OK |
| **Agency** | Walden Ponds Wildlife Habitat, Boulder County Open Space |
| **Map(s)** | Boulder County Open Space *Walden Ponds Wildlife Habitat*; Latitude 40° *Boulder-Nederland Trails* |
| **Facilities** | Restrooms, picnic table, and a group shelter at trailhead |

**HIGHLIGHTS**  More than 19 small ponds and wetlands, once mined for gravel, are scattered on 113 acres of restored habitat. Some of it is rough around the edges, as the restoration began only in 1975, but a great deal of natural beauty shines through; the Sawhill Ponds are the more attractive of the two areas. It is a nice setting for enjoying a variety of feathered friends, including pelicans, great blue herons, belted kingfishers, gulls, and geese, to name just a few of the 20 species spotted regularly here.

**DIRECTIONS**  From Boulder, take Valmont Road east to 75th Street. Turn left onto 75th Street, and drive north. The preserve is 0.5 mile south of Jay Road on the west side of 75th Street.

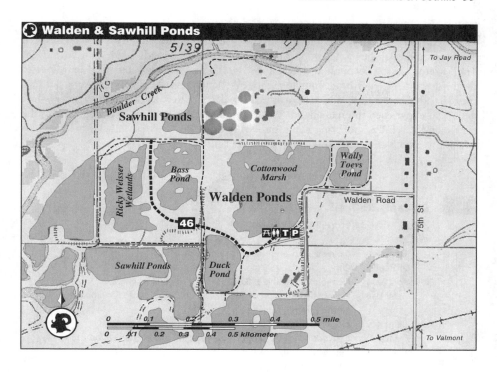

*Just one of the great spots to fish on Sawhill Ponds*

Though you might not be impressed when you pull into the parking lot, persevere and take the Cottonwood Marsh Trail to the west. Keep an eye out for the bird-watching boardwalk on the right (north) side of the trail, and take a little detour to experience the marshland. Walk slowly and carefully, and bring some binoculars to watch the waterfowl. Sink into the serenity of the place.

Walk on toward Duck Pond to the left (south) of the boardwalk. Walk south between the ponds, and then turn right (west) and go between the Ricky Weiser Wetlands and Bass Pond. Take a left and walk south to Sawhill Ponds. Wander where your spirit takes you, weaving among the water, reeds, grasses, and birds—no goals permitted.

## 47   Streamside Trail

### ELDORADO CANYON STATE PARK

| | |
|---|---|
| **Distance** | 0.6 miles, out-and-back |
| **Difficulty** | Easy |
| **Elevation Gain** | Negligible (starting at 5,800') |
| **Trail Use** | Hiking, biking, great for kids, wheelchair-accessible first 300 feet, leashed dogs OK |
| **Agency** | Eldorado Canyon State Park |
| **Map(s)** | *Eldorado Canyon State Park*; Latitude 40° *Boulder-Nederland Trails* |
| **Facilities** | Restrooms at trailhead |
| **Note(s)** | Park fee required. |

**HIGHLIGHTS** Ideal for mellow family strolls and contemplation if you arrive early. This short and easy walk along South Boulder Creek accesses the climbing routes. You will likely see the rock jocks up close and get a breathtaking view of them on the Bastille rock south across the creek and road. If the climbers look glassy-eyed, it is because they have once again defied the mortal grasp of gravity.

**DIRECTIONS** From Boulder, take CO 93 south. Turn right on CO 170 and continue to the park entrance west of Eldorado Springs, about 8 miles southwest of Boulder. From Denver, take I-25 north to US 36 (west toward Boulder). Exit at Louisville-Superior and turn left (south) at the light. Take the first right (west) onto CO 170, and follow it 7.4 miles to Eldorado Canyon State Park. Park immediately after you pass the entrance station.

Walk on the trail on the right (north) side of the road, and cross the footbridge that is 50 yards from the stylish restrooms and changing rooms. Cross the stream and go another 0.3 mile before the trail dead-ends into rocks and trees. You can continue by climbing up, over, and around, but that isn't recommended for children. You'll see several small side slot canyons that are used for climbing access. Bring your climbing gear—harness, hard hat, rope, and so forth—if you really want to explore them. If not, contemplate the ageless rock and babbling brook.

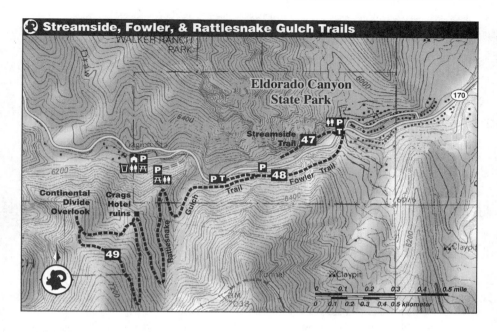

## Streamside, Fowler, & Rattlesnake Gulch Trails

**48** **Fowler Trail**

ELDORADO CANYON STATE PARK

| | |
|---|---|
| **Distance** | 1.4–4 miles, out-and-back |
| **Difficulty** | Easy |
| **Elevation Gain** | 100' (starting at 6,000') |
| **Trail Use** | Hiking, stroller and wheelchair accessible, leashed dogs OK |
| **Agency** | Eldorado Canyon State Park |
| **Map(s)** | *Eldorado Canyon State Park*; Latitude 40° *Boulder Nederland Trails* |
| **Facilities** | Restrooms at visitor center; none at trailhead |
| **Note(s)** | Park fee required. |

**HIGHLIGHTS** This short, easy uphill climb's chief advantage is that it allows hikers to savor the soaring cliffs and the rock climbers perched on them or dancing their way to the top across the valley. The trail provides views of the magnificent rock garden made of grayish quartzite rock that started off as eroded sand 1.6 billion years ago. The reddish Fountain Formation rocks were compacted into sandstone 300 million years ago and are the same formation and from the same era as Boulder's Flatirons and the Red Rocks amphitheater. The Lyons Formation sandstone rocks are the youngsters of the canyon at 240 million years old. These silent monuments give you a new perspective on the precious, brief span of a human's life and the necessity of savoring every moment. Combining this hike with the longer Rattlesnake Gulch Trail is a very doable adventure.

**DIRECTIONS** From Boulder, take CO 93 south. Turn right on CO 170, and continue to the park entrance west of Eldorado Springs, about 8 miles southwest of Boulder. From Denver, take I-25 north to US 36 (west toward Boulder). Exit at Louisville-Superior and turn left (south) at the light. Take the first right (west) onto CO 170 and follow it 7.4 miles to Eldorado Canyon State Park.

The trailheads for the Fowler and Rattlesnake Gulch Trails are one and the same and are 0.5 mile uphill from the entrance station. There is limited parking so you might have to walk up the road from the entrance or back from the visitor center. The latter is the better, shorter option for walking on the road.

Once you find the trailhead, simply walk up the gradual incline to the east and follow the nature guide stations. Gaze across the canyon to see a wonderful rock-climbing exhibition as climbers test their skills. There is even a free telescope if you want an up-close and personal view of these limber and fearless rock aficionados. You see the magnificent panorama of rock ridges, from west to east: Quartzite Ridge, Nest Ridge, Redgarden Wall, Hawk Eagle Ridge, and Rotwand Wall. They are topped off by Rincon Wall and 7,240-foot Shirt Tail Peak. The trail continues gradually uphill until you are above the out-of-view, famous Bastille rock wall, which is on the same side of the canyon as the trail.

Beyond the state park boundary, the trail travels slightly downhill until it intersects a dirt road. There is no access to the entrance station, and it meanders with the curving, low ridgeline for another 1.3 miles until it dead-ends at private property. Though this trip has some great views, more interesting scenery can be found in nearby Rattlesnake Gulch.

## 49 Rattlesnake Gulch Trail
### ELDORADO CANYON STATE PARK

see map on p. 101

| | |
|---|---|
| **Distance** | 2.8–3.6 miles, balloon |
| **Difficulty** | Moderate |
| **Elevation Gain** | Crags Hotel ruins: 800'; Loop: 1,200' (starting at 6,000') |
| **Trail Use** | Hiking, mountain biking, leashed dogs OK |
| **Agency** | Eldorado Canyon State Park |
| **Map(s)** | *Eldorado Canyon State Park*; Latitude 40° *Boulder-Nederland Trails* |
| **Facilities** | Restrooms at visitor center; none at trailhead |
| **Note(s)** | Park fee required. |

**HIGHLIGHTS** This trail features excellent views of the main canyon, an interesting side canyon, ruins of the Crags Hotel, the Continental Divide, and the Burlington Northern Santa Fe/Amtrak rail line. The switchbacks are almost as ambitious as the Eldorado Trail if you complete the entire loop. You gain 800 feet in a little more than 0.6 mile on the widely sweeping, fairly gradual switchbacks to reach the ruins of the Crags Hotel, which burned down in 1912, only four years after it was built. A historical marker tells more about the hotel at the site, where you have a limited view of the Indian Peaks. If you also want to see the Continental Divide, it is a short, easy stroll uphill from the ruins. If you'd like, it's quite possible to combine this hike with the short Fowler Trail.

**DIRECTIONS** From Boulder, take CO 93 south. Turn right on CO 170 and continue to the park entrance west of Eldorado Springs, about 8 miles southwest of Boulder. From Denver, take I-25 north to US 36 (west toward Boulder). Exit at Louisville-Superior and turn left (south) at the light. Take the first right (west) onto CO 170 and follow it 7.4 miles to Eldorado Canyon State Park.

The trailheads for the Fowler and Rattlesnake Gulch Trails are one and the same and are 0.5 mile uphill from the entrance station. There is limited parking so you might have to walk up the road from the entrance or back from the visitor center. The latter is the better, shorter option for walking on the road.

Go up the Fowler Trail, and access the Rattlesnake Gulch Trail approximately 100 yards up on the right. The trail starts sharply uphill through trees and is rocky but opens up fairly quickly and widens. Because it is a former road, it is often wide enough for two. It has very good sun exposure, so snow and ice can melt much of the year, making it accessible to hikers well into the late fall. The first 0.3 mile is a little steep, but then the trail mellows and even goes downhill. After the S turn, you see some minor ruins, but the trail to them is blocked off; stay on the trail. The next 0.3 mile is uphill, and the bright red hematite and iron ore hillsides are precipitous and striking high above. The Burlington Northern Santa Fe/Amtrak train line comes into view; the rail line is also the route of the ski train to Winter Park Resort.

You next come upon the Crags Hotel ruins with a superb 180-degree view back to the east of the soaring cliffs and a snow-capped Indian Peak or two to the north-west. An old wall or fireplace still stands from a century ago. This is a good place for a water and rest break, and there is a bench. The overlook is closer than it appears to be on the state park map. It is a fairly easy 0.1-mile jaunt up an easy hill to the overlook. The overlook has limited space, so use the ruins area if you want more breathing space for your snack or lunch break. The overlook

has another bench and features an even better view of the Continental Divide.

You see the loop option as you leave the overlook; it is well worth the extra effort and extends what might otherwise be a short hike. The 0.8-mile loop is best taken counterclockwise from the overlook because it is less steep and rocky in that direction. You can save the steep and rocky sections for the downhill trip. The trail goes steeply uphill on the right (west) side of the trail. As it climbs you realize that you are climbing toward the railroad tracks. The loop levels after the 0.25-mile mark and then climbs more gradually until you are almost next to the stretch of train track framed by two tunnels. If you're lucky and are there either first thing in the morning or in early evening, you'll see an Amtrak train go by. The trail goes steeply and then more gradually downhill through the trees back to the main trail. Once you reach the main trail, retrace your steps to the trailhead.

## 50  Switzerland Trail
### ROOSEVELT NATIONAL FOREST

see map on p. 104

| | |
|---|---|
| **Distance** | 3–5 miles, out-and-back |
| **Difficulty** | Easy |
| **Elevation Loss** | 300' (starting at 5,900') |
| **Trail Use** | Hiking, mountain biking, motorized recreation, snowshoeing, leashed dogs OK |
| **Agency** | Boulder Ranger District, Roosevelt National Forest |
| **Map(s)** | *Arapaho and Roosevelt National Forests South Half*; Latitude 40° *Boulder-Nederland Trails* |
| **Facilities** | Picnic area along the trail |

**HIGHLIGHTS** This beautiful trail near Gold Hill is used primarily for mountain biking but can also be a fun hike. It starts high and then is a gradual descent on a wide doubletrack, four-wheel-drive road that is almost passable for regular cars. There are great views of the ridgelines, valleys, and some distant peaks. Unfortunately there is some motorized use, especially on the weekends, but it is worth dodging the infrequent usage. This was the route of a mining train, and then an excursion train, from the late 1880s until the early 1900s.

**DIRECTIONS** From Boulder take Mapleton Avenue to Sunshine Canyon and then on to Gold Hill. The trail is 3 miles west of Gold Hill at a four-way intersection with a large brown sign labeled Little Switzerland.

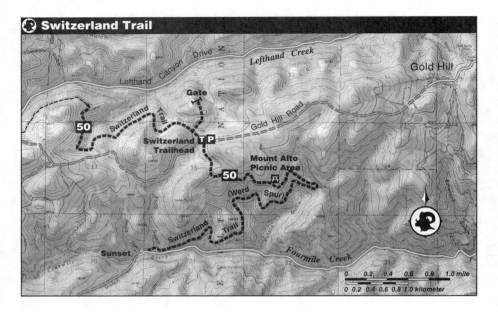

From the above intersection, you can go left to reach the Mount Alto Picnic Area in 1 mile and the Sunset town site in 4 miles. I recommend going right on a more scenic part of the trail that starts on a gradual downhill. In 0.25 mile you come to a short secondary trail on the right (north) side of the road that is closed to motorized vehicles. If you want a quiet meadow for a picnic, this is a good spot. There are lots of aspens and ponderosa pines. It is a better trail for hiking than biking because of how short it is. The first 0.1 mile switchbacks downhill from Little Switzerland and then levels into the expansive meadow, bordered by private property, cabins, and a ridgeline palace.

Lots of wildflowers and the soft trail make it an inviting side trip. Unfortunately, the trail ends at a locked gate in only 0.5 mile.

Back on the trail, continue downhill as the constantly changing scenery opens up with mountains, valleys, rock formations, and sweeping ridgelines of trees. The trail levels after around 0.5 mile and then turns north in a wide arc. You can go up, over, or around a hillock. Avoid the trail that goes straight up a hillside unless you want your heart to pound. The trail continues fairly level and enters tree cover for another mile before plunging downhill in earnest for the valley below. Turn around at any point for an experience of your choice. Extend your ride on other gravel roads.

*Contemplative reflections in Heron Lake (see page 96)*

*A great view of the Continental Divide*

# chapter 3

# Denver Area: Mountains

## 1–2 HOURS FROM DENVER

The mountains west of Denver are the magic kingdoms that attract sojourners from around the world, but if you're a resident, they're at your feet. If you can, avoid the weekend snarls to truly enjoy the experiences. Though many of the treks are day trips, I encourage you to spend the night in tents or lodges whenever possible so that you can spend more time on the trails and less time in your car. Quite a few of these trips aren't easily doable in a day, but they are too incredible to leave out of the book. From South Park and Como to Vail and Summit County, there is enough to explore for a lifetime. So clear your schedule, travel at off-peak times, carpool, and savor this amazing panorama of experiences.

### Staunton State Park

This 2013 addition to the Colorado State Park system is another gem in the system's natural crown. It is a foothills park near Bailey, and it features pretty rolling hills and striking rock formations. You can find a hike to match the ambitions and abilities of every hiker and mountain biker.

### Georgetown & Guanella Pass Area

This popular area south of Georgetown offers many recreational options that are close to Denver and don't require a trip through the Eisenhower Tunnel. Established in the mid-1850s, mining village Georgetown is a bonus, with restored Victorian architecture and a wide variety of great dining options. Allow for a snack or meal break in Georgetown to add to your appreciation of this once bustling mining region.

### Berthoud Pass Area

As you approach Berthoud Pass, you will have the option of exploring two scenic trails: Butler Gulch and Jones Pass. They both edge up to the Continental Divide and offer wildflower-rimmed climbs to spectacular vistas. The trails atop Berthoud Pass offer spectacular, serene views. The easy access from US 40, however, means that they don't necessarily offer complete serenity, but the 360-degree vista is ample compensation. The top of the pass is a former downhill ski area that operated from 1937 to 2001, when it went bust. It has now become a de facto backcountry, earn-your-turns ski and snowshoeing area that also offers many opportunities for summer recreation.

### Summit County & Loveland Pass

The hike to Lily Pad Lake gives you a chance to explore a bit of the wildly scenic Eagles Nest Wilderness with minimal effort. That might just whet your appetite for panoramic views, and the top of the Loveland Pass is one of the best places in the state for those nonstop views. The 12,000- to 13,000-foot ridgelines are stairways to mountain heaven and are often above the clouds. You can see 14,000-foot Grey and Torrey Peaks, as well as 13,000-foot Grizzly Peak and Sniktau Mountain; 12,500-foot Baker Mountain; and the Loveland, A-Basin, and Keystone ski areas. You will also see the Continental Divide and the more distant Gore and Tenmile mountain ranges. Take short strolls to enhance the view or climb the aforementioned thirteeners with a major head start by launching your expedition from 12,000 feet. If you want to summit a 13,000-foot peak and take in the bracing views from the top of Colorado's world with a lot less effort, this is one of the best opportunities. It is wise to have foul-weather gear and warm backup clothes, as the weather in the mountains can change without warning. Heavy hailstorms and sudden summer snowstorms are not uncommon, and a stiff, cool breeze is the norm.

## Mount Evans Wilderness/Clear Creek Ranger District

This wilderness area offers fun, almost flat family routes with sweeping views of the Front Range peaks or longer treks to where you feel like you could fly right on over to the Mount Evans massif and its lofty neighbors. These are high-altitude trails, so prepare accordingly for sudden drops in temperature, wind, and afternoon thunderstorms.

## Kenosha Pass & Colorado Trail

Kenosha Pass is in a splendid location for gazing down upon the unique high country plains of South Park and the soaring mountains that surround and majestically frame it. Accessible from Kenosha Pass, the Colorado Trail begins at 10,000 feet. Superb views of South Park and the 14,000-foot peaks of the Mosquito Range are just off-trail.

---

### 51  Davis Ponds Loop
STAUNTON STATE PARK

| | |
|---|---|
| **Distance** | 2.2 miles, loop |
| **Difficulty** | Easy |
| **Elevation Gain** | 100' (starting at 5,430') |
| **Trail Use** | Hiking, snowshoeing, skiing, good for kids, leashed dogs OK |
| **Agency** | Staunton State Park |
| **Map(s)** | *Staunton State Park* |
| **Facilities** | Restrooms at trailhead |
| **Note(s)** | Park fee required. |

**HIGHLIGHTS** The Davis Ponds Loop trail is a gently rolling trail that goes out to the picturesque ponds. From the ponds you have views of the distant rock formations.

**DIRECTIONS** From Denver, take US 285 south to Shaffers Crossing, about 6 miles west of Conifer. Turn north on Elk Creek Road and follow the signs 1.5 miles to the park entrance.

Park in the first parking area, on the left, after you come through the main entrance. Go to the north end of the parking lot and cross Elk Road. Take the trail on the left (west) after you cross the road. Bear left to enter the figure eight trails. (If you see the picnic area on the right, 0.8 mile past the parking lot, you have gone too far north.)

You can choose which way you want to travel on the loop. If you bear right at the first intersection, you will arrive at the first pond more quickly than if you bear left.

---

### 52  Staunton Ranch Trail
STAUNTON STATE PARK

| | |
|---|---|
| **Distance** | 6.6 miles, out-and-back |
| **Difficulty** | Easy–moderate |
| **Elevation Gain** | 500' (starting at 8,200') |

## Davis Ponds Loop & Staunton Ranch Trail

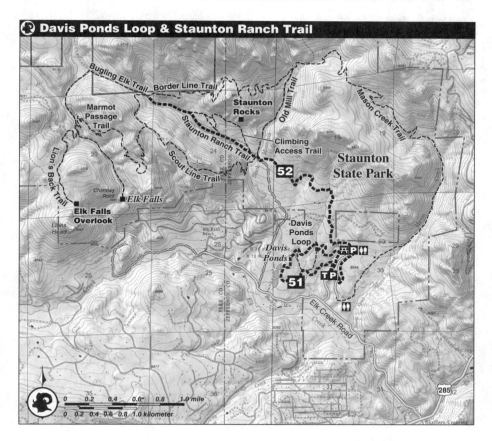

| | |
|---|---|
| **Trail Use** | Hiking, biking, horseback riding, snowshoeing, skiing, leashed dogs OK |
| **Agency** | Staunton State Park |
| **Map(s)** | *Staunton State Park* |
| **Facilities** | Restrooms at trailhead |
| **Note(s)** | Park fee required. |

**HIGHLIGHTS** This hike can be a 6.6-mile out-and-back that rolls mostly uphill for the first 1.5 miles and passes the striking Staunton Rocks. You can get closer to the rocks on the 0.5-mile climbers' access trail. It is a trail that offers views in almost every direction as it rolls across the hills.

**DIRECTIONS** From Denver, take US 285 south to Shaffers Crossing, about 6 miles west of Conifer. Turn north on Elk Creek Road and follow the signs 1.5 miles to the park entrance.

Park in the first parking lot after you enter the main gate. The trailhead is due north from the lot. Don't take the path on the left; it goes to the Davis Ponds Loop. There is a road between the ponds trail and the Staunton Ranch Trail. The trail climbs slowly from the trailhead on the right side of the road. You will pass restrooms on the left (west) side of the road. After 0.5 mile

the trail tracks northeast away from the road and begins to switchback more steeply uphill. It then tracks northwest and continues to climb through the mixed forest. It climbs 300 feet with views to the west and northeast. The Staunton Ranch Trail tops out at around 8,700 feet and then descends toward a road. Go 100 feet to the right to get back on the trail, passing a stream. Pass

*The Climbing Access Trail at Staunton Ranch*

the Old Mill Trail. At around 1.8 miles enjoy the mottled rock outcrops, and use the Climbing Access Trail if you want a close-up view of the Staunton Rocks. Continue another 1.5 miles to reach the Border Line Trail, where you can turn around.

## 53 Butler Gulch
### ARAPAHO NATIONAL FOREST

see map on p. 111

| | |
|---|---|
| **Distance** | Up to 5 miles, out-and-back |
| **Difficulty** | Moderate |
| **Elevation Gain** | 1,200' (starting at 10,400') |
| **Trail Use** | Hiking, mountain biking, snowshoeing, skiing, leashed dogs OK |
| **Agency** | Clear Creek Ranger District, Arapaho National Forest |
| **Map(s)** | Latitude 40° *Summit County Trails* |
| **Facilities** | None |

**HIGHLIGHTS** This trailhead is also the access point for the Jones Pass road/trail near Henderson Mine. Butler Gulch is vehicle-free, making it a more attractive option. You can combine a climb of Butler Gulch with a descent down the Jones Pass road (or vice versa) to see a stunning panorama from the top of the ridgeline. Thick wildflowers will be your magic carpet after you climb above treeline.

**DIRECTIONS** Take I-70 west from Denver and exit at Empire for Berthoud Pass/Winter Park. Drive through Empire toward the pass. When you come to the first sharp bend to the right, exit to the left for Henderson Mine. Continue north on the mine road until you reach the designated parking area. The road is closed at the trailhead that serves both the Jones Pass trail/four-wheel-drive road, and the Butler Gulch trail. Travel west through the trees on the joint trail until a junction at approximately 0.25 mile. Bear right for the Jones Pass trail or left for the more difficult but beautiful Butler Gulch trail.

The Butler Gulch trail is also a road, but it is closed to vehicles and is much narrower than the Jones Pass road. It is covered by a thick mixed forest and starts off quite gradually but then steepens. It is well marked. You will start off on a joint trail for Jones Pass and Butler Gulch. After 0.25 mile or so Butler Gulch will split off

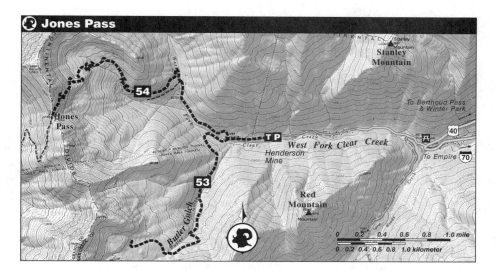

**Jones Pass**

to the left (south). You will climb a steeper mile, and you will see a small waterfall on the right after this first mile; this is a good place for a water and rest break. The trail traverses south and then turns to the west with a rapid ascent to treeline at around 11,000 feet. When the route breaks out of the trees you will see an open bowl, great for winter skiing or summer enjoyment of wildflowers. The trail levels a bit as it travels to the west and then climbs to the top of the ridgeline and an even more impressive 360-degree vista. You can traverse to the northwest along the trail on the ridgeline if you want to reach the top of Jones Pass and go down the other way for variety.

*A magic carpet of wildflowers in Butler Gulch*

**54** Jones Pass

ARAPAHO NATIONAL FOREST

see map on p. 111

| | |
|---|---|
| **Distance** | Up to 8 miles, out-and-back |
| **Difficulty** | Easy–challenging |
| **Elevation Gain** | 2,600' (starting at 10,000') |
| **Trail Use** | Hiking, mountain biking, snowshoeing, skiing, leashed dogs OK |
| **Agency** | Clear Creek Ranger District, Arapaho National Forest |
| **Map(s)** | Latitude 40° *Summit County Trails* |
| **Facilities** | None |

**HIGHLIGHTS** This beautiful mountain valley is close to Denver and doesn't require a drive over Berthoud Pass. There are several trails you can explore at this popular location near the Henderson Mine, but you share this trail with some off-road vehicles (all-terrain vehicles and motorcycles). Enjoy a hike of any length, and soak in the views. You can combine this hike with Butler Gulch, and make it a loop hike. The Butler half will be vehicle-free.

**DIRECTIONS** Take I-70 west from Denver and exit at Empire for Berthoud Pass/Winter Park. Drive through Empire toward the pass. When you come to the first sharp bend to the right, exit to the left for Henderson Mine. Continue north on the mine road until you reach the designated parking area. The road is closed at the trailhead that serves both the Jones Pass trail and the Butler Gulch trail. Travel west through the trees on the joint trail until a junction at approximately 0.25 mile. Bear right for the Jones Pass trail or left for the more difficult and advanced Butler Gulch trail.

You have some glimpses of the ridgeline as you travel through the trees. At a little less than 0.5 mile you break out of the trees and enjoy the panorama of the valley and soaring ridgeline. Avalanche runout zones are observable on the steep slopes to the west. The trail/road steepens as it switchbacks. It then travels through a varied landscape of high mountain meadows and trees. You can go all the way to the summit of the pass or turn around whenever you wish. If you continue to the top of the pass, you will see a trail that goes south. You can take this to the top of Butler Gulch for a loop hike. Route-finding is easier if you start with Butler Gulch and travel clockwise.

**55** Guanella Pass: Silver Dollar Lake Trail

ARAPAHO NATIONAL FOREST

| | |
|---|---|
| **Distance** | Up to 3 miles, out-and-back |
| **Difficulty** | Easy |
| **Elevation Gain** | 1,000' (starting at 11,000') |
| **Trail Use** | Hiking, mountain biking, snowshoeing, skiing, good for kids, leashed dogs OK |
| **Agency** | Mount Evans Wilderness, Clear Creek Ranger District, Arapaho National Forest |
| **Map(s)** | Trails Illustrated *Idaho Springs, Georgetown, Loveland Pass* |
| **Facilities** | Campground about 0.5 mile away |

**HIGHLIGHTS** This short, fairly easy trail to a pristine lake surrounded by soaring mountains is one of the best trails on Guanella Pass and within easy driving distance from Denver. Before July, you may encounter snow on the trail.

**DIRECTIONS** Take I-70 west from Denver. Take Exit 228 for Georgetown, and drive into town, following signs to Guanella Pass. On the first road past Guanella Pass Campground, turn right and park. The picnic ground turnoff is on the right side of the road.

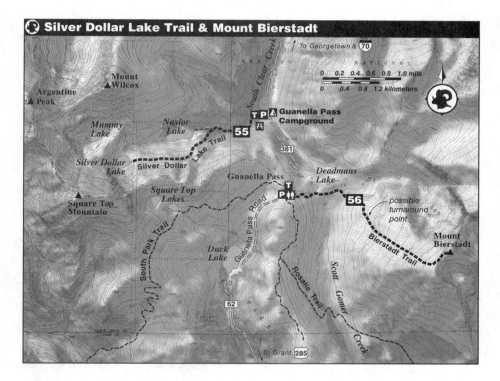

## Silver Dollar Lake Trail & Mount Bierstadt

Take the road approximately 0.4 mile to the trailhead, which is on the left and well marked. The road to the trailhead is steep. Once you reach the trailhead, the route levels somewhat, and you follow a small creek for a short distance. The trail then leaves the drainage, tracking to the right (west), and winds through the trees back toward the road. It then climbs out of a hollow and along a narrow section with a small drop-off until you emerge from the trees to a spectacular view of the lake and the surrounding rock wall cirque that towers above. From the lake you can climb one of the surrounding 12,000- to 13,000-foot peaks, with a good topographic map and compass and mountaineering preparation.

**56**   ## Mount Bierstadt
ARAPAHO NATIONAL FOREST

| | |
|---|---|
| **Distance** | 6 miles to summit, out-and-back |
| **Difficulty** | Difficult |
| **Elevation Gain** | 2,930' to Mount Bierstadt (starting at 11,130') |
| **Trail Use** | Hiking, snowshoeing, skiing, option for kids, leashed dogs OK but not permitted near water sources |
| **Agency** | Mount Evans Wilderness, Clear Creek Ranger District, Arapaho National Forest |
| **Map(s)** | Trails Illustrated *Winter Park, Central City, Rollins Pass* |
| **Facilities** | Restrooms at trailhead |

**HIGHLIGHTS**  One of Colorado's most accessible fourteeners and much shorter and easier than Longs Peak, Mount Bierstadt can be climbed almost any time of the year and is a short drive from the Denver metro area. Safe, short excursions in the awe-inspiring terrain at the base of the Evans-Bierstadt massif can also be rewarding. The town of Georgetown is always a treat to visit and has a variety of food and beverage opportunities.

**DIRECTIONS**  Take I-70 west from Denver to Georgetown. Take Exit 228 for Georgetown and head toward town. Turn right toward Georgetown at the first four-way stop. Pass through Georgetown before climbing west and then south out of town toward the pass. Look for the Guanella Pass Trailhead for Bierstadt on the left (east) side of the road when you break out into the open and see the striking view of the Evans-Bierstadt massif to the east.

A t 14,060 feet Mount Bierstadt is one of Colorado's highest mountains. As with any fourteener, high altitude is challenging, but you can take a nice 2-mile hike (round-trip) before encountering lung burn. Plus, the panoramic setting is superb.

Start at the Guanella Pass Trailhead and go as far as you like. Your starting time and your company will determine the scope of your adventure. It is not advisable to climb high mountains alone or start late and expect to summit safely. The first part of the trail actually goes downhill for 1 mile. Just using the first mile as an out-and-back trek is worth the trip. At that point you are near Scott Gomer Creek at around 11,400 feet. You previously would have encountered challenging willows and marshes here, but now there is an easy-to-follow trail and footbridge through the willows.

The trail is well marked with cairns all the way to the summit, but you sometimes have to look for them with a keen eye to stay on course. I recommend using one of the many books providing detailed routes on the fourteeners for a complete description of the route. After you have made your way across the boardwalk, look for the cairns that mark the switchbacking trail to the top. You will come to a saddle about 200 feet below the summit, where you will want to take a breather before the final summit push.

*The route up Mount Bierstadt*

South Park Trail on the other side of the road from the Bierstadt Trail can be used for another short out-and-back trek with great views. It starts out on a short hill, travels around 100 yards or so on a flat area, and then descends before climbing again. After another 100 yards it starts to meander and climb steeply.

*GREAT FAMILY HIKE*

The first mile of this trail descends gently, crosses a creek and winds through willows and marshes along an easy-to-follow trail. Turn back here or, if your young people want a bit steeper challenge, go another 0.5 mile to see more views.

**57**  **Loveland Pass Ridgetop**

LOVELAND PASS, CONTINENTAL DIVIDE TRAIL

see map on p. 116

| | |
|---|---|
| **Distance** | 2 miles, out-and-back |
| **Difficulty** | Moderate |
| **Elevation Gain** | 1,110' (starting at 12,000') |
| **Trail Use** | Hiking, option for kids, leashed dogs OK |
| **Agency** | Clear Creek Ranger District, Arapaho National Forest |
| **Map(s)** | Trails Illustrated *Vail, Frisco, Dillon* |
| **Facilities** | None |

**HIGHLIGHTS** The view from the 13,117-foot-high unnamed point along the Sniktau-Grizzly ridgeline is impressive; this trip is an easier jaunt than the summits of Sniktau and Grizzly.

**DIRECTIONS** From Denver take I-70 west to the Loveland Pass exit just before the Eisenhower Tunnel. Drive to the parking areas on top of the pass; arrive early to beat the crowds and the thunderstorms. Carpool if possible. Sniktau and Grizzly are on the south side of the pass, left if you are traveling west. Park on either side of the road and climb east from it.

For the first 0.3 mile, the start of the trek is the same for both mountains, Grizzly and Sniktau, and the viewpoint on top of the ridge. Go straight uphill on the broad trail that's wide enough to be a road. You are immediately treated to awesome 360-degree scenery. The first 0.3 mile gains more than 200 feet—you feel every step at this elevation.

If you are well prepared, take a right and go southwest at the first trail intersection. You travel slightly downhill at first as you traverse the steep slope on a trail that provides good footing and no exposure. You will feel like an eagle or hawk soaring through the air and looking down on the traffic and A-Basin ski area. There are some hardy Indian paintbrush flowers along the trail in season. After 0.25 mile the trail starts to climb, at first gradually and then more steeply. You lose a bit of elevation and then gain around 150 feet over the first 1.5 miles.

Then the real climbing begins as you clamber up a steep slope to the saddle, gaining 100 feet in 0.25 mile. You have a great view from the saddle that makes the whole trip worthwhile—the huge valley between Loveland Pass and the Grays and Torrey massif makes you feel like you have already summited. This is a good turnaround point if members of your party

aren't partying. The top-of-the-ridge viewpoint is to the right (west). There is an easy trail to follow, though the going is slow as you reach a couple of level spots on the way up and catch your breath. As you get near the top, you have a view of the Gore range to the northwest. The trail traverses around an unnamed high point and stays lower than the summit for a more direct route to Grizzly Peak.

If the skyscraper ridgetop viewpoint is your goal, leave the trail and track

*The views are awesome from the Loveland Pass ridgetop trail.*

Loveland Pass Ridgetop, Grizzly Peak, & Mount Sniktau

left (south) toward the 13,117-foot high point. You can climb more than 13,000 feet, enjoy the magnificent view, and see the sinuous ridges to Sniktau and Grizzly, while lording your status over the lowly pass road below.

***GREAT FOR KIDS***

If you are a family hiking with small children or are unaccustomed to high altitudes, climb as high as you want to, take a few snapshots, enjoy the views, and reverse course. Altitude can cause dizziness and headaches, so ascend slowly.

## 58  Grizzly Peak

### LOVELAND PASS, CONTINENTAL DIVIDE TRAIL

|  |  |
|---|---|
| **Distance** | 5 miles, out-and-back |
| **Difficulty** | Moderate |
| **Elevation Gain** | 1,635' (starting at 11,990') |
| **Trail Use** | Hiking, leashed dogs OK |
| **Agency** | Clear Creek Ranger District, Arapaho National Forest |
| **Map(s)** | Trails Illustrated *Vail, Frisco, Dillon* |
| **Facilities** | None |

**HIGHLIGHTS** This mountain looks like a grizzly bear in comparison to the soft, round, teddy bear shapes of Mount Sniktau. It is a spectacular ridge walk and steep scramble at the end that is clearly worth the effort for the views. It requires a bit of a roller-coaster climb because the ridge between Sniktau and Grizzly drops more than 150 feet, and that altitude has to be regained going and coming. Though you can continue to Grays and Torrey Peaks from Grizzly, that would be a very long trek.

**DIRECTIONS** From Denver take I-70 west to the Loveland Pass exit just before the Eisenhower Tunnel. Drive to the parking areas on top of the pass; arrive early to beat the crowds and the thunderstorms. Carpool if possible. Sniktau and Grizzly are on the south side of the pass, left if you are traveling west. Park on either side of the road and climb east from it.

The start of the trek is the same for both Grizzly and Sniktau for the first 0.3 mile. Go straight uphill on the broad trail that is wide enough to be a road. You are immediately treated to awesome 360-degree views. The first 0.3 mile gains more than 100 feet—you feel every step at this elevation. Take a right and go southwest at the first trail intersection. You travel slightly downhill at first as you traverse the steep slope on a trail that provides good footing and no exposure. You will feel like an eagle or hawk soaring through the air and looking down on the traffic and

A-Basin ski area. There are some hardy Indian paintbrush flowers along the trail in season. After 0.25 mile the trail starts to climb, at first gradually and then more steeply. You lose a bit of elevation and then gain around 150 feet over the first 1.5 miles.

Then the real climbing begins as you clamber up a steep slope to the saddle, gaining 100 feet in 0.25 mile. You have a great view from the saddle that makes the whole trip worthwhile—the huge valley between Loveland Pass and the Grays and Torrey massif makes you feel as though you have already summited. This is a good

*The trail winds its way up the ridge toward Grizzly Peak.*

turnaround point if members of your party aren't partying. From here, there is an easy trail to follow, though the going is slow as you reach a couple of level spots on the way up and catch your breath. As you get near the top, you have a view of the Gore range to the northwest. The trail traverses over the westernmost part of the Baker Mountain ridge and then plunges down to the first saddle between the peaks. Edge your way as low as possible around the first hump, and then drop down a bit lower before you have to climb up steep switchbacks to the summit of 13,427-foot Grizzly.

## 59 Mount Sniktau

LOVELAND PASS, CONTINENTAL DIVIDE TRAIL

see map on p. 116

| | |
|---|---|
| **Distance** | 4 miles, out-and-back |
| **Difficulty** | Moderate |
| **Elevation Gain** | 1,635' (starting at 11,990') |
| **Trail Use** | Hiking, leashed dogs OK |
| **Agency** | Clear Creek Ranger District, Arapaho National Forest |
| **Map(s)** | Latitude 40° *Summit County Trails* |
| **Facilities** | None |

**HIGHLIGHTS** The most popular peak climb from Loveland Pass heads across the undulating southwest ridge of Sniktau and crosses at least three false summits on the way up. Each step provides its own rewards—you don't have to summit to take in the view. Of the three choices from this trailhead, this hike has the most sustained view of I-70 and the Eisenhower Tunnel, but the highway noise fades and the views of Grays, Torrey, and Grizzly Peaks make the trek worthwhile.

**DIRECTIONS** From Denver take I-70 west to the Loveland Pass exit just before the Eisenhower Tunnel. Drive to the parking areas on top of the pass; arrive early to beat the crowds and the thunderstorms. Carpool if possible. Baker Mountain and its loftier compadres, Sniktau and Grizzly, are all on the south side of the pass, left if you are traveling west. Park on either side of the road and climb south from it.

From the parking area on the southwest side of US 6, climb up either of the two paths. Go straight up the steep ridge, and ignore the side trail that departs to the right (west) for Grizzly about 0.3 mile uphill. Climb until you reach the ridgeline and the first "summit," where you even get a bit of a windbreak. Many hikers enjoy the trail to this point and head back to their vehicles—an achievement because you will have already climbed 1,000 feet in short order.

If you want to continue to the peak, take a left and waltz up the wide ridge to the north side of the next "summit" at 13,152 feet. Though you will feel good about making the next "top," you will likely be unhappy to see the descending rocky path you have to follow down about 100 feet to a saddle before you start climbing again. You ascend 200 feet over the next 0.3 mile, bearing left to avoid unnecessary scrambling, and are rewarded with such great views of Grays, Torrey, and Grizzly that you will be tempted to make it a three-summit day.

### *GREAT FOR KIDS*

Another option goes up from the other side of the road and follows the northwest side of the ridge to gain a view of the Loveland Pass Ski Area and the Continental Divide. It's an easier trek than any of these three mountains but still has great views. The trail immediately climbs 100 feet but then mellows as it more gradually climbs another 100 feet while offering a commanding vista of Loveland Pass Ski Area.

**60** **Eastside Trail: Continental Divide Trail**
BERTHOUD PASS, CONTINENTAL DIVIDE TRAIL

see map on p. 120

| | |
|---|---|
| **Distance** | 4 miles, out-and-back |
| **Difficulty** | Moderate |
| **Elevation Gain** | 1,000' (starting at 10,435') |
| **Trail Use** | Hiking, horseback riding, snowshoeing, skiing, leashed dogs OK |
| **Agency** | Clear Creek Ranger District, Arapaho National Forest |
| **Map(s)** | Latitude 40° *Summit County*; Latitude 40° *Colorado Front Range* |
| **Facilities** | Restrooms at trailhead |

**HIGHLIGHTS** This trail offers a wide, easy-to-follow route and a gradual climb to nonstop, magnificent views. Much of the trail is above treeline, so keep an eye on the weather and make sure you use lots of sunscreen. It originates next to the parking area and restrooms on the east side of the Berthoud Pass Summit.

**DIRECTIONS** From Denver, take I-70 west to US 40. Drive 14 miles west to the summit of Berthoud Pass. Park in the large lot on the east side of the summit.

The Continental Divide Trail is on the south side of the parking area. If you are facing the steep hill, with the restrooms on the left (north), it is on the right. From the south side of the parking lot, go southeast into the trees. It is a wide trail that was probably a service road or catwalk for the ski area. You will see a sign on the right side of the trail. The trail travels east, gradually uphill, for about 0.25 mile, before turning sharply to the north and continuing uphill. After 0.5 mile it intersects other northbound trails and a former ski run. A Nordic trail continues on the other side of the ski run; instead, turn sharply to the southeast, and continue to follow the very long switchbacking trail uphill, out of the trees.

As you clear the trees, the panorama begins to unfold to the west and you see the south side of Berthoud Pass and the Grays

*View from the summit of Coal Mines Peak*

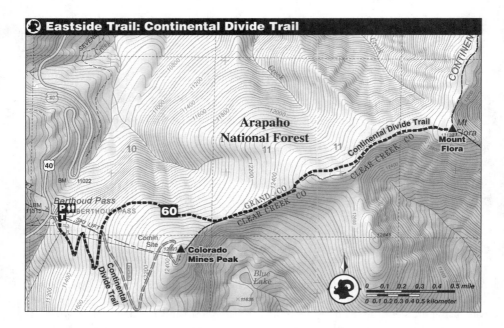

and Torrey massif to the southwest. Continue to follow the trail/road as it widely switchbacks and slowly climbs toward Mount Flora as far as you wish before turning around. With every traverse and turn you will have amazing views in every direction. The former ski area facilities are at 12,200 feet, and the summit offers an even more commanding view of the Continental Divide to the north and Mount Evans to the south. You will have a good view of the trails on the west side of the pass and can decide if you want to go for a second adventure.

### 61  Lily Pad Lake
WHITE RIVER NATIONAL FOREST

|  |  |
|---|---|
| **Distance** | 3 miles, out-and-back |
| **Difficulty** | Easy |
| **Elevation Gain** | 200' (starting at 9,700') |
| **Trail Use** | Hiking, snowshoeing, skiing, great for kids, leashed dogs OK |
| **Agency** | Eagles Nest Wilderness, Dillon Ranger District, White River National Forest |
| **Map(s)** | Latitude 40° *Summit County Trails* |
| **Facilities** | None |
| **Note(s)** | Bikes are prohibited, and dogs must be leashed because of the wilderness designation. |

**HIGHLIGHTS**  This hike takes you to a delightful series of small lakes and ponds in Eagles Nest Wilderness on a path that is lavishly decorated with wildflowers in the early summer. Few hikes offer this much beauty with such easy access and minimal effort.

**DIRECTIONS**  Even though the trail is in the wilderness, the trailhead is next to urban development and easy walking distance from many condominiums in Silverthorne. You can also take advantage of the local bus service; the parking lot is small.

## Lily Pad Lake

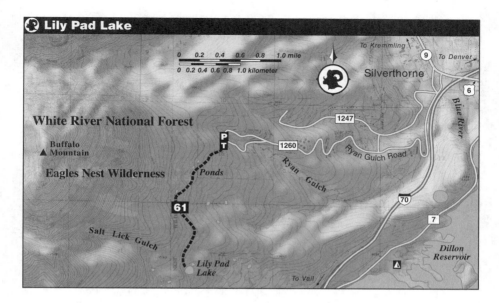

From I-70, take the Silverthorne exit and go north on CO 9. Turn west on Ryan Gulch Road. Take the road until it ends in a loop, where there is a parking area for Buffalo Pass and Lily Pad Lake Trailheads. Lily Pad Lake Trail is an unpaved road to the right of a paved road, with a cable hung from red posts across it.

Proceed west from the parking area toward the far trailhead and take the unpaved (right), closed road. The only steep section is at the very beginning of the hike and lasts less than 0.25 mile, so don't be dismayed if you have tykes in tow. Once you crest the top of the hill, you see a large brown pipe sticking out of the top of a water storage tank on the left. Bear right/straight to reach the Eagles Nest Wilderness boundary as the trail descends. The trail levels, enters a thick lodgepole pine forest, and then crosses a footbridge at 0.25 mile that takes you over wetlands in the early summer. The trail then climbs on a short, rocky section. It then roller-coasters along and finishes downhill at the first pond that is surrounded by evergreens and offers a small peephole to the bright blue sky and wispy clouds floating by. The trail turns left (south) and goes downhill, and you see a variety of wildflowers in season, including chiming bells.

The trail rolls gently as it turns southwest at 0.5 mile, where you can savor the vivid green of a pretty wetlands meadow accented by aspens. At around 0.75 mile you are encircled by wildflowers in season

*Lily Pad Lake*

as the trail descends to 9,600 feet and parallels the meadow before going southwest uphill. You cross the drainage again in very thick trees, good shelter on a hot day. The trail climbs up and tops out at around 9,800 feet, and you see another trail entering as you begin to descend. You roller-coaster through a mixed forest, finishing downhill at Lily Pad Lake, which is covered by some of the thickest and hardiest lily pads

in the state. If you are lucky, they will be blooming.

Climb over the next small hill for a spectacular view of an often snowcapped peak reflected in a clear, lily pad–free, and somewhat larger lake. Take your pick of superb settings for a snack, water, or lunch break before returning. When you do, be careful to bear right as you go uphill, and don't take the closed trail on the left.

## 62  Echo Lake & Chicago Lakes Trails
### ARAPAHO NATIONAL FOREST

| | |
|---|---|
| **Distance** | Echo Lake: 0.8 mile; round-trip with Chicago Lakes: up to 9 miles; out-and-back |
| **Difficulty** | Easy–moderate |
| **Elevation Gain** | Echo Lake: 50'; Chicago Lakes: 1,500' with return climb (starting at 10,600') |
| **Trail Use** | Hiking, snowshoeing, skiing, option for kids, leashed dogs OK |
| **Agency** | Mount Evans Wilderness, Clear Creek Ranger District, Arapaho National Forest |
| **Map(s)** | Trails Illustrated *Winter Park, Central City, Rollins Pass* |
| **Facilities** | Pit toilets and picnic tables |
| **Note(s)** | No bikes in the wilderness. |

**HIGHLIGHTS** The Echo Lake portion of this route is an easy, almost flat family route around the lake, surrounded by multiple views of Front Range peaks. You can add a much longer out-and-back on a spectacular tour of the Chicago Lakes Trail. The extension on the rolling Chicago Lakes Trail will give you outstanding views of the Mount Evans massif and its lofty neighbors as you enter the Mount Evans Wilderness area. Snow arrives early and stays late because of the elevation.

**DIRECTIONS** Take I-70 to Idaho Springs and take Exit 40, for Mount Evans. Take CO 103 south 14 miles, to the shoreline of Echo Lake. There is parking at the Echo Lake picnic area or 1 mile farther south at the entrance to Echo Lake Campground, its seasonal restaurant, and the Mount Evans Scenic Byway.

From the picnic area, the trail goes west and then south, counterclockwise around the lake. Go right from the picnic area and restrooms. Enjoy the immediate views of Mount Evans before entering thick trees. When you round the end of the lake in 0.25 mile, you will see a sign for the Chicago Lakes Trail going straight, while the Echo Lake Trail turns left. Go left if you want a short out-and-back. If you want to see an impressive view, go over the small hill and descend onto the Chicago Lakes

Trail. In 0.25 mile you will see the impressive cirques and peaks of Mounts Roger, Warren, Spalding, and Evans on the horizon. This is a good time to snap a photo and turn around if you aren't ambitious.

The Chicago Lakes Trail is bordered by avalanche terrain for the next 0.5 mile, so check conditions if it is snow season. The trail is narrow and has a 500-foot drop on the right side, making it a good idea to leash dogs. The trail descends around 500 feet to the Idaho Springs Reservoir road.

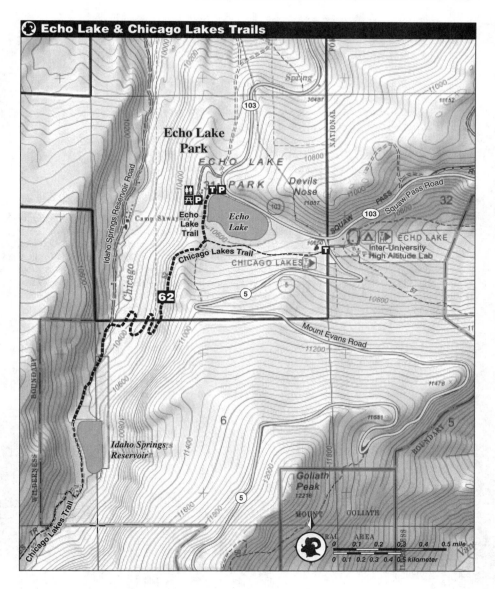

Echo Lake & Chicago Lakes Trails

Turn left on the road, and it will climb up slowly to the reservoir. This is another good turnaround for a short excursion. The trail continues south around the west side of the reservoir with spectacular views of the high cliffs above. The rocky trail climbs southwest slowly, above the sparkling riparian valley, rolling over small hills as it climbs. The soaring, eastside ridgeline climbs to 13,391 feet on Rogers Peak. The trail climbs to 11,500 feet before it descends to 11,400 at Chicago Lakes.

## 63  Colorado Trail: West Branch

PIKE NATIONAL FOREST

| | |
|---|---|
| **Distance** | Up to 11.4 miles (round-trip) to Jefferson Creek Campground, out-and-back |
| **Difficulty** | Easy–moderate, depending on distance traveled |
| **Elevation Gain** | 800' (starting at 10,000') |
| **Trail Use** | Hiking, mountain biking, snowshoeing, skiing, option for kids, leashed dogs OK |
| **Agency** | South Park Ranger District, Pike National Forest |
| **Map(s)** | Trails Illustrated *Tarryall Mountains & Kenosha Pass* |
| **Facilities** | Restrooms near trailhead and a campground |

**HIGHLIGHTS** Kenosha Pass is a splendid location for gazing down upon the unique high country plains of South Park and the soaring mountains that surround and majestically frame it. The Colorado Trail is accessible from Kenosha Pass, and you get the benefits of starting off at 10,000 feet. Superb views of South Park and the 14,000-foot peaks of the Mosquito Range are just off-trail. It is popular with both mountain bikers and hikers. You can choose short, easy family hikes or more ambitious treks. It is often not clear of snow and dried out until mid- to late June in heavy snow years.

**DIRECTIONS** Kenosha Pass is approximately 65 miles southwest of Denver on US 285. Park on the east side of the highway outside the Kenosha Pass Campground. Assume at least 1.5 hours of drive time from Denver.

From the west side of the highway, you see a sign for the Colorado Trail. From the road, bear left around the restrooms and keep going (do not walk into the campground area on the right), and you eventually come to another sign for the Colorado Trail. Go to the right (north) on the trail. You are in a very thick tree tunnel

*Tarryall Mountains from the Rock Creek segment of the Colorado Trail*

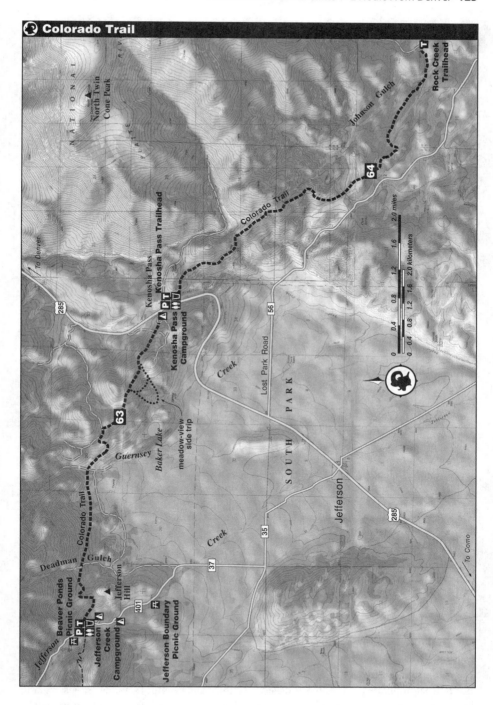

## Colorado Trail

at first as you climb steadily but gradually for 0.5 mile. You gain another 100 feet before it levels off and then starts to go downhill before emerging from the trees. You are treated to an eagle-high overview of South Park. This is a great spot for a photo or snack break. The trail is on the part of the slope that slants to the south, so it features intense summer midday sun, with a pleasant breeze—don't forget your sunscreen.

After about 200 yards of downhill travel, it reenters trees. You lose around 250 feet if you walk all the way down near Baker Lake—the low point of this section of the trail. You regain all of the lost elevation, plus another 250 feet, gradually if you continue toward Jefferson Creek. Baker Lake is just short of 1.5 miles from the trailhead; if you turn around there, you will have about a 3-mile trek round-trip and about 350 feet in total elevation gain.

From Baker Lake you climb steadily but gradually as you cross Guernsey Creek and Deadman Gulch and meander into and out of the trees on your way to Jefferson Creek Campground at around 10,300 feet. As always, be cautious and turn around early if the weather changes and cumulus clouds start forming.

### GREAT FOR KIDS

The first 2–3 miles of the trail climb very gradually, and the trail emerges out of the trees to a panoramic view of South Park and the massive backdrop of the 14,000-foot wall of fourteeners in the Mosquito Range, with some scenic glimpses of the Tarryall Range to the east, too. Because the trail travels at first gradually and then steeply downhill to the west from this point, you might want to have a snack or water break and then turn around. Going to Baker Lake will require a relatively long, moderate uphill climb on the return.

---

## 64 Colorado Trail: East Branch

PIKE NATIONAL FOREST

see map on p. 125

| | |
|---|---|
| **Distance** | Up to 14.4 miles to Rock Creek Trailhead, out-and-back |
| **Difficulty** | Easy–moderate, depending on distance traveled |
| **Elevation Gain** | 800' (starting at 10,000') |
| **Trail Use** | Hiking, mountain biking, snowshoeing, skiing, leashed dogs OK |
| **Agency** | South Park Ranger District, Pike National Forest |
| **Map(s)** | Trails Illustrated *Tarryall Mountains & Kenosha Pass* |
| **Facilities** | Restrooms and a campground nearby |
| **Note(s)** | Day-use fee required. |

**HIGHLIGHTS** This segment of the Colorado Trail is on the east side of US 285. The entire Colorado Trail can be used for an out-and-back outing of up to 30 miles or a one-way car shuttle of around 15 miles. The trail features sweeping views of South Park and the Mosquito Range as it rolls gently through some thick aspen glens—great for viewing fall or summer foliage.

**DIRECTIONS** Kenosha Pass is approximately 65 miles southwest of Denver on US 285. Park on the east side of the highway outside the Kenosha Pass Campground. Assume at least 1.5 hours of drive time from Denver.

The trail starts uphill and then levels near a log bench and railroad history marker. The area's railroad history is remarkable—four railroads operated in the area: the Denver, South Park, and Pacific over the pass; the Denver & Rio Grande from Pueblo; the Colorado Midland from Woodland Park;

and the Colorado & Southern through Jefferson and Como.

After leveling, the trail rolls gently through a thick and beautiful stand of aspens, making this an ideal spot for fall or summer foliage. The forest thins in about 0.5 mile, and you get great views of South Park and the

*Thick stands of aspen on the Colorado Trail turn red and gold in the fall.*

Mosquito Range. An informal side trail on the right (south) of the main trail leads down to a small meadow that is good for picnics, as well as enjoying the view.

The trail gradually climbs 360 feet over the next mile, topping out at around 10,360 feet, leaving traffic noise behind. It levels at around the 1.5-mile mark, offering even better views of the east side of South Park. The forest transitions into conifers as the trail descends gradually and then more steeply into the valley—a good place to turn around. The views back to the trailhead are even better because you are directly facing the towering 13,000- and 14,000-foot mountains on the horizon. You can backpack to the Rock Creek Trailhead.

# chapter 4

# Boulder Area: Indian Peaks

## 1 HOUR OR LESS FROM BOULDER

**B**oulder is one of the most popular places to live in the United States because it is surrounded by wonderful places to escape urban living. The mountains west of the city, the Indian Peaks, a magnificent subset of the Front Range, are among the best landscapes for escape and rejuvenation in North America. This rugged mountain range is lesser known to visitors but is extremely popular among locals for reasons that will become obvious should you have time to savor this awe-inspiring landscape. Ironically, they are virtually the only geographically significant natural or man-made wonders in the state that bear the names of the American Indians who preceded Europeans by thousands of years. Take either of the following routes west from Boulder: CO 119 through Boulder Canyon to CO 72 (the Peak to Peak Scenic Byway) or US 36 north to Lyons and then west on CO 7 and south on CO 72.

### Indian Peaks Wilderness Boundary & Brainard Lake Road

This borderline of a wilderness area is one of the most popular places in the state for hiking, biking, and picnics. When you see the stunning setting you will know why. The Indian Peaks, including Navajo (13,409 feet), Apache (13,441 feet), Shoshone (12,699 feet), Pawnee (12,943 feet),

Mount Toll (12,979 feet), Paiute (13,088 feet), and Audubon (13,223 feet), form a formidable and thoroughly enticing backdrop. This glacier-carved mountain "wall" along the Continental Divide was once considered as an addition to Rocky Mountain National Park to protect it, but many feared the designation would cause it to be overrun with people. Its beauty still makes it very popular.

The 1970s wilderness designation for the area means that a permit system for camping and backpacking is now in place for summer—a regulation that was badly needed. I could see some point in the future when day use might require a permit too. I highly recommend that you visit during the week if you want to avoid your fellow *Homo sapiens,* though weekend visits are still enjoyable because of the sheer number of options. If you do plan to visit on the weekend, particularly in the more popular areas, arrive early to make sure you can secure a parking space. The U.S. Forest Service has made an effort to help users spread out and to maintain the wilderness appeal of the area; they ask that, if at all possible, you leave your pets at home. Some trails are designated as dog-free, but your furry friends are still allowed on many of the trails if you must bring them, though they must be leashed.

*Longs Peak from Niwot Ridge*

### 65  Middle Saint Vrain

ROOSEVELT NATIONAL FOREST

| | |
|---|---|
| **Distance** | Up to 9 miles, out-and-back |
| **Difficulty** | Easy |
| **Elevation Gain** | 1,000' (starting at 8,500') |
| **Trail Use** | Hiking, mountain biking, camping, fishing, snowshoeing, skiing, option for kids, leashed dogs OK |
| **Agency** | Boulder Ranger District, Roosevelt National Forest |
| **Map(s)** | Latitude 40° *Boulder-Nederland Trails* |
| **Facilities** | Restrooms at campground |
| **Note(s)** | Moose are commonly spotted in this area, near trails and in the parking lots. Give these animals a wide berth; they have been known to attack people and dogs, especially when protecting their young. This is a fee area. |

**HIGHLIGHTS** This area features multiple campgrounds, a beautiful mountain stream, access to Buchanan Pass, and some Indian Peak summits. It is an easy trek on a heavily used trail, starting on the road and then paralleling it from across Middle Saint Vrain Creek, while passing through rolling, heavily forested terrain. It is wise to arrive early to avoid the large weekend crowds, or visit the area midweek.

**DIRECTIONS** Drive north from the Nederland and Ward area on CO 72; the trailhead is approximately 6 miles north of Ward. You can also reach it by driving toward Allenspark from Lyons and then turning left (south) on the Peak to Peak Scenic Byway (CO 72) toward Nederland and Peaceful Valley. Continue south when you see the turnoff for Peaceful Valley, which you're not taking. Do take the second turnoff west (right) after Peaceful Valley. Look for signs that say Forest Access or Camp Dick. Drive through the campground to the end of the road to reach the actual trailhead.

*Middle Saint Vrain Trail*

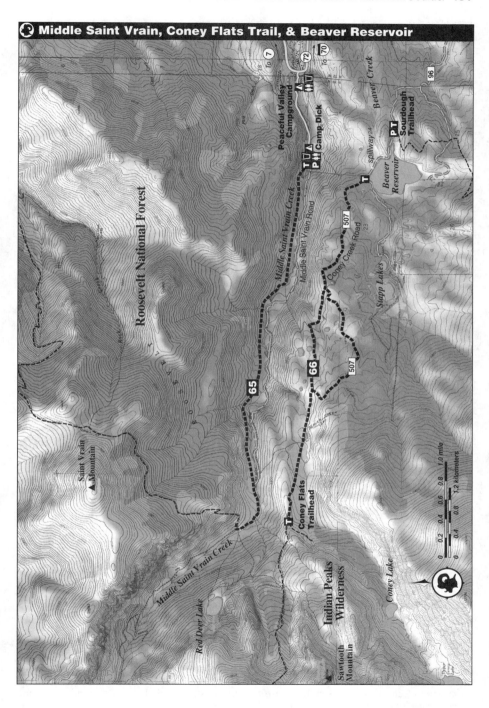

**Middle Saint Vrain, Coney Flats Trail, & Beaver Reservoir**

This trailhead also leads to the Sourdough Trail, which goes south toward Beaver Reservoir, Red Rocks Lake, and Rainbow Lakes Road in what is a major adventure. When you reach the trailhead parking lot, where the off-road vehicle trail begins, look for the Sourdough Trail on the left (south) side of the road. It is well marked. Remember that the four-wheel-drive road is not the rolling, mellow trail. The crossover trail is on the right (north), just beyond the Sourdough Trail. It is 200 yards from the parking lot and goes downhill to the stream on a wide, sturdy bridge. The trail is closed to motorized vehicles.

Some of the best views for photography are at the beginning of the trail and in the campground; if you want pictures of peaks, snap away before you reach the heavily forested trail. The trail scenery is varied, with riparian areas, open meadows, some aspens, and every species of evergreen: spruce and lodgepole, limber, and ponderosa pine. Go as far as you like before turning around. You have to start early and move fast if you want to make it to treeline and back. Buchanan Pass and the high mountain glacial cirques of the Indian Peaks await you if you make the complete trek. You can go over the Continental Divide on Buchanan Pass and trek all the way to Monarch, Granby, and Grand Lakes. The farther you go, the rockier the trail gets and the more stunning the high mountain scenery becomes.

### GREAT FOR KIDS

Good for hikers of all ages and skill levels, this trail through a wide valley climbs gently to its high point, where it offers a variety of mountain scenery. It is a good place to go on windy or hot days because of the heavy tree cover that will shield you once you get beyond the campground. The trail parallels a beautiful mountain stream, and there are lots of informal spots where you can have a picnic when you have gone far enough to enjoy the riparian beauty. Drive to the end of the road for the closest access to the trailhead. Cross over to the trail from the four-wheel-drive road, and then stroll as far as you wish, until you find a picnic spot.

## 66 Coney Flats Trail & Beaver Reservoir
ROOSEVELT NATIONAL FOREST

see map on p. 131

| | |
|---|---|
| **Distance** | Up to 7.5 miles, balloon |
| **Difficulty** | Easy–moderate |
| **Elevation Gain** | 600' (starting at 9,200') |
| **Trail Use** | Hiking, mountain biking, snowshoeing, skiing |
| **Agency** | Boulder Ranger District, Roosevelt National Forest |
| **Map(s)** | Latitude 40° Boulder-Nederland Trails |
| **Facilities** | None |
| **Note(s)** | Moose are commonly spotted in this area, near trails and in the parking lots. Give these animals a wide berth; they have been known to attack people and dogs, especially when protecting their young. |

**HIGHLIGHTS** This easy trek on a lesser known trail starts on a four-wheel-drive road and then parallels it while passing through rolling, heavily forested terrain. The trail rolls through the trees, offering some pretty vistas of the Indian Peaks along the way.

**DIRECTIONS** Drive south from Allenspark on the Peak to Peak Scenic Byway (CO 72), and take the turnoff south of Middle Saint Vrain/Camp Dick Campground. The only sign, which says Boy Scout Camp and Forest Road 96, is on the west side of the highway. Or drive approximately 5 miles north on the Peak to Peak Scenic Byway from Ward and look for the Boy Scout Camp sign on the west side of the road. It's easy to miss, especially if you're driving too fast; if you reach Camp Dick, you've gone too far. Drive west past the entrance to the Boy Scout Camp until you reach the spillway of the reservoir, and then look for the trail on the right (north) side of the road. You can turn around at a wide spot about 0.25 mile west, because the parking is tight when it fills up, and then park as close as you can get. You pass two access points for the Sourdough Trail on the left (south) side of the road before the reservoir on the way in; the first heads south, and the second, north. The second access is marked as the Beaver Reservoir trailhead for the Sourdough Trail.

There are some great views of the Indian Peaks, especially Sawtooth, from the reservoir. If the weather is iffy and you want peak pictures, take them before hiking the trail in case the weather socks it in. The trail starts a bit steeply, levels, and then rolls gently as you pass several smaller lakes. You are in a tunnel of lodgepole pine and then mixed aspen and pine for the first mile or so, and then the trees open up to views of Sawtooth Mountain and Paiute Peak. When you reach a trail junction where Forest Road 507 leaves the trail and branches off to the south, you can use the gravel road for a short side trip, but it isn't marked well and eventually becomes difficult to follow. Stay on the trail, which is closed to bikes, or backtrack to it, unless you are experienced with a compass and topographic map or a GPS unit.

The northern route begins at the Coney Flats Trailhead, which you pass on the east side of the trail about 50 yards from the start. It goes downhill to the Middle Saint Vrain and Camp Dick area and is a hilly, heavily forested route that can be a fun short car shuttle.

If you'd like a longer trip, take the Sourdough Trail south to the access at Brainard Lake Road (see trip 67). It starts about 0.25 mile short of the reservoir on the south side of the road and intersects with the Baptiste and Wapiti Ski Trails as it travels down—and then uphill—until it finally joins the South Saint Vrain Trail. From there you can go either to Red Rock Lake Trailhead or up to Brainard Lake. It is a long trek in any case.

More accessible, popular access points for the Sourdough Trail include the Brainard Lake Road and Red Rock Trailhead; you could even go farther south to the Rainbow Lakes Road Trailhead (see trip 68) on County Road 116.

*Taking a break on the Coney Flats Trail*

## 67  Sourdough Trail: Red Rock Trailhead to Beaver Reservoir

ROOSEVELT NATIONAL FOREST

| | |
|---|---|
| **Distance** | Up to 15 miles, out-and-back |
| **Difficulty** | Easy–moderate |
| **Elevation Gain** | 860' (starting at 10,000') |
| **Trail Use** | Hiking, mountain biking, snowshoeing, skiing, leashed dogs OK |
| **Agency** | Brainard Lake Recreation Area, Boulder Ranger District, Roosevelt National Forest |
| **Map(s)** | Latitude 40° *Boulder-Nederland Trails* |
| **Facilities** | Restrooms at parking lot |
| **Note(s)** | Moose are commonly spotted in the Brainard Lake area, near trails and in the parking lots. Give these animals a wide berth; they have been known to attack people and dogs, especially when protecting their young. |

**HIGHLIGHTS** This section of the Sourdough Trail is less popular for hiking and more popular with intermediate mountain bikers, despite being generally much rockier than going south. You break out of the thick tree cover from time to time for pleasing views but are sheltered from wind and sun most of the time.

**DIRECTIONS** The Brainard access to this trail is just east of the fee station for the recreation area and crosses the road at the Red Rock Trailhead parking area. From Boulder, take Boulder Canyon Road to Nederland. At the roundabout in Nederland, turn north on the Peak to Peak Scenic Byway (CO 72) for approximately 9 miles. Pass the historic town of Ward on the right (east) side of the road, and in 0.25 mile turn left (west) onto Brainard Lake Road. From Boulder, you could also take US 36 toward Lyons and then turn left (west) on Left Hand Canyon Road to Ward. Bear right at all intersections along the way.

If you are coming from the north, take CO 66 west to Lyons and CO 7 west to Peaceful Valley. Then turn south on CO 72 toward Ward, and in 10 miles, turn right (west) onto Brainard Lake Road. In another 2.2 miles, parking, along with restrooms and a warming hut, is available in the lot on the right side of the road. You can also access the trail near Beaver Reservoir on the north end (see directions for Coney Flats & Beaver Reservoir).

Going north from the Red Rock trailhead and parking lot, you have a slight climb over the first 0.25 mile and then a slowly descending stretch (a loss of about 200 feet) until just under a mile. Then the rocky trail descends another 200 feet to an intersection with the South Saint Vrain Trail. This means, of course, that you'll have a bit of a climb on the way back. The next 0.5 mile is fairly level, and you come to another trail intersection, where you should bear right to go toward Beaver Reservoir. You'll pass a small, seasonal pond and then roll over a 100-foot-high ridge, as the trail trends northwest and then turns sharply to the east and northeast over the next mile. The last mile includes climbs, descents, and switchbacks near the reservoir and then descends to the road. The last mile opens up with peak views.

*The trail to Beaver Reservoir winds through stately pine trees.*

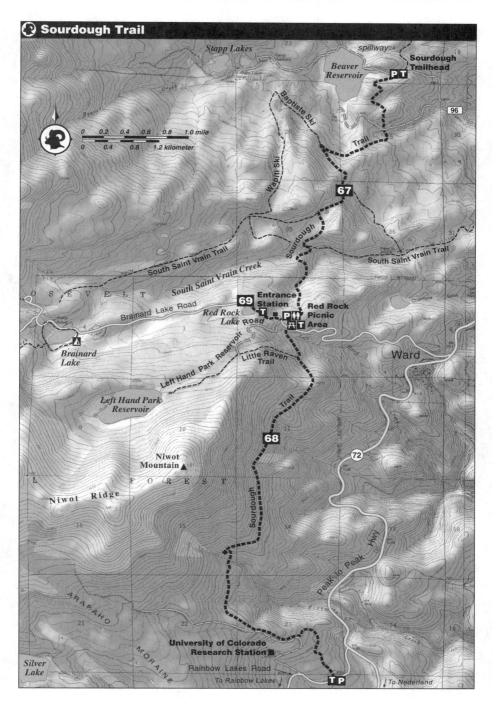

## Sourdough Trail

*Stapp Lakes*

spillway

*Beaver Reservoir*

**Sourdough Trailhead**

P T

96

Baptiste Ski Trail

Wapiti Ski Trail

67

Sourdough

South Saint Vrain Trail

South Saint Vrain Creek

South Saint Vrain Trail

0   0.2   0.4   0.6   0.8   1.0 mile
0      0.4      0.8    1.2 kilometer

R O O S E V E L T

Brainard Lake Road

Red Rock Lake Road

69

**Entrance Station**

**Red Rock Picnic Area**

T

P

*Brainard Lake*

Little Raven Trail

**Ward**

*Left Hand Park Reservoir*

*Left Hand Park Reservoir*

**Niwot Mountain**

N i w o t   R i d g e

N A T I O N A L   F O R E S T

68

Sourdough Trail

72

Peak to Peak Hwy

A R A P A H O   M O R A I N E

**University of Colorado Research Station**

Rainbow Lakes Road

*To Rainbow Lakes*

*Silver Lake*

T P

To Nederland

## 68  Sourdough Trail: Red Rock Trailhead to Rainbow Lakes

see map on p. 135

ROOSEVELT NATIONAL FOREST

| | |
|---|---|
| **Distance** | 11 miles, out-and-back |
| **Difficulty** | Moderate |
| **Elevation Gain** | 900' (starting at 10,000') |
| **Trail Use** | Hiking, mountain biking, snowshoeing, skiing, leashed dogs OK |
| **Agency** | Brainard Lake Recreation Area, Boulder Ranger District, Roosevelt National Forest |
| **Map(s)** | Latitude 40° *Boulder-Nederland Trails* |
| **Facilities** | Restrooms at parking lot |
| **Note(s)** | Moose are commonly spotted in the Brainard Lake area, near trails and in the parking lots. Give these animals a wide berth; they have been known to attack people and dogs, especially when protecting their young. |

**HIGHLIGHTS** The Sourdough Trail, though popular, has much less traffic than trails in and around Brainard Lake. You won't get quite the stunning views of the Indian Peaks, but you get beautiful views of the foothills, plains, and even snowcapped peaks in the distance. As you can see from the altitude information (gained and lost) on the map, both trail segments roller-coaster, but the trail segment from Brainard to the south is more level overall, until you get near Rainbow Lakes, where the trail descends significantly.

**DIRECTIONS** The most accessible and popular access points for the Sourdough Trail are from Brainard Lake Road or the Rainbow Lakes Road (County Road 116) parking area and trailhead. The Brainard access to this trail is just east of the fee station for the recreation area and crosses the road at the Red Rock trailhead parking area. From Boulder, take Boulder Canyon Road to Nederland. At the roundabout in Nederland, turn north on the Peak to Peak Scenic Byway (CO 72) for approximately 9 miles. Pass the historic town of Ward on the right (east) side of the road, and in 0.25 mile turn left (west) onto Brainard Lake Road. From Boulder, you could also take US 36 toward Lyons and then turn left (west) on Left Hand Canyon Road to Ward. Bear right at all intersections along the way.

If you are coming from the north, take CO 66 west to Lyons and CO 7 west to Peaceful Valley. Then turn south on CO 72 toward Ward, and in 10 miles, turn right (west) onto Brainard Lake Road. In another 2.2 miles, parking, along with restrooms and a warming hut, is available in the lot on the right side of the road. You can also access the trail near Beaver Reservoir on the north end (see directions for Coney Flats & Beaver Reservoir).

This most popular segment of the Sourdough Trail winds 7 miles south from the Red Rock Trailhead to the parking lot at Rainbow Lakes Trailhead. A car shuttle is a good way to ride the trail, though out-and-back romps are also nice. Much of the trail is sheltered by trees, a major bonus on the frequent windy days.

The route to the south is a bit easier overall than going north toward Beaver Reservoir. The trail does climb a bit initially, and you pass the Little Raven Trail in a little less than 0.5 mile, coming in from the west. After climbing up to 10,200 feet in the first mile, the trail mellows and stays fairly level until you near Rainbow Lakes, where it descends 1,100 feet to the Rainbow Lakes Road.

## 69 Red Rock Lake
ROOSEVELT NATIONAL FOREST

see map on p. 135

| | |
|---|---|
| **Distance** | 100 yards, out-and-back |
| **Difficulty** | Easy |
| **Elevation Gain** | Negligible (starting at 10,000') |
| **Trail Use** | Hiking, fishing, snowshoeing, skiing, great for kids |
| **Agency** | Brainard Lake Recreation Area, Boulder Ranger District, Roosevelt National Forest |
| **Map(s)** | Latitude 40° *Boulder-Nederland Trails* |
| **Facilities** | Restrooms at parking lot |
| **Note(s)** | Moose are commonly spotted in the Brainard Lake area, near trails and in the parking lots. Give these animals a wide berth; they have been known to attack people and dogs, especially when protecting their young. |

**HIGHLIGHTS** This short, easy side excursion on the left (south) side of Brainard Lake Road takes you 100 yards to the lake and gives you a spectacular view of the peaks, as well as a look at a beautiful small lake and riparian area. If you have young children, start with this scenic round-trip to Red Rock Lake. You can wander around the north side of the lake for an easy excursion of any length.

**DIRECTIONS** From Boulder, take Boulder Canyon Road to Nederland. At the roundabout in Nederland, turn north on the Peak to Peak Scenic Byway (CO 72) for approximately 9 miles. Pass the historic town of Ward on the right (east) side of the road, and in 0.25 mile turn left (west) onto Brainard Lake Road. From Boulder, you could also take US 36 toward Lyons and then turn left (west) on Left Hand Canyon Road to Ward. Bear right at all intersections along the way.

If you are coming from the north, you can take CO 66 west to Lyons and CO 7 west to Peaceful Valley. Then turn south on CO 72 toward Ward, and in 10 miles, turn right (west) onto Brainard Lake Road. In another 2.6 miles, park on the right side of the road, across from the trailhead.

The Red Rock Lake Trail and side road are on the left. Be careful not to confuse this with the Red Rock Trailhead. Out-and-back on the side road is the easiest way to go, or if you feel a little more adventuresome and don't mind a small hill, take the right edge of the shoreline around the lake to the west, where you are rewarded with additional views of the peaks and a view of the lake.

*Lily pads, peaks, and fun at Red Rock Lake*

## 70  Mitchell Lake & Blue Lake Trail

ROOSEVELT NATIONAL FOREST

| | |
|---|---|
| **Distance** | 1 mile to Mitchell Lake, 4.8 miles to Blue Lake; out-and-back |
| **Difficulty** | Easy–moderate |
| **Elevation Gain** | Mitchell Lake: 400'; Blue Lake: 1,000' (starting at 10,300') |
| **Trail Use** | Hiking, snowshoeing, skiing, option for kids |
| **Agency** | Brainard Lake Recreation Area, Indian Peaks Wilderness, Boulder Ranger District, Roosevelt National Forest |
| **Map(s)** | Latitude 40° *Boulder-Nederland Trails* |
| **Facilities** | Restrooms at trailhead |
| **Note(s)** | Brainard Lake is a fee area. Dogs are not permitted. Moose are commonly spotted in the Brainard Lake area, near trails and in the parking lots. Give these animals a wide berth; they have been known to attack people and dogs, especially when protecting their young. Bikes are not allowed in the Indian Peaks Wilderness Area. |

**HIGHLIGHTS**  High, pristine mountain lakes with the Indian Peaks as a backdrop are what you'll see for your efforts. The lakes are a popular destination, so arrive early to find a parking spot. Mitchell Lake is an easy family stroll, while Blue Lake is a pleasant hike.

**DIRECTIONS**  From Boulder, take Boulder Canyon Road to Nederland. At the roundabout in Nederland, turn north on the Peak to Peak Scenic Byway (CO 72) for approximately 9 miles. Pass the historic town of Ward on the right (east) side of the road, and in 0.25 mile turn left (west) onto Brainard Lake Road. From Boulder, you could also take US 36 toward Lyons and then turn left (west) onto Left Hand Canyon Road to Ward. Bear right at all intersections along the way.

If you are coming from the north, you can take CO 66 west to Lyons and CO 7 west to Peaceful Valley. Then turn south onto CO 72 toward Ward, and in 10 miles, turn right (west) onto Brainard Lake Road. Follow Brainard Lake Road 2.2 miles to the entrance station and then another 2.5 miles to reach the turnoff for Mitchell and Long Lakes on the right. Turn right at the fork in the road to get to the parking lot.

*Mitchell Lake sits in a glacial cirque.*

The trail climbs steadily and gradually 1 mile up to Mitchell Lake. You cross Mitchell Creek on a footbridge, and then the trail goes north away from the creek 0.1 mile before turning southwest toward the lake. It slowly climbs and winds through the pretty mixed forest before rejoining Mitchell Creek and getting steeper. You then climb in earnest and pass a small unnamed lake often mistaken for Mitchell Lake. After the first shoreline access to Mitchell Lake, you continue to climb and pass several more opportunities to descend to the lakeshore. You get views of the glacial cirque and the pointed summit of Mount Toll at the lake.

If you continue, you can hike another 2 miles up to Blue Lake, which is well above treeline. If you don't want to go all the way to Blue Lake but would like a view above the trees, climb the steep hill just beyond Mitchell Lake. It is worth the price of admission to see the view and won't add much to the return trip.

The trail from Mitchell Lake to Blue Lake is much steeper than the Mitchell Lake Trail, though there are a few flat stretches. It is not a good early season trail, unless you don't mind lots of water and mud. It is much more enjoyable when it has dried out. You are out of the trees after the first steep hill beyond Mitchell Lake and can start enjoying spectacular ridgeline and peak views. On a clear day, the trail offers a steady diet of views all the way over the numerous waves of ridges rolling away under your feet, as you climb one false summit ridge after another. As with many of the trails in this book, even if you turn around short of Blue Lake, you will have had an enjoyable, physically satisfying adventure. Just remember that the return trip will seem much longer and might actually take more time than your trip out because you will be tired.

### GREAT FOR KIDS

By definition and distance, the trek to Mitchell Lake is an easy, short, and highly scenic trip for families with small children or those not wanting an arduous outing. The trail goes up, over, and around rocks as it winds to the lake with a gradual climb and crosses a stream on a small footbridge. There are lots of intermediary sites and sounds to enjoy in the lodgepole pine and aspen forest. Take a picnic or snack for the lakeshore, and enjoy the sparkling water, cool breeze across the lake, and soaring cliffs before returning to your car. If you have additional time and energy, continue another 0.5 mile toward Blue Lake, and enjoy more spectacular views of Niwot Ridge and the high mountain scenery that surrounds you. Bring an extra layer, snacks, water, and sunscreen.

  **Long Lake & Jean Lunning Trails**
ROOSEVELT NATIONAL FOREST

see map on p. 139

| | |
|---|---|
| **Distance** | 0.6 mile to the lake, out-and-back; 1.5 miles, around-the-lake loop |
| **Difficulty** | Easy |
| **Elevation Gain** | 100' (starting at 10,500') |
| **Trail Use** | Hiking, snowshoeing, skiing, option for kids |

*The spectacular Indian Peaks from Long Lake*

| | |
|---|---|
| **Agency** | Brainard Lake Recreation Area, Indian Peaks Wilderness, Boulder Ranger District, Roosevelt National Forest |
| **Map(s)** | Latitude 40° *Boulder-Nederland Trails* |
| **Facilities** | Restrooms at trailhead |
| **Note(s)** | Brainard Lake is a fee area. Moose are commonly spotted in the Brainard Lake area, near trails and in the parking lots. Give these animals a wide berth; they have been known to attack people and dogs, especially when protecting their young. Bikes are not allowed in the Indian Peaks Wilderness Area. Dogs are not allowed on the Jean Lunning or Pawnee Pass Trails. |

**HIGHLIGHTS** This family stroll for the uninitiated has views of Niwot Ridge along the way and a spectacular and unique view of the Indian Peaks across the sparkling lake. The lakeshore is a delightful place for a lunch or snack break. The Jean Lunning Trail follows the south side of Long Lake and is a highly scenic, wildflower-studded path.

**DIRECTIONS** From Boulder, take Boulder Canyon Road to Nederland. At the roundabout in Nederland, turn north on the Peak to Peak Scenic Byway (CO 72) for approximately 9 miles. Pass the historic town of Ward on the right (east) side of the road, and in 0.25 mile turn left (west) onto Brainard Lake Road. From Boulder, you could also take US 36 toward Lyons and then turn left (west) on Left Hand Canyon Road to Ward. Bear right at all intersections along the way.

If you are coming from the north, you can take CO 66 west to Lyons and CO 7 west to Peaceful Valley. Then turn south on CO 72 toward Ward, and in 10 miles, turn right (west) onto Brainard Lake Road. Follow Brainard Lake Road 2.2 miles to the entrance station and then another 2.5 miles to reach the turnoff for Mitchell and Long Lakes on the right. Bear left at the intersection to the trailhead.

This high-altitude stroll leads to a beautiful mountain lake in a spectacular setting. Just follow the trail gradually uphill as it wends its way through the forest, up, over, and around rocks and across one stream (on a footbridge) to the lake. Be sure to take a camera and a picnic or snack.

If you keep going past the east end of the lake, you'll enjoy other views of the lake and the high mountain ridgeline. Cross the footbridge to the south side of the lake, and take the Jean Lunning Trail west for the best views. A boardwalk keeps your feet dry in the spring. Turning around and retracing your steps is a good alternative for the return trip. If you prefer to see the north side of the lake on the way back, return via the Pawnee Pass Trail; go right (east) at the intersection to go back to the parking area.

**72** **Lake Isabelle**

ROOSEVELT NATIONAL FOREST

see map on p. 139

| | |
|---|---|
| **Distance** | 3 miles, out-and-back |
| **Difficulty** | Easy |
| **Elevation Gain** | 300' (starting at 10,500') |
| **Trail Use** | Hiking, snowshoeing, skiing |
| **Agency** | Brainard Lake Recreation Area, Indian Peaks Wilderness, Boulder Ranger District, Roosevelt National Forest |
| **Map(s)** | Latitude 40° *Boulder-Nederland Trails* |
| **Facilities** | Restrooms at trailhead |
| **Note(s)** | Brainard Lake is a fee area. Dogs are not allowed. Moose are commonly spotted in the Brainard Lake area, near trails and in the parking lots. Give these animals a wide berth; they have been known to attack people and dogs, especially when protecting their young. Bikes are not allowed in the Indian Peaks Wilderness Area. |

**HIGHLIGHTS** Lake Isabelle is another mile beyond Long Lake and is one of the more beautiful trails in the Front Range, with spectacular Indian Peaks views. It is a steady climb from Long Lake but not particularly steep, until very near the lake.

**DIRECTIONS** From Boulder, take Boulder Canyon Road to Nederland. At the roundabout in Nederland, turn north on the Peak to Peak Scenic Byway (CO 72) for approximately 9 miles. Pass the historic town of Ward on the right (east) side of the road, and in 0.25 mile turn left (west) onto Brainard Lake Road. From Boulder, you could also take US 36 toward Lyons and then turn left (west) on Left Hand Canyon Road to Ward. Bear right at all intersections along the way.

If you are coming from the north, you can take CO 66 west to Lyons and CO 7 west to Peaceful Valley. Then turn south on CO 72 toward Ward, and in 10 miles, turn right (west) onto Brainard Lake Road. Follow Brainard Lake Road 2.2 miles to the entrance station and then another 2.5 miles to reach the turnoff for Mitchell and Long Lakes on the right.

You are rewarded with superb views almost all the way because most of the trail has openings through the trees to Niwot Ridge. At about 0.75 mile beyond Long Lake, you come to an open meadow area that affords a terrific view of the ridge and some of the peaks beyond—a good place for a rest break because of its sunny southern exposure and relative shelter from the wind. After this point the trail steepens considerably and switchbacks up through trees to Lake Isabelle. The view from the lake of this section of the Indian Peaks is no less than stunning. From the lake you can continue higher up the Pawnee Pass Trail if you're looking for a longer trek, or turn around and return to your starting point.

## 73  Pawnee Pass & Peak
### ROOSEVELT NATIONAL FOREST

see map on p. 139

| | |
|---|---|
| **Distance** | 9.8 miles to the pass, 11 miles to the peak; out-and-back |
| **Difficulty** | Moderate–challenging |
| **Elevation Gain** | 2,500' to pass; 2,800' to peak (starting at 10,500') |
| **Trail Use** | Hiking |
| **Agency** | Brainard Lake Recreation Area, Indian Peaks Wilderness, Boulder Ranger District, Roosevelt National Forest |
| **Map(s)** | Latitude 40° *Boulder-Nederland Trails* |
| **Facilities** | Restrooms at trailhead |
| **Note(s)** | Brainard Lake is a fee area. Dogs are not allowed. Moose are commonly spotted in the Brainard Lake area, near trails and in the parking lots. Give these animals a wide berth; they have been known to attack people and dogs, especially when protecting their young. Bikes are not allowed in the Indian Peaks Wilderness Area. |

**HIGHLIGHTS** The hike up to the top of Pawnee Pass is, along with climbing Mount Audubon, one of the most enjoyable moderate to challenging outings in the area. When you make the top of the pass, it is only a short scramble to the north to climb Pawnee Peak. From the top you not only have a great view of the Indian Peaks, but you can also see all the way over the Continental Divide and into the Monarch Lake and Winter Park area.

**DIRECTIONS** From Boulder, take Boulder Canyon Road to Nederland. At the roundabout in Nederland, turn north on the Peak to Peak Scenic Byway (CO 72) for approximately 9 miles. Pass the historic town of Ward on the right (east) side of the road, and in 0.25 mile turn left (west) onto Brainard Lake Road. From Boulder, you could also take US 36 toward Lyons and then turn left (west) on Left Hand Canyon Road to Ward. Bear right at all intersections along the way.

*Grand Lake from Pawnee Pass*

If you are coming from the north, you can take CO 66 west to Lyons and CO 7 west to Peaceful Valley. Then turn south on CO 72 toward Ward, and in 10 miles, turn right (west) onto Brainard Lake Road. Follow Brainard Lake Road 2.2 miles to the entrance station and then another 2.5 miles to reach the turnoff for Mitchell and Long Lakes on the right.

You are rewarded with superb views almost all the way to Lake Isabelle because of openings through the trees to Niwot Ridge. At about 0.75 mile beyond Long Lake, you come to an open meadow area that affords a terrific view of the ridge and some of the peaks beyond—a good place for a rest break because of its southern exposure and relative shelter from the wind. After this point the trail steepens considerably and switchbacks up through trees to the lake. The view from the lake of this section of the Indian Peaks is no less than stunning.

From Lake Isabelle continue up the Pawnee Pass Trail, so well marked and well worn that it's almost impossible to lose. The trail switchbacks northeast from the lake and gradually gains elevation as it tracks mostly west, offering ever more spectacular views along the way. After the initial switchbacks, the trail turns gradually to the west, narrowing and passing under and around some noteworthy rock formations. It then travels on a broader but somewhat rocky trail for about 0.5 mile before hitting a stretch of short but very steep switchbacks—the crux of the climb to the pass. The peak is a short, nontechnical scramble to the right (north) from the pass. Do a car shuttle if you want to go all the way over the pass to beautiful Monarch Lake, ending in the Fraser/Granby area. From Brainard to Monarch Lake is approximately 14 miles one way.

## 74  Mount Audubon
### ROOSEVELT NATIONAL FOREST

see map on p. 139

| | |
|---|---|
| **Distance** | 7 miles, out-and-back |
| **Difficulty** | Moderate–difficult |
| **Elevation Gain** | 2,730' (starting at 10,500') |
| **Trail Use** | Hiking, snowshoeing, skiing, leashed dogs OK |
| **Agency** | Brainard Lake Recreation Area, Indian Peaks Wilderness, Boulder Ranger District, Roosevelt National Forest |
| **Map(s)** | Latitude 40° *Boulder-Nederland Trails* |
| **Facilities** | Restroom at trailhead |
| **Note(s)** | Brainard Lake is a fee area. The small parking lot usually fills up early (8 a.m.). Climb during the week if possible to avoid the crowds. Moose are commonly spotted in the Brainard Lake area, near trails and in the parking lots. Give these animals a wide berth; they have been known to attack people and dogs, especially when protecting their young. Bikes are not allowed in the Indian Peaks Wilderness Area. |

**HIGHLIGHTS** This gentle giant is one of the most popular and accessible thirteeners in the Front Range. The trail offers superb views of lakes and peaks as you climb from the subalpine forest to the treeless tundra.

**DIRECTIONS** From Boulder, take Boulder Canyon Road to Nederland. At the roundabout in Nederland, turn north on the Peak to Peak Scenic Byway (CO 72) for approximately 9 miles. Pass the historic town of Ward on the right (east) side of the road, and in 0.25 mile turn left (west) onto Brainard Lake Road. From Boulder, you could also take US 36 toward Lyons and then turn left (west) on Left Hand Canyon Road to Ward. Bear right at all intersections along the way.

If you are coming from the north, take CO 66 west to Lyons and CO 7 west to Peaceful Valley. Then turn south on CO 72 toward Ward, and in 10 miles, turn right (west) onto Brainard Lake Road. Follow Brainard Lake Road 2.2 miles to the entrance station and then another 2.5 miles to reach the turnoff for Mitchell and Long Lakes on the left. Bear right at the intersection to the trailhead shared with Mitchell Lake.

Look for the trailhead at the north end of the Mitchell Lake parking lot. The trail travels west-northwest in thick tree cover that preserves snow into late spring. Be prepared for wet conditions; if you're early in the season, the trail can be a stream. You will reach a steeper, rockier section of the route in about 0.6 mile as you break out of the thick trees and ascend switchbacks in a more northerly direction. Look to the west for spectacular views of Mitchell Lake and Navajo and Apache Peaks. At around the 1.5-mile mark, the Beaver Creek Trail goes right; stay left. The trail goes more westerly and you can see the false summit to the northwest. It then climbs steadily north, rounding the bottom of the shoulder of the mountain. The trail to the north ends, and you can pick your trail to the left (west) for your final summit climb. There is no one set trail, but lots are marked with cairns and will take you to the summit. You can hug the right (north) ridge and enjoy views of Meeker and Longs, but keep in mind that the summit is a little bit southwest. The rock scrambling is fun but can be tricky if it is partially snow-covered. When you reach the summit enjoy the expansive views of Grand Lake and Paiute, Toll, Pawnee, Shoshoni, Apache, and Navajo Peaks to the south. If you have lots of time—at least 2 hours—you can also summit Paiute Peak by using the ridge that travels to the west.

## 75 Niwot Ridge
ROOSEVELT NATIONAL FOREST

see map on p. 139

| | |
|---|---|
| **Distance** | 8 miles via Long Lake to U.C. Biosphere, out-and-back; 8 miles via U.C. Research Center Road to Biosphere, out-and-back |
| **Difficulty** | Moderate |
| **Elevation Gain** | Via Long Lake Trailhead to end of U.C. Research Center Road: 1,750' (starting at 10,600'); Via U.C. Research Center Road to end: 2,750' (starting at 9,500') |
| **Trail Use** | Hiking, mountain biking (on U.C. Research Center Road; not allowed in Indian Peaks Wilderness), snowshoeing, skiing, leashed dogs OK |
| **Agency** | Boulder Ranger District, Roosevelt National Forest |
| **Map(s)** | Latitude 40° *Boulder-Nederland Trails* |
| **Facilities** | Restrooms at Long Lake Trailhead |
| **Note(s)** | Brainard Lake is a fee area. Moose are commonly spotted in this area, near trails and in the parking lots. Give these animals a wide berth; they have been known to attack people and dogs, especially when protecting their young. |

**HIGHLIGHTS** Towering above Brainard Lake, this high ridge can be a fun adventure and offers a grand and unique view of the majestic Indian Peaks and Longs Peak. This climb is best attempted on a calm, warm day because Niwot Ridge and Mountain are often windswept. Always bring extra layers. There are two approaches to Niwot Ridge: a trail from the Jean Lunning Trail on the south side of Long Lake, or the University of Colorado Research Center Road near the Rainbow Lakes end of the Sourdough Trail.

*Navajo Peak from the Niwot Ridge Biosphere*

**DIRECTIONS** From Boulder, take Boulder Canyon Road to Nederland. At the roundabout in Nederland, turn north on the Peak to Peak Scenic Byway (CO 72) for approximately 9 miles. Pass the historic town of Ward on the right (east) side of the road, and in 0.25 mile turn left (west) onto Brainard Lake Road.

For the University of Colorado Research Center Road, turn left on the Rainbow Lakes Road turnoff, approximately 3 miles north of the Sugarloaf Road turnoff on CO 72. Drive 1 mile to the Rainbow Lakes Road intersection; then bear right/uphill to the research station parking area.

The access from Long Lake and the Jean Lunning Trail is not well marked. Go across the footbridge toward Long Lake, take the Jean Lunning Trail left (west), and then look for an unmarked trail 100 yards from the start of the Lunning Trail on the left (south). It is around 2.6 miles from this point to the intersection with U.C. Research Center Road. The trail switchbacks through thick tree cover for around a mile and climbs 400 feet to a rockslide area. Another 100 yards gives you a great view of a waterfall near Lake Isabelle and an Indian Peaks panorama. The best views are over the next mile. The trail tracks southeast around 11,000 feet, and then back to the southwest toward a large cairn. This is a good turnaround point unless you want to gain another 400 feet to the end of U.C. Research Center Road, which is 800 feet higher at 12,250 feet. To climb Niwot Ridge, get out your map and compass and head southeast when you are halfway to the road.

U.C. Research Center Road is treecovered for the first 1,500 feet. If you travel to the end of the very rocky road, you will be at the spectacular foot of Navajo Mountain (13,409 feet).

## 76  Rainbow Lakes & Arapaho Glacier Overlook Trails
ROOSEVELT NATIONAL FOREST

| | |
|---|---|
| **Distance** | 2–12 miles, out-and-back |
| **Difficulty** | Easy–moderate |
| **Elevation Gain** | Caribou Ridge: 300'; Arapaho Trail: 1,100' (starting at 10,100') |
| **Trail Use** | Hiking, fishing, camping, snowshoeing, skiing, option for kids |
| **Agency** | Boulder Ranger District, Roosevelt National Forest |
| **Map(s)** | Latitude 40° *Boulder-Nederland Trails* |
| **Facilities** | Campground and restrooms |
| **Note(s)** | Moose are commonly spotted in this area, near trails and in the parking lots. Give these animals a wide berth; they have been known to attack people and dogs, especially when protecting their young. Dogs are not allowed in the Indian Peaks Wilderness Area. |

**HIGHLIGHTS** The four small Rainbow Lakes are in a spectacular high-mountain setting nestled next to the soaring tundra and glacier-carved Caribou ridgeline. The real treat is the view from the lakes. Plus there's good fishing if the thunder isn't rolling. The Arapaho Glacier Overlook Trail is more challenging but an even more stunning spectacle. These trails and the campground are heavily used in the summer. The area melts out, and dries out, later in the summer (July–August) in an average snow year because of the elevation. Bring insect repellent.

**DIRECTIONS** From Boulder, take Boulder Canyon Drive (CO 119) 17 miles to Nederland. Follow CO 72 West for 6.8 miles. County Road 116 is between Nederland and Ward on the west side of the road. It is also the entry to the University of Colorado Research Station. There is a large parking lot for the southern terminus of the Sourdough Trail and a rough but drivable road from that point 4.2 miles to the trailhead. Both trailheads are at the end of Rainbow Lakes Road (CR 116), and at the western edge of the Rainbow Lakes Campground.

# Rainbow Lakes & Arapaho Glacier Overlook Trails

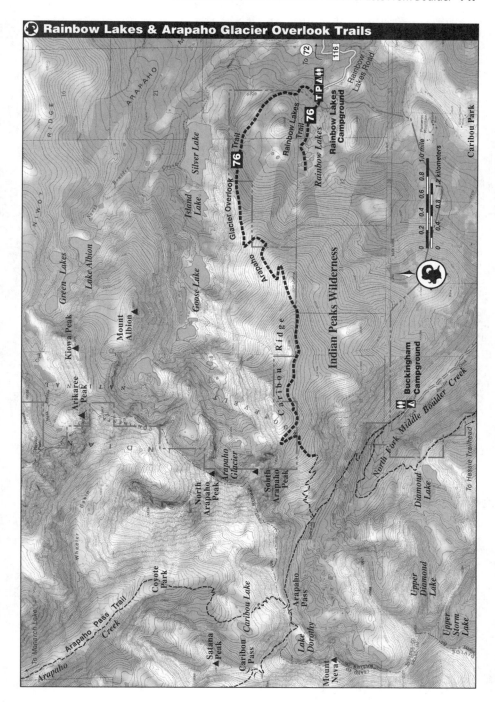

## Rainbow Lakes Trail

This trailhead is at the very end of the road at the southwest end of the parking lot and is well signed. It rolls gently for 1 mile to the lakes, and you'll have some views along the way. The trail turns left (south) and then west at the watershed boundary sign. It gets steeper as you walk through the pretty mixed aspen and conifer forest. It widens and levels after climbing 150 feet and 0.5 mile to 10,250 feet. It is then only another 50 yards down to the first lake, making this an easy jaunt for small children or the less ambitious. There is a slight climb to the second lake and overview. The first two lakes are essentially adjacent. The second lake offers a great peak view.

From there the trail gets very rocky, climbs up to 10,300 feet, passes wetlands, and then levels. In 0.25 mile you cross a stream that can be deep during spring runoff. Lakes 3 and 4 are like twin sisters and feature another peak view—a good lunch spot. If you go south and east around Lake 4 you will see a small pond with an informal campsite and illegal fire ring. I recommend going south and west between the lakes to the sheltered stream for quiet contemplation or a snack break. Pick your way around the rocks. It turns into a meadow stroll as the trail meanders southwest. Reverse course to the trailhead at your leisure.

## Arapaho Glacier Overlook Trail

This trailhead is on the northwest end of the campground. The actual overlook is a distant 6 miles one-way from the trailhead, but you can make it to treeline and a stunning view in approximately 3 miles one-way. The trailhead is well marked, and the initial mile or so the trail is easy to track because it runs along the city of Boulder's watershed fence and then has a few blue ribbons once you leave the watershed boundary and enter a mixed conifer and aspen forest. Once the trail starts to climb and steepen, the switchbacks are difficult to see and are not well marked. You'll need a topographic map and good route-finding skills, but if you keep the lakes to your left (south) and the ridgeline to the right (north) you are generally traveling first north and then west on the south side of the ridge. There is much fallen timber everywhere except the trail, which is always a good clue as to its location.

After following the winding trail to treeline, walk over to the north side of the ridge to enjoy a superb view of the Boulder Watershed that includes the panorama of the Indian Peaks glacier-carved moraine. You have a great view of the rest of the Caribou Ridge route to North and South Arapaho Peaks as well as the glacier itself and Kiowa Peak and Niwot Ridge. The prevailing west wind makes your visit above treeline an air-conditioned one even on hot days. The trail continues another 3 miles one-way to the actual overlook of the small glacier.

*GREAT FOR KIDS*

---

The trail to the four Rainbow Lakes is short and sweet, with easy walking and views all around. This area is popular for fishing, camping and hiking with families. It is a gently rolling, 1-mile trail to the lakes, so it is ideal for small children or casual excursions.

You have options for two of the Rainbow Lakes upon arrival: one to the right (west-northwest) and another to the left (southwest). The other two lakes are farther than 1 mile (approximately 0.5 mile beyond the first two). The trails around the lakes are quite narrow, but some lakeside spots are good for a snack or picnic stop between the lakes.

---

## 77 Saint Vrain Mountain & Meadow Mountain

ROOSEVELT NATIONAL FOREST,
ROCKY MOUNTAIN NATIONAL PARK

| | |
|---|---|
| **Distance** | 8 miles, out-and-back |
| **Difficulty** | Moderate |
| **Elevation Gain** | Saint Vrain Mountain: 3,190'; Meadow Mountain: 2,660' (starting at 8,970') |
| **Trail Use** | Hiking, backpacking, snowshoeing, skiing |
| **Agency** | Boulder Ranger District, Roosevelt National Forest; Rocky Mountain National Park |
| **Map(s)** | Latitude 40° *Boulder County Trails* |
| **Facilities** | No toilets; restaurant and lodges in Allenspark |
| **Note(s)** | Bikes and dogs are not allowed inside Rocky Mountain National Park or Indian Peaks Wilderness Area. |

**HIGHLIGHTS** This is a great small-peak climb into the Indian Peaks Wilderness and Rocky Mountain National Park near Allenspark, with sweeping Continental Divide views. You can climb either Meadow Mountain or Saint Vrain Mountain, or just enjoy the spectacular panorama at the saddle. The trail travels along the RMNP border with superb views of Mount Meeker, Longs Peak, Chiefs Head Peak, and Wild Basin, as well as Twin Sisters and the plains sprawling to the east.

**DIRECTIONS** Take CO 7 to Allenspark, and then go west on the right (north) side of the Allenspark Post Office. Turn left and follow gravel Ski Road (Forest Road 107) south approximately 2 miles to the trailhead. Stay right on Forest Road 1161 when the road forks.

The trail goes gradually uphill through thick, mixed, beautiful aspen and lodgepole pines, making it a good fall-color hike. It rolls uphill fairly gently through the trees for the first 0.75 mile, where it enters the Indian Peaks Wilderness. As the fir trees open up, the trail tracks into a broad drainage, steepens, and then switchbacks broadly. You'll parallel Saint Vrain Creek below and hear the sounds of the small seasonal waterfall. Enjoy the cascading stream sounds as you climb and cross several small spring streams.

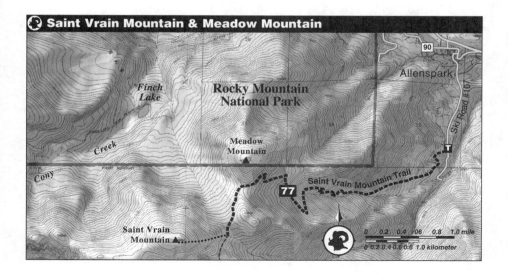

**Saint Vrain Mountain & Meadow Mountain**

The trail leaves the drainage as the switchback goes north through a very rocky section, and then the trail levels a little as it turns south at around 1.9 miles, crosses a small stream, and then travels southwest steeply uphill, closing the distance to treeline. Early in the summer, you are treated to abundant wildflowers. At the start of the tundra, the trail tracks southwest and crosses the Rocky Mountain National Park (RMNP) boundary at around 11,200 feet. Meadow Mountain's summit is north at 11,632 feet. There appear to be several ways up the broad slope to the summit of Saint Vrain Mountain, but the main trail is on the southern edge of the saddle, on the southeast side of the mountain at around 11,400 feet. Climb west steeply another 700 feet in 0.5 mile to the summit. Late in the snow season after avalanche danger is over, this is a popular slope for Telemark skiing and snowboarding.

Look around and savor the mixed alpine flora and fauna and the 180-degree view. You can make the route a little less steep by making your own mini switchbacks as you ascend the steep ridge. You will see the soaring thirteener Continental Divide mountains in RMNP on the way up, and great views of Mount Meeker, Longs Peak, and the other monarchs of Wild Basin. Near the summit you also see a trail descending southeast that eventually ends up near Buchanan Pass. If you plant a car at Camp Dick, you can do a long car shuttle hike that ends there. The summit view is one of the best in the Front Range; enjoy the peaks of RMNP to the north and the Indian Peaks and Audubon and Paiute Peaks to the south.

*Jean Lunning Trail (see page 140); photographed by Kay Turnbaugh*

*The Hessie trailhead*

# chapter 5

# Nederland Area

## 35 MINUTES FROM BOULDER

## 1–2 HOURS FROM DENVER

The Nederland area, 18 miles from Boulder, offers a variety of trails at the foot of the Indian Peaks. The magnificent backdrop of the Continental Divide invites the uninitiated into the high foothills and mountains of the Front Range. Enjoy the windswept meadows, sparkling lakes and streams, and aspen and conifer forests of both Indian Peaks and James Peak Wilderness Areas.

Nederland is surrounded by Roosevelt National Forest and is within easy driving distance of trails of varying difficulty. The rolling Magnolia trails network is minutes from town, as are Caribou Ranch and Mud Lake, both Boulder County Open Spaces. The Hessie and Fourth of July trailheads are a bit farther and have easy to moderate trails into the Indian Peaks Wilderness, and the Rollinsville/East Portal Trails a few more miles from town offer forest excursions to austere, high mountain lakes in the James Peak Wilderness. The town of Nederland features more than the annual Frozen Dead Guy Days festival; a dozen excellent restaurants, bakeries, coffee shops, and brewpubs fortify body and soul. There are also affordable and unique lodging options and Regional Transportation District (RTD) buses, if you don't want to make the drive.

### Hessie Trailhead

The Hessie trailhead just west of the town of Eldora is a popular spot where parking fills up by 7:30 or 8 a.m. on summer weekends. The trailhead is now served by shuttle buses that run every 15–20 minutes on summer weekends. The bus runs 8 a.m.–7 p.m. and departs from the Nederland High School parking lot on the road to Eldora. It is a

pleasant, much less stressful way to get to the trailhead.

### Fourth of July Trailhead

This is a popular access point for some of the most spectacular scenery in the Indian Peaks Wilderness. It sits at 10,150 feet and provides access to North and South Arapaho Peaks; Mount Neva and Jasper Peak; Arapaho and Caribou Passes; and Diamond, Jasper, and Dorothy Lakes. In the height of summer, the area is blanketed with wildflowers, and the gradual, nontechnical trails attract people of all ages and abilities. The parking lot is small, relative to the popularity, so plan to carpool and arrive early.

### East Portal Trailhead

Rollinsville is a mountain town that was created to serve not only the numerous mines and miners, but also as a railroad stop on the way to the famous Moffat Tunnel that bored under the Continental Divide to Winter Park. It is now the turnoff to the Moffat Road and the popular trailhead 9 miles west, at the East Portal of one of the highest (9,239 feet) and longest (6.2 miles) railroad tunnels in the world. There is a bar/restaurant and a quick-stop grocery in Rollinsville.

You are likely to see coal and freight trains plying their way through the expansive and beautiful mountain valley as you drive west from Rollinsville, or even Amtrak's California Zephyr going to or from the West Coast. The tunnel was holed through in 1926, in a blast triggered by President Calvin Coolidge. The first railroad traffic went through in 1928. It is still a very busy, often clogged route for

Union Pacific and Burlington Northern Santa Fe trains.

The Rogers and Heart Lake, Forest Lakes, and Crater Lakes Trails all start at the East Portal of the tunnel and are scenic routes to high mountain lakes, with spectacular views of the riparian and glacier-carved valley from the Crater Lakes Trail.

## 78  Caribou Ranch Open Space
### BOULDER COUNTY OPEN SPACE

| | |
|---|---|
| **Distance** | 3.1 miles (DeLonde Homestead: 1.2 miles, Blue Bird Loop: 1.9 miles), balloon |
| **Difficulty** | Easy |
| **Elevation Gain** | 200' (starting at 8,500') |
| **Trail Use** | Hiking, horseback riding, snowshoeing, skiing, option for kids |
| **Agency** | Boulder County Open Space |
| **Map(s)** | Latitude 40° *Boulder-Nederland Trails* |
| **Facilities** | Restrooms, picnic areas |
| **Note(s)** | Dogs and bicycles are prohibited, and the ranch is closed April 1–June 30 to protect calving elk and migratory birds. |

**HIGHLIGHTS**  This Boulder County Open Space area includes the historic DeLonde Homestead with a striking, aspen- and pine-ringed high mountain meadow, as well as the 19th-century Blue Bird Mine complex. The ranch was used for movies, including the 1966 remake of *Stagecoach*. Most of the buildings have been preserved, and though they aren't open to the public, you can look in the windows and see the close quarters the miners used. You can enjoy a stream, small waterfall, diverse trees, and animals. The aspens make it a great fall hike.

**DIRECTIONS**  From Boulder, take Canyon Boulevard/CO 119 west 18 miles to Nederland. Go through the roundabout and bear right to take Peak to Peak Scenic Byway (CO 72) north 2 miles to County Road 126; turn left (west) on CR 126, and go 1 mile to the Caribou Ranch parking lot.

### GREAT FOR KIDS

The trek to the DeLonde Homestead, where you can often spot moose while having a snack at the picnic tables and viewpoint of the beaver ponds, is well suited for kids who need a shorter destination for motivation. Some might also like going the extra distance to the Blue Bird Mine complex, where they can explore the history of mining and have lunch or more snacks next to the small waterfall.

You will travel northwest from the parking area and go gradually uphill in thick trees. In 0.5 mile you will crest the ridge and have a sweeping view of part of the ranch and the hilly, forested terrain stretching to the north and west. You will descend a short hill and reenter the trees, reaching a comely, small meadow. The trail turns sharply north and goes downhill, with a historical marker about the Switzerland excursion train that ran until the early 1900s. You will reach an intersection in 0.25 mile.

If you aren't sure you want to hike the entire loop, turn right and go down a short hill to begin a counterclockwise circuit. This will take you to the historic DeLonde homestead, beaver pond, and Blue Bird Mine compound at the beginning of your trek. There are plaques about the movie, mining, and resort history of the ranch, as well as the wildlife. You will reach the homestead in approximately 0.5 mile. You can make a slight detour to the southeast to see the beaver pond and wildlife description before continuing north toward the mine. The next section is uphill, through rocky terrain, for more than 0.5 mile. You will see signage for the stream (Boulder

## Caribou Ranch Open Space

Creek) and then the Blue Bird mine on the north side of the trail. If you visit the mine, continue past the structures 0.25 mile to reach the streamside picnic area and small waterfall. When you go back downhill, look to your left for the trail you came in on; it is easy to miss the trail and end up on the service road, which is gated.

When you return to the trail from the mine, you can continue for another 1.5 miles back to the trailhead by traveling right (west), or make your trek a somewhat shorter route by retracing your steps. It is worth completing the entire circuit, so you can enjoy the meadow and hill vistas along the way and walk through the stately stands of aspen. If you continue west, the trail crests a small hill and then goes downhill before leveling. There is a viewpoint less than 0.5 mile on the left that is good for photos. When you round the bend in the trail, it travels southeast and begins a gentle climb back to where you started.

### *OUR OWN SWITZERLAND*

The Switzerland Trail was a narrow-gage mining train and then an excursion train that ran west of Boulder from 1883 to 1919. Around the turn of the 20th century, it was one of the primary means of transportation for people and goods into the mines and mountain towns it served. When the mines started closing, the railroad began offering wildflower and scenic excursions into the mountains that were likened to those in Switzerland. The railbed is now popular for hiking and biking.

### *FROM CATTLE TO MUSIC TO OPEN SPACE*

Caribou Ranch was a working cattle ranch and boys camp in the 1930s and then became a famous Arabian horse ranch. When music producer Jim Guercio bought it in the 1970s, it became famous as a recording studio. Elton John, U2, John Lennon, Joe Walsh, and other well-known musicians recorded there. After a fire ruined much of the recording equipment, the property was used for a gated, high-end real estate development. The Guercio family donated about half of the ranch to Boulder County for open space.

### 79   Mud Lake Open Space
BOULDER COUNTY OPEN SPACE

| | |
|---|---|
| **Distance** | 2.6 miles (Kinnickinnick Loop: 1.1 miles, Tungsten Loop: 0.8 mile, Caribou Ranch Connector Trail: 0.5 mile), figure eight |
| **Difficulty** | Easy |
| **Elevation Gain** | 200' (starting at 8,400') |
| **Trail Use** | Hiking, mountain biking, horseback riding, snowshoeing, skiing, great for kids, leashed dogs OK |
| **Agency** | Boulder County Open Space |
| **Map(s)** | Latitude 40° *Boulder-Nederland Trails* |
| **Facilities** | Restroom, picnic pavilion, picnic tables |
| **Note(s)** | Moose can often be found in the open space. Give them a wide berth; they can become aggressive around dogs and when with a calf. |

**HIGHLIGHTS**  This is a beautiful, small Boulder County Open Space area featuring stately aspens and a lake. It is an easy figure eight in gently rolling terrain that also features a pine, fir, and spruce forest with views of Bald and Pomeroy Mountains. A 50-person picnic pavilion near the lake can be reserved through Boulder County Open Space. Leashed dogs are allowed in Mud Lake but not in Caribou Ranch.

**DIRECTIONS**  From Boulder, take Canyon Boulevard/CO 119 west 18 miles to Nederland. Enter the roundabout and bear right to take Peak to Peak Scenic Byway (CO 72) north 2 miles to County Road 126; turn left (west) on CR 126 for 0.5 mile. Turn left into the Mud Lake parking lot.

The trailhead is on the northwest edge of the parking lot. There is a map at the trailhead. You will travel uphill 50 yards to an intersection with the Tungsten Loop. Go left to immediately reach Mud Lake, much lovelier than its name. Waterfowl will be there until it freezes solid in winter. You can circumnavigate the lake for a very short, easy stroll. Or follow the entire slightly hilly Tungsten Loop for an almost 1-mile jaunt, and enjoy the views of both sides of the lake. Be sure to trek over to the east side for the best photography. You will see a sweeping view of the lake, with Pomeroy Mountain (a subpeak of South Arapaho Peak) in the background.

If you want a more extended adventure, with a bit more uphill and views, add the 1.1 miles of the Kinnickinnick Loop. You will climb around 200 feet to include it, but the trail is well worth it and not very steep. Going counterclockwise on Kinnickinnick,

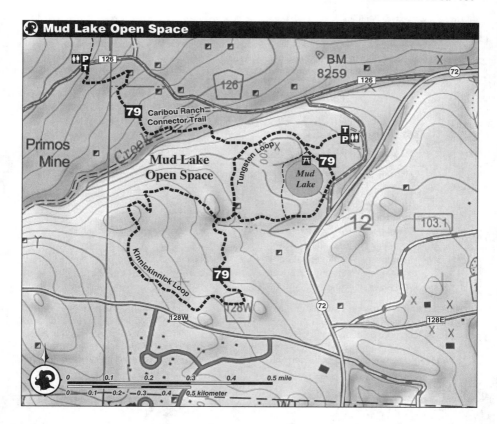

**Mud Lake Open Space**

from Tungsten, means you will climb the steepest (northwest) section first, and then have a mellow downhill. As you wind your way uphill on gentle switchbacks, you will see a bench at the top of the hill. This is also an excellent spot for pictures of Pomeroy and Bald Mountains, and if it's a clear day you might even see Mount Audubon peeking over the top in the distance. If you prefer a mellower climb first, go clockwise (southeast), and enjoy a beautiful stand of aspens on the way up.

If you want to lengthen the enjoyment, include the Caribou Ranch Connector Trail to add another mile round-trip. It is a beautiful, gradual hill route, with pretty meadows and ponderosa pines, and is frequented by deer, elk, and moose. The trail intersections are well marked, and blue diamonds on the trees mark the trails themselves.

*Family fun on the shores of Mud Lake*

## GREAT FOR KIDS

The Mud Lake loops can be negotiated by kids of almost any age, whether they're beginning bikers or seasoned hikers—especially the short Tungsten Loop. Wild Bear Ecology Center has a small loop north of the Tungsten loop for children in their program that sometimes includes tepees. It is open to the public.

### 80  West Magnolia Trails
ROOSEVELT NATIONAL FOREST

| | |
|---|---|
| **Distance** | Up to 8 (Trails 925A, 925B, and 342: 1.5 miles; Trails 925A and 925B: 1 mile; Trail 355A: 1 mile), loop |
| **Difficulty** | Easy |
| **Elevation Gain** | 400' (starting at 8,600') |
| **Trail Use** | Hiking, mountain biking, horseback riding, snowshoeing, skiing, leashed dogs OK |
| **Agency** | Boulder Ranger District, Roosevelt National Forest |
| **Map(s)** | Latitude 40° *Boulder-Nederland Trails* |
| **Facilities** | None |

**HIGHLIGHTS**  This is a large network of easy trails in gently rolling terrain in an aspen, pine, fir, and spruce forest, with views of South Arapaho Peak, Bald, and Pomeroy Mountains, and the Eldora ski area. The loops can be confusing, but it is difficult to get lost. They are well used by mountain bikers and have enough snow for skiing only after a major upslope storm. The area was recently thinned, leaving big clear-cut patches, but when you get into the trees, the hiking or biking can be delightful.

*Aspen Alley is a popular trail in the West Magnolia area.*

## West Magnolia Trails

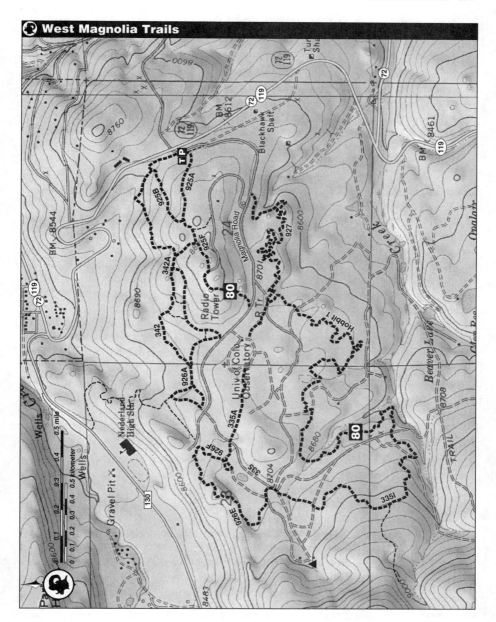

**DIRECTIONS** From Boulder, take Canyon Boulevard/CO 119 west 18 miles to Nederland. From the roundabout, go right (south) onto CO 72/119, and drive 2.7 miles to Magnolia Road/County Road 132W; turn right (northwest), and you will see a small parking area on the right. Or continue west another mile, and park outside the second forest gate that is closed for the winter. Walk southwest around the gate and you will see the trailhead on the right (west) side of the summer parking lot.

### Trails 925A/B, 342A, and 926A

From the first parking area, you will see a 925A trail sign on the left (west) uphill side of the trailhead. This goes gradually uphill into the trees to the north and then west. In a little over 0.25 mile you will come to the intersection with the 925B and 925F trails. If you continue straight, you will end up on 925F, which will take you over a hill and through the trees to Magnolia Road in about 1 mile. If you go right (north) on 925B, you will go downhill and around back to the parking area in only 0.75 mile. If you go downhill on 925B and then left on 342A, you will enjoy a longer, additional 0.75-mile loop through a beautiful aspen grove. You can loop the grove on 342 and 926A, and then return uphill to the parking area. The signage doesn't tell you if the trail is the A or B loop. So from the first parking area next to the Peak to Peak Highway, bear left at the first sign and then right at the next sign for the Aspen Alley loop (342A). It is better for hiking than it is for mountain biking because the sand is deep in many places, and 342 is very rocky.

### Trail 355

These trails/roads are from the summer trailhead that is 1 mile west of CO 119.

### Hobbit Trail and Trails 355A, 355, 926E, and 926F

This is an easy, rolling out-and-back that travels west from the trailhead. You will probably want to continue to the 926E and 926F trail to extend your trip through the forested, rolling, rocky hills with views to the north of Eldora Mountain Resort ski area and South Arapaho Peak. When 355A dead-ends into campground loop 355, turn right to pick up 926E and 926F. They will take you to a small ridgetop and then back around to 355, which is primarily the summer campground road. Trail 355 can also be used to extend your trek through the thick, lodgepole pine portion of the forest. If you want to go farther, take 355I past the 355 campground road and south onto Hobbit I. The 927 trail is a good intermediate mountain biking trail or easy hike.

---

### 81  Arapaho Pass

ROOSEVELT NATIONAL FOREST

|  |  |
|---|---|
| **Distance** | 4 miles to Fourth of July Mine, 6 miles to Pass summit, 25.5 miles to Monarch Lake; out-and-back |
| **Difficulty** | Easy–difficult |
| **Elevation Gain** | 1,090' (starting at 10,150') |
| **Trail Use** | Hiking, leashed dogs OK |
| **Agency** | Indian Peaks Wilderness, Boulder Ranger District, Roosevelt National Forest |
| **Map(s)** | Latitude 40° *Boulder-Nederland Trails*; Latitude 40° *Boulder County Trails* if going to Monarch Lake |
| **Facilities** | Pit toilet and campground at trailhead |

**HIGHLIGHTS**  You can enjoy a wildflower-studded hike to stunning views of Neva and Jasper peaks and Dorothy and Diamond Lakes. It is a nonstop Rocky Mountain panorama on a gradually ascending trail. You can also visit the ruins of the Fourth of July Mine at 11,245 feet. If you are ambitious, you can take this trail across the Continental Divide and into the Grand Valley. You can also summit Mount Neva (12,814 feet) from Caribou Pass, but it is an exposed, difficult rock route.

**DIRECTIONS**  Go 0.5 mile south from Nederland on CO 119, and turn right (west) on the road to the town of Eldora. It is 3 miles from CO 119 to the town (do not turn left on the Shelf Road to the ski area). From Sixth Street in Eldora it is 1.5 miles on what becomes a rough dirt road to the Hessie intersection; bear right uphill. It is another 4.5 miles to the parking area, just above the Buckingham Campground. The road from the Hessie intersection is steep and rough but passable by passenger cars if you avoid obvious obstacles.

## Arapaho Pass, South Arapaho Peak, & Diamond Lake Trails

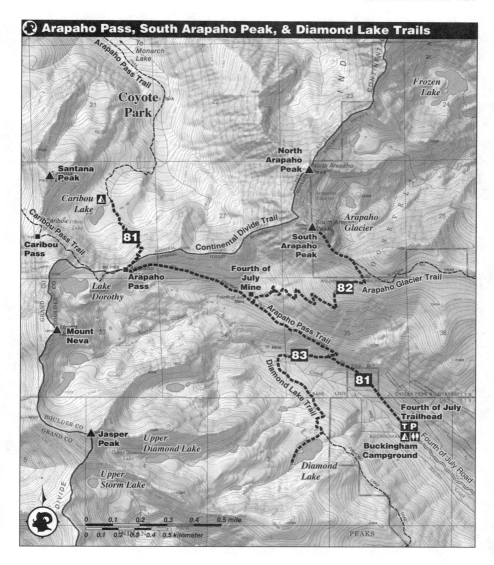

Starting at the Fourth of July Trailhead, you will begin a gradual climb through tree cover that is welcome on warm summer days. It can be a little wet in early spring or late summer, but there are footbridges to get across the wet spots. At 0.5 mile you will see the trail to Diamond Lake to the left (south); bear right (west). You will encounter some switchbacks around 1 mile. In a little less than 0.5 mile you will pass a pretty waterfall that crosses the trail. This is a nice photo spot of the riparian valley below, though it is a bit short of the lake and peak views. The trail climbs more steeply as the views to the south and west expand.

You will reach the photogenic Fourth of July Mine ruins at 11,245 feet after 2 miles. This is a good place for a break or a turnaround point for families with young children. This is also the point where you pick up the Arapaho Glacier Trail that travels north, if you want to climb South Arapaho Peak (13,397 feet).

*Arapaho Pass is especially beautiful when the wildflowers are blooming.*

The 11,900-foot high point of the pass is another mile straight ahead. You will see Caribou Pass, which can be icy and treacherous even in the middle of summer, going northwest toward Meadow Creek Reservoir and Tabernash; bear right and start downhill toward Caribou Lake, Coyote Park, and Monarch Lake. Another mile of switchbacks will take you down to Caribou Lake, a good turnaround point unless you have a car shuttle near Monarch Lake or want a long round-trip. It is around 12.7 miles one-way to Monarch Lake.

 **82  South Arapaho Peak**
ROOSEVELT NATIONAL FOREST

see map on p. 161

| | |
|---|---|
| **Distance** | 8 miles, out-and-back |
| **Difficulty** | Difficult |
| **Elevation Gain** | 3,250' (starting at 10,150') |
| **Trail Use** | Hiking, leashed dogs OK but not recommended |
| **Agency** | Indian Peaks Wilderness, Boulder Ranger District, Roosevelt National Forest |
| **Map(s)** | Latitude 40° *Boulder-Nederland Trails* |
| **Facilities** | Pit toilet and campground at trailhead |
| **Note(s)** | Try to climb it during the week to avoid the overflowing parking lot and crowded road. |

**HIGHLIGHTS** South Arapaho Peak is one of the most striking and accessible 13,000-foot mountains in Colorado's Front Range, making it one of the most popular nontechnical climbs in the state. The final steep, rocky summit yields breathtaking views. Craggy North Arapaho should not be attempted alone as it requires more skillful rock scrambling and serious exposure not found on the South Arapaho route.

**DIRECTIONS** Go 0.5 mile south from Nederland on CO 119, and turn right (west) on the road to the town of Eldora. It is 3 miles from CO 119 to the town (do not turn left on the Shelf Road to the ski area). From Sixth Street in Eldora it is 1.5 miles on what becomes a rough dirt road to the Hessie intersection; bear right uphill. It is another 4.5 miles to the parking area, just beyond the Buckingham Campground. The road from the Hessie intersection is steep and rough but passable by passenger cars if you avoid obvious obstacles.

Take the Arapaho Pass Trail from the parking lot at the Fourth of July Trailhead, and bear right at the Diamond Lake Trail intersection. You will cross a stream with a pretty waterfall after 1.5 miles. The trail then climbs more steeply as the trees thin near treeline, and you encounter the Fourth of July Mine at around 11,245 feet. Take the Arapaho Glacier Trail to the right (north). Another 2,150 feet will put you on top. You will cross the creek again; watch for the trail to the northeast if there is snow cover. The first switchback travels almost due east as it climbs. You will have another 1.5 miles of long, gradually climbing switchbacks on the Glacier Trail that will take you to the saddle. At the saddle you will turn west to face your final 600-foot steep and rocky challenge. The Glacier Trail continues to the northeast. Gird yourself with a solid snack and water break, and enjoy the expansive views to the south of Mount Neva and Jasper Peak and Lake Dorothy.

There is no one marked trail to the summit from the saddle. One route is close to the end of the crest of the southeast ridge to the north. Whatever route you pick, remember that the summit is still west and north of you, rather than straight north. Don't take chances near the drop-off, but enjoy the view into the glacier-carved cirque. The 360-degree views of the Indian Peaks, the western slope, and the Rocky Mountain National Park peaks to the north are well worth it. Be prepared for cool or cold high winds on top regardless of the time of the year.

*Remnants of the Fourth of July Mine at the Arapaho Glacier Trail intersection*

## 83  Diamond Lake

ROOSEVELT NATIONAL FOREST

see
map on
p. 161

| | |
|---|---|
| **Distance** | 5 miles, out-and-back |
| **Difficulty** | Moderate |
| **Elevation Gain** | 850' (starting at 10,150') |
| **Trail Use** | Hiking, snowshoeing, skiing, leashed dogs OK |
| **Agency** | Indian Peaks Wilderness, Boulder Ranger District, Roosevelt National Forest |
| **Map(s)** | Latitude 40° *Boulder-Nederland Trails* |
| **Facilities** | Pit toilet and campground at trailhead |
| **Note(s)** | Try to hike during the week to avoid the overflowing parking lot and crowded road. Diamond Lake is stocked for fishing. |

**HIGHLIGHTS**  This sparkling lake sits below the picturesque shoulder of Jasper Peak and is one of the two closest lake hikes in the area, the other being Lost Lake. You can combine this with a hike to Jasper Lake if you want a more challenging, superscenic day. That combination could be an out-and-back, a car shuttle to the Hessie trailhead, or an overnight backpack.

**DIRECTIONS**  Go 0.5 mile south from Nederland on CO 119, and turn right (west) on the road to the town of Eldora. It is 3 miles from CO 119 to the town (do not turn left on the Shelf Road to the ski area). From Sixth Street in Eldora it is 1.5 miles on what becomes a rough dirt road to the Hessie intersection; bear right uphill. It is another 4.5 miles to the parking area, just beyond the Buckingham Campground. The road from the Hessie intersection is steep and rough but passable by passenger cars if you avoid obvious obstacles.

You will be climbing on the Arapaho Pass Trail (904) for the first 0.5 mile. Watch for the Diamond Lake Trail turnoff on the left (south) side of the trail. You will hike west up the Middle Boulder Creek drainage and descend to a creek crossing after around 1.5 miles. The trail travels southeast and then south. You will cross two more creeks before beginning the final, steeper climb on switchbacks, under thick tree cover. When you break out of the trees, you will be impressed at the size of this natural diamond. You can continue on a trail to the west to the far end of the lake. There are lots of great spots for lunch or fishing.

*Parry's primrose frames the view of a waterfall on the Diamond Lake Trail.*

## 84  Lost Lake

ROOSEVELT NATIONAL FOREST

see map on p. 166

| | |
|---|---|
| **Distance** | 5.2 miles, out-and-back |
| **Difficulty** | Easy–moderate |
| **Elevation Gain** | 700' (starting at 9,000') |
| **Trail Use** | Hiking, fishing, camping/backpacking, snowshoeing, skiing, options for kids, leashed dogs OK |
| **Agency** | Boulder Ranger District, Roosevelt National Forest |
| **Map(s)** | Latitude 40° *Boulder-Nederland Trails* |
| **Facilities** | Portable toilet at trailhead only during summer months; camping |
| **Note(s)** | Dogs must be leashed in wilderness. Backcountry camping permit needed for campsites. |

**HIGHLIGHTS** Lakes get lost in Colorado, and this one is a sparkling gem just outside the Indian Peaks Wilderness Area. It features a pleasing view of the soaring Jasper–Neva Peak massif in the distance and is surrounded by backcountry campsites nestled among the conifers. This highly scenic lake route is a popular short journey from Hessie, so expect lots of company—people and dogs. Weekdays or early starts are a good idea.

**DIRECTIONS** The Hessie trailhead west of the town of Eldora is a gateway to many excellent trails to serene high mountain lakes. To get there, go south at the roundabout in Nederland to CO 72/119. Turn right (west) on County Road 130, where you'll see a sign for the Eldora ski area. Continue straight past the second turnoff that goes up to the ski area; the Eldora town site and Hessie Road are straight ahead. There is limited parking near the trailhead that fills early (7:30 a.m.) during the summer months. On summer weekends, there is a shuttle for the Hessie trailhead from Nederland High School on CR 130 that runs every 15–20 minutes from 8 a.m. to 7 p.m.

If you drive, continue through the town of Eldora. After the road turns to gravel, Hessie is left at the first major road intersection, less than 0.5 mile from the Eldora town site. Do not go straight up toward Buckingham Campground. Parking along the road is limited; pay attention to the signs—the fines for illegal parking can be hefty, and you don't want to block emergency vehicles.

After parking or disembarking the shuttle, look for a trail on the right side of the lower road to the trailhead. The trail is built up with boardwalks through wet sections and will exit onto a four-wheel-drive road, which is often underwater. An intermittent trail on the right circumvents the puddles. Cross the bridge and you will be at the sign that marks the beginning of the trails in this section.

**B**ear left downhill on foot at the first intersection after the road turns to gravel; the Fourth of July Road goes straight/right uphill. The next 0.7 mile of trail, next to the four-wheel-drive road, will take you through conifers to the old Hessie town site, marked with a sign. You will pass ponds with ducks and geese, and possibly some moose on the way to the site. The road/trail continues past the town site to a footbridge over Middle Boulder Creek. You will see a large sign for the trailhead after crossing the bridge, with mileage given for individual lake trailheads that are 1.2 miles uphill. Ignore the road that goes to the left 100 yards beyond the sign; it dead-ends at

the creek. The road you want bears right (northwest) uphill, and you will go through a very rocky section as it switchbacks to the southwest over larger rocks. The views of the riparian valley open up as you climb, and you can see Eldora Mountain Resort ski runs to the south. The trail climbs steeply past beautiful wildflowers and then levels briefly before climbing again.

Once you reach broad rocks after the level spot, you can venture off-trail to the left over more rocks and see a small waterfall. The trail climbs another 200 yards, levels, and turns south through welcome tree cover. You will be next to the cascading stream as you climb to the second bridge

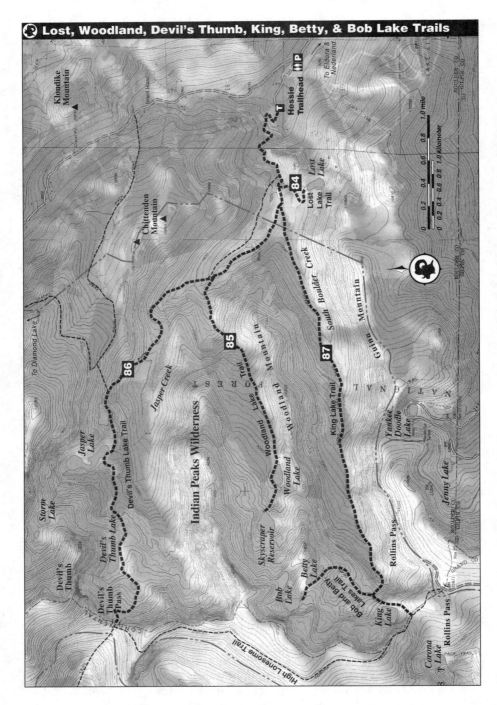

**Lost, Woodland, Devil's Thumb, King, Betty, & Bob Lake Trails**

over the creek. There is good signage for lake destinations. Bear left over the bridge for Lost Lake, which is 0.8 mile away. In 50 feet you will see an impressive waterfall on the right as the rocky trail steepens. You will reenter trees, and the next 0.5 mile can be very wet in early spring. The trail veers west and levels at an intersection. Bear left for Lost Lake, as the King–Woodland Lake

Trail goes straight across a meadow. Detour over to the meadow briefly for a pretty view that is a preview of what you will see from the lake. If anyone in your party is too weary, you can make this the turnaround. Lost Lake is another steep 0.5 mile. Once you reach the lake, you can circumnavigate around it in either direction. The view from the far shore is worth the trek.

## 85  Woodland Lake Trail
ROOSEVELT NATIONAL FOREST

| | |
|---|---|
| **Distance** | 10 miles, out-and-back |
| **Difficulty** | Moderate |
| **Elevation Gain** | 300' (starting at 10,000') |
| **Trail Use** | Hiking, fishing, snowshoeing, skiing, leashed dogs OK |
| **Agency** | Indian Peaks Wilderness, Boulder Ranger District, Roosevelt National Forest |
| **Map(s)** | Latitude 40° *Boulder-Nederland Trails* |
| **Facilities** | Pit toilet at intersection of Hessie and Fourth of July Roads |

**HIGHLIGHTS** Waterfalls, alpine meadows, and wildflowers abound along the trail to Woodland Lake. This route to one of the closer lakes in this spectacular mountain park can be snowy or wet in late May or early June.

**DIRECTIONS** The Hessie trailhead, west of the town of Eldora, is a gateway to many excellent trails to serene high mountain lakes. To get there, go south at the roundabout in Nederland to CO 72/119. Turn right (west) on County Road 130, where you'll see a sign for the Eldora ski area. Continue straight past the second turnoff that goes up to the ski area; the Eldora town site and Hessie Road are straight ahead. There is limited parking near the trailhead that fills early (7:30 a.m.) during the summer months. On summer weekends, there is a shuttle for the Hessie trailhead from Nederland High School on CR 130 that runs every 15–20 minutes from 8 a.m. to 7 p.m.

If you drive, continue through the town of Eldora. After the road turns to gravel, Hessie is left at the first major road intersection, less than 0.5 mile from the Eldora town site. Do not go straight up toward Buckingham Campground. Parking along the road is limited; pay attention to the signs—the fines for illegal parking can be hefty, and you don't want to block emergency vehicles.

After parking or disembarking the shuttle, look for a trail on the right side of the lower road to the trailhead. The trail is built up with boardwalks through wet sections and will exit onto a four-wheel-drive road, which is often underwater. An intermittent trail on the right circumvents the puddles. Cross the bridge and you will be at the sign that marks the beginning of the trails in this section.

After the footbridge and stream crossing at the Hessie trailhead, you will travel on a rapidly ascending old mining road at the rate of 100 feet every 0.25 mile. The trail breaks out of the trees with a panorama of the high mountain valley at 9,100 feet. It levels a little in another 0.25 mile, around 9,200 feet; or I should say that it is a little less steep before

climbing another 200 feet over the next 0.25 mile, to 9,400 feet, reentering trees in the process. The next trail intersection signage gives the distances to some of the lakes—1.5 miles to Lost Lake, 4 miles to Woodland Lake, 5 miles to King Lake, 4 miles to Jasper, and 5 miles to Devil's Thumb. Bear left across the footbridge toward Lost Lake.

You have another footbridge stream crossing and reach another trail intersection at just under the 2-mile mark, around 9,500 feet. Go right for Devil's Thumb Lake, left for your destination, Woodland and King Lakes. Enjoy great views and a pretty wetland lake in the next 0.25-mile climb, a place where you could declare victory and turn around if your party has weary feet or lungs. The trail goes left back into the trees and then takes a sharp right northwest to another footbridge stream crossing. You'll encounter a beautiful wildflower meadow and a view of Jasper Peak. When you reach the wilderness boundary in 0.3 mile, the trail levels and climbs more gradually, as it crosses more meadows with gorgeous wildflowers while meandering next to the stream. (Yes, people can imitate nature and meander.) Look to the right to see a small waterfall just before you reach another trail intersection with signs telling you to bear left for Woodland Lake.

At 9,600 feet the trail climbs more steeply at 100 feet per 0.1 mile. You have a great overview of the entire glacial moraine, or drainage, and several petite waterfalls at 9,800 feet. At 9,900 feet the trail levels again briefly and crosses a narrow footbridge to the south. It then turns west and back to the south sharply. You climb some steep switchbacks up to 10,000 feet, take a breath, and then climb in earnest up to 10,300 feet before leveling with a waterfall. Lots of shade will keep you from overheating as you cross wetlands. The trail then turns south again and crosses open meadows with a ridgeline view at 10,600 feet. It actually descends a little before climbing to an even more spectacular view of the ridge at 10,800 feet and then levels as it reaches and skirts the lake.

Stay on the trail and climb up to a little less than 11,000 feet for an even better panorama of the lake. The trail continues in a stairstep fashion up to Skyscraper Reservoir. It isn't a

*On the way to Woodland Lake*

pristine mountain lake like Woodland, but it does have a great eagle's-eye view of the plains. The topmost ridge is surmountable from here, but because it would be a very steep scramble over scree and tundra, I don't recommend it. Tiptoe across wetlands, meadows, or rocks. Look at the infinite variations of rock, sky, trees, flowers, grasses, and every angle of the universe at your feet. On the way down keep your eyes peeled for the gorgeous waterfall on the west side of the trail, near the second stream crossing if you missed it, as I did, on the way up.

## 86  Devil's Thumb Lake Trail

ROOSEVELT NATIONAL FOREST

see map on p. 166

| | |
|---|---|
| **Distance** | 13 miles, out-and-back |
| **Difficulty** | Difficult |
| **Elevation Gain** | 2,200' (starting at 9,000') |
| **Trail Use** | Hiking, snowshoeing, skiing, leashed dogs OK |
| **Agency** | Indian Peaks Wilderness, Boulder Ranger District, Roosevelt National Forest |
| **Map(s)** | Latitude 40° *Boulder-Nederland Trails* |
| **Facilities** | Pit toilet at intersection of Hessie and Fourth of July Roads |

**HIGHLIGHTS** Devil's Thumb Lake is pristine and sits in a magical setting just below Devil's Thumb Pass. Along the way you will get to embrace waterfalls, tiptoe around meadows with carpets of wildflowers, and gaze upon Jasper Peak in the distance. You can cruise past lovely Jasper Lake along the way. Once at Devil's Thumb Lake, you get a close-up view of its namesake rock. It is a long day hike or an easier overnight backpack.

**DIRECTIONS** The Hessie trailhead west of the town of Eldora is a gateway to many excellent trails to serene high mountain lakes. To get there, go south at the roundabout in Nederland to CO 72/119. Turn right (west) on County Road 130, where you'll see a sign for the Eldora ski area. Continue straight past the second turnoff that goes up to the ski area; the Eldora town site and Hessie Road are straight ahead. There is limited parking near the trailhead that fills early (7:30 a.m.) during the summer months. On summer weekends, there is a shuttle for the Hessie trailhead from Nederland High School on CR 130 that runs every 15–20 minutes from 8 a.m. to 7 p.m.

If you drive, continue through the town of Eldora. After the road turns to gravel, Hessie is left at the first major road intersection, less than 0.5 mile from the Eldora town site. Do not go straight up toward Buckingham Campground. Parking along the road is limited; pay attention to the signs—the fines for illegal parking can be hefty, and you don't want to block emergency vehicles.

After parking or disembarking the shuttle, look for a trail on the right side of the lower road to the trailhead. The trail is built up with boardwalks through wet sections and will exit onto a four-wheel-drive road, which is often underwater. An intermittent trail on the right circumvents the puddles. Cross the bridge and you will be at the sign that marks the beginning of the trails in this section.

**A**fter the footbridge and stream crossing at the Hessie trailhead, you will travel on a rapidly ascending old mining road at the rate of 100 feet every 0.25 mile. The trail breaks out of the trees with a panorama of the high mountain valley at 9,100 feet. The trail levels a little in another 0.25 mile, around 9,200 feet; or I should say that it is a little less steep before climbing another 200 feet over the next 0.25 mile, to 9,400 feet, reentering trees in the process. The next trail intersection signage gives the distances to some of the lakes—1.5 miles to Lost Lake, 4 miles to Woodland Lake, 5 miles to King Lake, 4 miles to Jasper, and 5 miles to Devil's Thumb. Bear left across the footbridge toward Lost Lake if it is late summer. If it's early season, going right

before the footbridge on the Devil's Thumb Bypass Trail is a better choice. The main Devil's Thumb Lake Trail is frequently very wet and muddy.

If you go left toward Lost Lake, you have another footbridge stream crossing and reach another trail intersection at just under the 2-mile mark, around 9,500 feet. Bear right for Devil's Thumb Lake. You enjoy great views of Jasper Peak and a wetland pond in the next 0.25-mile climb. At this point you could declare victory and turn around if your party has weary feet or lungs. The next 0.5 mile of trail can be soggy with lots of social trails avoiding the mud; go northwest. You will be traveling streamside with some small waterfalls to view. Another 0.6 mile takes you to the intersection with the Devil's Thumb Bypass Trail, where you will turn left (west). This is where some real climbing begins as the trail ascends out of the valley, gets much rockier, and approaches Jasper Lake. The valley views expand as you ascend. You will see the Diamond Lake Trail intersect from the north about 0.5 mile from Jasper Lake. After a very steep and rocky section, the trail mellows as you approach the breezy shore of Jasper Lake, with its namesake mountain soaring above. This is a great place for a break, because Devil's Thumb Lake is still another mile. The trail goes downhill briefly from Jasper before resuming its ascent toward the magnificent high mountain valley of the Thumb.

*The Devil's Thumb stands tall over its namesake lake.*

## 87 King, Betty, & Bob Lakes Trail
### ROOSEVELT NATIONAL FOREST

| | |
|---|---|
| **Distance** | King Lake: 12.6 miles, Betty Lake: 12.7 miles, Bob Lake: 13 miles; out-and-back |
| **Difficulty** | Difficult |
| **Elevation Gain** | King: 2,430'; Betty and Bob Lakes: 2,895' (starting at 9,000') |
| **Trail Use** | Hiking, snowshoeing, skiing, leashed dogs OK |
| **Agency** | Indian Peaks Wilderness, Boulder Ranger District, Roosevelt National Forest |
| **Map(s)** | Latitude 40° *Boulder-Nederland Trails* |
| **Facilities** | Pit toilet at intersection of Hessie and Fourth of July Roads |

**HIGHLIGHTS** Betty and Bob Lakes are nestled in a spectacular setting in a high mountain glacial cirque just below the Continental Divide. You will have a sweeping view of the Divide and these sparkling lakes. You can also "summit" the Divide for even more stunning views to the west. The route features waterfalls and some streamside hiking, as well as lots of tree cover before you reach wildflower-bordered tundra trekking.

**DIRECTIONS** The Hessie trailhead, west of the town of Eldora, is a gateway to many excellent trails to serene high mountain lakes. To get there, go south at the roundabout in Nederland to CO 72/119. Turn right (west) on County Road 130, where you'll see a sign for the Eldora ski area. Continue straight past the second turnoff that goes up to the ski area; the Eldora town site and Hessie Road are straight ahead. There is limited parking near the trailhead that fills early (7:30 a.m.) during the summer months. On summer weekends, there is a shuttle for the Hessie trailhead from Nederland High School on CR 130 that runs every 15–20 minutes from 8 a.m. to 7 p.m.

If you drive, continue through the town of Eldora. After the road turns to gravel, Hessie is left at the first major road intersection, less than 0.5 mile from the Eldora town site. Do not go straight up toward Buckingham Campground. Parking along the road is limited; pay attention to the signs—the fines for illegal parking can be hefty, and you don't want to block emergency vehicles.

After parking or disembarking the shuttle, look for a trail on the right side of the lower road to the trailhead. The trail is built up with boardwalks through wet sections and will exit onto a four-wheel-drive road, which is often underwater. An intermittent trail on the right circumvents the puddles. Cross the bridge and you will be at the sign that marks the beginning of the trails in this section.

After the footbridge and stream crossing at the Hessie trailhead, you will travel on a rapidly ascending old mining road at the rate of 100 feet every 0.25 mile. The trail breaks out of the trees with a panorama of the high mountain valley at 9,100 feet. The trail levels a little in another 0.25 mile, around 9,200 feet; or I should say that it is a little less steep before climbing another 200 feet over the next 0.25 mile, to 9,400 feet, reentering trees in the process. The next trail intersection signage gives the distances to some of the lakes—1.5 miles to Lost Lake, 4 miles to Woodland Lake, 5 miles to King Lake, 4 miles to Jasper, and 5 miles to Devil's Thumb. Because you have already walked at least a mile, add another 5 to your outing one-way from here. Bear left across the footbridge toward Lost and King Lakes. Enjoy the waterfall next to the rocky trail as you climb toward Lost Lake and another intersection. The trail levels when you reach the Lost Lake turnoff at 1.5 miles; bear right/straight west at the intersection. Enjoy the

great view of Jasper Peak across the pretty meadow. Bear left/straight (west-southwest) at the intersection with the Woodland Lake Trail, as it goes northwest.

You will reach the Indian Peaks Wilderness and gradually climb 1,200 feet in 4 miles. If you look south around 4 miles out, on the high ridge west of Guinn Mountain, you will see the Twin Trestles of the original Moffat Road railroad that went over Rollins Pass. You will encounter switchbacks about 1 mile from King Lake that climb more steeply, and they rapidly take you over treeline with sweeping views of Rollins Pass and James Peak to the south. You will see the Betty and Bob Lakes Trail going north from the main trail at a stream crossing just 0.3 mile east of King Lake. You can continue past King Lake and on to the Continental Divide Trail for grins. You will intersect the High Lonesome Trail, which can take you all the way to Devil's Thumb. The extra 0.4 mile to Betty and Bob Lakes is a worthwhile scenic excursion.

## 88  Rogers Pass Lake/Heart Lake
ROOSEVELT NATIONAL FOREST

see map on p. 172

| | |
|---|---|
| **Distance** | 8.2 miles, out-and-back |
| **Difficulty** | Moderate–challenging |
| **Elevation Gain** | 2,100' (starting at 9,240') |
| **Trail Use** | Hiking, fishing, snowshoeing, skiing, leashed dogs OK |
| **Agency** | James Peak Wilderness, Boulder Ranger District, Roosevelt National Forest |
| **Map(s)** | Latitude 40° *Boulder County Trails* |
| **Facilities** | Pit toilet at trailhead |

**HIGHLIGHTS** Hike any portion of this popular trail, and you will have an enjoyable trek in a stately old-growth forest, with a few ridgetop views along the way. To make it to Rogers Pass and Heart Lake you will need all day and an early start to avoid thunderstorms. The lakes are sparklers, cupped by the soaring mountaintops of the Continental Divide. The trail has many steep sections, with intermittent level spots. This is a popular trail on weekends, with lots of dogs. The trail is marked with intermittent blue diamonds.

**DIRECTIONS** From Boulder, take Canyon Boulevard/CO 119 west 18 miles to Nederland. Go left (south) through the roundabout, onto Peak to Peak Scenic Byway (CO 119), and drive 4.5 miles to Rollinsville. Turn right (west) on narrow, gravel County Road 16; drive 8 more miles to the Moffat Tunnel and the East Portal Trailhead. There is a large parking area.

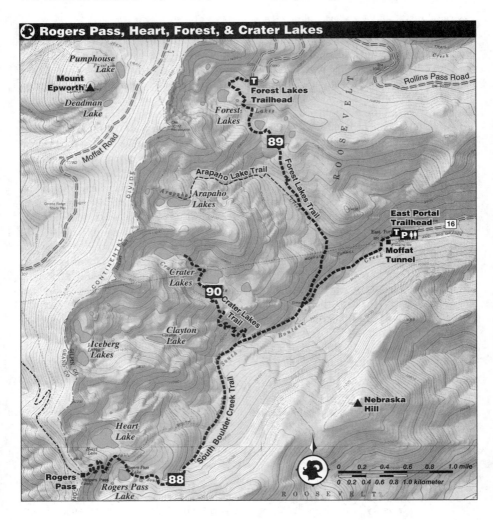

**Rogers Pass, Heart, Forest, & Crater Lakes**

Go around the right (north) side of the tunnel on the South Boulder Creek Trail (900). The trail can be very wet in early or late season; snow often melts slowly. After the first mile, the thick tree cover will make nice shade for hot days. At 1.2 miles, you will reach the intersection with the Forest Lakes Trail; continue straight ahead. In another 0.3 mile you will reach a fork in the trail as it steepens. Bear left for a mellower switchback; the shortcut straight ahead is much steeper and off-trail. In about 0.25 mile the trail turns sharply right uphill on a switchback that goes north-northeast. At around another 0.4 mile

you might see the Crater Lakes Trail (819) on the right; continue straight ahead as the trail climbs more steeply. You will see another false trail on the right, as the trail levels briefly then goes steeply over 10,000 feet, crossing a tributary of South Boulder Creek and turning due south.

Take a minute to enjoy the old-growth forest of stately trees; many are draped in Spanish moss. Look to the left and you can see the snowcapped high ridgeline tracking west, often with spindrift looking like wispy clouds being blown over the top. You will be protected from the wind by the thick tree cover. A somewhat less steep section will catapult you up to 10,300 feet, where there will be a stream crossing and the trees open up, with more views to the south of the high ridge and the ridge to the north as well.

You will pass through a lot of pretty glades as the trail climbs more gradually over the next mile to around 10,400 feet, and you will enjoy another sunny break in the trees with a small meadow on the right. The trail goes south and actually levels and goes temporarily downhill. Then it swings west, and the next mile to Heart Lake is much steeper, climbing 700 feet (gasp). Look for potential side trails to the lakes, which are both at just over 11,000 feet—Heart at 11,300 feet and Rogers Pass at 11,100 feet. Take a long lunch break, and enjoy the trek down.

## 89  Forest Lakes

ROOSEVELT NATIONAL FOREST

| | |
|---|---|
| **Distance** | Upper Lake: 7 miles, Lower Lake: 6.5 miles; out-and-back |
| **Difficulty** | Moderate |
| **Elevation Gain** | Upper Lake: 1,620'; Lower Lake: 1,400' (starting at 9,240') |
| **Trail Use** | Hiking, snowshoeing, skiing, leashed dogs OK |
| **Agency** | James Peak Wilderness, Boulder Ranger District, Roosevelt National Forest |
| **Map(s)** | Latitude 40° *Boulder County Trails* |
| **Facilities** | Pit toilet at trailhead |

**HIGHLIGHTS** This trail offers everything: a waterfall, sparkling streams, patches of wildflowers, and dazzling high mountain lakes, with good views of the Continental Divide for the last 1.5 miles. Hiking any portion of this route can be rewarding. You will be in the James Peak Wilderness Area, so no open fires are permitted, and dogs must be leashed, for their safety.

**DIRECTIONS** From Boulder, take Canyon Boulevard/CO 119 west 18 miles to Nederland. From the roundabout, go right (south) onto Peak to Peak Scenic Byway (CO 119), and drive 4.5 miles to Rollinsville. Turn right (west) on narrow, gravel County Road 16; drive 8 more miles to the Moffat Tunnel and the East Portal Trailhead. There is a large parking area.

Go around the right (north) side of the tunnel on the South Boulder Creek Trail (900). The trail can be very wet and resemble a small stream early in the season. At 1.2 miles, you will reach the intersection with the Forest Lakes Trail (809); go right (northeast). The trail is initially an old road that traverses a steep slope, climbing 300 feet in around 0.75 mile. You will cross Arapaho Creek in about 0.5 mile for a total gain of more than 600 feet from the trailhead. Cross a footbridge, and you will have intermittent views of the riparian valley as you climb through the thick trees.

The road ends as the trail swings northwest and rolls more gradually uphill through a mixed forest. The trail gradually breaks from the trees and you will have excellent views of the high mountain ridgeline on your left from the pretty glade, at around 10,000 feet. The trail climbs more gradually for the next 0.75 mile. When you pass the intersection with the Arapaho Lakes Trail, you will be around 1 mile from the lower lake and will reach 10,400 feet gradually. (Some like to see the Arapaho Lakes too, but the route is sketchy with lots of fallen trees, is not maintained, and is very steep.) The last 0.5 mile is steeper, as the trail climbs another 200 feet in short order. Enjoy the beautiful lake, with the Continental Divide as the backdrop. If you continue to the upper lake, you might hear jeeps on the Rollins Pass Road, which is only 0.25 mile beyond it.

*A fisherman tries his luck at Lower Forest Lake.*

## 90 Crater Lakes

ROOSEVELT NATIONAL FOREST

see
map on
p. 172

| | |
|---|---|
| **Distance** | 6 miles, out-and-back |
| **Difficulty** | Moderate to lower lake |
| **Elevation Gain** | Lower lake: 1,500'; Upper lake: 2,000' (starting at 9,240') |
| **Trail Use** | Hiking, leashed dogs OK |
| **Agency** | James Peak Wilderness, Boulder Ranger District, Roosevelt National Forest |
| **Map(s)** | Latitude 40° *Boulder County Trails* |
| **Facilities** | Pit toilet at trailhead |
| **Note(s)** | You will be in the James Peak Wilderness Area, so no open fires are permitted, and dogs must be leashed. |

**HIGHLIGHTS** This is the easiest and shortest route from the East Portal Trailhead. You will reach the trail junction for Crater Lakes in just under 2 miles, and the short, steep climb from that point rewards you with immediate views of the glacier-carved valley and soaring ridgeline. The lakes are small but pretty, and there are good picnic spots.

**DIRECTIONS** From Boulder, take Canyon Boulevard/CO 119 west 18 miles to Nederland. From the roundabout go right (south) onto Peak to Peak Scenic Byway (CO 119), and drive 4.5 miles to Rollinsville. Turn right (west) on narrow, gravel County Road 16; drive 8 more miles to the Moffat Tunnel and the East Portal Trailhead. There is a large parking area.

There is a trail marker on the right side of the parking lot. Go around the right (north) side of the tunnel on the South Boulder Creek Trail (900); the road next to the tunnel will also get you there, but the trail is more scenic. The trail can be very wet and resemble a small stream early in the season; there are footbridges that will keep your feet almost dry. Enjoy the sounds of rushing water. After 1.2 miles, and around 500 feet of gain, you will reach a meadow and the intersection with the Forest Lakes Trail (809); stay straight on the South Boulder Creek Trail. When in doubt, keep in mind that the trail bears right, and travel away from the creek. There are social trails that stay next to the creek and peter out.

After another 0.5 mile, at around 10,000 feet, you will come to another intersection, with much improved signage pointing you to the Crater Lakes Trail that goes right, while the Heart Lake/South Boulder Creek Trail goes straight/left. This is where the trail steepens and starts to switchback. Don't despair if you have people who are struggling, the steep section is relatively short. Enjoy the views as you climb. The trail takes a sharp right at the 2.4-mile point and travels between two very large boulders and goes left. The gradient lessens, and you will reach a footbridge at just under 3 miles. The trail flattens somewhat and opens up as it makes the final, more gradual ascent to the first lake at 10,600 feet. You will see faint spur trails that go to south Crater Lake and north Crater Lake. The south lake is surrounded by steep walls, and the more distant north lake has more places for picnics. The higher lake, nestled in the glacial cirque, is another 500 feet of elevation gain with steep rock scrambling.

*Hikers on the trek to Crater Lakes*

*Longs Peak from Chasm Lake Trail*

# chapter 6

# Rocky Mountain National Park: South

## 1 HOUR FROM DENVER-BOULDER-FORT COLLINS

One of the beautiful things about Rocky Mountain National Park (RMNP) is its size, making it an ecosystem unto itself, where the deer, elk, moose, and bears can play, unscathed, unless they wander into the adjacent national forests. The relatively tame elk, deer, bear, moose, and bighorn sheep are common but striking sights throughout the park. This area is the geographically closest part of RMNP to Boulder and Denver because it is the farthest south, but it is often overlooked because the town of Estes Park is associated as the east side entrance to the park. Wild Basin, a U-shaped, glacier-carved valley, is a primary access point and a spectacular one at that, with cascading streams, waterfalls, ridgetops, soaring peaks, and a magnificent forest. The highest mountain in northern Colorado and one of the highest in the state, Longs Peak is easily accessible just south of Estes Park and north of Allenspark and is one of the most challenging fourteeners to climb.

To reach this section of the park, take CO 66 to Lyons and then CO 7 to CO 72. (Don't take CO 36 from Lyons to Estes Park because you will bypass Wild Basin and have to backtrack from Estes Park.) You can access Wild Basin and Longs Peak from CO 72, the Peak to Peak Scenic Byway, as you travel north toward Estes Park. If you live in Fort Collins, Loveland, or other points north, you can drive to Estes Park and then south on CO 72.

### Longs Peak Area

As Walter Borneman and Lyndon Lampert claim in *A Climbing Guide to Colorado's Fourteeners,* "Longs Peak is undisputedly the monarch of the northern Front Range, and one of the outstanding peaks of the entire North American continent." It was considered to be unclimbable from the time of its discovery by Stephen Long in 1820 until fearless, one-armed, Grand Canyon navigator John Wesley Powell did it in 1868 from the south side. His approach was especially remarkable because his party had to climb all the way up and over the Continental Divide and through uncharted terrain from Grand Lake before attempting the summit. It is, however, likely that American Indians climbed the peak before he did.

It is one of those places, like many in Rocky Mountain National Park, that you never tire of, no matter how many times you have visited, summited, or attempted to summit it. It is a place that imparts a feeling of timeless immortality to us mere mortals. And the soaring and forbidding Diamond rock face never ceases to astonish climbers of all skill levels. Many an expert climber has spent an unplanned night bivouacked among its frigid granite cliffs praying for dawn.

The true beauty of Longs is the wide variety of trails that crisscross its massive expanse and make it possible for trekkers of all skill levels to partake of some piece of its high-altitude glory. In fact, during the frenzy of the summer months, thousands of poorly prepared hikers line up to be treated to the rigors of climbing almost 5,000 feet in a little less than 7 miles and are rewarded with a down-climb of 5,000 feet when their knees and feet are begging for an errant helicopter to whisk them away. Unfortunately the combination of geologic drama, death-defying heights, very fickle weather, and foolhardy trekkers has exacted a price of more than 40 fatalities since 1884. If you want to climb Longs, use any of the many excellent fourteener guidebooks.

### Wild Basin

This part of Rocky Mountain National Park offers its own kind of magic—sculpted by glaciers, sequestered by the stunning Mount Meeker massif to the south with Chiefs Head in view, bordered on the west by the Continental Divide peaks (Ouzel, Tanima, and Mahana) and highlighted by Copeland Mountain. Few panoramas are its equal. You will also be inspired by the creativity of North Saint Vrain, Ouzel, and Coney Creeks as they tumble and fall through the valley from serene lakes like Ouzel and Sand Beach. It is well south of Estes Park, making it a closer destination from the metro Denver and Boulder areas.

## 91  Lily Lake & Ridge
### ROCKY MOUNTAIN NATIONAL PARK: SOUTH

| | |
|---|---|
| **Distance** | 1 mile, balloon |
| **Difficulty** | Easy |
| **Elevation Gain** | 200' (starting at 8,925') |
| **Trail Use** | Hiking, fishing, snowshoeing, skiing, great for kids |
| **Agency** | Rocky Mountain National Park |
| **Map(s)** | Trails Illustrated *Rocky Mountain National Park* |
| **Facilities** | Pit toilets, picnic area, and fishing dock |
| **Note(s)** | This trail is wheelchair accessible. Bikes and dogs are not allowed on trails in Rocky Mountain National Park. |

*Lily Lake with Longs Peak and Estes Cone (right)*

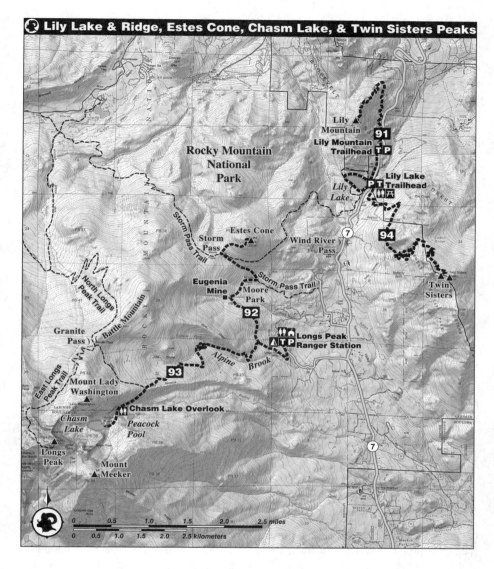

## ☉ Lily Lake & Ridge, Estes Cone, Chasm Lake, & Twin Sisters Peaks

Lily
Mountain

**91**
**T P**

Lily Mountain
Trailhead

**Rocky Mountain
National
Park**

Lily Lake
**P T** Trailhead

*Lily
Lake*

**94**

**7**

Estes Cone

Storm
Pass

Wind River
Pass

North Longs
Peak Trail

*Storm Pass Trail*

*Storm Pass Trail*

Eugenia
Mine

Moore
Park

**92**

Twin
Sisters

Granite
Pass

East Longs
Peak Trail

Battle Mountain

**93**

*Alpine*  *Brook*

Longs Peak
Ranger Station
**T P**

Mount Lady
Washington

Chasm Lake Overlook

*Chasm
Lake*

*Peacock
Pool*

**7**

Longs
Peak

Mount
Meeker

0    0.5    1.0    1.5    2.0    2.5 miles

0    0.5    1.0    1.5    2.0    2.5 kilometers

**HIGHLIGHTS** Lily Lake has no lily pads, but wild lilies do grow nearby, or perhaps it was named for a woman. This short, easy stroll around the sparkling lake, surrounded by the sandstone cliffs of Lily Mountain and the magnificent massif of Meeker and Longs Peaks and Estes Cone, is suitable for people of all ages.

**DIRECTIONS** Take the Peak to Peak Scenic Byway (CO 7) south from Estes Park approximately 5.5 miles to the turnoff on the west side of the road.

For a spectacular view of Meeker and Longs Peaks and Estes Cone from on high, go counterclockwise, north from the parking area. In 0.25 mile take the fainter trail to the north that will take you on a 200-foot climb onto the ridge of Lily Mountain. The trail travels north and switchbacks south through trees to the overlook. From the top of the trail you can enjoy the dazzling water of the lake and the impressive mountain backdrop. The ridge trail rollercoasters a bit before descending back down to the main trail, and it's well marked. When you reach the main trail, go right for the parking area or left to circle the lake.

If you are happy just circling the enchanting lake with no elevation gain,

go clockwise for a circumnavigation, and enjoy some tree cover on the south side of the lake. As you continue to the west and then north, you will see a side trail going northwest. For an additional view of a beautiful high mountain valley and more distant mountains in Rocky Mountain National Park, go left and add another 0.5-mile round-trip to your stroll.

## 92   Estes Cone

### ROCKY MOUNTAIN NATIONAL PARK: SOUTH

see map on p. 179

|  |  |
|---|---|
| **Distance** | 6.4 miles, out-and-back |
| **Difficulty** | Moderate |
| **Elevation Gain** | 1,500' (starting at 9,500') |
| **Trail Use** | Hiking, snowshoeing |
| **Agency** | Rocky Mountain National Park |
| **Map(s)** | Trails Illustrated *Rocky Mountain National Park* |
| **Facilities** | Restrooms, ranger station, and campground |
| **Note(s)** | Bikes and dogs are not allowed on trails in Rocky Mountain National Park. |

**HIGHLIGHTS**  If you want a unique perspective and view of Longs Peak and Mount Meeker as well as Twin Sisters, this hike is for you; it's an interesting ramble past an abandoned mining site with a minor rock scramble to reach the summit.

**DIRECTIONS**  Take the Peak to Peak Scenic Byway (CO 7) south from Estes Park 7.5 miles to the turnoff on the west side of the road for the Longs Peak Trail and campground. Turn right (west) and go up the hill to the intersection; bear left into the parking lot. You can also reach the trailhead by driving north on CO 7 from either Lyons or Nederland. If you are driving north from the Denver area, the route through Lyons is the best alternative.

The Longs Peak Trail is the starting point for this hike, but you share the trail with the legions climbing that summit for only 0.5 mile of relatively steep climbing through lodgepole pine forest. The trail then veers to the northwest and levels off somewhat before climbing gradually to Eugenia Mine, where some aspen trees are mixed in with the pine. The area surrounding the abandoned mining site is a good place for a snack and water break.

After crossing the Inn Brook drainage, the trail travels northeast downhill into Moore Park. It then joins the Storm Pass Trail and goes northwest (left) gradually uphill to Storm Pass. Here the trees begin to thin out before the trail turns northeast

(right) and switchbacks more steeply uphill to the rock summit of Estes Cone. The most challenging section is the last, long switchback section because it climbs 1,000 feet in approximately the last 0.5 mile, but this part of the trail rewards you with the best views of Longs Peak and Mount Meeker. Climb carefully on the sometimes slick, wet, and icy rock to reach the top of the summit rocks. The last climb to the summit is not recommended for young children. If you prefer not to climb the summit, you can go as far as Storm Pass and walk up enough of the switchbacks or to the summit rocks to enjoy a few photo opportunities and then turn around. Storm Pass can take you to Sprague Lake.

*View of Longs Peak, Estes Cone, and Lily Lake from Lily Mountain*

You can also hike to Estes Cone from the Storm Pass Trailhead at the south end of Lily Lake. The trail begins as a road. Stay to the left at 0.2 mile; the trail to the right circles back to the lake. At about 0.6 mile, you will come to an intersection; continue over the footbridge and start the climb up the eastern slopes of Estes Cone with occasional views of the cone and of Longs Peak. At a little over 3 miles, you'll come to another intersection; turn right to summit Estes Cone. This route is about 7.5 miles round-trip.

## 93 Chasm Lake

ROCKY MOUNTAIN NATIONAL PARK: SOUTH

see map on p. 179

| | |
|---|---|
| **Distance** | 8.4 miles, out-and-back |
| **Difficulty** | Moderate |
| **Elevation Gain** | 2,300' (starting at 9,500') |
| **Trail Use** | Hiking, camping, snowshoeing, skiing |
| **Agency** | Rocky Mountain National Park |
| **Map(s)** | Trails Illustrated *Rocky Mountain National Park* |
| **Facilities** | Restrooms, ranger station, and campground |
| **Note(s)** | Bikes and dogs are not allowed on trails in Rocky Mountain National Park. |

**HIGHLIGHTS** Once you are above treeline, you enjoy 360-degree views that include Longs Peak and Mount Meeker as well as Twin Sisters. The lake is in a magnificent setting with the heights of the Loft between Meeker and Longs soaring above. Hiking early in the season, before Longs Peak is accessible to climbers, means far fewer crowds.

**DIRECTIONS** Take the Peak to Peak Scenic Byway (CO 7) south from Estes Park 7.5 miles to the turnoff on the west side of the road for the Longs Peak Trail and campground. Turn right (west), go up the hill to the intersection, and bear left into the parking lot. You can also reach the trailhead by driving north on CO 7 from either Lyons or Nederland. If you are driving north from the Denver area, the route through Lyons is the best alternative.

As with most of the trails described in this book, you can have a satisfying, moderate family adventure by planning a 2- to 3-hour round-trip adventure on the first 1.5 miles of the trail. Until you reach around 10,000 feet (around 1 hour into the hike), the trail is in a tree tunnel with tantalizing peeks; then you are afforded views of the summit of Longs Peak. At that point you could simply enjoy lunch or a snack and head back to the trailhead. The 500-foot climb is a good workout. This and the Longs Peak Trail are one and the same for most of the route, until you reach the junction on the ridge where the Longs Peak Trail goes straight (northwest) to Granite Pass while the Chasm Lake Trail takes Mills Moraine left (south and then west) to Chasm Lake Overlook.

Start at the Longs Peak Ranger Station, and walk 0.5 mile to the intersection where the Storm Pass Trail splits off to the north; you continue straight/left (southwest) on a trail that steepens, climbing with occasional short switchbacks. When you aren't sufficiently warmed up to enjoy it, the trail is steep; it climbs up to 10,000 feet fairly quickly in thick tree cover over the next 0.5 mile. It then levels a little and more gradually climbs for the next 0.25 mile before steeply gaining another 500 feet. The trees thin out and allow you partial views of the summit of Longs, looking down from on high and daring you to climb it. On a clear day you enjoy an impressive view of the famous Diamond climbing route.

The trail climbs again, switchbacks, and turns more south, edging its way up toward the stunted wind- and weather-gnarled trees of Goblin's Forest. Cross the small footbridge over Alpine Brook. Don't hesitate to turn around if conditions become challenging, particularly if early season snow or ice is present. Soon the krummholz trees reveal a spectacular view of the slope all the way to the summit. Once you are above treeline at 11,000 feet, you enjoy a panoramic view. Always keep an eye on the weather, keep in mind that the trail down might not be as straightforward as you remember, and allow extra time for slower members of your party to make it back to the trailhead without the duress of a too-rapid descent.

Once above treeline you gradually switchback your way to a ridge and steep slope that you have to traverse to the south to reach the final stretch up Mills Moraine to Chasm Lake Overlook, where there is a privy. Here the trail splits again, with the right branch going almost due north to Granite Pass while you veer to the south toward the lake. Follow the spectacular 11,600-foot-high ridge around the corner and be startled by the views of Longs Peak, Mount Meeker, and Chasm Lake itself. The final 200 feet to the lake from the privy can be a difficult and precarious ridge walk, depending on whether ice or snow lingers early in the season.

*Chasm Lake Trail*

## 94 Twin Sisters Peaks

ROCKY MOUNTAIN NATIONAL PARK: SOUTH

see map on p. 179

| | |
|---|---|
| **Distance** | 7.5 miles, out-and-back |
| **Difficulty** | Moderate |
| **Elevation Gain** | East summit: 2,305'; West summit: 2,320' (starting at 9,110') |
| **Trail Use** | Hiking, snowshoeing |
| **Agency** | Rocky Mountain National Park |
| **Map(s)** | Trails Illustrated *Rocky Mountain National Park* |
| **Facilities** | None |
| **Note(s)** | Bikes and dogs are not allowed on trails in Rocky Mountain National Park. |

**HIGHLIGHTS** These are the two easternmost summits in Rocky Mountain National Park. Their position gives hikers awesome views of Longs Peak and Mount Meeker, and tiny Estes Cone. You can also see a more distant view of the Continental Divide in Rocky Park. This gradual ascent is a fun climb with minor rock scrambling for the final summits. It is a great family summit.

**DIRECTIONS** From Estes Park, go south on CO 7 for 6 miles (or go 7 miles north from Allenspark) and turn east on the Twin Sisters Trail road 0.5 mile to parking.

The trail starts off gradually with very long switchbacks in a fairly thick mixed forest. This is a real switchback-trail mountain, with around 20 switchbacks over the first 2 miles. That means it is a nice gradual ascent. At just under 2 miles you will reach the Lookout Springs junction; stay right. You will have another 10 or so switchbacks with ever-expanding views, and a rockier trail over the next 1.5 miles until you reach a saddle between the two summits. The established west summit trail goes past a building and climbs steadily to a point where you can rock-scramble on to the top and soak in the views. Descend to the saddle, and use a variety of social trails if you want to ascend to the more challenging but not difficult east summit. The best unobstructed views are from the west summit. Far fewer people climb the east summit.

## 95 Copeland Falls

ROCKY MOUNTAIN NATIONAL PARK: SOUTH

see map on p. 184

| | |
|---|---|
| **Distance** | 2.6 miles, out-and-back |
| **Difficulty** | Easy |
| **Elevation Gain** | 195' (starting at 8,320') |
| **Trail Use** | Hiking, snowshoeing, skiing, great for kids |
| **Agency** | Rocky Mountain National Park |
| **Map(s)** | Trails Illustrated *Rocky Mountain National Park* |
| **Facilities** | Restrooms at trailhead |
| **Note(s)** | Bikes and dogs are not allowed on trails in Rocky Mountain National Park. |

**HIGHLIGHTS** This is a great family option because it is a short, easy hike to a spectacular, small waterfall in the magical Glacier Gorge, which also makes it a popular destination, so arrive early or enjoy the national park camaraderie.

**DIRECTIONS** To reach Wild Basin from Estes Park, take CO 7 south approximately 12 miles. After you drive through Meeker, look for the sign on the right. Turn right (west) and proceed past the lodge and around the lake to the left. The road narrows to almost one lane. From Boulder or Denver, take CO 66 through Lyons to CO 7 past Allenspark. The close-in parking fills up early and that means an extra 1.5 miles of walking on the road or the trail next to it to reach the actual trailhead (the trail next to the road is more scenic).

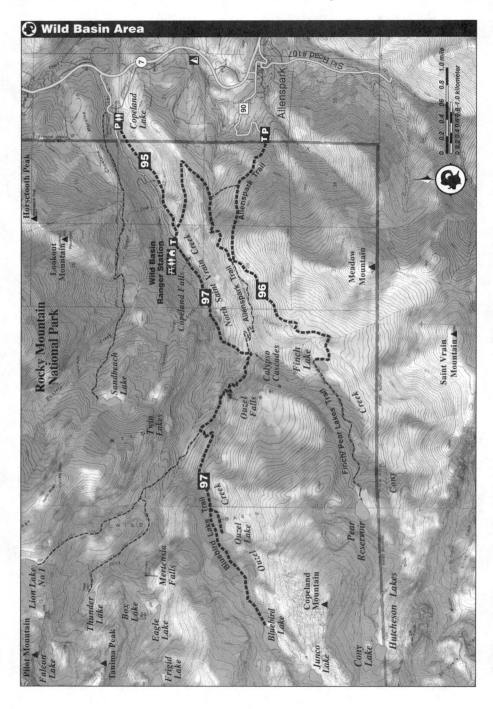

*Copeland Falls*

The trail gains approximately 200 feet from distant secondary parking to Wild Basin Ranger Station (8,500 feet). If the close-in parking is full or if you have young children who prefer short hikes, Copeland Falls might be enough. You can always go farther if you want. The streamside stroll to the ranger station even features meadows along the way. When you reach the Wild Basin Ranger Station parking lot, bear left to see the falls off a well-marked side trail 0.25 mile from the ranger station. At that point you can rest and decide if you want to venture farther up the enchanted land of Wild Basin.

## 96  Allenspark & Finch Lake Trails to Wild Basin
ROCKY MOUNTAIN NATIONAL PARK: SOUTH

| | |
|---|---|
| **Distance** | 13.4 miles from Wild Basin to Finch Lake, 6 miles from Allenspark to overlook, 13.4 miles from Allenspark to Finch Lake; out-and-back |
| **Difficulty** | Easy to overlook, moderate to Finch Lake |
| **Elevation Gain** | 950' (starting at 8,960') |
| **Trail Use** | Hiking, snowshoeing, skiing |
| **Agency** | Rocky Mountain National Park |
| **Map(s)** | Trails Illustrated *Rocky Mountain National Park* |
| **Facilities** | Restrooms, picnic area, and ranger station at Wild Basin Trailhead |
| **Note(s)** | Bikes and dogs are not allowed on trails in Rocky Mountain National Park. |

**HIGHLIGHTS** This trek offers two alternatives that go high above Wild Basin. You can hike to either the overlook at the trail intersection or to Finch Lake. You can reach these destinations from either the Allenspark Trail or the Wild Basin Trailhead. The overlook offers spectacular views of this glacier-carved wonderland from above. You are also treated to great views of Mount Meeker and Chiefs Head to name just a couple. You can reach the overlook or Finch Lake by taking a side trip, climbing up from the Wild Basin Valley, or starting higher up on the Allenspark Trailhead.

**DIRECTIONS**  You can access this trail from either the Allenspark Trailhead or Wild Basin. To reach Wild Basin from Estes Park, take CO 7 south approximately 12 miles. After you drive through Meeker, look for the sign on the right. Turn right (west) and proceed past the lodge and around the lake to the left. The road narrows to almost one lane. From Boulder or Denver, take CO 66 through Lyons to CO 7 past Allenspark. The close-in parking fills up early, and that means an extra 1.5 miles of walking on the road or the trail next to it to reach the actual trailhead (the trail next to the road is more scenic).

To reach Allenspark Trailhead, take CO 7 approximately 10 miles south to Allenspark. Go to the post office and turn west on County Road 90. Drive a few miles until you see Meadow Mountain Drive, turn right, and look for the parking lot.

The trail gains approximately 200 feet from the distant secondary parking lot to the Wild Basin Ranger Station (8,500 feet). Starting at Wild Basin requires climbing up from the valley floor. The Allenspark Trailhead is about 490 feet higher than the Wild Basin/Finch Lake Trailhead. The hiking distance on the main trails is about the same from either starting point.

## Wild Basin Trailhead to Overlook

You will pass the Pear Lake/Finch Lake/Allenspark Trail on the left before you reach the ranger station. You don't have to hike to Finch Lake to enjoy a great view of Wild Basin. It is an interesting, short, out-and-back side trip to climb to the ridge above Wild Basin, where you are rewarded with a terrific view of the glacier-carved valley and the peaks that surround it. It is about a 1.5-mile trek from the trailhead and a little less than 3 miles (one-way) to the viewpoint near the ridgetop, with an 800-foot-plus climb on gradual switchbacks to reach it. When you arrive, great views of Mount Meeker, Longs Peak, Chiefs Head, Pagoda Peak, and the entire Wild Basin stretch before you. At this point you can turn around and have a satisfying round-trip of less than 6 miles.

*Wild Basin rest stop*

## Allenspark Trail

The Allenspark Trail is more scenic than the trailhead on the valley floor. After approximately the first mile, you have breaks in the trees and start getting views of Chiefs Head, Pagoda Mountain, Mount Meeker, and Longs Peak. The last 0.5 mile to the overlook point provides even more views, with the grand finale being the overlook, where you get a 180-degree view of the peaks and the valley. It is a steady climb with variations all the way to the overlook. From the overlook you'll see the Finch/Pear Lakes Trail. Hike part of that trail for more great views.

## Finch Lake

Once you reach the overlook and trail intersection, follow the Finch/Pear Lakes Trail left (southwest). You reenter the trees and climb steadily toward the lake and pass through a small section of trail that was burned in the fire in 1978. After the first stream crossing, you dip into and out of the drainage. There is another stream crossing in about 0.5 mile; the trail then follows a small ridge down to the lake. Once there you have an impressive view of Copeland Mountain, a beautiful riparian area, and a dazzling lake.

## 97 Calypso Cascades, Ouzel Falls, & Ouzel Lake
ROCKY MOUNTAIN NATIONAL PARK: SOUTH

see map on p. 184

| | |
|---|---|
| **Distance** | 3.6 miles to the cascades, 5.4 miles to the falls, 10 miles to Ouzel Lake, 13 miles to Bluebird Lake; out-and-back |
| **Difficulty** | Easy to cascades and falls, moderate to either of the lakes |
| **Elevation Gain** | Cascades: 880'; Falls: 1,130'; Ouzel Lake: 1,500'; Bluebird Lake: 2,500' (starting at 8,320') |
| **Trail Use** | Hiking, snowshoeing, skiing, option for kids |
| **Agency** | Rocky Mountain National Park |
| **Map(s)** | Trails Illustrated *Rocky Mountain National Park* |
| **Facilities** | Restrooms at trailhead |
| **Note(s)** | Bikes and dogs are not allowed on trails in Rocky Mountain National Park. Park fee required during the summer months at the Wild Basin entrance. |

**HIGHLIGHTS** Calypso Cascades and Ouzel Falls are popular, easy, short hikes in Wild Basin that feature the beauty of a cascading stream and can be enjoyed by adventurers of all ages and abilities. It is most dramatic during spring runoff but fun year-round. Ouzel and Bluebird Lakes are moderate, almost all-day treks through almost every mountain climate zone. Ouzel is a pristine lake at the foot of Copeland Mountain, and higher Bluebird Lake affords a view of the Continental Divide.

**DIRECTIONS** To reach Wild Basin from Estes Park, take CO 7 south approximately 12 miles. After you drive through Meeker, look for the sign on the right. Turn right (west) and proceed past the lodge and around the lake to the left. The road will narrow to almost one lane. You can drive to the parking lot near the ranger station, but start early because it frequently fills up on weekends. The ranger station parking lot is approximately 1.5 miles from the highway. Take CO 66 and CO 7 west and north from Lyons if you're coming from Denver/Boulder.

Proceed to the left through the parking lot to a route map and sign. Bear left and take the trail across the bridge. This trail offers a lot of variety as it winds, rolls, and steadily climbs through a pretty mixed forest of aspen and evergreens. The trail is next to the crystal-clear water and small waterfalls of North Saint Vrain Creek, while at times you move some distance from it. Eventually you come to the bridge that crosses the creek about 0.4 mile below Calypso Cascades—a good spot for a snack break that usually offers photo opportunities of the stream. This bridge is approximately 1 mile beyond Copeland Falls; it is approximately another 0.25-mile climb to the intersection of North Saint Vrain Creek and Coney Creek and the magical cascades that never look the same.

From the cascades it is another climb 0.7 mile to Ouzel Falls. At the cascades you see the Finch Lake/Allenspark Trail on the left, which has descended from the heights above to the floor of Wild Basin. Bear right and cross Coney Creek over two more bridges. At this point the trail levels for a bit and then steepens as it switchbacks straight uphill. Even if you don't plan to go all the way to Ouzel Falls, it is worth another 200 yards to enjoy the views of the west slopes of Longs Peak and Mount Meeker that open up. When you break out of the trees, you also see the dramatic scenery from the 1978 lightning-ignited fire that swept through this area and burned more than 1,000 acres. Once you get beyond the steep switchbacks, cross Ouzel Creek and you see Ouzel Falls. In another 100 yards you reach an overlook with spectacular views of Longs Peak, Mount Meeker to the northwest, Meadow Mountain to the southeast, and Wild Basin and the North Saint Vrain Creek below to the north.

At this point, you have a choice—continue up the trail steeply on switchbacks for the next 0.5 mile and then climb more gradually all the way to pristine Ouzel Lake or Bluebird Lake, or turn around and head for the parking lot. The hike to Ouzel Lake is one of my favorites in the park, but the later you start, the more people you will see. You also have to consider getting caught in thunderstorms if you start late. If you see large clouds forming on the Continental Divide mountains to the west, it would be smart to turn around. If the sky is still clear and it is not yet midday, continue on the rolling, steadily climbing trail that offers a spectacular panorama of Wild Basin. In less than a mile you come to a fork in the trail, with the right fork going to Thunder Lake and the left to Ouzel and Bluebird Lakes; bear left. Thunder Lake is 1 mile farther one-way and offers access to a route over the Continental Divide.

When you are 0.5 mile from Ouzel Lake, you will reach another signed trail intersection. Go right 1.5 miles, and climb steeply for another 1,000 feet to reach the spectacular setting of Bluebird Lake. Go straight/left on a rolling but relatively flat trail for the subtler beauty of Ouzel Lake's surroundings at the foot of Copeland Mountain.

### GREAT FOR KIDS

If you're hiking with young children, you might take a snack break at the bridge that crosses the creek. Continue to the intersection of North Saint Vrain and Coney Creeks to enjoy the cascades and turn around to retrace your steps to the trailhead.

### AMERICAN DIPPER

The American dipper, also called the water ouzel, is a rather nondescript, small bird with large feet that feeds on aquatic insects underwater. You can often see it walking on the gravelly bottom of streams and even underwater as deep as 6 feet. Usually you can spot one standing on a rock in the middle of the stream, bobbing its head—the behavior that gives it its name.

*Ouzel Lake*

*The trail to Jewel and Black Lakes in Rocky Mountain National Park*

# chapter 7

# Rocky Mountain National Park: East

## 1–2 HOURS FROM DENVER-BOULDER-FORT COLLINS

Rocky Mountain National Park (RMNP) features some of the most spectacular scenery in North America. The east, west, and south sides of the park are each covered in a separate chapter of this book. Most of the park is within easy driving distance of the Denver, Boulder, and Fort Collins areas, making it a popular destination for locals, as well as nature lovers from around the globe. The uplift of the ancient Rocky Mountains and the enormous glaciers that carved out characteristic U-shaped valleys and glacial moraines created the soaring cliffs and majestic peaks. The mystical beauty of this landscape can enthrall you for a lifetime. The park offers some of the best hiking and backpacking trails in North America. Backpacking does require inexpensive national park permits.

Visit during the week if you want to avoid the crush; it is still well worth the visit even if you can only visit on a weekend because most visitors don't venture more than a mile from their cars or the trailheads. You can avoid the weekend crowds by hiking the lesser-known trails that I describe in this and the other two chapters. A wide variety of ranger-led hikes, as well as nightly campfire talks during the summer months, are free to the public. Pick up the schedules at the visitor centers or campgrounds, call the visitor center, or visit the park's website, **nps.gov/romo,** for details.

Biking in the park is possible only on the extensive paved and gravel roads. A popular but somewhat hazardous ride is

Trail Ridge Road. It is a spectacular bike ride with steep drop-offs of several thousand feet and narrow shoulders. It is not appropriate for beginners or children. It is also possible to bike one-way (west) on unpaved Fall River Road. Mountain bikers like to use gravel Fall River Road for the uphill to the visitor center and Trail Ridge Road for the downhill back to Estes Park. It is well worth starting at sunrise to avoid the wide motor homes that share the dizzying heights of the highest (12,000 feet) through-highway in the United States.

Dogs are not allowed on the trails in Rocky Mountain National Park due to the millions of visitors. (Imagine the impact of millions of dogs.) They are allowed in campgrounds.

Don't feed the elk, moose, bears, mountain goats, deer, or birds any time of the year. They become addicted to treats and become pests with bad habits that sometimes have to be relocated or destroyed to protect humans. Don't approach any wild animals— it is against park rules and is very dangerous, especially if they have their young with them. Though they might look docile, they are wild animals that have been known to pursue and even forcefully evict tourists from their turf. You will likely see elk herds on the east side of the Continental Divide and moose on the west. They sometimes wander into the town of Estes Park, much to the dismay of the town's residents. Hundreds of elk can be seen in the Moraine Park area in the fall during the mating season; their eerie, whistling mating call is a unique auditory nature experience. Though stopping along the park's narrow roads is frowned upon, it is hard not to gawk at these magnificent animals, and there is ample designated parking.

The east side of RMNP is 70 miles from Denver. Allow at least 2 hours to get to Estes Park from Denver or about 1 hour from Boulder and Fort Collins, depending on the route you choose. Plan for additional time to find the trailheads; plus, it is a scenic drive, so take your time and enjoy it.

From Denver take I-25 north and exit at Loveland and CO 34. Take CO 34 west through the spectacular Big Thompson Canyon. Alternatively, you can go through Lyons on CO 7, past the southernmost section of the park, Wild Basin, on the way to Estes Park. From Boulder this alternate route can be accessed on CO 36; it intersects CO 34 in Estes Park. When you reach Estes Park on CO 34, continue to the third traffic light and you will see a sign for RMNP. Turn left at the sign and go up a hill, bear right at the stop sign, and then bear right at the intersection 0.5 mile after the next traffic light. You will see signs for the Beaver Meadows Visitor Center, which is worth a stop to see the overall map of the park, the fairly specific trail maps for areas such as Bear Lake, and a 3-D map graphically depicting the dramatic terrain you will be immersed in. You can also fill your water bottles there. A second visitor center at the Fall River Road entrance features a restaurant.

## Moraine Park

This magnificent glacial moraine is where you will find two popular trails—the Cub Lake and Fern Lake Trails. Moraine Park has a majestic setting, one of the most impressive in the park. The ever-changing mountain weather and light make it a magical place where large herds of elk roam freely, especially in the fall mating season. Many people know that this is the place to hear bull elks bugling in the fall, an eerie sound seemingly unworthy of such large, masculine animals.

If you want to enjoy the bugling without the crowds, come early, or snag a campsite on a full-moon weekend. Because it is relatively low (8,100 feet) and stays relatively warm until the depths of winter, it's good for hiking early and late in the season. A campground in Moraine Park is open year-round.

## Bear Lake

With easy accessibility, including for those in wheelchairs; a wide variety of trails; and a classic rocky mountain setting, the Bear Lake area is one of the most popular and populated areas in the park year-round. The area is high, at 9,475 feet, so visitors might have a little difficulty catching their breath if they charge uphill before becoming acclimatized. The throngs of summer can be avoided by getting an early start. On weekends, especially by afternoon, the parking lot and the trails fill up. If you want to sleep in and have a late breakfast, plan to take the Bear Lake Shuttle; it stops in the parking lot across from Glacier Basin Campground and on Bear Lake Road to pick up passengers and is well marked with signs. Most people don't get far from the parking lot or Bear Lake, but enough do to make an early start a good idea. Remember to bring lots of warm clothing even if it is balmy in the flatlands. The mountains create their own climate, and it can be cool and windy when it isn't at lower elevations. There are restrooms, but there isn't any water.

Bear Lake is the starting point for a wide variety of trails; challenge yourself by attempting to climb 12,300-plus-foot Flattop Mountain, or enjoy short and easy family trails. The Dream, Nymph, and Emerald Lakes system is the easiest place to explore but rewarding nonetheless, while the Flattop Trail is the entry point for more challenging terrain.

## Glacier Gorge Trailhead

An entry point to one of the most magical parts of the park, Glacier Gorge Trailhead resembles the ethereal pictures of the Rocky Mountains painted by Albert

Bierstadt in the late 19th century. Massive granite walls, waterfalls, cascading streams, and the majestic cliffs of Mt. Lady Washington and Longs Peak soar above, while views of the Mummy Range grace the horizon to the northeast. The first part of this trail is a popular hiking destination; fortunately, the population thins out as you go deeper into the backcountry. Alberta Falls is good for beginners and family trips. The trails to Alberta Falls, the Loch, Mills Lake, Jewel Lake, and Black Lake all originate at this trailhead. You can also connect to the North Longs Peak Trail from the Glacier Gorge Trail.

## Other Trails to Explore: Fall River Road

Spectacular Chapin, Chiquita, and Ypsilon Mountains look daunting from Deer Ridge and Trail Ridge Road, but they are climbable from their tame but steep, tundra-covered back sides. Though they are not described in detail in this book, you can reach the trailhead from Fall River Road and climb all three in a long day or just one while enjoying the panoramic view.

 **McGregor Ranch**

ROCKY MOUNTAIN NATIONAL PARK: EAST

see map on p. 194

| | |
|---|---|
| **Distance** | Up to 10 miles for the loop, 4 miles for out-and-back to Gem Lake |
| **Difficulty** | Easy–moderate |
| **Elevation Gain** | 1,130' (starting at 7,730') |
| **Trail Use** | Hiking, running, rock climbing, snowshoeing, skiing, option for kids |
| **Agency** | Rocky Mountain National Park |
| **Map(s)** | Trails Illustrated *Rocky Mountain National Park* |
| **Facilities** | Restrooms at trailhead |
| **Note(s)** | Bikes and dogs are not allowed on trails in Rocky Mountain National Park. |

**HIGHLIGHTS** The ranch is in a unique setting on the northeast edge of Estes Park. It is a working ranch with the dual backdrops of the rock climbers' paradise of lofty Lumpy Ridge on the north and views of majestic Longs Peak and the Rocky Mountain National Park massif in the distance to the southwest and west. Most of the trails are easy and can be hiked year-round because of the ranch's relatively low elevation. Enjoy gorgeous meadows with grazing stock, soaring monolithic granite cliffs, and rolling easy-to-moderate trails with hidden lakes tucked away on the north side of the ridge. If you're daring and fleet-footed, you can watch the spectacle of lightning storms reaching across Estes Valley, as the usual afternoon parade of thunderstorms roll off the high mountain ridges, and you can run to shelter before they reach the ranch.

**DIRECTIONS** From CO 34 turn right at the first light in Estes Park, and go uphill past the Stanley Hotel. At the next intersection turn right on Devil's Gulch/Glen Haven Road (County Road 43) northeast from Estes Park. There is a large parking lot on the north side of Devil's Gulch Road, 0.5 mile from the ranch's front gate. Many of the trails are sun-drenched and can get quite warm in the midday sun, so getting an early start is a good idea.

Once you reach the parking lot, you have two choices. The large loop that circles Lumpy Ridge can be an all-day, moderate hike that visits part of the Cow Creek Trail in McGraw Ranch, and Gem Lake—the long way around. (There is not adequate parking at McGraw Ranch, so this is the only recommended access to the Cow Creek Trail.) It is easier but just as enjoyable to savor smaller chunks of the loop by either going left (roughly northwest) or right (roughly east and then north). The route to the left is a much easier and more gradual, rolling climb than the straight uphill route to the right (east). If you don't want to see Gem Lake and would rather stay on the southwest side of Lumpy Ridge, the latter is the way to go; it's an enjoyable

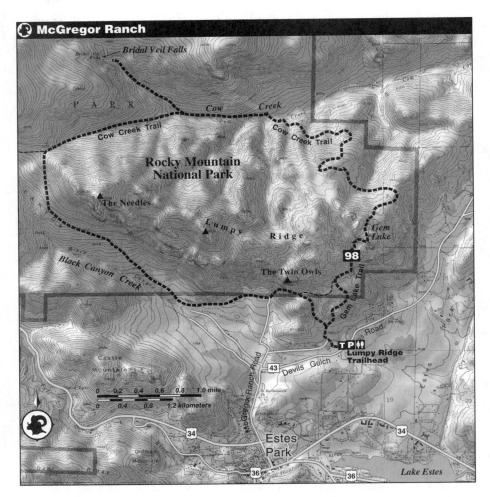

out-and-back trek that you can approach at a leisurely pace with pretty views and no steep sections. If you want to see Gem Lake, go right (east) straight uphill; for this route see the latter part of this trail description.

You can imagine the vistas on Twin Owls while strolling below, but don't attempt the routes unless you are a skilled technical rock climber and have the necessary equipment with you—even the lower routes can be deceiving and deadly. Excellent guide services in Estes Park can safely teach you the necessary skills and accompany you on the climb.

Pass through several gates, being sure to fasten them behind you to prevent cattle

from roaming onto your return path. The trail rolls along for almost 1.5 miles before it enters trees and begins to climb in earnest. In another 0.5 mile, round the end of Lumpy Ridge and trek around to the north side and the edge of Black Canyon, intersecting Cow Creek Trail in McGraw Ranch. You traverse the back side of the ridge on a narrower trail and enjoy obstructed views through thick tree cover and rock outcrops as the trail descends into the valley. Once you have accomplished that, you still face a moderate trek that ends with a rock garden, sweeping views, a steep uphill, and then a descent back to the parking lot. Turn around and retrace your steps if you've

## GREAT FOR KIDS

If you want an easy out-and-back trek, go to the left (west), the recommended route for families with young children. The trail travels uphill gradually from the parking lot and then goes gradually downhill for the first 0.5 mile. At the bottom of the hill, you cross the former, closed parking lot to get to the trailhead. It is back up a short hill. You will pass the Twin Owls Trail on the right (north) side of the trail on the way.

At the trailhead, go downhill to the left; uphill to the right is a rock climbers' side trail that goes straight and then veers north. Stay on the main trail, bear left, and go downhill to follow the gently rolling trail. Enjoy the views to the south and west, and take photos as soon as you can before the afternoon thunderstorm clouds roll in and the sun travels to the west, making good pictures difficult. As you walk, study the rock faces to the right (north) side of the trail. You will likely see rock climbers dangling high and defying gravity on the granite ridges.

When the trail begins to climb steeply, enjoy a picnic and turn around unless you want to follow the trail as it evolves into a moderate though shady climb through the captivating ponderosa pine forest. When your legs have had enough, reverse course and call it good.

had enough; if you're just getting warmed up, however, and don't hear or see thunderstorms, plunge ahead. Stop for a long break and study Gem Lake's unique rock-carved setting. The rest of the trail is a stroll through a granite sculpture garden that winds its way east and then southeast, gradually rolling over and around the east end of Lumpy Ridge. Don't take the trail that branches north and then east to McGraw Ranch. Once you have rounded the ridge, take the first trail that heads down to the new parking lot, or you will have a longer loop on the Twin Owls Trail back to the lot.

### Shorter Route to Gem Lake

If your primary goal is to see lovely Gem Lake, then start up the right (east) trail from the parking lot and travel straight uphill. Though the trail starts very steep, it mellows

*Gem Lake*

considerably after the first 0.75 mile. The first mile features a magnificent rock garden that is worth the trip for even a short, strenuous out-and-back hike that doesn't include the whole trek to the pond. After the trail levels temporarily, it travels more northerly and rounds the east end of Lumpy Ridge as you climb lots of steep steps. In another long mile, you reach Gem Lake, where you can enjoy a break before your return. Your total round-trip will be around 4 miles with a gain of 1,000 feet. If you'd like to make the 10-mile loop from this end, continue on the trail and complete the loop by rounding the west end of Lumpy Ridge. As you travel into the thicker tree cover, you get glimpses of the McGraw Ranch valley 800 feet below. To complete the loop, you descend 800 feet into the valley and then climb back out at the other end from Black Canyon around 500 feet.

## 99  Horseshoe Park

ROCKY MOUNTAIN NATIONAL PARK: EAST

| | |
|---|---|
| **Distance** | 2 miles, balloon |
| **Difficulty** | Easy |
| **Elevation Gain** | 100' (starting at 8,600') |
| **Trail Use** | Hiking, snowshoeing, skiing, great for kids |
| **Agency** | Rocky Mountain National Park |
| **Map(s)** | Trails Illustrated *Rocky Mountain National Park* |
| **Facilities** | Restroom at campground |
| **Note(s)** | Bikes and dogs are not allowed on trails in Rocky Mountain National Park. Park fee required. |

**HIGHLIGHTS**  This short and easy walk is at most a 2-mile round-trip suitable for families or for someone out for a nice, easy workout. It can be turned into a more challenging trek by continuing up to Deer Mountain. Early in the season you will encounter a fair amount of moisture on the trail.

**DIRECTIONS**  When you reach Estes Park on CO 34, continue to the third traffic light and you will see a sign for RMNP. Turn left at the sign and go up a hill, bear right at the stop sign, and then bear right at the intersection 0.5 mile after the next traffic light. You will see signs for the Beaver Meadows Visitor Center, which is worth a stop to see the overall map of the park, the fairly specific trail maps for areas such as Bear Lake, and a 3-D map graphically depicting the dramatic terrain you will be immersed in. You can also fill your water bottles there. A second visitor center at the Fall River Road entrance features a restaurant. From the Beaver Meadows entrance, drive toward Trail Ridge Road and climb the long hill to the Deer Junction and the Deer Mountain Trailhead. Just after Deer Junction turn right (north) toward Fall River Road. At the bottom of the hill, Horseshoe Park Trailhead parking lot is on the right (east). The trailhead is on the right back toward Deer Mountain.

From the Fall River entrance follow the signs toward Trail Ridge Road; it is closed in the winter, as is the western extension of Fall River Road. Pass the turnoff on the right (west) for Fall River Road; the trailhead is the next parking lot on the left (east) side of the road.

The trees on the trail are a colorful mixture of pine, fir, and aspen; the trail's proximity to the road is not a problem because of the thick cover. The trail starts to climb gently after about 0.5 mile and never gets steep, leveling out several times along the way. Bear right at the trail intersection to go up to the closed Horseshoe Park Lodge. The trail levels and then heads down a slight downhill when you reach the group campground and old lodge and picnic tables. The lodge is a good place to enjoy a snack, water, or photo break. Before turning around, walk downhill into the beautiful meadow that gives the horseshoe-shaped park its name.

You can circle the meadow and walk up toward Deer Mountain or just turn around.

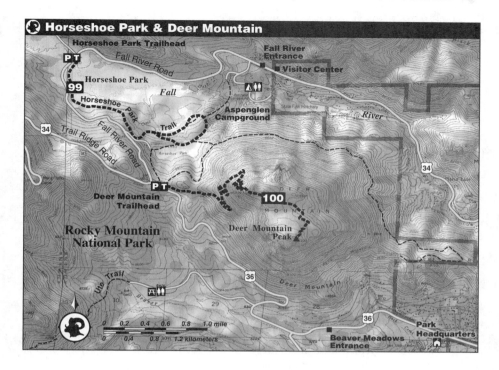

If you go into the meadow and turn left, you will see the loop trail on the left. If you see it around the end of the hill (it will eventually intersect the trail you came in on), you can take it as an alternate route back to the parking lot. If it isn't obvious, retrace your steps to the trailhead.

## 100  Deer Mountain

ROCKY MOUNTAIN NATIONAL PARK: EAST

| | |
|---|---|
| **Distance** | 2–6 miles, out-and-back |
| **Difficulty** | Easy–moderate |
| **Elevation Gain** | 1,075' (starting at 9,910') |
| **Trail Use** | Hiking, snowshoeing, skiing, great for kids |
| **Agency** | Rocky Mountain National Park |
| **Map(s)** | Trails Illustrated *Rocky Mountain National Park* |
| **Facilities** | None |
| **Note(s)** | Bikes and dogs are not allowed on trails in Rocky Mountain National Park. Park fee required. |

**HIGHLIGHTS** The Continental Divide and Longs Peak are the magnificent backdrop for this trail when you fix your gaze on the southwest horizon. To the northwest is the Mummy Range with the soaring massif of Chapin, Chiquita, and Ypsilon Mountains. Best of all, the views are immediate. Wander only 100 yards from the trailhead to enjoy the spectacle, making this ideal for flatland visitors and for families with young children looking for short excursions. Hiking all the way to the top is a moderate climb for more ambitious hikers.

**DIRECTIONS**  When you reach Estes Park on CO 34, continue to the third traffic light and you will see a sign for RMNP. Turn left at the sign and go up a hill, bear right at the stop sign, and then bear right at the intersection 0.5 mile after the next traffic light. You will see signs for the visitor center, which is worth a stop to see the overall map of the park, the fairly specific trail maps for areas such as Bear Lake, and a 3-D map graphically depicting the dramatic terrain in which you will be immersed. You can also fill your water bottles there. A second visitor center at the Fall River Road entrance features a restaurant. From park headquarters near the Beaver Meadows entrance, disregard the Bear Lake Road turnoff on the left, and drive 4.5 miles to Deer Ridge Junction. There is parking on both sides of the road. From the Fall River entrance follow the signs toward Trail Ridge Road. Pass the turnoff on the right for Fall River Road. When you reach the intersection at the top of the hill, turn left (east) and park immediately at Deer Trail Junction and the trailhead for Deer Mountain.

The trail starts up some stone steps; slightly hidden on the left is a great view of the Chapin, Chiquita, and Ypsilon Mountain massif. Find your way through the ponderosa pines and onto the rocks, and dig out your camera to prepare for the upcoming magnificent vistas; in another 0.25 mile you'll have a superb view of Longs Peak and the Continental Divide. The trail climbs, goes downhill for a short stretch, turns east, and begins to climb more steeply. Enjoy the beautiful aspen, lodgepole pine, and limber pine trees as you climb the ridge, where there are some good viewpoints on the right. You'll likely see some chipmunks too. The view continues until you enter trees, and the switchbacks begin after the first 0.5 mile. There is good shade from the hot sun on summer days if you didn't get up early and chilly winds to keep you cool in spring or fall. Broad, gradual switchbacks are the heart of the climb. You gain a wide ridge around the 2-mile mark. In another 0.8 mile you come to the side trail on the right that takes you to the top, where you will enjoy a superb panorama.

*View of Chapin, Chiquita, and Ypsilon Mountains from Deer Mountain Trail; photographed by Joe Grim*

## 101 Cub Lake

ROCKY MOUNTAIN NATIONAL PARK: EAST

see map on p. 200

| | |
|---|---|
| **Distance** | Up to 4.6 miles, out-and-back |
| **Difficulty** | Easy |
| **Elevation Gain** | 550' (starting at 8,100') |
| **Trail Use** | Hiking, snowshoeing, skiing |
| **Agency** | Rocky Mountain National Park |
| **Map(s)** | Trails Illustrated *Rocky Mountain National Park* |
| **Facilities** | Restrooms and picnic area |
| **Note(s)** | Bikes and dogs are not allowed on trails in Rocky Mountain National Park. Park fee required. |

**HIGHLIGHTS** This trail is popular year-round. In fall large herds of bugling elk are exceeded only by the flocks of people there to hear them dueling for romance. The height of the elk bugling is in the beautiful fall season (mid-September through early October), which is also often warm but can feature a chilly breeze. You can hike the route as a loop, with your return on the Fern Lake Trail, but you will end up 1 mile short of the Cub Lake Trailhead, with 1 mile of walking along the road to get back to your car. To intersect the Fern Lake Trail, walk past Cub Lake and follow the trail as it climbs the ridgeline on the north side of the trail up about 200 feet to meet the Fern Lake Trail.

**DIRECTIONS** When you reach Estes Park on CO 34, continue to the third traffic light and you will see a sign for RMNP. Turn left at the sign and go up a hill, bear right at the stop sign, and then bear right at the intersection 0.5 mile after the next traffic light. You will see signs for the visitor center, which is worth a stop to see the overall map of the park, the fairly specific trail maps for areas such as Bear Lake, and a 3-D map graphically depicting the dramatic terrain in which you will be immersed. You can also fill your water bottles there. A second visitor center at the Fall River Road entrance features a restaurant. After going through the Beaver Meadows entrance take the first left onto Bear Lake Road. After a hairpin S turn, pass the sign for Moraine Park, take the next right, and then turn left at the sign for the Cub Lake and Fern Lake Trailheads. Continuing straight takes you into the Moraine Park Campground, which remains open in the winter.

The trail immediately crosses two streams on wooden bridges. The first mile or so borders the open expanses of Moraine Park and offers views back to the east and south. It's also the most likely section to see elk or moose. Clamber over some large rocks in about 0.5 mile. The trail rolls over more rock formations while bordering the willow-highlighted riparian area. It climbs gradually through colorful wetlands with a variety of eye candy—magnificent ponderosa pines, rock formations, reeds, willows, water, and distant peaks. Eventually the trail climbs more steeply (not for long, though) under thicker tree cover to the edge of the lake. Once you reach the lake, climb over to Fern Lake for the return, veer south and hike through Hollowell Park to Bierstadt and Bear Lakes, or simply return to the trailhead.

*Cub Lake Trail*

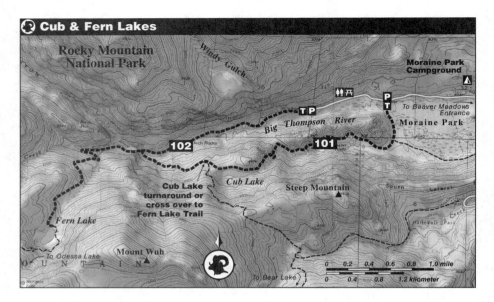

**102**  **Fern Lake**

ROCKY MOUNTAIN NATIONAL PARK: EAST

| | |
|---|---|
| **Distance** | Up to 7.6 miles, out-and-back |
| **Difficulty** | Moderate |
| **Elevation Gain** | 1,380' (starting at 8,120') |
| **Trail Use** | Hiking, snowshoeing, skiing, option for kids |
| **Agency** | Rocky Mountain National Park |
| **Map(s)** | Trails Illustrated *Rocky Mountain National Park* |
| **Facilities** | Restrooms and picnic area |
| **Note(s)** | Bikes and dogs are not allowed on trails in Rocky Mountain National Park. Park fee required. |

**HIGHLIGHTS**  This trail can be used for a short, easy hike just to the featured lake or a major adventure by starting at Moraine Park and finishing at Bear Lake. If you do that, start early to avoid storms, and use a car shuttle or the park shuttle. You can also use this trailhead to climb all the way up to Odessa Lake another 500 feet in elevation and 0.6 mile beyond Fern Lake. That part of the trail is very steep and makes the trek a moderate to challenging hike if you then go all the way to or return from Bear Lake.

**DIRECTIONS**  When you reach Estes Park on CO 34, continue to the third traffic light and you will see a sign for RMNP. Turn left at the sign and go up a hill, bear right at the stop sign, and then bear right at the intersection 0.5 mile after the next traffic light. You will see signs for the Beaver Meadows Visitor Center, which is worth a stop to see the overall map of the park, the fairly specific trail maps for areas such as Bear Lake, and a 3-D map graphically depicting the dramatic terrain in which you will be immersed. You can also fill your water bottles there. A second visitor center at the Fall River Road entrance features a restaurant. After going through the main entrance take the first left onto Bear Lake Road. After a hairpin S turn, pass the sign for Moraine Park, take the next right, and turn left at the sign for the Cub and Fern Lake Trailheads. Continuing straight takes you into Moraine Park Campground, which remains open in the winter.

The trail covers terrain similar to that of Cub Lake Trail. It starts as a gradual climb and then steepens considerably as it leaves the Moraine Park lowlands and surmounts a higher plateau to Fern Lake. From there, if you have the time and ambition, you can switchback high onto the ridge and have impressive views of the entire Moraine Park valley and climb up and over into the Glacier Gorge/Bear Lake drainage. It is one of the more spectacular jaunts you can take in the park without going up to the highest reaches.

The trail begins easy and rolling. At around the 0.5-mile mark you will reach a large monolithic rock. This can be your turnaround point (see sidebar). You can also create a loop out of this and the Cub Lake Trail, which intersects this trail at approximately 1.8 miles and around 8,500 feet. If you stay on the Fern Lake Trail, you climb another 1,000 feet from this trail intersection to Fern Lake.

You have a commanding view of the Moraine Park valley on the way up before you enter thick tree cover. You then see two picturesque waterfalls, the second about 0.25 mile from the lake. Once you reach the lake, some impressive cliffs are visible high above, and you will likely see evidence of some busy beavers.

*The large rock can make a good turnaround spot.*

### GREAT FOR KIDS

If you're hiking with young children and want a very easy jaunt, take this trail 0.5 mile past the intersection with the Fern Lake Trail to a large monolithic rock. This is a good turnaround point because the elevation gain to this point is negligible. From here, the trail steepens and climbs another 400 feet to the intersection with Cub Lake Trail. If your group is up to hiking farther, continue to that intersection, where there is a natural pool and footbridge that is a good picnic spot. After that intersection the trail gets much steeper and switchbacks up from the valley.

---

**103** **Mill Creek Basin**

ROCKY MOUNTAIN NATIONAL PARK: EAST

see map on p. 202

| | |
|---|---|
| **Distance** | Up to 5 miles to Cub Lake overlook (out-and-back), 6.4 miles to Cub Lake Trailhead (point to point) |
| **Difficulty** | Easy–moderate |
| **Elevation Gain** | 1,000' (starting at 8,200') |
| **Trail Use** | Hiking, snowshoeing, skiing |
| **Agency** | Rocky Mountain National Park |
| **Map(s)** | Trails Illustrated *Rocky Mountain National Park* |
| **Facilities** | Restrooms and picnic area at trailhead |
| **Note(s)** | Bikes and dogs are not allowed on trails in Rocky Mountain National Park. Park fee required. |

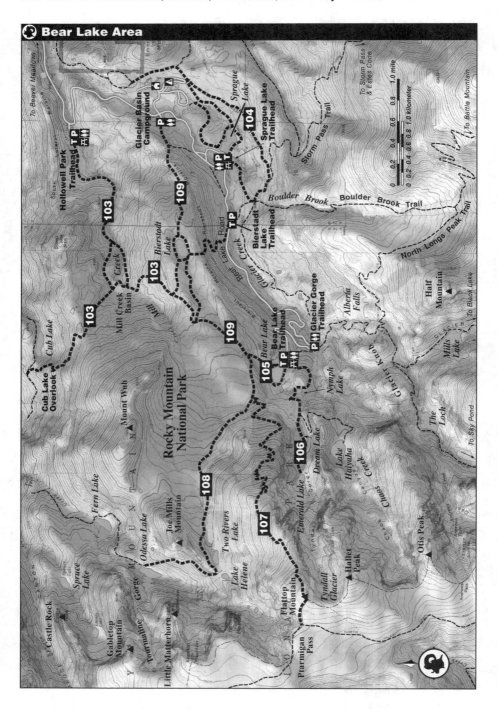

Bear Lake Area

**HIGHLIGHTS** This is the next trailhead you come to on Bear Lake Road after Moraine Park. The park starts off as a magnificent high mountain meadow, ringed by ponderosa pines and aspens, with a pleasing view of the surrounding hills. It can also be used as a less busy alternate route to Cub Lake or to access Bierstadt or Bear Lake. The fairly gradual climb can be turned into an out-and-back trek of any length and offers a view of Cub Lake from on high if you don't want to go the entire 6.5 miles past the lake to the Cub Lake Trailhead.

**DIRECTIONS** When you reach Estes Park on CO 34, continue to the third traffic light and you will see a sign for RMNP. Turn left at the sign and go up a hill, bear right at the stop sign, and then bear right at the intersection 0.5 mile after the next traffic light. You will see signs for the Beaver Meadows Visitor Center, which is worth a stop to see the overall map of the park, the fairly specific trail maps for areas such as Bear Lake, and a 3-D map graphically depicting the dramatic terrain in which you will be immersed. You can also fill your water bottles there. A second visitor center at the Fall River Road entrance features a restaurant. From the Beaver Meadows entrance, drive 0.5 mile and turn left on Bear Lake Road. Drive approximately 3.5 miles from the Beaver Meadows entrance, traveling downhill past the Moraine Park Campground and Museum and then uphill through a pine forest adjacent to a YMCA camp. When you emerge from the trees, Hollowell Park is straight ahead. As the road reaches the turnoff and makes a hairpin turn to the left, turn right into the parking area for the trailhead.

This fairly easy and relatively short hike to an overview of Cub Lake is a fun out-and-back hike. This trailhead can also be used for a somewhat steeper 1-mile climb to Bierstadt Lake or the beginning of a loop back to the Cub Lake Trailhead. When you start your hike, read the sign about the log sluice that was used until 1907. From the trail you can see the aspens descending the mountainside where the sluice used to be. The aspen trees are the canopy for the route to Bierstadt Lake; it is magical when the leaves are resplendent in the fall.

Regardless of your destination, take the trailhead across the meadow and bear left in 0.25 mile at the first intersection. The right branch at that first intersection is a horse trail over to Moraine Park. If it isn't the height of horse season, it is a pleasant rolling stretch that parallels the road but is high enough to avoid the highway noise. It is a rather long stroll, which can make the Cub Lake Overlook route to the left (west) the better choice.

If you turn left, you will cross the level meadow for 0.25 mile and then go

*A view from the Mill Creek Basin Trail*

gradually uphill into the trees. It is always fun to hike next to a cascading stream; this treat is Mill Creek. At the next intersection, at approximately the 1.25-mile mark, go left again and climb a moderate mile up to Bierstadt Lake, or go straight (west and northwest) for the overview of Cub Lake. Don't follow the first stream crossing to the left (southwest), which goes up to Bierstadt, to remain on the Cub Lake overview branch of the trail. The overview trail climbs gradually through the trees, crests, and then descends as it opens up to a pretty meadow. It then winds back into the trees, with steeper and flatter sections alternating for more than a mile, until it opens up into a great view down the moraine onto Cub Lake.

The trail to Bierstadt Lake is wide, rocky in some sections, and primarily a tree tunnel (with lots of shade from quaking aspens on warm days) until you get to the ephemeral lake that does a disappearing act in dry years. Even if you encounter a dry lake bed, you will still, weather permitting, have a spectacular view of Hallet Peak.

## 104  Glacier Basin & Sprague Lake
ROCKY MOUNTAIN NATIONAL PARK: EAST

see map on p. 202

| | |
|---|---|
| **Distance** | Up to 3 miles, loop |
| **Difficulty** | Easy |
| **Elevation Gain** | 200' (starting at 8,710') |
| **Trail Use** | Hiking, snowshoeing, skiing, option for kids, wheelchair accessible |
| **Agency** | Rocky Mountain National Park |
| **Map(s)** | Trails Illustrated *Rocky Mountain National Park* |
| **Facilities** | Restrooms, picnic areas, and a horse stable |
| **Note(s)** | Bikes and dogs are not allowed on trails in Rocky Mountain National Park. Park fee required. |

**HIGHLIGHTS**  The Sprague Lake area offers a couple of easy loops, as well as the trailheads for more ambitious adventures such as the Boulder Brook/North Longs Peak and Storm Pass Trails. The easiest trip is simply around the lake itself, only 0.5 mile with no elevation gain; it's wheelchair accessible and offers great views of the peaks on the Continental Divide—the usual suspects: Flattop, Hallet, and friends.

**DIRECTIONS**  When you reach Estes Park on CO 34, continue to the third traffic light and you will see a sign for RMNP. Turn left at the sign and go up a hill, bear right at the stop sign, and then bear right at the intersection 0.5 mile after the next traffic light. You will see signs for the Beaver Meadows Visitor Center, which is worth a stop to see the overall map of the park, the fairly specific trail maps for areas such as Bear Lake, and a 3-D map graphically depicting the dramatic terrain in which you will be immersed. You can also fill your water bottles there. Take the first left after the Beaver Meadows Visitor Center onto Bear Lake Road. Approximately 1 mile from Hollowell Park or 4.5 miles from the Beaver Meadows entrance, take a left on Bear Lake Road and drive until you come to Glacier Basin Campground. Parking is on the right (west) side of road, and the trailhead is on the east side of the campground. The Sprague Lake area and parking lot are the next left on the south side of the road and are approximately 0.5 mile from the Glacier Basin Campground parking lot.

You can start the easy longer loops at either Glacier Basin Campground, which is closed during winter months, or Sprague Lake. The best views are seen at Sprague Lake or at the campground, with limited but nice views along the way. There is ample parking at either end of the loop, with parking lots across from the campground off Bear Lake Road and at the Sprague Lake picnic area. If you want a very easy one-way trek for small children or people who aren't acclimated to the altitude, this can be done as a point to point with a two-car shuttle.

If you want a longer hike, start the entire 3-mile loop from the Sprague Lake Picnic Area across from the livery. Start by walking toward the lake, edging along the left (counterclockwise) side of the lake, and then looking for a trail connection on the left side of the lake before you come to a picnic area beside the trail. Take the trail downhill into the trees toward the campground. Take the right (uphill) fork in 0.5 mile and switchback to the top of the ridge, to the best view of the route, with the Mummy Mountains in the distance along with Flattop and Hallet. You then loop back along the ridgeline toward the Storm Pass and Boulder Brook Trails, passing both trails as you roller-coaster southwest and then northwest, looping back toward Sprague Lake. The trail descends the ridge and crosses a creek as you bear right toward the lake. Do not take the trail marked as a return route to the Glacier Gorge Campground.

If you prefer to go the other way around the loop, start at the picnic area next to the Sprague Lake parking lot, ascend a short (200 yards), steep hill that turns into an easy climb, and enter a lodgepole pine forest. Look for and follow the orange markers on the tree limbs. A trail entering from the left is marked Glacier Gorge/Bear Lake; take

it left to climb to an intersection with the Boulder Brook and Glacier Gorge Trails. Follow the sign to the left toward the Glacier Basin Campground. The trail goes downhill, over Boulder Brook twice, and rolls before another short climb. Crest the hill and intersect the Storm Pass Trail on the right. Continue downhill to the left and toward the campground. Enjoy the best view of the route, with the Mummy Mountains in the distance and Flattop and Hallet Peaks back to the west. This is a good place for a break. Continue straight ahead another 0.5 mile to the campground, or take the first trail on the left to Sprague Lake.

## Boulder Brook & North Longs Peak Trails

If you'd like a longer trek than that previously described, try the quiet but steep hike from Sprague Lake up the Boulder Brook Trail all the way to the North Longs Peak Trail. Follow the previous directions to where the trail intersects with the Boulder Brook Trail; instead of turning toward the campground, go straight uphill on the Boulder Brook Trail. After a gradual start, the trail becomes very steep as it follows the brook. It finally levels briefly and opens up, with sparkling brook and wildflowers providing superb entertainment. It travels through a narrow grassy area, crosses the stream twice, reenters sparser aspen trees, and goes steeply

*A jaunt around Sprague Lake is an easy adventure.*

uphill. The trail is a little hard to follow at times because it isn't heavily used, but you will eventually intersect the North Longs Peak Trail. There you can travel it left (east) toward Granite Pass or enjoy the sweeping view and return to Sprague Lake.

### Sprague Lake & Storm Pass

The Storm Pass Trail can be accessed from either Sprague Lake or near Lily Lake and the Longs Peak and Estes Cone Trailhead. It is a great candidate for a car shuttle, if you want to hike only 5 miles; otherwise, it's a 10-mile out-and-back. Follow the main route description above, and when you reach the Storm Pass Trail intersection go straight or bear right (east-southeast)

and climb the hill gradually rather than descending to Glacier Basin Campground. Climb steadily for almost 0.5 mile; the trail swings due south and gives you a view of the north side of Longs Peak. You then travel downhill, losing at least 100 feet, into a pretty valley and meadow.

The pass is another 3 miles, mostly uphill after the sign marking Wind River and Storm Pass. The trail edges the meadow and reenters the trees in about 100 yards and begins to climb at first gradually and then more steeply. It is not well marked but is used frequently enough to be visible as it winds through the trees. It alternately steepens and levels as it steadily climbs through the thick tree cover.

---

*GREAT FOR KIDS*

The easiest adventure is simply circumnavigating the flat trail 0.5 mile around the lake. There are a few picnic spots and benches along the way. If you would like to do more, the next easiest one-way trek for families with young children is to start at the high point at Sprague Lake and walk downhill to the Glacier Basin Campground, using a car shuttle. If you want to avoid a shuttle, do a simple out-and-back adventure of any length to be determined by the participants' motivation. If you are going to go out and back, I suggest starting from Glacier Basin Campground (park across the road) because it is the flattest part of the route and you can avoid the ridge walk trail on the left entirely. Starting at Sprague Lake is doable as an out-and-back but is more challenging terrain because it is somewhat uphill on the way back. All of the options are easy.

---

 **Around Bear Lake**

ROCKY MOUNTAIN NATIONAL PARK: EAST

see map on p. 202

| | |
|---|---|
| **Distance** | 1 mile, loop |
| **Difficulty** | Easy |
| **Elevation Gain** | Negligible (starting at 9,475') |
| **Trail Use** | Hiking, snowshoeing, skiing, great for kids, wheelchair accessible |
| **Agency** | Rocky Mountain National Park |
| **Map(s)** | Trails Illustrated *Rocky Mountain National Park* |
| **Facilities** | Restrooms and picnic shelter at trailhead |
| **Note(s)** | Bikes and dogs are not allowed on trails in Rocky Mountain National Park. Park fee required. |

**HIGHLIGHTS** This short, wheelchair-accessible stroll around Bear Lake is ideal for families with small children or people having difficulty adjusting to the altitude. The views are nonstop, from soaring mountains to quaking aspens.

**DIRECTIONS** When you reach Estes Park on CO 34, continue to the third traffic light and you will see a sign for RMNP. Turn left at the sign and go up a hill, bear right at the stop sign, and then bear right at the intersection 0.5 mile after the next traffic light. You will see signs for the Beaver Meadows Visitor Center, which is worth a stop to see the overall map of the park, the fairly specific trail maps for

*Bear Lake views*

areas such as Bear Lake, and a 3-D map graphically depicting the dramatic terrain in which you will be immersed. You can also fill your water bottles there. Take the first left after the Beaver Meadows Visitor Center onto Bear Lake Road. Drive to the Bear Lake parking lot, or take the shuttle in the parking lot across from Glacier Basin Campground. The Beaver Meadows entrance near RMNP head-quarters is the best entry point for access to Bear Lake Road, which is approximately 0.25 mile from the entrance station. Turn left (south) onto Bear Lake Road and follow it to its terminus at the Bear Lake parking lot, passing Moraine Park, Hollowell Park, Glacier Basin Campground, Sprague Lake, and the Glacier Gorge Trailhead along the way.

Circumnavigate in either direction with your camera out and ready. Maintain a leisurely pace, and stop frequently to enjoy the magnificent setting and scenery. If you have the energy, take a short jaunt uphill toward the other smaller lakes described on the next page: Nymph, Dream, and Emerald.

## GLACIATION

Volcanoes and uplift provided the building blocks for the beautiful Bear Lake and Glacier Gorge areas. But the real artisans of nature were the glaciers that formed about 2 million years ago and slowly "walked" down the stream-cut, U-shaped valleys. In the highest valleys the deep snow compacted into blue ice and then flowed as glaciers widened the erosion, carving out the characteristic U-shaped valleys. These converging rivers of ice flowed into the lower valleys where the ice melted and dropped debris along the valley sides, known as lateral moraines. The last glaciers started about 28,000 years ago and flowed together from Odessa Lake Gorge and other tributary valleys to form a large glacier that melted into Moraine Park, which you cross on the way to Bear Lake. Terminal moraines, material left at the farthest extent of a glacier, naturally dam Bear Lake.

## 106  Nymph, Dream, & Emerald Lakes
ROCKY MOUNTAIN NATIONAL PARK: EAST

see map on p. 202

| | |
|---|---|
| **Distance** | 3.6 miles, out-and-back |
| **Difficulty** | Easy |
| **Elevation Gain** | 605' (starting at 9,475') |
| **Trail Use** | Hiking, snowshoeing, skiing, great for kids |
| **Agency** | Rocky Mountain National Park |
| **Map(s)** | Trails Illustrated *Rocky Mountain National Park* |
| **Facilities** | Restrooms and picnic shelter at trailhead |
| **Note(s)** | Bikes and dogs are not allowed on trails in Rocky Mountain National Park. Park fee required. |

**HIGHLIGHTS** It is easy to understand why these Bear Lake trails are among the most popular. They are relatively short and easy to navigate, and they feature some of the most beautiful scenery in the park.

**DIRECTIONS** When you reach Estes Park on CO 34, continue to the third traffic light and you will see a sign for RMNP. Turn left at the sign and go up a hill, bear right at the stop sign, and then bear right at the intersection 0.5 mile after the next traffic light. You will see signs for the Beaver Meadows Visitor Center, which is worth a stop to see the overall map of the park, the fairly specific trail maps for areas such as Bear Lake, and a 3-D map graphically depicting the dramatic terrain in which you will be immersed. You can also fill your water bottles there. Take the first left after the Beaver Meadows Visitor Center onto Bear Lake Road. Drive to the Bear Lake parking lot, or take the shuttle in the parking lot across from Glacier Basin Campground. The Beaver Meadows entrance near RMNP headquarters is the best entry point for access to Bear Lake Road, which is approximately 0.25 mile from the entrance station. Turn left (south) onto Bear Lake Road and follow it to its terminus at the Bear Lake parking lot, passing Moraine Park, Hollowell Park, Glacier Basin Campground, Sprague Lake, and the Glacier Gorge Trailhead along the way.

It is only 0.5 mile and a 225-foot gain to Nymph Lake, so it is not a difficult hike. Because the trail starts at almost 10,000 feet and is uphill, small children might find it to be quite enough. For an average, fit adult it is a stroll in the park and well worth the effort. Loop the lake around to the right in or very near the trees to enjoy views of Hallet, Thatchtop, and Flattop. Touring around Nymph Lake is a short family outing and can be combined with a circuit of Bear Lake.

Another 0.6 mile and 200 feet get you to the sleepy shoreline of Dream Lake. The hike from Nymph to Dream Lake is also a real treat (eye candy, if you will). From the other side of Nymph Lake, the trail continues uphill to the left; you soon see a striking view of Longs Peak. Don't be drawn to go straight uphill to the right, even though you are likely to see tracks going that way—that route leads onto a cliff. Bear left and continue at a fairly low angle, staying above the picturesque valley spreading out on the

*Emerald Lake*

left and below the impressive rock cliffs on the right. Stately, magnificently healthy evergreens climb the mountainsides; their branches and needles seem etched in crystal because of the high-altitude atmosphere.

The various paths to the lake eventually merge at the top, with bearing to the right as the most common route. Weave your way through a few rocks, and then see the stunning setting for Dream Lake, true to its name. This is a terrific photo opportunity spot because of its exquisite surroundings, towering mountains and cliffs, and scruffy wind-sculpted trees with gnarled roots.

Another 0.7 mile and 200 more feet of elevation gain get you to Emerald Lake, at approximately 10,300 feet, which also has an impressive setting. The shoulder and cliffs of Flattop Mountain soar on the north, while Hallet Peak and Tyndall Glacier complete the panorama of this high mountain jewel.

## 107  Flattop Mountain & Hallet Peak
ROCKY MOUNTAIN NATIONAL PARK: EAST

see map on p. 202

| | |
|---|---|
| **Distance** | 8.8 miles to summit of Flattop Mountain, 10 miles to summit of Hallet Peak; out-and-back |
| **Difficulty** | Moderate–challenging |
| **Elevation Gain** | 2,850' (starting at 9,475') |
| **Trail Use** | Hiking, snowshoeing, skiing, option for kids |
| **Agency** | Rocky Mountain National Park |
| **Map(s)** | Trails Illustrated *Rocky Mountain National Park* |
| **Facilities** | Restrooms and picnic shelter at Bear Lake Trailhead |
| **Note(s)** | Bikes and dogs are not allowed on trails in Rocky Mountain National Park. Park fee required. |

**HIGHLIGHTS**  This moderate to challenging hike features some of the best views of the sheer, granite west side of Longs Peak and the magical, glacier sculpture of Glacier Gorge, with a majestic, bird's-eye view of Bierstadt, Sprague, Bear, Dream, and Black Lakes. The west side of Longs Peak and the famous Keyboard of the Winds (ridgetop rock sentinels) sweep into Black Lake, and Hallet's sharp prow becomes ever more impressive as you climb into the sky. You can enjoy these views by taking the trail to the overlooks, without summiting Flattop.

**DIRECTIONS**  When you reach Estes Park on CO 34, continue to the third traffic light and you will see a sign for RMNP. Turn left at the sign and go up a hill, bear right at the stop sign, and then bear right at the intersection 0.5 mile after the next traffic light. You will see signs for the Beaver Meadows Visitor Center, which is worth a stop to see the overall map of the park, the fairly specific trail maps for areas such as Bear Lake, and a 3-D map graphically depicting the dramatic terrain in which you will be immersed. You can also fill your water bottles there. Take the first left after the Beaver Meadows Visitor Center onto Bear Lake Road. Drive to the Bear Lake parking lot, or take the shuttle in the parking lot across from Glacier Basin Campground. The Beaver Meadows entrance near RMNP headquarters is the best entry point for access to Bear Lake Road, which is approximately 0.25 mile from the entrance station. Turn left (south) onto Bear Lake Road and follow it to its terminus at the Bear Lake parking lot, passing Moraine Park, Hollowell Park, Glacier Basin Campground, Sprague Lake, and the Glacier Gorge Trailhead along the way.

While summiting Flattop is a noteworthy achievement, hiking part of the way is also something you can thoroughly enjoy because of the panoramic views and the flora and fauna of the various alpine zones along the way. At treeline the stunted, wind-shaped krummholz forest looks like something out of a child's fairy tale. If you get an early start and the weather holds, summiting is doable for anyone of average fitness, as long as you allow enough time to adjust to the altitude and for water and snack breaks. If you have a compulsive, goal-oriented side that tries to convince you to ascend quickly at the outset, restrain it; otherwise, you'll have too little energy for the steep upper slopes.

From the Bear Lake parking lot, walk right toward the lake. When you reach the shoreline, you can see the impressive massif of Hallet Peak, but the summits of Flattop and Hallet are out of sight. Go to the right and watch for the signed route that takes you gradually uphill through the pretty aspens that frame the lake and Hallet Peak. At the first major switchback, at about 0.25 mile, you reach the Bierstadt Lake Trail, a short hike covered in Trail 109. Go left to stay on the Flattop Mountain Trail, which climbs steeply and opens up to spectacular views to the south. The next stretch parallels Bear Lake and affords some of the best views of Longs Peak, Bear Lake, Glacier Gorge, and the glacier-carved, U-shaped valleys—a perfect place for photographs as you will soon be in the trees again, and it will be a while before you emerge.

After about another 100 yards, the trail levels and veers north into the shade of Engelmann spruce trees and then opens up enough for you to see east into Mill Creek Basin. If you look up high straight ahead, you can see the route up Flattop and the prow of Hallet peeking over the top. The flat stretch lasts about 0.25 mile, and then you climb steadily for 0.5 mile to reach the intersection with the Flattop Mountain Trail, which switchbacks more steeply up to the left, while the Odessa Lake Trail continues to climb straight ahead. Continue to Flattop, switchbacking narrowly and then widely and climbing steadily, mostly in fir and spruce trees. In about 0.25 mile you reach a view of Mill Creek Basin before the trail turns sharply left. You can see all the way down to McGregor Ranch and Lumpy Ridge. This viewpoint is another possible family turnaround point, until you reach the Dream Lake Overlook, another steeper 0.5 mile or more. The trail bears southwest as it climbs to the edge of the

cliffs and the overlook, where you once again have great views of both Longs and Hallet Peaks. This popular destination is another turnaround spot for those not climbing the peak. At this point you will be approximately one-third of the way to the top in terms of overall effort.

After this, just getting to treeline can easily take another 30–45 minutes or more if you stop frequently for breaks and are not a runner. Treeline (usually around 11,000 feet) is approximately 2.5 miles from Bear Lake; leaving about another 2 steep miles and 1,300 feet to the summit. From the overlook, the trail switchbacks widely and tracks more toward the north, passing next to a small rock outcrop; some cairns along the way mark it. The trail travels almost to the northern ridge and outcrops before tracking back to the south and reaching treeline. At this point you get good views of the Mummy Range—Chapin, Chiquita, and Ypsilon Mountains—and Mummy Mountain. If you are determined and very fit and take few breaks, you can reach treeline in a little more than 1 hour; most of the time you will encounter at least a breeze at that point. You might need an extra layer of clothing, depending on the time of year, or a cool drink if the sun is beating down. This is a good time to have a snack and a drink and decide if discretion is the better part of valor, given the time of the day and the clouds in the sky.

Depending on the time of the year, particularly early in the hiking season, you might need to avoid some snowfields and small streams of water. How long it takes you to hike from the treeline to the summit depends on your condition and that of the trail. I highly recommend that you turn around if it is raining or thunder is rumbling. The trail traverses and climbs steadily first northwest and then southwest to the top of the next ridgeline to a false summit; the actual summit is out of view to the west. If you're hiking on a beautiful day and have plenty of time to make the return trip, you can have a lot of fun. The views are nonstop

*Flattop Mountain and Hallet Peak*

once you reach treeline. As you near the summit, there are breathtaking views of Dream Lake's valley and both the pointy false summit and actual summit of Hallet Peak. You will also see the Tyndall Glacier. From the flat, windswept top you can see over the Continental Divide and into the west side of Rocky Mountain National Park, the trail that goes all the way to Grand Lake, and the origin of the Colorado River.

## Hallet Peak

Hallet Peak, almost 400 feet higher at 12,713 feet, is on the other side of the cirque and Tyndall Glacier from Flattop Mountain. You don't have to summit Flattop to climb Hallet, though many people like to climb both in the same day. Once you reach the top of the last ridge on Flattop, you can see the routes up both peaks and decide if you have enough energy and good weather for both or if one summit will do. The critical issues are the likelihood of a drenching or lightning storm and the fall of darkness before you reach Bear Lake—the mountains will be there for another day.

### GREAT FOR KIDS

Though hiking time will vary by group, making it to the stretch that parallels Bear Lake and then circling the lake could be an hour-plus family jaunt—a good goal with small children. There's a nice uphill stroll option switchbacking on the Bierstadt Lake and Flattop Mountain Trail, through a pretty aspen grove and some great views before returning to crowded Bear Lake.

**Odessa Lake**

ROCKY MOUNTAIN NATIONAL PARK: EAST

see map on p. 202

| | |
|---|---|
| **Distance** | 8.2 miles, out-and-back |
| **Difficulty** | Moderate |
| **Elevation Gain** | 1,205' (starting at 9,475') |
| **Trail Use** | Hiking |
| **Agency** | Rocky Mountain National Park |
| **Map(s)** | Trails Illustrated *Rocky Mountain National Park* |
| **Facilities** | Restrooms and picnic shelter at Bear Lake Trailhead |
| **Note(s)** | Bikes and dogs are not allowed on trails in Rocky Mountain National Park. Park fee required. |

**HIGHLIGHTS** This traversing trail is a moderate jaunt that branches off from the Flattop Mountain Trail about 1.4 miles from Bear Lake. When you emerge from the trees, you'll be enraptured by the views of Mills Mountain and Mount Wuh, and the high mountain splendor of Odessa. If you make it to Odessa Lake, three 12,000-foot peaks and the impressive Odessa Gorge will be your reward. You can even complete a superbly scenic, point to point all the way to Fern Lake and Moraine Park if you park a car there or don't mind trekking back uphill to Bear Lake.

**DIRECTIONS** When you reach Estes Park on CO 34, continue to the third traffic light and you will see a sign for RMNP. Turn left at the sign and go up a hill, bear right at the stop sign, and then bear right at the intersection 0.5 mile after the next traffic light. You will see signs for the Beaver Meadows Visitor Center, which is worth a stop to see the overall map of the park, the fairly specific trail maps for areas such as Bear Lake, and a 3-D map graphically depicting the dramatic terrain in which you will be immersed. You can also fill your water bottles there. Take the first left after the Beaver Meadows Visitor Center onto Bear Lake Road. Drive to the Bear Lake parking lot, or take the shuttle in the parking lot across from Glacier Basin Campground. The Beaver Meadows entrance near RMNP headquarters is the best entry point for access to Bear Lake Road, which is approximately 0.25 mile from the entrance station. Turn left (south) onto Bear Lake Road and follow it to its terminus at the Bear Lake parking lot, passing Moraine Park, Hollowell Park, Glacier Basin Campground, Sprague Lake, and the Glacier Gorge Trailhead along the way.

From Bear Lake you start on a fairly steady and somewhat steep climb that eventually levels. In less than 0.5 mile the Bierstadt Lake Trail continues straight (northeast), while the Flattop Mountain and Odessa Lake Trail takes a sharp left (west) uphill. After the intersection, climb above Bear Lake and look out across the valley at Glacier Gorge and Longs Peak—a good place for photos. The trail then enters the trees, but after 100 yards it affords a view of Mill Creek Basin and the rounded, thickly forested shoulder of Mount Wuh. It travels more northwesterly, levels out, and climbs at a slower rate.

Where the Flattop Mountain Trail switchbacks sharply left (west) uphill, continue straight (northwest) on the Odessa Lake Trail. Though the trail isn't steep, the slope into which it is carved is. The trail is usually well traveled and obvious but might be obscured in the trees you have to navigate and somewhat difficult to negotiate if you are one of the first ones on it in early spring before the snow has completely melted. It is not well marked beyond this point, but it climbs steadily to the left (northwest) and does not descend into the Mill Creek drainage toward the right (northeast), as some routes indicate. You can generally follow tracks another mile until you reach treeline. At that point the trail is easier to find, but you need good route-finding skills if you lose the trail and have to angle your way left (northwest) first up to Two Rivers Lake and then to Odessa Lake. Look for the trail carefully when you break out of the trees; you don't want to unnecessarily climb the steep, open slopes of Mills Mountain left (west) of the trail.

From 10,000 feet the trail steadily climbs in and out of the more sporadic and wind-twisted trees for the next approximately 1.5 miles and 600-plus feet, winding past the small Two Rivers Lake and Lake Helene. The mind has a way of shortening or lengthening distance, depending on the body's level of exertion. You reach the impressive Odessa Lake Gorge after you round a bend to the left and are treated to the majestic, windswept vistas of Notchtop (12,129 feet), Knobtop (12,331 feet), and Little Matterhorn (11,586 feet). Their majestic presence makes this casual jaunt more of an achievement and wilderness experience.

If it is late in the day, reverse course to make sure you are below treeline before the afternoon thunderstorms start. The way back is much easier because you can often enjoy the downhill, rather than gasping your way up. If you do get off track, keep Mill Creek Basin on your left and go south until you reach the Bear Lake cliff and basin, and then take another left (east) turn. If you started early and are up for the exertion, continue from Odessa Lake all the way to Fern Lake and even Moraine Park.

## 109  Bierstadt Lake
### ROCKY MOUNTAIN NATIONAL PARK: EAST

see map on p. 202

| | |
|---|---|
| **Distance** | 2.8 miles, out-and-back |
| **Difficulty** | Easy |
| **Elevation Gain** | 565' (starting at 8,850') |
| **Trail Use** | Hiking, snowshoeing, skiing, good for kids |
| **Agency** | Rocky Mountain National Park |
| **Map(s)** | Trails Illustrated *Rocky Mountain National Park* |
| **Facilities** | Restrooms and picnic shelter at Bear Lake Trailhead |
| **Note(s)** | Bikes and dogs are not allowed on trails in Rocky Mountain National Park. Park fee required. |

**HIGHLIGHTS** This short jaunt for families and beginners starting from Bear Lake offers great views of the entire glacier-carved valley back to Sprague Lake and up Glacier Gorge to Longs Peak. It is one of the most popular routes from Bear Lake; avoid crowds by starting early or hiking during the week.

**DIRECTIONS** When you reach Estes Park on CO 34, continue to the third traffic light and you will see a sign for RMNP. Turn left at the sign and go up a hill, bear right at the stop sign, and then bear right at the intersection 0.5 mile after the next traffic light. You will see signs for the Beaver Meadows Visitor Center, which is worth a stop to see the overall map of the park, the fairly specific trail maps for areas such as Bear Lake, and a 3-D map graphically depicting the dramatic terrain in which you will be immersed. You can also fill your water bottles there. Take the first left after the Beaver Meadows Visitor Center onto Bear Lake Road. Drive to the Bear Lake parking lot, or take the shuttle in the parking lot across from Glacier Basin Campground. Though starting at Bear Lake makes it a slightly longer hike (about 0.25 mile), it is a much easier, gradual climb. Because the Bierstadt Lake Trailhead parking lot is often full early, the shuttle bus is the best option. If you want a steep, moderate, somewhat shorter climb, however, the parking lot is the way to go.

When you start at the Bierstadt Lake Trailhead, it switchbacks up the side of the moraine from the valley floor through a stand of aspen trees. You have great views in all directions: Storm Peak and Mount Lady Washington to the west and Longs Peak to the south. As the trail starts to level, the aspens give way to lodgepole pine. You soon intersect Bear Lake Trail coming in from the west (left). Turn right at this intersection, and bear right at the next two trail junctions as well. You eventually round the southern end of the lake and end up on the lake's west side. From there reverse course to your starting point or continue downhill to Bear Lake if you have arranged a shuttle.

From Bear Lake, you wind through the aspens and pines, and when the Flattop and Odessa Trail veers left (about 0.5 mile), go right or straight toward Bierstadt Lake. The trail continues to climb gradually as the aspens give way to pines but actually goes downhill for about 0.3 mile before leveling and reaching the lake, meaning you'll have a bit of uphill on the way back to Bear Lake. The trail meanders to the west end of the lake, where the trees open up a bit more and you can see the spectacular setting better. There is an even better view of the mountain backdrop from the east end of the lake. You can pick up the trail down to Mill Creek Basin from the east side of the lake; if you would like a nice downhill loop, plant a car at that trailhead.

### BIGHORN SHEEP

In spring you are most likely to see bighorn sheep at lower elevations. In winter you are more likely to see them in Big Thompson Canyon and at lower elevations near Horseshoe Park and Sheep Lake. You might also encounter the sheep high above Wild Basin. They are, however, a rare sight in most parts of the park. The bighorn's recovery from near extinction in the park is a remarkable conservation story.

Though they were able to exist symbiotically with American Indians for hundreds of years, they almost didn't survive the arrival of European hunters in the late 1800s. They numbered only 200 by the end of the 19th century. Protection has revived these hardy dwellers of the highest reaches of the park and they now number more than 800. They are extremely well adapted to eating even the roughest of forage with their multiple-stomach digestive tracts, and their unique hooves allow them to leap and cling to the rocky, high-mountain precipices with breathtaking ease, making them the envy of climbers and hikers. Recent research has shown the size of the herd is declining; Rocky Mountain National Park and wildlife biologists are investigating this alarming turn of events.

*Bierstadt Lake twinkles in the distance.*

## 110   Alberta Falls

ROCKY MOUNTAIN NATIONAL PARK: EAST

see
map on
p. 216

| | |
|---|---|
| **Distance** | 1 mile, out-and-back |
| **Difficulty** | Easy |
| **Elevation Gain** | 100' (starting at 9,240') |
| **Trail Use** | Hiking, snowshoeing, skiing, great for kids |
| **Agency** | Rocky Mountain National Park |
| **Map(s)** | Trails Illustrated *Rocky Mountain National Park* |
| **Facilities** | Restrooms at trailhead |
| **Note(s)** | Bikes and dogs are not allowed on trails in Rocky Mountain National Park. Park fee required. |

**HIGHLIGHTS** This is a great family or photography excursion if you have small children or people not prepared for or uninterested in long hikes or altitude. A short, easy round-trip, it can easily be extended once you've reached the falls if you want; the trail is a gateway to gorgeous Glacier Gorge.

**DIRECTIONS** When you reach Estes Park on CO 34, continue to the third traffic light and you will see a sign for RMNP. Turn left at the sign and go up a hill, bear right at the stop sign, and then bear right at the intersection 0.5 mile after the next traffic light. You will see signs for the Beaver Meadows Visitor Center, which is worth a stop to see the overall map of the park, the fairly specific trail maps for areas such as Bear Lake, and a 3-D map graphically depicting the dramatic terrain in which you will be immersed. You can also fill your water bottles there. Take the first left after the Beaver Meadows Visitor Center onto Bear Lake Road. Drive to the Glacier Gorge parking lot. Glacier Gorge Trailhead is easy to locate on the way to Bear Lake. The parking lot is approximately 1.2 miles before the Bear Lake lot. If it is full, park in the Bear Lake lot and take the pleasant, short jaunt on the trail from the Dream Lake Trail to the Glacier Gorge Trail. If you want to sleep in and start late, using the park shuttle bus eliminates the stress you'd experience trying to park in the full lots.

The trail travels west from the parking lot, paralleling the small gorge before turning south and crossing a footbridge. It then begins a steady but not very steep climb. It eventually climbs back to the petite canyon carved by a small stream that can flow dramatically for a short time during the spring runoff. The intensity of the falls varies widely during the year according to stream flow and is most impressive during spring runoff as well. While the trail is usually quite safe when it's not wet and slick, it is a good idea to keep children close and away from the edge of the cliffs. If you go up the trail beyond the 0.5 mile to the falls, the views of the Mummy Range in the distance and the cliffs of the Bierstadt Moraine across Prospect Canyon improve with every step. From Alberta Falls the trail is steady but not very steep.

*Alberta Falls*

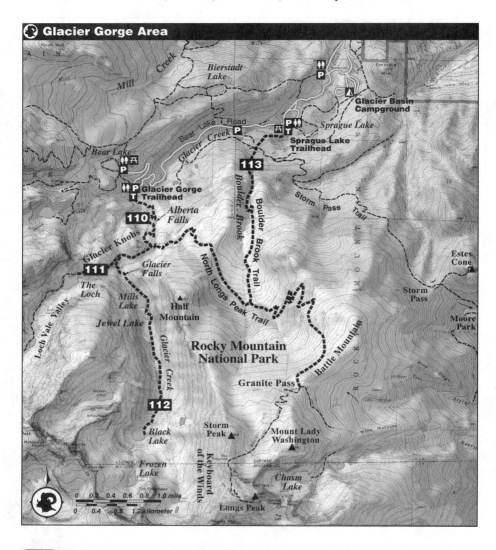

Glacier Gorge Area

## 111    The Loch

ROCKY MOUNTAIN NATIONAL PARK: EAST

| | |
|---|---|
| **Distance** | 5.4 miles, out-and-back |
| **Difficulty** | Moderate |
| **Elevation Gain** | 940' (starting at 9,240') |
| **Trail Use** | Hiking, snowshoeing, skiing |
| **Agency** | Rocky Mountain National Park |
| **Map(s)** | Trails Illustrated *Rocky Mountain National Park* |
| **Facilities** | Restrooms at trailhead |
| **Note(s)** | Bikes and dogs are not allowed on trails in Rocky Mountain National Park. Park fee required. |

**HIGHLIGHTS** One of the most rewarding in the park, this hike is also very popular. The Loch, Scottish for "lake," is in a magnificent setting, surrounded by Otis, Taylor, and Powell Peaks, and offers great photographic opportunities.

**DIRECTIONS** When you reach Estes Park on CO 34, continue to the third traffic light and you will see a sign for RMNP. Turn left at the sign and go up a hill, bear right at the stop sign, and then bear right at the intersection 0.5 mile after the next traffic light. You will see signs for the Beaver Meadows Visitor Center, which is worth a stop to see the overall map of the park, the fairly specific trail maps for areas such as Bear Lake, and a 3-D map graphically depicting the dramatic terrain in which you will be immersed. You can also fill your water bottles there. Take the first left after the Beaver Meadows Visitor Center onto Bear Lake Road. Drive to the Glacier Gorge parking lot. Glacier Gorge Trailhead is easy to locate on the way to Bear Lake. The parking lot is approximately 1.2 miles before the Bear Lake lot. If it is full, you will have to park in the Bear Lake lot and take the pleasant, short jaunt from the Dream Lake Trail to the Glacier Gorge Trail. If you want to sleep in and start late, using the park shuttle bus eliminates the stress you'd experience trying to park in the full lots.

This hike starts at the same trailhead as all other destinations in Glacier Gorge. After passing Alberta Falls, the trail climbs steadily through loose switchbacks to the intersection with the North Longs Peak Trail. Go right at this intersection. The trail then climbs around Glacier Knob, with interesting parapets all around. It continues up on the north side of the Icy Brook drainage that wends its way through the rock. After the intersection the trail narrows and scenery is rewarding as you near the entrance of the Loch Vale Valley. The switchbacks level out, and you continue between impressive, steep canyon walls. After winding through the canyon, the trail opens up and climbs again, with switchbacks virtually all the way to the lake.

If you want a longer, more challenging, and bracing wilderness hike, this is one of the better ones in the park that is easily accessible. It takes you below the west side of Longs Peak and the aptly named Keyboard of the Winds, rock sentinels that whistle and moan in the frequent high winds. The glacier-sculpted valley of rock art has some amazing sights; as with many of the destinations in Rocky Mountain National Park, the farther you go, the more enchanting it becomes.

*The Loch is surrounded by peaks.*

## 112  Jewel & Black Lakes

ROCKY MOUNTAIN NATIONAL PARK: EAST

see map on p. 216

| | |
|---|---|
| **Distance** | 10 miles, out-and-back |
| **Difficulty** | Moderate |
| **Elevation Gain** | 1,400' (starting at 9,200') |
| **Trail Use** | Hiking, backpacking, snowshoeing, skiing |
| **Agency** | Rocky Mountain National Park |
| **Map(s)** | Trails Illustrated *Rocky Mountain National Park* |
| **Facilities** | Restrooms at trailhead |
| **Note(s)** | Bikes and dogs are not allowed on trails in Rocky Mountain National Park. Park fee required. |

**HIGHLIGHTS** If you want a longer, more challenging, and bracing wilderness hike, this is one of the better ones in the park that is easily accessible. It takes you below the west side of Longs Peak and the aptly named Keyboard of the Winds, rock sentinels that whistle and moan in the frequent high winds; you're likely to see some amazing sights in this glacier-sculpted valley of rock art. As with many of these destinations, the farther you go, the more enchanting it becomes. If you want to visit three lakes in magnificent settings, this trek is for you. The journey to the first two can be day trips in and of themselves. Black Lake is a moderate to challenging hike, depending on conditions. On a calm summer's day it is delightful; fall and spring offer ice and wind chill that keep you on your toes. Hearing high winds approaching from the Keyboard of the Winds on Longs Peak on an unsettled day is an experience you won't want to miss.

**DIRECTIONS** When you reach Estes Park on CO 34, continue to the third traffic light and you will see a sign for RMNP. Turn left at the sign and go up a hill, bear right at the stop sign, and then bear right at the intersection 0.5 mile after the next traffic light. You will see signs for the Beaver Meadows Visitor Center, which is worth a stop to see the overall map of the park, the fairly specific trail maps for areas such as Bear Lake, and a 3-D map graphically depicting the dramatic terrain in which you will be immersed. You can also fill your water bottles there. Take the first left after the Beaver Meadows Visitor Center onto Bear Lake Road. Drive to the Glacier Gorge parking lot. Glacier Gorge Trailhead is easy to locate on the way to Bear Lake. The parking lot is approximately 1.2 miles before the Bear Lake lot. If it is full, you will have to park in the Bear Lake lot and take the pleasant, short jaunt from the Dream Lake Trail to the Glacier Gorge Trail. If you want to sleep in and start late, using the park shuttle bus eliminates the stress you'd experience trying to park in the full lots.

A day hike to any of the lakes is quite enjoyable because of the great scenery you see in all directions. Once you get beyond Alberta Falls, you continue to wind back and forth over Glacier Creek next to the small gorge that gives you more than one overlook and photo opportunity. Eventually the gorge opens up, with cliffs soaring above on both sides of the trail.

The first trail junction you come to is the North Longs Peak Trail that splits to the left and goes toward Granite Pass (high on the flank of Longs Peak), Boulder Brook, and the infamous boulder field on Longs Peak. Take the right branch toward Mills Lake and Loch Vale. The trail steepens but

you are treated to views of Arrowhead and Chiefs Head Peak in the distance ahead, with the gorge on your left and Glacier Gorge Canyon an inviting entry point to this majestic topography.

The trail goes downhill for a short distance and eventually goes back into the trees. You then reach the next major intersection. To the left is the Black Lake Trail (the lake is 2.8 miles from here); to the right is the trail to Loch Vale, also known as the Loch. You encounter a second stream crossing in a relatively short distance that features wooden steps and rocks. You see some cairns as well as wooden steps for route-finding.

### A BLACK LAKE OVERNIGHT

Warm weather in the flatlands or even at the beginning of a trip means nothing in the rapidly changing and localized weather of the higher reaches of the Rockies. It was a delightful winter's day in Boulder, a quite tolerable 49°F, balmy for mid-January, and my companions and I were sure that our venture to Black Lake for a midwinter camping trip would be blessed with unseasonably sultry weather. When we arrived at the trailhead, we were greeted by 30-mile-per-hour gusts that felt tolerable at 40°F. When we arrived at Mills Lake hours later, we had enough snow to put on our snowshoes half the time. The winds had increased and were pushing us around in gusts that we estimated were about 50 miles per hour, and the temperature was about 20°F. The lake surface was several inches of thick ice. A protracted hour-long struggle took us another mile to Jewel Lake as the winter sun sank low on the horizon.

At that point the wind was performing a sound and light show of its own. It was like watching huge surf rolling in off the Pacific. We could see the wind hit the ridgeline of Mount Lady Washington 2,000 feet above and drive spindrift high into the beams of golden sunlight through the wispy cloud cover. The wind went through our down jackets and drove snow onto our necks; the winds were later clocked at just under 100 miles per hour in Rocky Mountain National Park, and the temperature sank to minus 25°F that night. It was a long night with only a single-burner stove to produce heat; so much for our sultry winter sojourn at Black Lake.

There are at least two good routes to Mills Lake from here. You can either surmount the rocks or take a more circuitous route through the trees if you don't like scrambling. You are very close to the lake so it is well worth the trouble. Once you reach the lakeshore, you are treated to stunning views of Mount Lady Washington and can see the Keyboard of the Winds on the southwest side of Longs Peak. This is a great place for photos or a snack or lunch break, but you might have to find a wind-sheltered spot to enjoy it. On a warm summer's day, though, the cool breeze is welcome.

Once you reach Mills you have walked 2.8 miles from the Glacier Gorge Trailhead and are 2.2 miles from Black Lake. There is a campground about 0.25 mile ahead, but you need a permit from Rocky Mountain National Park to spend the night. This is a good place to turn around if you are hiking it in the early spring, find the mixture of rocks and mud annoying, and don't want to encounter more of the same. One of

*From the Black Lake Trail, you can see Keyboard of the Winds on the west side of Longs Peak, as well as Chiefs Head Peak.*

the interesting aspects of more challenging and remote trails is that they require more flexibility and creativity than just marching down an easy path.

If you keep going, the trail winds around the east edge of the lake with lots of interesting options over, under, and around large outcrops and towering trees. Eventually the main trail wanders rather far to the east away from the lakeshore. You also eventually reach an open meadow area with great views of Stone Man Pass and Arrowhead, as well as Chiefs Head and McHenrys Peaks. You are then only about 200 yards from the very steep stretch that takes you up to the edge of Black Lake. At the south end of the lake is pretty Ribbon Falls. The standard trail is to the left (east) of the falls.

## 113  North Longs Peak Trail

ROCKY MOUNTAIN NATIONAL PARK: EAST

see map on p. 216

| | |
|---|---|
| **Distance** | 13.6 miles to Granite Pass, out-and-back |
| **Difficulty** | Moderate; varies depending on distance hiked |
| **Elevation Gain** | 2,840' (starting at 9,240') |
| **Trail Use** | Hiking, backpacking, rock climbing, snowshoeing, skiing |
| **Agency** | Rocky Mountain National Park |
| **Map(s)** | Trails Illustrated *Rocky Mountain National Park* |
| **Facilities** | Restrooms at trailhead |
| **Note(s)** | Bikes and dogs are not allowed on trails in Rocky Mountain National Park. Park fee required. |

**HIGHLIGHTS** This trail is lightly used, a surprise given the unique terrain and beautiful views. The first mile or so to the Boulder Brook Trail intersection offers superb views of Glacier Gorge, Flattop and Hallet Peaks, the Mummies, and the entire valley on the return. This trail can also be used for climbs of Storm Peak, Mount Lady Washington, and even Longs Peak if you want to avoid the crowds of the main Longs Peak Trail and don't mind the extra distance.

**DIRECTIONS** When you reach Estes Park on CO 34, continue to the third traffic light and you will see a sign for RMNP. Turn left at the sign and go up a hill, bear right at the stop sign, and then bear right at the intersection 0.5 mile after the next traffic light. You will see signs for the Beaver Meadows Visitor Center, which is worth a stop to see the overall map of the park, the fairly specific trail maps for areas such as Bear Lake, and a 3-D map graphically depicting the dramatic terrain in which you will be immersed. You can also fill your water bottles there. Take the first left after the Beaver Meadows Visitor Center onto Bear Lake Road. Drive to the Glacier Gorge parking lot. Glacier Gorge Trailhead is easy to locate on the way to Bear Lake. The new parking lot and restrooms are a major improvement; the parking lot is approximately 1.2 miles before the Bear Lake lot. If it is full, park in the Bear Lake lot and take the pleasant, short jaunt from Dream Lake Trail to Glacier Gorge Trail. If you want to sleep in and start late, using the park shuttle bus eliminates the stress you'd experience trying to park in the full lots.

From the starting point at the Glacier Gorge Trailhead, the trail climbs 400 feet gradually to the intersection with the North Longs Peak Trail at 0.75 mile. From there it is a little less than 2 miles to the Boulder Brook Trail intersection. This alone makes a great round-trip trek of approximately 5.5 miles. If you continue, it's another 4 miles one-way from the intersection, or a total of 6.8 miles one-way to Granite Pass at 12,080 feet, an ambitious but spectacular round-trip.

The trail goes downhill from the intersection for approximately 100–200 feet, immediately greeting you with great views of the Mummy Range and valley as well as Glacier Gorge. This part of the trail is very open to sun and wind, but don't be dismayed if it is a hot day because you will soon be on a north-facing and tree-shaded section of the trail. Climb back out of the draw after a small stream crossing. It then levels out and enters a short new-growth forest of lodgepole and spruce. After another 0.5 mile or so, round the bend into the Boulder Brook drainage for an impressive view of the summit of Longs Peak. You can also see the north shoulder of the mountain's massif soaring above and daring you to make the climb above treeline to Granite Pass.

About 4 miles from the trailhead you enter a more mature forest of taller trees. This is a reasonable turnaround point because views are obscured from here until you near treeline; plus, the trail tops out at this point at approximately 10,000 feet, giving you a 1,000-foot gain for the day. If you want to continue, going above treeline is a great climb; the trail is easy to follow and switchbacks widely across the mountainside before sprinting steeply next to some rock outcrops, where you enjoy panoramic views as Mount Lady Washington and Storm Peak come into view. Reaching Granite Pass is always a thrill because it is part of the summit route on Longs Peak. In early spring the trail to the boulder field can virtually be a running stream, so wear waterproof boots if you're hiking the top of this trail in late spring or early summer. Storm Peak is another 1.25 miles (one-way) and 1,300 feet of vertical if you have the irresistible urge to summit a peak.

## Sprague Lake Access

For a route with far fewer people than the Glacier Gorge Trail has and for a more subtle beauty to accompany the solitude, start at the Sprague Lake Picnic Area across from the livery. When you enter the Sprague Lake parking area, follow a one-way spur to the right to the small picnic area and the trailhead. After ascending a short (200 yards), somewhat steep hill, the trail levels out to an easy climb in the lodgepole pine forest. The trail is marked with orange markers on tree limbs. After about 0.5 mile turn left onto a trail signed GLACIER GORGE/BEAR LAKE, and continue to climb to an intersection with the Boulder Brook and Glacier Gorge Trails. Bear straight (south) onto Boulder Brook Trail.

This trail starts gradually for more than 0.3 mile or so and then begins to climb more steeply, eventually narrowing above Boulder Brook. It is a beautiful riparian area and tree-covered glade; the steep trail is a little difficult to follow when you leave the stream. It leaves the stream and wanders between two separate streams before finally intersecting the North Longs Peak Trail. It is impossible not to intersect this trail, but how efficiently you do so depends on your route-finding skills. If you lose the faint trail, continue south until you intersect it. Once you reach the North Longs Peak Trail, turn east (left) to continue to Granite Pass.

*View of the Mummy Range from North Longs Peak Trail*

*Moose are a common sight in Rocky Mountain National Park.*

# chapter 8

# Rocky Mountain National Park: West

## 2–3 HOURS FROM
## DENVER-BOULDER-FORT COLLINS

West of the Continental Divide and over Trail Ridge Road lies another part of the magical kingdom of Rocky Mountain National Park (RMNP). It features the aptly named and majestic Never Summer mountain range; the headwaters of the mighty Colorado River, which is no more than a sparkling stream at this point; the lush, glacier-created Kawuneeche River Valley; and the delights of adjacent Grand Lake, Shadow Mountain Reservoir, Lake Granby, and Monarch Lake. This part of the park is popular but not as crowded as the heavily used eastern slope and has cooler temperatures and more frequent rain showers. It is most easily accessible Memorial Day–mid-October, while Trail Ridge Road is open, and it closes when the snows make it too dangerous to navigate.

### Trail Ridge Road

Trail Ridge Road is the highest continuous road in the United States, topping out at more than 12,000 feet, and is one of the most spectacular rides on the planet. It is a worthwhile drive, in spite of the slow traffic and crowds. Some prefer to experience the ride on a bike. Get an early start to avoid the afternoon thunderstorms and the heavy motor home and trailer traffic, as well as the fumes and hazards that come with them.

There are some short high-altitude hikes on top near the visitor center for those who can tolerate altitude. Driving the entire route, taking short family jaunts, enjoying the viewpoints, and stopping at the visitor center can take up most of a day. You'll need warm clothing because the temperatures rarely exceed the 60s and the breeze is usually chilly, regardless of the season. The temperature is usually at least 20 degrees cooler than Estes Park or Grand Lake, especially early in the morning or late in the afternoon or evening. The road can close suddenly (temporarily) at any time if it is hit by a hailstorm or snowstorm—not unusual during any month of the year. When you see the lack of guardrails and the thousands of feet you would plummet if you drove off the road, you will understand that it cannot be navigated when it's slick. The road usually opens Memorial Day weekend and closes for the winter by late October or early November.

---

**114** **Ute Trail**

ROCKY MOUNTAIN NATIONAL PARK: WEST

see map on p. 225

| | |
|---|---|
| **Distance** | Up to 8 miles, out-and-back and point to point options |
| **Difficulty** | Easy–challenging |
| **Elevation Gain** | From Trail Ridge trailhead: 300' (starting at 11,500'); |
| | From Upper Beaver Meadows trailhead: 3,000' (starting at 8,400') |
| **Trail Use** | Hiking, snowshoeing, skiing, option for kids |

| | |
|---|---|
| **Agency** | Rocky Mountain National Park |
| **Map(s)** | Trails Illustrated *Rocky Mountain National Park* |
| **Facilities** | Restrooms at Upper Beaver Meadows |
| **Note(s)** | Bikes and dogs are not allowed on trails in Rocky Mountain National Park. Be aware that lightning strikes are common and deadly above treeline on this trail. If a storm is approaching, descend as quickly as you can and take precautions. Park fee required. |

**HIGHLIGHTS** This first trail you reach as you crest Trail Ridge Road is above treeline through the tundra and has sensational views of Forest Canyon and one of the more amazing alpine massifs in the world. The parking lot is tiny, so carpooling and an early start are necessary to beat fellow hikers and the common lightning and thunderstorms that often start around 11 a.m. You can also climb up from the Lower Beaver Meadows Trailhead, where there is ample parking.

**DIRECTIONS** When you reach Estes Park on CO 34, continue to the third traffic light and you will see a sign for RMNP. Turn left at the sign and go up a hill, bear right at the stop sign, and then bear right at the intersection 0.5 mile after the next traffic light. You will see signs for the Beaver Meadows Visitor Center, which is worth a stop to see the overall map of the park, the fairly specific trail maps for areas such as Bear Lake, and a 3-D map graphically depicting the dramatic terrain in which you will be immersed. You can also fill your water bottles there. One trailhead for this route is on Trail Ridge Road, 13.5 miles west of Beaver Meadows and approximately 5 miles east of the Alpine Visitor Center. The parking is limited to only about three vehicles, but there is space for another three about 0.5 mile west. The other trailhead is at the bottom of Trail Ridge Road, 0.8 mile from the Beaver Meadows entrance; turn left and drive less than a mile up the dirt road to the Upper Beaver Meadows Trailhead. The Upper Beaver Meadows Trailhead takes you to the Ute Trail.

An easy and breathtaking jaunt above treeline with little elevation gain or loss, this route will have you walking on the clouds. Or you can take a challenging car-shuttle hike downhill 3,000 feet to Upper Beaver Meadows or uphill 3,000 feet from Upper Beaver Meadows to the trailhead on top of Trail Ridge. If you want, you can do a simple out-and-back trip for up to 3 miles and only have to climb about 100 feet; this option takes you uphill 100 feet for the first 0.25 mile from the parking area. You enjoy immediate and continuously exciting views and are surrounded by a marvelous rock garden. When you catch your breath, you have 0.25 mile of level trail before descending about 80 feet over the next 0.5 mile.

The trail climbs to top out around 11,600 feet, with a view of nature's rock sculpture on Tombstone Ridge, and then descends 100 feet past the ridge and reaches Timberline Pass in about 0.75 mile, 2 miles from the upper trailhead. There, you can enjoy the view of Beaver Mountain before the path plunges 2,000 feet over the next 2 miles into Windy Gulch and then traverses around Beaver Mountain with great views of Longs Peak and the Continental Divide massif. As you descend, you see the artistically twisted krummholz trees that have been stunted by the severe environment. Descend another 1,000 feet, more gradually, over the next 2.5 miles into Beaver Meadows.

In case you're interested, the Ute Trail also has a segment from the Alpine Visitor Center that parallels the road downhill to Milner Pass.

### GREAT FOR KIDS

At the 1-mile mark you are only 0.5 mile from getting an impressive peek at Tombstone Ridge. If you have had enough and want to avoid additional climbing at high altitude, have a snack or some water and turn around. But if you and your party are, however, feeling well at altitude, climb up a little to a high point around 11,600 feet, and enjoy Tombstone Ridge before reversing course.

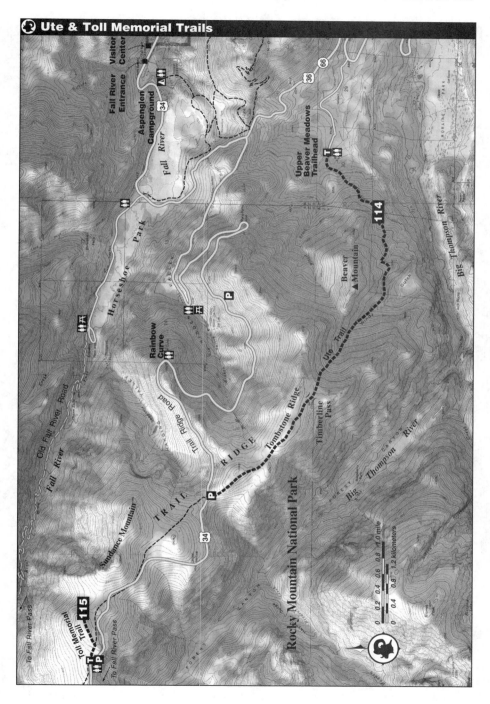

Ute & Toll Memorial Trails

## 115 Toll Memorial Trail

ROCKY MOUNTAIN NATIONAL PARK: WEST

| | |
|---|---|
| **Distance** | 1 mile, out-and-back |
| **Difficulty** | Easy |
| **Elevation Gain** | 260' (starting at 12,110') |
| **Trail Use** | Hiking, great for kids |
| **Agency** | Rocky Mountain National Park |
| **Map(s)** | Trails Illustrated *Rocky Mountain National Park* |
| **Facilities** | Restrooms at trailhead |
| **Note(s)** | Bikes and dogs are not allowed on trails in Rocky Mountain National Park. Park fee required. |

**HIGHLIGHTS** This exciting, short, high-altitude tundra stroll features superb views and pretty wildflowers.
**DIRECTIONS** When you reach Estes Park on CO 34, continue to the third traffic light and you will see a sign for RMNP. Turn left at the sign and go up a hill, bear right at the stop sign, and then bear right at the intersection 0.5 mile after the next traffic light. You will see signs for the Beaver Meadows Visitor Center, which is worth a stop to see the overall map of the park, the fairly specific trail maps for areas such as Bear Lake, and a 3-D map graphically depicting the dramatic terrain in which you will be immersed. You can also fill your water bottles there. From either entrance, take Trail Ridge Road (CO 34) up to the world of tundra at just under 12,000 feet. This is your third opportunity to stop once you crest the ridge and will be on the right (north) side of the road where you see a sign and restrooms.

**W**alk slowly uphill to avoid becoming light-headed if you aren't used to high altitudes. The trail is bordered by rock formations on the right that are fun for scrambling if you feel OK. When you reach the end of the trail, you'll have a great view of the Mummy Range to the north; Chapin, Chiquita, and Ypsilon Mountains are the closest summits.

## 116 Mount Ida

ROCKY MOUNTAIN NATIONAL PARK: WEST

| | |
|---|---|
| **Distance** | 11.5 miles, out-and-back |
| **Difficulty** | Moderate |
| **Elevation Gain** | 2,110' (starting at 10,700') |
| **Trail Use** | Hiking, snowshoeing |
| **Agency** | Rocky Mountain National Park |
| **Map(s)** | Trails Illustrated *Rocky Mountain National Park* |
| **Facilities** | Restrooms at trailhead |
| **Note(s)** | Bikes and dogs are not allowed on trails in Rocky Mountain National Park. Park fee required. |

**HIGHLIGHTS** One of the most accessible high peaks in the park with a very high trailhead, this is a mountaineering experience and summit climb that can be accomplished with much less exertion than most. You will enjoy a spectacular 360-degree view from the top and nonstop views along the way.
**DIRECTIONS** When you reach Estes Park on CO 34, continue to the third traffic light and you will see a sign for RMNP. Turn left at the sign on Moraine Street and go up a hill, bear right at the stop sign, and then bear right at the intersection 0.5 mile after the next traffic light. You will see signs for the Beaver Meadows Visitor Center, which is worth a stop to see the overall map of the park, the fairly specific trail maps for areas such as Bear Lake, and a 3-D map graphically depicting the dramatic terrain in which you will be immersed. You can also fill your water bottles there. Take Trail Ridge Road west, up and over the Continental Divide, and past the Alpine Visitor Center. Go to the Milner Pass parking lot that is about 4 miles west of the Alpine Visitor Center.

**D**on't be lulled by the easy accessibility of this peak climb, as I once was. You should not undertake this trek unless you are well acclimated, fit, and well prepared for thunderstorms. Take the usual precautions by getting an early start and bringing waterproof cool weather gear. The T-shirt, shorts, and poncho I wore when I hiked Ida the first time were inadequate.

The somewhat steep switchbacks start from the back of the parking lot and travel gradually to the east as they climb the steep slope toward treeline. As you climb toward the ridgetop, you have impressive views down-valley to the Never Summer Range. Once it tops out, the trail travels more gradually in a traversing fashion to the south and enters the world of tundra in another mile, approximately 2 miles from the trailhead. You are rolling next to the tundra, with unnamed high spots nearby. The trail levels somewhat and then climbs gently. The trail climbs more steeply for the last 2 miles and becomes sketchier, but the route to the distant high spot is fairly obvious.

*View of Mount Ida*

---

**117** **Colorado River Trail to Little Yellowstone Canyon**
ROCKY MOUNTAIN NATIONAL PARK: WEST

see map on p. 228

| | |
|---|---|
| **Distance** | 7.4 miles to Lulu City, up to 10 miles to Little Yellowstone; out-and-back |
| **Difficulty** | Easy–moderate, depending on distance |
| **Elevation Gain** | Lulu City: 350'; Little Yellowstone: 990' (starting at 8,950') |
| **Trail Use** | Hiking, snowshoeing, skiing, option for kids |
| **Agency** | Rocky Mountain National Park |
| **Map(s)** | Trails Illustrated *Rocky Mountain National Park* |
| **Facilities** | Restrooms at trailhead |
| **Note(s)** | Bikes and dogs are not allowed on trails in Rocky Mountain National Park. Park fee required. |

**HIGHLIGHTS** This interesting, easy trail up a beautiful riparian valley goes through a mining ghost town that was home to 200 people and has many historic memories. Climbing up to see the appropriately named small canyon is a treat, not only for the canyon view but also because of the commanding, peaceful view of one of the most idyllic-looking river valleys on the continent.

**DIRECTIONS** You can reach Grand Lake from Denver by driving west on I-70 to Berthoud Pass and then north on US 40, through Winter Park and Grandby. Follow signs to CO 34 and RMNP, Grand Lake entrance station. The Colorado River Trail parking lot is 10 miles east from the Grand Lake entrance station. It is the last lot before Trail Ridge Road goes steeply uphill. If you're approaching RMNP on CO 34, when you reach Estes Park continue to the third traffic light and you will see a sign for the park. Turn left at the sign on Moraine Street, and go up a hill, bear right at the stop sign, and then bear right at the

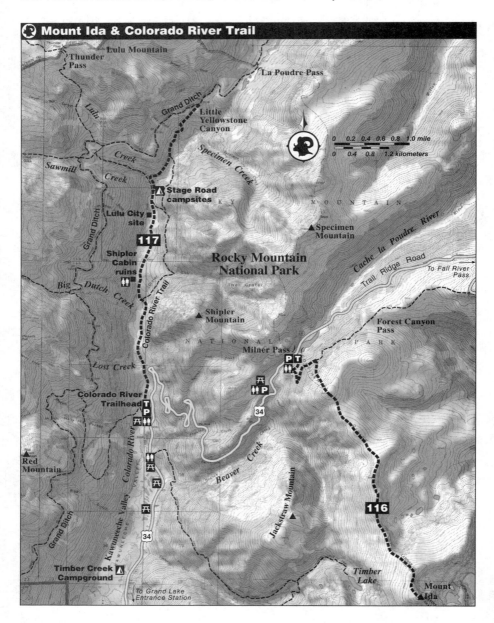

**Mount Ida & Colorado River Trail**

intersection 0.5 mile after the next traffic light. You will see signs for the Beaver Meadows Visitor Center, which is worth a stop to see the overall map of the park, the fairly specific trail maps for areas such as Bear Lake, and a 3-D map graphically depicting the dramatic terrain in which you will be immersed. You can also fill your water bottles there. Drive up and over Trail Ridge Road and look for the first trailhead on the right after reaching the bottom, or the last trailhead from the west.

The trail starts at the east end of the parking lot and goes straight uphill on a steep switchback before leveling off into a fairly gentle roll all the way to Lulu. It starts in unremarkable lodgepole pine for the first 0.25 mile but then gets interesting over the next 0.5 mile as the trail crosses the tributary streams (maybe even Squeak Creek) of the Colorado River three times. The trail is then riverside, and the small meadows and stream bank make good picnic spots for those with small children or ambitions. At the 0.5-mile mark continue straight when you reach an intersection with a trail to Thunder Pass (9.2 miles) and the Grand Ditch (2.8 miles). You will be 3.2 miles from Lulu, 4 miles from the lower part of Little Yellowstone Canyon, and 1.8 miles from the ruins of the Shipler Cabin. The meadows offer tantalizing peak views of Howard Mountain and Mount Cirrus to the north through the spruce trees and columbine flowers that grace the trail. At just more than 1 mile, the trail climbs again, ascending about 70 feet as it tracks away from the river.

At 1.5 miles it climbs again in earnest, ascending another 100 feet, and then drops through a meadow, with cliffs soaring above. For the next 0.5 mile, the trail edges next to the thousands of tons of rockslides that have thundered into the valley over time. You cross Crater Creek as Lead Mountain comes into view across the pretty meadow. You reach what is left of the Shipler Cabin at approximately 2.3 miles; there is a hikers' privy on the north side of the trail.

The trail steepens again and climbs around 200 feet over the next mile through thick trees; mosquitoes will keep you company if you feel lonely. Around the 3-mile mark you notice that the trees are draped with fungi commonly called Spanish moss. It is actually a parasite that can strangle a tree over time in its green gossamer web. When you reach another trail intersection, signs explain that you are 0.2 mile from Lulu, 2 miles from the Michigan Ditch, 3.7 miles from Thunder Pass, 1 mile from Little Yellowstone, and 4 miles from Poudre Pass. Cross Sawmill/Specimen Creek, and the trees open up into mixed forest, with aspen joining the Engelmann spruce and pine. Go downhill to the left (north) to the Lulu site if that is your goal. If you want to go all the way to Little Yellowstone Canyon, continue straight along an almost level path that travels along a low ridge around 9,500 feet that gives you a commanding view of the multicolored greens of the riparian valley at your feet.

The trail then turns to the northeast as it climbs steeply into a wide, eroded drainage, showing nature in action carving a canyon. You come to another trail intersection, where you can go back 0.8 mile to Lulu or 1 mile to the Stage Road campsites. There is an impressive view back across the valley as you climb up and cross a bridge. Then you reenter trees and switchback uphill as the trail climbs quickly to 9,800 feet. As you top the ridge, part of the Little Yellowstone opens up before you, and there is a two-person rock, good for lunch or a snack. That is approximately the 4.5-mile mark projected as your destination. If you are willing to climb another 100 feet and hike another 0.5 mile you are in for a real treat—a much better view of the canyon, a spectacular view of the Kawuneeche (Arapaho Indian for "coyote") Valley, a few peaks in the background, and a graceful waterfall. Cross two more drainages and climb to 9,900 feet for your reward. If you didn't see Lulu on the way up, take one of the two available detours on the way back to see the town site; then merge with the main trail and head back to your starting point.

### GREAT FOR KIDS

The Shipler Cabin is a good turnaround point for families with small children or those hikers with modest goals. The cabin ruins are much more than you will see at Lulu City, where most traces of the town are long gone.

### 118   Baker Gulch to Mount Nimbus & Mount Stratus

ROCKY MOUNTAIN NATIONAL PARK: WEST, ARAPAHO NATIONAL FOREST

|  |  |
|---|---|
| **Distance** | 7.4 miles to Baker Gulch, 10 miles to Baker Pass, 12 miles to Mount Nimbus, 12.8 miles to Mount Stratus; out-and-back |
| **Difficulty** | Moderate–challenging |
| **Elevation Gain** | Baker Pass: 2,305'; Mount Nimbus: 3,755'; Mount Stratus: 3,555' (starting at 8,950') |
| **Trail Use** | Hiking, snowshoeing |
| **Agency** | Rocky Mountain National Park; Never Summer Wilderness, Sulphur Ranger District, Arapaho National Forest |
| **Map(s)** | Trails Illustrated *Rocky Mountain National Park* |
| **Facilities** | Restrooms and picnic area at trailhead |
| **Note(s)** | Bikes and dogs are not allowed on trails in Rocky Mountain National Park. Park fee required. |

**HIGHLIGHTS** This is a hike across a river valley, through trees and vales and into a gorgeous valley bordered by mountains with a riot of wildflowers in the spring and early summer, meadows that roll to the horizon, and the possibility of more challenging climbs to either Parika Lake or the top of Mount Nimbus.

**DIRECTIONS** You can reach Grand Lake from Denver by driving west on I-70 to Berthoud Pass and then north on US 40, through Winter Park and Grandby. Follow signs to CO 34 and RMNP, Grand Lake entrance station. The Colorado River Trail parking lot is 6.5 miles east from the Grand Lake entrance station. It is the last lot before Trail Ridge Road goes steeply uphill. If you're approaching RMNP on CO 34, when you reach Estes Park continue to the third traffic light and you will see a sign for the park. Turn left at the sign on Moraine Street and go up a hill, bear right at the stop sign, and then bear right at the intersection 0.5 mile after the next traffic light. You will see signs for the Beaver Meadows Visitor Center, which is worth a stop to see the overall map of the park, the fairly specific trail maps for areas such as Bear Lake, and a 3-D map graphically depicting the dramatic terrain in which you will be immersed. You can also fill your water bottles there. Drive up and over Trail Ridge Road and look for the second trailhead on the right after reaching the bottom. Use the Baker and Bowen Trailhead, 6.5 miles from the Grand Lake entrance station and visitor center.

From the trailhead you cross a long meadows area with beautiful views of the riparian valley and towering peaks. You then enter a lodgepole pine forest that might make you think this will be a dull hike. Your trek through the trees takes you out of Rocky Mountain National Park and into Roosevelt National Forest. Once you hit Baker Gulch, the fun begins as you trek west and northwest. The lodgepoles give way to a beautiful mixed aspen forest, and then wildflowers begin to dot the landscape. The trail winds upward, opening up with a view of a very steep shoulder of Baker Mountain.

After 3.5 miles you reach the magnificent meadows of Baker Pass. If you go no farther, you will be happy. If, however, you are mesmerized by the high mountain meadows and drawn by the blanket of wildflowers to go all the way up, north to the top of Baker Pass, continue to the peaks. Around 5 miles from the trailhead, you see the tempting summit of Mount Nimbus with an unalluring scree and rock route to the top; scramble away because from the top of Mount Nimbus, you will enjoy an unparalleled panorama. Thunderstorms permitting, you are but a short ridge walk away from Mount Stratus.

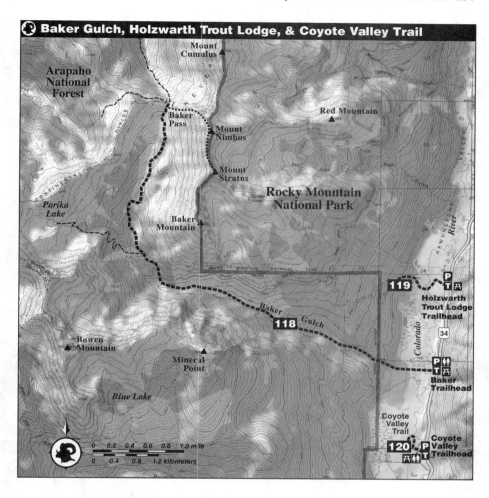

### Baker Gulch, Holzwarth Trout Lodge, & Coyote Valley Trail

---

**119**  **Holzwarth Trout Lodge**

ROCKY MOUNTAIN NATIONAL PARK: WEST

| | |
|---|---|
| **Distance** | 1 mile, out-and-back |
| **Difficulty** | Easy |
| **Elevation Gain** | Negligible (starting at 9,000') |
| **Trail Use** | Hiking, snowshoeing, skiing, great for kids |
| **Agency** | Rocky Mountain National Park |
| **Map(s)** | Trails Illustrated *Rocky Mountain National Park* |
| **Facilities** | Restrooms and picnic area at trailhead |
| **Note(s)** | Bikes and dogs are not allowed on trails in Rocky Mountain National Park. Park fee required. |

**HIGHLIGHTS**  This is the largest group of restored, historic structures in the park. This stroll through the middle of the Colorado River Valley includes a view of the Zirkel range in the distance and gives you a sense of what life was like more than a century ago in what was once a remote piece of paradise.

You might even see moose lurking about. During the summer months (June–September) a golf cart shuttle is available for the disabled.

**DIRECTIONS**  You can reach Grand Lake from Denver by driving west on I-70 to Berthoud Pass and then north on US 40, through Winter Park and Grandby. Follow signs to CO 34 and RMNP, Grand Lake entrance station. The Colorado River Trail parking lot is 8 miles east of the Grand Lake entrance station. It is the last lot before Trail Ridge Road goes steeply uphill. If you're approaching RMNP on CO 34, when you reach Estes Park continue to the third traffic light and you will see a sign for RMNP. Turn left at the sign on Moraine Street and go up a hill, bear right at the stop sign, and then bear right at the intersection 0.5 mile after the next traffic light. You will see signs for the Beaver Meadows Visitor Center, which is worth a stop to see the overall map of the park, the fairly specific trail maps for areas such as Bear Lake, and a 3-D map graphically depicting the dramatic terrain in which you will be immersed. You can also fill your water bottles there. Drive up and over Trail Ridge Road and look for the first trailhead on the right after reaching the bottom. The lodge is 8 miles from the Grand Lake entrance station and visitor center.

One of the cabins is next to the parking lot, while the others are a short, flat hop away on a doubletrack dirt road that is ideal for family strolls. When you cross the Colorado River, look west and enjoy the view of the distant Zirkel range. Bear left when you reach the edge of the forest. The road splits, and you will see the cabins slightly uphill. There is a golf cart shuttle for the disabled. The walk up to the cabins is short and easy and worth the trip back in time to a different era.

*Holzwarth Trout Lodge*

**120** **Coyote Valley Trail**

ROCKY MOUNTAIN NATIONAL PARK: WEST

see
map on
p. 231

| | |
|---|---|
| **Distance** | 1 mile, out-and-back |
| **Difficulty** | Easy |
| **Elevation Gain** | Negligible (starting at 9,000') |
| **Trail Use** | Hiking, snowshoeing, skiing, great for kids |
| **Agency** | Rocky Mountain National Park |
| **Map(s)** | Trails Illustrated *Rocky Mountain National Park* |
| **Facilities** | Restrooms and picnic tables at trailhead |
| **Note(s)** | Bikes and dogs are not allowed on trails in Rocky Mountain National Park. Park fee required. |

**HIGHLIGHTS** Another terrific handicapped-accessible trail, this route is frequented by moose, elk, musk-rats, otters, osprey, red-tailed hawks, voles, and shrews, to mention a few of the critters highlighted in the nature stops. This pretty trail accompanies the river on a short loop with views of Baker Mountain.

**DIRECTIONS** You can reach Grand Lake from Denver by driving west on I-70 to Berthoud Pass and then north on US 40, through Winter Park and Grandby. Follow signs to CO 34 and RMNP, Grand Lake entrance station. The Colorado River Trail parking lot is 6 miles east of the Grand Lake entrance station. It is the last lot before Trail Ridge Road goes steeply uphill. If you're approaching RMNP on CO 34, when you reach Estes Park continue to the third traffic light and you will see a sign for RMNP. Turn left at the sign on Moraine Street and go up a hill, bear right at the stop sign, and then bear right at the intersection 0.5 mile after the next traffic light. You will see signs for the Beaver Meadows Visitor Center, which is worth a stop to see the overall map of the park, the fairly specific trail maps for areas such as Bear Lake, and a 3-D map graphically depicting the dramatic terrain in which you will be immersed. You can also fill your water bottles there. Drive up and over Trail Ridge Road and look for the first trailhead on the right after reaching the bottom. The trailhead is 6 miles from the Grand Lake entrance station and visitor center.

The trail goes north from the parking lot and restrooms. After you cross the river, go left for a short picnic table loop or right for the guided nature tour along the river. There is a nice detour down to the river at the first stop. You pass some Engelmann spruce and lodgepole pine trees on the way, along with wildflowers and, if you're lucky, wildlife. You can enjoy views of Baker Mountain (12,397 feet) from anywhere along the trail. The farther you go, the more of the valley view you'll see. Plus you get to enjoy the Colorado River in its "infancy." Hawks often soar above the valley. Watch for moose and elk among the trees.

*Coyote Valley Trail*

### 121  East Inlet & Thunder Lake Trails

ROCKY MOUNTAIN NATIONAL PARK: WEST

| | |
|---|---|
| **Distance** | 0.3 mile–11 miles, point to point |
| **Difficulty** | Easy–challenging |
| **Elevation Gain** | Adams Falls: 80'; Wild Basin Trailhead: 3,600' (starting at 8,400') |
| **Trail Use** | Hiking, snowshoeing, skiing, option for kids (Adams Falls) |
| **Agency** | Rocky Mountain National Park |
| **Map(s)** | Trails Illustrated *Rocky Mountain National Park* |
| **Facilities** | Restrooms, picnic area, and ranger station at trailhead |
| **Note(s)** | Bikes and dogs are not allowed on trails in Rocky Mountain National Park. |

**HIGHLIGHTS** This stroll is ideal for photographers who don't want a major adventure but are looking for a real treat. The short trail offers several vantage points of the waterfall and the arroyo in which it resides. The lush meadows and wetlands just around the bend of the East Inlet Trail will tempt you to take a longer hike. You can take the trail for enjoyable hikes of almost any length, even an 11-mile trek to beautiful Lone Pine Lake or 17 miles one-way over the Continental Divide to Wild Basin if you like bushwhacking and route-finding, or take the all-day moderate hike to Lone Pine Lake.

**DIRECTIONS** You can reach Grand Lake from Denver by driving west on I-70 to Berthoud Pass and then north on US 40, through Winter Park and Granby. Follow signs to CO 34, RMNP, and the town of Grand Lake. Drive to the Grand Lake town entrance. Take an immediate left on the first paved road and follow it to the end 2.3 miles ahead. If you prefer, you can reach Grand Lake over Trail Ridge Road from Estes Park.

*Thunder Lake*

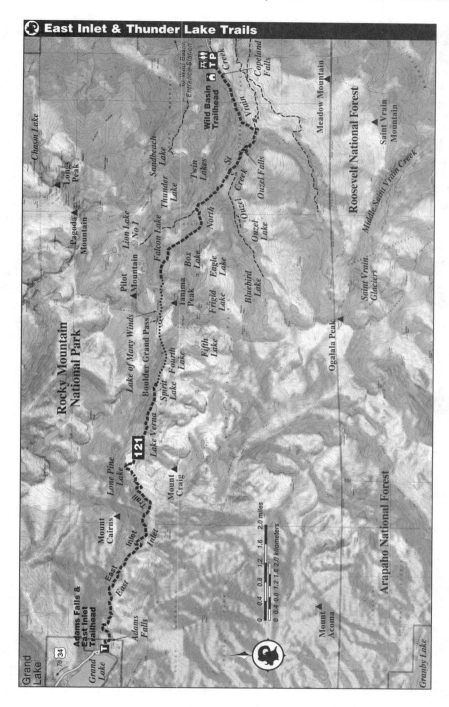

**East Inlet & Thunder Lake Trails**

Go downhill immediately after leaving the parking lot and then uphill through aspen and lodgepole pine trees. When you reach the trail intersection, turn right and go downhill to Adams Falls. To complete the loop, go somewhat steeply uphill and intersect the main trail, where you turn left to return to the lot. I highly recommend going at least another 200 yards to the right to take in a little more of East Inlet Trail. After rounding the bend, enjoy a magnificent view of the expansive grassy meadows and distant rock outcrops carved by glaciers.

If you have time to explore farther, take the trail as it edges the lake before finally climbing gently after 0.75 mile. The farther you go, the higher you will go, letting you enjoy a more sweeping view of this gorgeous riparian scene. The trail rolls gently for 3 miles before it climbs steeply out of the valley up to Lone Pine Lake, which is 5.5 miles from the trailhead. The trail to Lone Pine Lake is worth an adventure of any length.

Just turn around when you become weary. The trail is a rolling route that steadily gains altitude to the lake with many viewpoints. If you have the time and energy and have set up a car shuttle at Wild Basin, you can continue over the Continental Divide and to the southern portion of Rocky Mountain National Park in Wild Basin.

I have only hiked the route from east to west from Wild Basin via Thunder Lake and Grand Pass to Grand Lake. Either way you can enjoy the string of lakes—Verna, Spirit, Fourth, and more—that sit nestled in the thick evergreen forest. The trickiest and most challenging part of the hike is connecting from Grand Pass to the East Inlet Trail or vice versa. You must have good map-and-compass skills to traverse successfully and complete your trek in a single, very long day. Alternatively, you can turn it into a more relaxing backpack or an out-and-back to as many lakes as you want to see in a day.

## 122  Monarch Lake to Brainard Lake

ARAPAHO NATIONAL FOREST

| | |
|---|---|
| **Distance** | 0.7 mile to end of Monarch Lake, 15 miles to Brainard Lake; point to point |
| **Difficulty** | Easy–challenging, depending on distance hiked |
| **Elevation Gain** | 4,000' (starting at 8,340') |
| **Trail Use** | Hiking, camping, fishing, snowshoeing, skiing, option for kids |
| **Agency** | Arapaho National Recreation Area and Indian Peaks Wilderness, Sulphur Ranger District, Arapaho National Forest |
| **Map(s)** | Trails Illustrated *Kremmling & Granby* |
| **Facilities** | Restroom and campground near trailhead |
| **Note(s)** | Bikes and dogs are not allowed on trails in Rocky Mountain National Park. |

**HIGHLIGHTS** Outside Rocky Mountain National Park, this hike offers anything from an easy lakeside, wetlands, and meadow stroll to a challenging out-and-back trek to Pawnee Pass in the Indian Peaks on the east side of the Continental Divide or even a point-to-point adventure over the Divide and to Brainard Lake. Along the way expect to hike next to a sparkling stream and to savor picturesque lakes. The trail is in Arapaho National Forest and is adjacent to RMNP.

**DIRECTIONS** The trailhead isn't easy to find, nor is it very difficult. You can reach Grand Lake from Denver by driving west on I-70 to Berthoud Pass, and then north on US 40, through Winter Park and Granby. Follow signs to CO 34 and RMNP, and the town of Grand Lake. Take CO 34 approximately 12 miles from Grand Lake to the south side of Granby Lake. Follow signs for Arapaho Bay left (east). The gravel road edges along Lake Granby and then Arapaho Bay, before winding its way back to the Monarch Lake Trailhead.

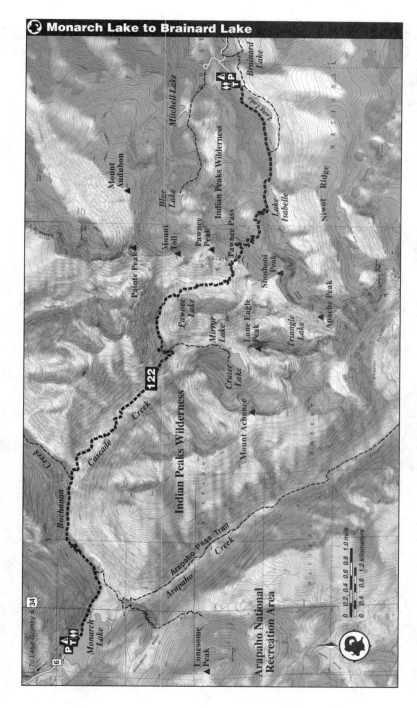

Monarch Lake to Brainard Lake

*The Continental Divide soars above Brainard Lake.*

You can enjoy the beauty of Monarch Lake at the trailhead. The trail follows the cascading creek most of the way to the Buchanan and Pawnee Pass intersection and is a very nice round-trip of approximately 6 miles.

To go to Pawnee Pass, bear right (southeast). The intersection is near the Shelter Rock backcountry campsite, a good place for lunch or a snack unless you prefer to be streamside. The climbing begins in earnest after this intersection but is highlighted by tumbling, babbling Cascade Creek. It is a steep trek to Pawnee Lake, more than 6 miles from the trailhead, but the lake is a marvelous destination. It is another mile up steep switchbacks to the top of Pawnee Pass. From there you can either reverse course for a challenging 14-mile day or continue to Brainard Lake, about 3 miles below, and your car shuttle.

## GREAT FOR KIDS

The first 0.75 mile of this trail is next to Monarch Lake and offers great scenery, wildlife, and photo opportunities. On hot days you might want to get your feet wet in the lake. You can take a family jaunt for a picnic hike and turn around when you have seen enough of pretty Buchanan Creek.

*Crosier Mountain trailhead; photographed by Jeff Eighmy*

# chapter 9

# Fort Collins Area

## 30 MINUTES–1 HOUR FROM FORT COLLINS
## 1–2 HOURS FROM DENVER-BOULDER

Fort Collins had the foresight to preserve and create a superb variety of city parks. The city is a relatively recent arrival to the natural area and open space arena, thanks to a dedicated group of local open space advocates. While Boulder was the first arrival to the open space altar, Fort Collins and Larimer County have done an outstanding job of acquisition, and their trails and natural areas are second to none.

### Fort Collins Trail System

The city of Fort Collins is surrounded by some of the best recreational trails in the nation, the kind that make you feel like you have escaped to the rivers, foothills, parks, and pastures of rural America. The trails essentially circle the city and provide not only recreation but also transportation opportunities that are far more pleasant than climbing behind the wheel of a car. My favorite part of the trail system is the section that runs along the Poudre River, though every section of the trail offers something to enjoy. At about 4,950 feet, Fort Collins is a little lower in elevation than Boulder and Denver, both of which are over 5,000 feet; Colorado Springs is around 6,000 feet. The trails on the west side of town are a bit higher, and the trails around the reservoir, including Centennial Drive, are between 5,500 and 6,000 feet high. So altitude isn't a major factor, unless you have just arrived from sea level.

I go out of my way to commute on my bike and incorporate as much of the trail system into my commutes and errands as possible. By using bike routes and the trail

system, you can create some pleasant commutes and avoid traffic. The city of Fort Collins can be commended for providing this great system that gives a real small town community feel to the big city Fort Collins is becoming, and the city is still building the system. In 2005 the city acquired the Soapstone Prairie Natural Area approximately 40 minutes north of Fort Collins and adjacent to the also magnificent Red Mountain Natural Area purchased by Larimer County in 2005. I have added trails in this impressive ecosystem to this edition. Short ranger-led annual hikes to archaeological sites, as well as longer options for hiking, biking, and horseback riding, are available.

### Lory State Park

One of the gems of the state park system, this once lightly used park has been discovered. Its easy access from Fort Collins (30–45 minutes) makes it even more attractive to hikers, mountain bikers, and horseback riders. There are easy, intermediate, and challenging trails, highlighted on the east by the serrated rocks of the hogback hills and blue water of the Horsetooth Reservoir. The steep foothills to the west are topped by dramatic Arthur's Rock and its craggy neighbors. A lot of picnic spots and even some overnight campsites are accessible to backpackers (reservations are required). The most striking feature of this state park is Arthur's Rock, a multifaceted summit of rock outcrops that is prominent from the east-side trails and involves a 1,200-foot moderate hike and rock scramble to enjoy its commanding panorama.

## Larimer County

Larimer County has also added significantly to its collection of beautiful open spaces and natural areas, with acquisitions such as the Devil's Backbone and Blue Sky trail system, Eagle's Nest, and the magnificent piece of the foothills ecosystem called Red Mountain, 30–40 minutes north of Fort Collins (adjacent to the Soapstone property acquired by the city of Fort Collins). Check **co.larimer.co.us** for updates and details.

The 16-mile Devil's Backbone and Blue Sky trail system rivals anything in the state for variety and scenery. It is a roller-coaster trail with an overall elevation change of 500 feet in, on, and around the unique environment of the Rocky Mountain foothills. Part of it is a technical mountain biking route, though there are sections that are easy to moderate. If you want to hike the entire trail in a single day, you'll need to arrange a car shuttle unless you are an ultra-marathoner in training. The three primary access points to this slice of paradise are from the north, Horsetooth Mountain Open Space or Inlet Bay west of Fort Collins; in the middle, from Coyote Ridge southwest of Fort Collins; and from the south, the Devil's Backbone Trail outside of Loveland.

## Horsetooth Mountain Open Space

Horsetooth Mountain and Rock are prominent features of the skyline west of Fort Collins. A landmark visible from remarkable distances, Horsetooth Rock visually morphs into shapes not resembling teeth from the south and west, making it an interesting geological feature. Horsetooth Mountain Open Space offers a large network of trails, some that connect to Lory State Park in the north and others that connect to the Blue Sky Trail in the south. The trail to the top of Horsetooth Rock is one of the most popular because of the 360-degree views that include 14,000-foot Longs Peak to the southwest and unfolding foothills and the sprawling plains to the east. It is a favorite hike for sunrise, sunset, and full-moon rambles.

## Glen Haven Trails

The Glen Haven Trails are on the way to Rocky Mountain National Park (RMNP) and Estes Park and offer access to beautiful areas near RMNP that are less known and less busy than some areas of the park. These foothills trails offer mountain vistas and gorgeous riparian areas. The North Fork Trail is a little-known backpacking access area to RMNP's Lost Lake. Glen Haven and Drake are small towns just east of Estes Park, west of Loveland, that consist of small stores, restaurants, and several houses visible from the road. The trails offer unique foothills experiences as a dramatic transition zone between the plains and the high mountains.

### 123 Poudre River Trail

CITY OF FORT COLLINS

| | |
|---|---|
| **Distance** | 16.8 miles, out-and-back |
| **Difficulty** | Easy |
| **Elevation Gain** | Negligible (starting at 4,980') |
| **Trail Use** | Hiking, biking, running, horseback riding (on some sections), leashed dogs OK |
| **Agency** | City of Fort Collins |
| **Map(s)** | City of Fort Collins *Trail Map* |
| **Facilities** | Restrooms, picnic areas, and ballfields at Lee Martinez Park; restrooms along trail at Lions Open Space and Environmental Learning Center |

**HIGHLIGHTS** This delightful trail runs near the river as it winds from northwest Fort Collins and Laporte, past lovely Lee Martinez Park, through old town, and past Riverbend Ponds, a large

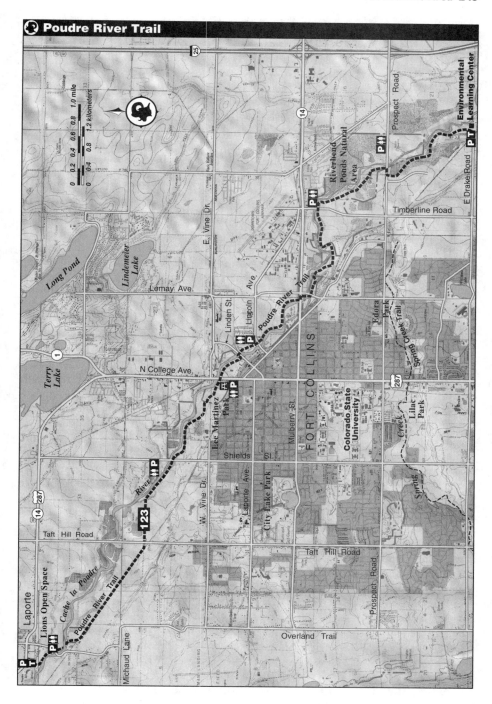

**Poudre River Trail**

open-space area, to East Prospect Road. Along the way you can enjoy the sparkling river's waters and the ever-changing surroundings as you go from rural to urban and back again. It is suitable for biking or hiking.

**DIRECTIONS** Fort Collins is 1–1.5 hours from Denver and Boulder, depending on traffic. You can access the trail from either end—the east end at East Prospect Road or the west end at Cache la Poudre Elementary and Middle Schools—or from the middle at Lee Martinez Park. The description below starts at the west end. If school isn't in session, you can park there and enjoy the small disc golf course before you start. (There is also a well-known source for cinnamon rolls nearby called Vern's.) The trail is next to the entryway for the school on the southwest side of Old US 287.

Starting at the west end, travel south and east around the school's ballfields and join up with the river after 0.5 mile of winding, tree-lined trail. When you reach Lions Open Space, a more reliable place to park when school is in session and a good place for picnics, stop briefly and enjoy a beautiful view of the river bend and foothills. From Lions Open Space the trail goes under Overland Trail Road and then crosses one of the best designed footbridges in Colorado. A walking loop from Lions Open Space to the school and then to the bridge lets you enjoy the river's beauty.

If you want to make a bike ride a little more challenging, take Overland Trail south over the river and turn west to climb Bingham Hill. This little loop won't add more than 3 miles to your journey but is guaranteed to pump up your heart rate to target levels. Catch your breath at the top of the hill, take a good look at the great view of the pastoral Bellvue valley, and return downhill to the trail.

After crossing the Cache la Poudre River on the footbridge, the trail bends east and rolls under power lines, giving you a view of gravel mining operations with the resultant ponds and some pastures. A soft path next to the bike trail is designated for hiking and running. In approximately 1 mile the trail crosses Taft Hill Road; signal lights warn motorists but don't stop them, so cross carefully. On the other side are a parking lot, picnic table, and solar-powered air hose for bikes.

The next stretch of trail is even prettier with two large ponds on both sides of the trail in the first 0.5 mile, and then the trail veers closer to the river. Hikers and mountain bikers can use the soft path that is a bit closer to the shore. Another mile takes you to Shields Street and an underpass. Now the tree-lined trail has interesting and varied soft-path options for snack and water breaks next to the water. You pass a bridge across the river to the north in about 0.5 mile. Hiking and mountain biking options are on the other side, located around two more ponds left by gravel mining that now have good vegetation for waterfowl and people.

At the next trail intersection, Lee Martinez Park, visible south of the trail, has good recreational options and open restrooms during nonfreezing months. Continuing east, cross under North College Avenue; soft-surface options are more limited, and the trail is better for biking than hiking unless you like to run or hike on hard surfaces. You go quite close to the river and then see the Northside Aztlan Center to the southwest, which has restrooms, basketball courts, and a weight room and charges an entry fee. When the trail dead-ends into Linden Street, turn left (north) and cross the river to pick up the trail on the northeast side of the bridge. The next mile follows the river and passes a golf course and then goes under Mulberry Street and to street level at the intersection of Mulberry and Lemay Avenue.

Go right (south) and cross the river again to pick up the bike trail on the right (west) side of the bridge. Cross under the Lemay Avenue river bridge, and continue your trek east. The winding path is lined with trees for the first 0.5 mile, climbs a small hill, and then makes a sharp turn downhill back toward the river. You pass Riverbend Ponds Natural Area and are away from the river until you go under Timberline Road. Enjoy a beautiful stretch of river and then pond views all the way to Prospect Road. The trail goes downhill past one of the ponds and turns south.

At the next trail intersection go left (south), rather than straight, to follow the river and go under Prospect Road. When you emerge on the south side of Prospect, turn left (south) and travel between some office buildings and a couple of ponds that often host blue herons and other impressive winged creatures. Turn left (east) to follow a dirt path between the ponds, which merges back into the paved path a little farther along. Go east and continue to the terminus of the trail at the Environmental Learning Center, where there are restrooms. If you

arrange for a car shuttle, have it fetch you here; otherwise, return to your starting point. If you prefer, you can retrace your route back under Prospect Road and then turn west until you join the Spring Creek Trail toward Edora Park, with a pool and an ice-skating rink.

Starting at Lee Martinez Park and traveling west on the trail also makes for a nice out-and-back; turn around wherever you like, but reaching the bridge across the Poudre River is well worth the effort. Starting at the Environmental Learning Center or from East Prospect Road (use the office building parking lots) makes for a great out-and-back journey along the river; turn around at the intersection at Lemay Avenue where the trail crosses under the road.

## 124  Spring Creek Trail
CITY OF FORT COLLINS

see map on p. 247

| | |
|---|---|
| **Distance** | Up to 13.1 miles, point to point |
| **Difficulty** | Easy |
| **Elevation Gain** | Heading west: 200' (starting at 4,940') |
| **Trail Use** | Hiking, biking, running, option for kids, leashed dogs OK |
| **Agency** | City of Fort Collins |
| **Map(s)** | City of Fort Collins *Trail Map* |
| **Facilities** | Restrooms, picnic areas, playgrounds, and ballfields |

**HIGHLIGHTS** The Spring Creek Trail offers a wide variety of scenery, parks, ponds, meadows, and foothills. This trail follows Spring Creek through several parks in the middle of Fort Collins. It currently extends from West Taft Hill Road to the confluence of Spring Creek and the Poudre River, where it joins the Poudre River Trail. The Spring Creek Trail extends through an underpass of Taft Hill Road. This highly popular segment of the trail goes to Southwest Community Park and the Foothills Natural Areas and offers its own beautiful brand of urban and suburban scenery near the foothills and through Rolland Moore and Edora Parks.

**DIRECTIONS** Fort Collins is 1–1.5 hours from Denver and Boulder, depending on traffic. Take I-25 north to the Prospect Road exit, and then drive west to Lemay Avenue. Turn left (south) to reach the Edora Pool and Ice Rink parking lot.

From the parking lot, travel west under Lemay Avenue, passing through some pretty meadows or wetlands with a good chance to see lots of birds, geese, and other wildlife. You then travel along Spring Creek, go past Spring Creek Park and fire station, join a sidewalk, and go west under College Avenue and through another small park. After proceeding under the railroad tracks

through a tunnel, cross a gravel road and weave around an open area before going under Centre Avenue. The community garden to the south is worth a stop. Continuing on the trail, go uphill past a pond populated with lots of ducks and geese, and then go under Shields Street and reach Rolland Moore Park.

*Foothills view from Spring Creek Trail*

If you still have lots of get-up-and-go, continue through the park, pass the tennis courts and the natural area, bear right, and go under Drake Road and then Taft Hill Road next to meadows. In another mile you reach the Cottonwood Glen Park next to the foothills and options in the Pineridge Natural Area (Trail 126) just over the ridge. Before you reach the park, you can turn left (south) at a trail intersection toward Cathy Fromme Prairie Natural Area.

**GREAT FOR KIDS**

Rolland Moore Park is a good place for a picnic and playground stop if you have children along. The trail beyond this point is another 1.5 miles uphill to the foothills, so you might want to enjoy a snack and water break at the park and then head back to Edora Park.

## 125 Cathy Fromme Prairie Natural Area
CITY OF FORT COLLINS

|  |  |
|---|---|
| **Distance** | 4.6 miles, point to point |
| **Difficulty** | Easy |
| **Elevation Gain** | 100' (starting at 4,980') |
| **Trail Use** | Hiking, biking, running, option for kids, leashed dogs OK |
| **Agency** | City of Fort Collins |
| **Map(s)** | City of Fort Collins *Cathy Fromme Prairie* |
| **Facilities** | Restrooms and parking on Shields and Taft Hill south of Harmony Road; restrooms at trailhead |

**HIGHLIGHTS** One of the earliest acquisitions of the natural areas program, this beautiful example of a short-grass prairie is named for a former Fort Collins City Council member who was an enthusiastic supporter of the program and died young of breast cancer. This paved trail offers foothills and prairie views and is popular with families with bikes and strollers. The western end of the trail offers a roundabout connection to the Foothills and Spring Creek Trails.

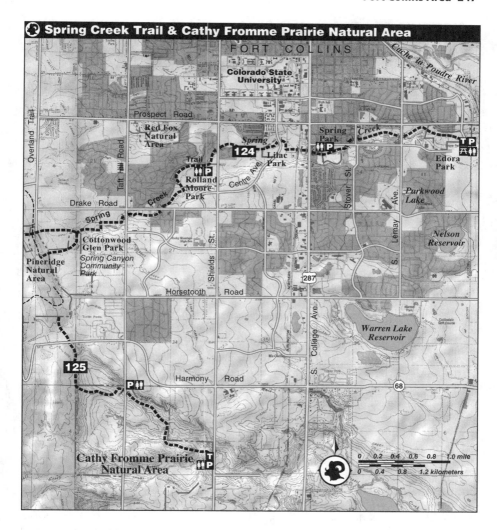

Spring Creek Trail & Cathy Fromme Prairie Natural Area

**DIRECTIONS** Fort Collins is 1–1.5 hours from Denver and Boulder, depending on traffic. The parking lot for the area is approximately 0.75 mile south of the intersection of Harmony Road and Shields Street, on the west side of Shields. There is also parking on Taft Hill Road, approximately 1 mile south of the Harmony Road intersection.

From the parking lot, head southwest for 0.25 mile and visit the raptor observation bunker, where, if you're lucky, you'll see hawks or eagles nesting. Please stay on the trail and hide in the shelter to increase your chances of seeing the birds. When you've enjoyed this area, turn around and go north and west for the main trail. The initial 0.3 mile is a gradual uphill west along the drainage and then goes more sharply northwest and then north as the trail meanders and rolls through the generally dry creek bed. In less than 0.5 mile a side trail connects to Dusty Sage Loop, a street in a residential area next to Harmony Road. In another 0.3 mile the trail crosses under Taft Hill Road and a little more steeply uphill into a foothills subdivision.

*The Cathy Fromme Prairie Natural Area*

In 0.3 mile a side trail connects to Plymouth Road and continues west-northwest uphill and then more directly north, paralleling Red Fox Road to County Road 38E. Turn right (east), go 0.25 mile, and turn left (north) onto Windom Street. Turn left on Baxter and right onto Platte to Horsetooth Road and Spring Canyon Community Park. You can either take a bike path through the park to the north, on the east or west side of the park, to connect to the Spring Creek Trail or go west on Horsetooth Road until it ends at the trailhead.

The biking and hiking trail goes downhill into the trees and then uphill toward the Pineridge Natural Area, where you connect with easy trails after going up and over the steep ridgeline trail that is straight ahead. If you go left (west) when you intersect the Pine Ridge Trail, you are traveling north on a trail with very rocky and steep downhill sections that brings you to the Dixon Dam parking lot. If you go right (north), you'll reach the small east ridge boundary of Pine Ridge. If you've chosen the latter option, look for the second trail on the left, beyond the dog park, that heads over the ridge and down the other side; it intersects with the Spring Creek Trail and ends in Cottonwood Glen Park.

### GREAT FOR KIDS

Taft Hill Road is a good point for people with small children to turn around. After crossing under Taft Hill the trail climbs uphill and ends in a neighborhood. Only continue if you want to add another mile of out and back with somewhat steep up- and downhill.

## 126  Foothills Trail: Pineridge Natural Area
### CITY OF FORT COLLINS AND LARIMER COUNTY PARKS AND OPEN SPACES

|  |  |
|---|---|
| **Distance** | Up to 5 miles, point to point |
| **Difficulty** | Easy |
| **Elevation Gain** | Negligible (starting at 4,980') |
| **Trail Use** | Hiking, mountain biking, running, great for kids, leashed dogs OK |
| **Agency** | City of Fort Collins, Larimer County Parks and Open Spaces |
| **Map(s)** | City of Fort Collins *Pineridge* |
| **Facilities** | Restrooms near parking lot |

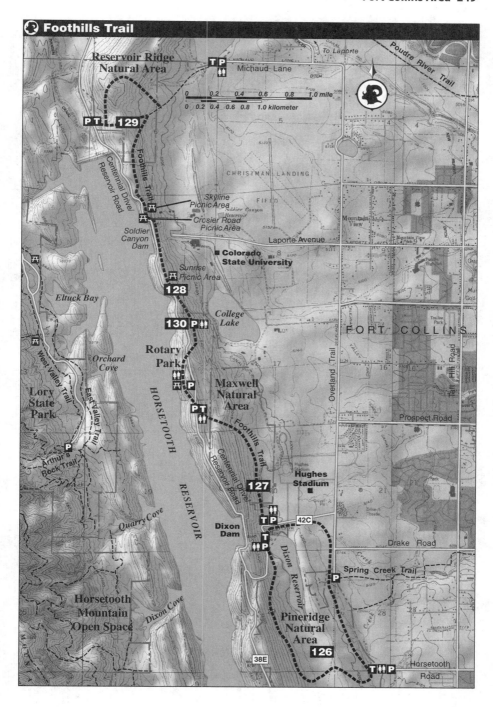

**Foothills Trail**

**HIGHLIGHTS** The Foothills Trail travels through three city natural areas as well as county recreation areas along Horsetooth Reservoir and features a wide variety of foothills topography with ponds, hills, valleys, climbs, and descents and great reservoir, city, and mountain views. It is an intermediate mountain biking trail but is easy to negotiate on foot. Making the entire round-trip on foot would be challenging; enjoying pieces of the trail is more fun.

This open space area in the foothills features some easy loop trails, a pretty foothills pond known as Dixon Reservoir, and some short hill options with views, and you may even see some prairie dogs. Adjoining a city park and a dog park, it is also the beginning of the Foothills Trail that travels north across County Road 42C.

**DIRECTIONS** Fort Collins is 1–1.5 hours from Denver and Boulder, depending on traffic. There are two formal parking lots for accessing this mini trail system—one on the road to Horsetooth Reservoir's Dixon Dam just south of Sonny Lubick Field at Hughes Stadium on CR 42C, which is off South Overland Trail, and the other at the south end of the Overland Trail Road where it dead-ends into a small city park. The Spring Creek Trail also enters Pineridge from the east.

## From Dixon Dam Parking Lot

Go either north or south on the trail that circles Dixon Reservoir and the open space. If you head north, you will go downhill, enter trees, and immediately circle the north end of Dixon Reservoir. The trail travels east and then south about 2 miles to the south end of the natural area. As you go south, you pass three options to go up the ridge on the east side of the natural area. The first, most northerly trail is much too steep, and the third, most southerly option is also steep, but the second option is a gradual switchback and the best choice to mount the east ridge.

When you reach the south end of the open space, the trail goes west uphill and skirts the foothills as it rolls north, with some rocky sections that can challenge novice bikers. This section of the trail tends to be wet in late spring and early summer; avoid the mud and help prevent trail erosion.

If you head south from the parking lot, you also go downhill and then immediately uphill as the trail veers to the west, away from the water, and then skirts the edge of the foothills and trees as it rolls south. When the trail reaches the south end, it swings east and then north for a couple of miles.

On the east side of the natural area, the two previously mentioned trails that go up and over the ridge take you either into the dog park area on the south or the small city park on the north. In both cases the trails

*The trail borders Horsetooth Reservoir in Pineridge Natural Area.*

are moderately fast, fun downhill trails with a few twists and turns; add them to your loop if you want.

If you want to take a longer walk or ride to the east side of the trail, pick up the Spring Creek Trail in the city park. It travels several miles east all the way to Edora Pool and Ice Rink or the Environmental Learning Center and Poudre River Trails on the east side of Fort Collins. If you feel compulsive and want to cover all of the Foothills Trail in one swoop from south to north, start at the Dixon Dam parking lot. It is 1.4 miles to the Maxwell Natural Area from there and another 0.8 mile to the top where the road intersects.

### From the West End of Horsetooth Road

Park where the road dead-ends and then take the footbridge across to the trailhead. You can do a short loop by going straight uphill approximately 0.5 mile to the top of the ridge and then downhill to circle the open space, for a total of approximately 5 miles. If you want a shorter hike or bike, turn north (right) on the ridgetop, and go about 0.25 mile to the trail that descends to the northeast and the small city park and small extension of Overland Trail Road. When you reach the bottom of the hill, turn south (right) and follow the dirt path back to your starting point next to the dog park.

---

**127**  ## Foothills Trail: Maxwell Natural Area
CITY OF FORT COLLINS AND LARIMER COUNTY PARKS AND OPEN SPACES

see map on p. 249

| | |
|---|---|
| **Distance** | Up to 4 miles, out-and-back |
| **Difficulty** | Easy–moderate |
| **Elevation Gain** | 300' (starting at 4,980') |
| **Trail Use** | Hiking, mountain biking, running, leashed dogs OK |
| **Agency** | City of Fort Collins, Larimer County Parks and Open Spaces |
| **Map(s)** | City of Fort Collins *Maxwell* |
| **Facilities** | Restrooms at top of the trail in county picnic area and parking lot on Reservoir Road |
| **Note(s)** | Rotary Park is a fee area. |

**HIGHLIGHTS** The Foothills Trail travels through three city natural areas, as well as county recreation areas along Horsetooth Reservoir, and features a wide variety of foothills topography with ponds, hills, valleys, climbs, and descents and great reservoir, city, and mountain views. It is an intermediate mountain biking trail but is easy to negotiate on foot. Making the entire round-trip on foot would be challenging; enjoying pieces of the trail is more fun.

This foothills open space area is west of Hughes Stadium and offers views of Fort Collins and foothills on moderate trails. You can climb to the top of the first foothill ridgeline above the famous Aggies A or up to Reservoir Road for a view. You can also start at the Dixon Dam parking lot and then take the Foothills Trail that edges the southwest stadium parking lot to access the area.

**DIRECTIONS** Fort Collins is 1–1.5 hours from Denver and Boulder, depending on traffic. You can access the trails in the area either from County Road 42C, just north of Pineridge Natural Area at the trailhead just west of Colorado State University's stadium parking lot, or from the end of Prospect Road where it enters the Two Ponds subdivision.

The trailhead on CR 42C is 1 mile west of the Overland Trail Road intersection, west of the stadium's south side parking lot. From the Maxwell Natural Area trailhead, the trail goes north, along a wide, level dirt road. The road eventually turns west onto a trail and then north and intersects the trail coming in from the Two Ponds subdivision up the hill from the east and coming downhill from the west at around

*The Foothills Trail wanders through three natural areas.*

the 0.5-mile mark. Turn west to go uphill past the water storage tank and switchback steeply uphill for 0.25 mile, gaining another 100 feet. The trail levels as it turns west and then south. When you reach an intersection in 0.25 mile, you can continue south on the trail that goes up gradually and then steeply for a short stretch above the famous Aggies A or turn right and go up a shorter steep hill to Reservoir Road and a view of the man-made lake. Once you cross Centennial Drive, also known as Reservoir Road, you enter a county fee area called Rotary Park; the trail continues downhill to the north along the edge of the reservoir.

If you access the natural area from the Two Ponds subdivision, take Prospect Road until it enters the subdivision by crossing Overland Trail Road. Take the first left and park, and the trail will be on right (west) side of the street. Take the trail straight uphill for about 0.5 mile to where it intersects the trail coming from the south. Then continue straight (west) until the trail starts to switchback to the north past the water tank. Another 0.5 mile leaves you near the top of the switchbacks with good views. If you continue west, the trail levels and enters a foothills grassy meadow area. Once you top the hill, 0.8 mile from the bottom, the trail levels and you can continue downhill right (north) and then left (south) to reach the top of the ridge above the A, or cross the road and enter the county's Rotary Park picnic area. The first two options are free, while using the county trail will cost you. It goes downhill all the way to the reservoir and then continues north for several scenic miles, passing near the Sunrise and Skyline picnic areas, which also require the county fee.

## 128  Foothills Trail: Centennial Drive

CITY OF FORT COLLINS AND LARIMER COUNTY
PARKS AND OPEN SPACES

see map on p. 249

| | |
|---|---|
| **Distance** | 4.4–8 miles, point to point |
| **Difficulty** | Moderate |
| **Elevation Gain** | Hiking/biking trail: 200'; Biking road: 600' (starting at 4,980') |
| **Trail Use** | Hiking, mountain biking, running, option for kids, leashed dogs OK |
| **Agency** | City of Fort Collins (east), Larimer County Parks and Open Spaces (west) |
| **Map(s)** | City of Fort Collins *Maxwell* |
| **Facilities** | Restrooms in the Larimer County picnic and parking area |
| **Note(s)** | County annual or day pass required for trail along east side of Horsetooth Reservoir |

**HIGHLIGHTS** The Foothills Trail travels through three city natural areas as well as county recreation areas along Horsetooth Reservoir and features a wide variety of foothills topography with ponds, hills, valleys, climbs, and descents and great reservoir, city, and mountain views. It is an intermediate mountain biking trail but is easy to negotiate on foot. The entire round-trip on foot makes a good running route; for hiking, enjoying pieces of the trail is more fun.

An intermediate mountain bike trail that's easy to negotiate on foot, this trail travels along the eastern shoreline of Horsetooth Reservoir. Enjoy the beauty of the sparkling water, the impressive foothills backdrop, and the richly colored rocks of hogbacks on this hilly trail that runs along the eastern edge of the reservoir, north of Dixon Dam. You can hike or mountain bike the fee trail or ride on the paved road (Centennial Drive) free. There are many picnic spots with sweeping views of the water and hills.

**DIRECTIONS** Fort Collins is 1–1.5 hours from Denver and Boulder, depending on traffic. This trail can be accessed either through the Maxwell Natural Area at no charge or from the various parking and picnic areas along the east side of the reservoir. If you want a longer hike with a significant hill climb, start at the bottom of Maxwell. If you want a shorter trek with easier rolling hills along the reservoir, drive up County Road 42C and climb uphill until it intersects with Reservoir Road. Then turn north (right) and cross Dixon Dam. Climb a very steep hill to the parking area (which charges a fee) on the left (west) side of the road. You get bonus points if you bike up.

From the parking area closest to Dixon Dam (Rotary Park Picnic Area), walk north to the trailhead. You have immediate, commanding views of the water and the hills that surround it, including Arthur's Rock on the ridgeline to the west. The trail goes gradually and then more steeply downhill for about 0.25 mile, where it reaches a Y junction. Turn left (west) and go down the wide stone steps toward the reservoir for the main trail. After the steep section, the trail turns north and continues to descend more gradually, eventually leveling fairly close to the lake.

Feel free to take a side trip to the lakeshore. When the water level is low, enjoy some Colorado beachfront with sand and bonus rocks and clay. If it is hot enough, you might take a quick dip to cool off. Because it is created by water that started as snowmelt, however, the reservoir doesn't ever get truly warm (68°–70°F is tops midsummer), so if it's not hot, your stay in the water will be refreshing but brief.

The trail continues for a 0.5-mile level stretch until it nears the Sunrise Picnic Area, where it climbs a small hill to reach 0.8 mile. An informal trail then descends back to the edge of the reservoir and ends at the dam face. Simply retracing your steps from here is a great 2-mile round-trip with views of the water.

At 1.5 miles, the Foothills Trail goes over the top of the small ridge and continues on the east side of the ridge above the Colorado State University research campus. The trail winds down 300 feet and then back up and enters Reservoir Ridge Natural Area 0.8 mile from the road crossing.

*GREAT FOR KIDS*

---

The only steep section of the Centennial Drive trail is the first 0.25 mile. Taking a short jaunt down to the lakeshore and beach can be a fun, short family excursion. The reservoir level does vary. At high, early summer levels, the beach can disappear, while later in the summer, as the reservoir level drops, it gets wider and wider. Stroll along the trail and enjoy the views before or after visiting the beach.

---

## 129  Foothills Trail: Reservoir Ridge Natural Area

CITY OF FORT COLLINS AND LARIMER COUNTY
PARKS AND OPEN SPACES

see map on p. 249

|  |  |
|---|---|
| **Distance** | 5 miles, loop |
| **Difficulty** | Easy |
| **Elevation Gain** | 300' (starting at 4,980') |
| **Trail Use** | Hiking, mountain biking, running, horseback riding, leashed dogs OK |
| **Agency** | City of Fort Collins, Larimer County Parks and Open Spaces |
| **Map(s)** | City of Fort Collins *Reservoir Ridge* |
| **Facilities** | Restrooms at trailhead |

**HIGHLIGHTS** The Foothills Trail travels through three city natural areas, as well as county recreation areas along Horsetooth Reservoir. It features a wide variety of foothills topography with ponds, hills, valleys, climbs, and descents and great reservoir, city, and mountain views. The trail is an intermediate mountain biking ride but is easy to negotiate on foot. Making the entire round-trip on foot would be challenging; enjoying pieces of the trail is more fun.

This trail segment can be accessed from either the east or west, but the most popular access is east from Michaud Lane and features a gradual climb with water and plains views and a loop trail on top. It is a visually rewarding and popular multiuse trail. The west side of the trail overlooks the north end of Horsetooth Reservoir while the east side features good foothills scenery and views. There is little shade, so start early, or be prepared for summer heat. This trail is usable almost year-round.

**DIRECTIONS** Fort Collins is 1–1.5 hours from Denver/Boulder on I-25, or US 287, depending on traffic. From either highway, take Prospect Road west to Overland Trail. Take Overland north to Michaud Lane, and turn west to where the road ends in a parking lot. There is also a parking lot on the west side of the Reservoir Ridge Natural Area, just below the northernmost dam of Horsetooth Reservoir. To reach it, take Centennial Drive north from the Maxwell and Pineridge Natural Areas, or go south from Bellvue on County Road 23 approximately 2 miles; the parking lot will be on the left (east) side of the road.

The trail climbs gradually for the first 0.5 mile and then climbs more steeply. Another 0.25 mile takes you to the loop trail intersection. You can take the enjoyable and scenic loop around in either direction: straight ahead/bear left (south) or take a sharp right (north). The loop trail is steeper uphill to the northwest (right), mellower to the left (south) at the start. The trail to the left (south) climbs approximately 0.5 mile, where it levels and reaches another intersection. If you go uphill to the west, you can hike all the way to the west edge of the area in 0.25 mile and then turn south to cross the road to the Foothills Trail, which travels along the east side of Horsetooth Reservoir.

*The Foothills Trail is well marked, making navigation easy.*

You can also follow the trail south another 0.5 mile to the Foothills campus of Colorado State University and a dam.

If you choose the northwest loop, the trail climbs steeply on a rocky, scenic trail for 0.5 mile until it levels, with views to the east and west. The trail then continues to the west 0.25 mile before turning south and gradually descending along the western boundary of the natural area. The downhill stretch goes for 0.5 mile, where you see the parking lot on the west side of Reservoir Ridge. The next 0.5 mile goes back uphill, switchbacks, crosses over the ridge, and meets up with the other side of the loop.

## 130  Reservoir Road/Centennial Drive

CITY OF FORT COLLINS AND LARIMER COUNTY
PARKS AND OPEN SPACES

see map on p. 249

| | |
|---|---|
| **Distance** | Up to 8 miles, loop |
| **Difficulty** | Challenging |
| **Elevation Gain** | 600' (starting at 4,980') |
| **Trail Use** | Biking, leashed dogs OK |
| **Agency** | City of Fort Collins, Larimer County Parks and Open Spaces |
| **Map(s)** | City of Fort Collins *Maxwell*; Larimer County Parks and Open Spaces *Horsetooth Reservoir* |
| **Facilities** | Restrooms at trailhead |

**HIGHLIGHTS** This roller-coaster road or mountain biking ride follows the ridgeline above the eastern edge of Horsetooth Reservoir on a paved county road. Commonly known as Reservoir Road, its formal name is Centennial Drive (County Road 23). It offers the sparkling scenery of reservoir water and foothills greenery that you can enjoy if you are strong of lung and loin. If you aren't, it is more fun at a leisurely pace on foot on the Foothills Trail, rather than the road.

**DIRECTIONS** Fort Collins is 1–1.5 hours from Denver and Boulder, depending on traffic. This trip is near the Maxwell Natural Area, where you can park. You can access the Reservoir Road from County Road 42C, just north of Pineridge Natural Area past the Colorado State University stadium. If you want a longer ride, access the road from County Road 38E, farther south on Taft Hill Road, at the intersection with Harmony Road. Turn west at that intersection, and you will be on CR 38E. If you start there, you will have to climb very steep Heartbreak Hill as you ride north.

**A**fter a warm-up of your choice, go up the steep CR 42C hill to Reservoir Road, which is also a good warm-up in and of itself at slow speeds. (A dandelion bouquet for those who can sprint up this hill.) Go right (north) at the intersection, and continue (likely gasping) uphill another 100 yards. Then enjoy a short downhill onto the top of Dixon Dam and a flat 0.25 mile. Enjoy the view of Fort Collins, and catch your breath because you are about to encounter the steepest hill of the ride. Keep your momentum purring and your legs twirling at 90 revolutions per minute for as long as you can. Stay seated as long as you can and shift those gears down, as your bike begs you to stand on the pedals. Ask yourself why your lungs don't hold more air and perhaps think about how you should have sprung for the more expensive bike. Keep pedaling and hope a foul diesel truck doesn't pass you. Finally crest the hill and take in the magnificent view as you cruise downhill.

Take a break at the picnic area or keep cruising downhill. Beware of the cattle guard about 0.5 mile downhill, and take the alternate route. Savor your downhill because it will only last about 1 mile. Then climb the first of three much easier summits with some sporadic downhill sections. The last steep downhill takes you past the final dam at 40 miles per hour and the turnoff for Lory State Park (see Arthur's Rock Trail and East & West Valley Trails for ideas if you want to take an all-day adventure detour), or turn around and reverse the ride.

*Reservoir Road is a great workout for bicyclists.*

If you continue, you have another 2 miles to go once you pass the north end of the reservoir, until you turn right (east) and climb the double hills of Bingham Hill Road to begin your return route. It is another 0.7 mile to the top of this significant climb. Maintain your speed on the downhill to make it over the second hill. Turn right (south) on Overland Trail Road and ride the easy rolling hills back to the stadium and your vehicle.

## 131  Arthur's Rock Trail

LORY STATE PARK

| | |
|---|---|
| **Distance** | 3.4 miles, loop and out-and-back options |
| **Difficulty** | Moderate |
| **Elevation Gain** | 1,280' (starting at 5,500') |
| **Trail Use** | Hiking, option for kids, leashed dogs OK |
| **Agency** | Lory State Park |
| **Map(s)** | *Lory State Park* |
| **Facilities** | Restrooms at trailhead and along trail; backcountry campsites; picnic areas |
| **Note(s)** | Park fee required. |

**HIGHLIGHTS** The most popular trail in the park is a moderate climb to the bottom of the sky on top of the rugged, rocky ridgeline that is the western backdrop of Lory State Park. It is a relatively short hike with great viewpoints all the way, so shorter pieces of the hike can be very enjoyable and easily negotiated with kids of all ages. The final mile features switchbacks, and the summit requires a short, steep, rocky scramble, providing a good artery-clearing workout. Several trails go to the summit; I cover the most popular, short trail first and then some alternate trails afterward.

**DIRECTIONS** From I-25, take the Prospect Road exit west. Take Prospect Road west, turn right (north) on Overland Trail Road to Bingham Hill Road, and turn west. Take the next left (south) at the next T junction, turn right (west) at the following intersection, and follow the road to the turnoff for Lory State Park on the left where the paved road ends. Drive to the end of the road to the southernmost parking lot in Lory.

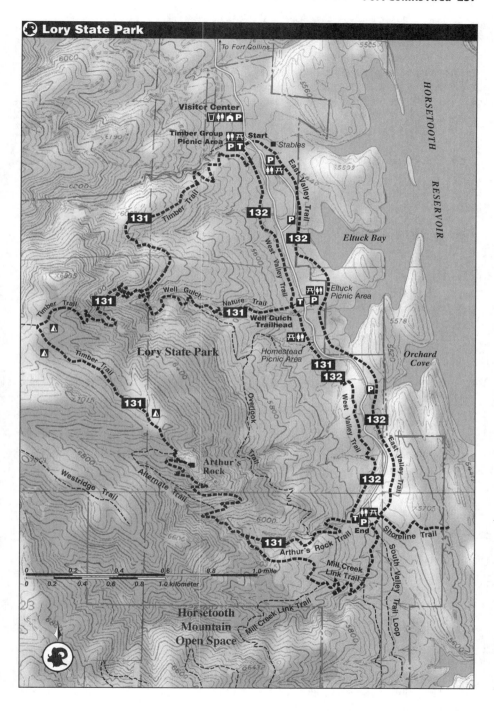

**Lory State Park**

This is the shortest, and therefore easiest, route to the top, though it is steep. It is also the busiest trail in the park. The trail begins on the west side of the parking lot. Be aware that the restroom next to the parking lot is the only one you will encounter. This parking lot is also the departure point for trails going east to the cool water of the reservoir and south to Horsetooth Mountain Open Space, as well as the East and West Valley Trails that go back to the north. A display at the trailhead includes an informative overview of the flora and fauna you might encounter and people-eating creatures such as mountain lions that you are unlikely to ever see. It includes hints on how to protect yourself from the asocial lions that generally prefer to feast on less contentious and tastier critters than *Homo sapiens*. Ticks aren't mentioned but are generally the only creatures that will really bother you.

Walk due west from the parking lot, passing the restroom and kiosk. When you reach the south terminus of the West Valley Trail in about 50 yards on the right (north), bear left (west). The trail enters a small arroyo that features a picturesque babbling brook and seasonal frogs. It winds through a rocky beginning that tests slick-soled footwear as it climbs in and around the rocks that can be wet in spring and frosty in late fall. After approximately 0.25 mile, the trail turns sharply south and then east and switchbacks more steeply uphill. If you continue straight, you will see a pretty waterfall in the spring or early summer.

When you reach the meadow, you will see a trail that goes north as a very steep alternate route toward the visible Arthur's Rock—not a good option for small children. The standard trail turns left, switchbacks, and then crosses the south edge of the meadow, leveling before beginning the next climb. On the left (south) side, the Mill Creek Link Trail heading into Horsetooth Mountain Open Space intersects your route. It is an easy alternate loop back southeast across the adjoining meadow. It crests the short hill at the intersection. Turn left (southeast) and

return to the parking lot, enjoying views to the south across the expansive meadows and rolling hills that lead to Horsetooth Mountain Open Space.

### GREAT FOR KIDS

Option 1: If you want an easy family outing for small children, linger along the way and enjoy the brook and abundant spring and early summer wildflowers or fall colors. Stop at the waterfall; then climb the short, steeper hill that switchbacks up, offers a view of the reservoir, and goes over the waterfall on a narrow, rocky section of trail. The Mill Creek Trail then veers southwest to a beautiful meadow and prominent rock outcrop before returning to the parking lot.

Option 2: The Timber Trail is a pleasant and easy out-and-back family hike with low population density. Just turn around when you reach the Well Gulch intersection. You could also continue down the Well Gulch Nature Trail and then take the West Valley Trail back to the picnic area.

At the junction with Mill Creek Link Trail, the Arthur's Rock Trail continues straight west and climbs a little more before leveling. The trees are a shady break spot. The trail narrows, and the thick tree cover can be a relief on a hot day. After about 0.25 mile from the junction with Mill Creek Link Trail, the trail turns north, crosses the usually dry drainage, and starts to climb in earnest, beginning the steepest part of the hike. As the trail climbs, it also opens up to the sun and the views. On the left (west) side of the trail is the steep shortcut to the rock for those who want to make their hearts race and test their quad and calf muscles. The standard route goes through several sweeping switchbacks as the steepness increases. You top the first ridge in another 0.25 mile, reaching a 180-degree viewpoint from the large rock to the right (east) from the trail, a popular turnaround point for many.

From here it is another 0.5 mile to the top up the steep, rocky path that climbs into the trees and then switchbacks to the north and east until it reaches the intersection with the Timber Trail. Bear straight/right and downhill to find and mount the

*View of Horsetooth Reservoir from Arthur's Rock Trail; photographed by Joe Grim*

final scramble to the summit that is actually on the left after a short downhill. The final 25 yards of rock scrambling requires some nonslip shoes and a bit of handiwork and good lungs. At the top of the chute, turn left (north), west, and then northwest to reach the actual summit rock. Enjoy the panorama that includes all of Fort Collins and its surroundings and north to the Wyoming border. There's even an unimpressive view of Horsetooth Rock on the distant southwest ridgeline.

## Timber Trail & Well Gulch Nature Trail Loop

After climbing Arthur's Rock, you can enjoy a moderate-plus loop hike, with or without a car shuttle, by continuing north on the Timber Trail to its intersection with the Well Gulch Nature Trail. Coming down from the summit, turn right (north), then right (north) again at the trail intersection, and climb up a short hill before leveling out. Then descend on a wide doubletrack trail. Pass a small meadow, enter tree cover, and then climb again to the Westridge Trail intersection. The Westridge Trail goes left (west-southwest), while the Timber Trail goes downhill to the right (north) and then northeast, where you will see a sign for campsites.

The Timber Trail continues east-southeast, switchbacking downhill, getting steeper as it goes along, offering nice views and then narrowing into a gulley that can be wet. It veers northeast and opens up to a 180-degree view of the state park, reservoir, and points beyond. It turns south and east, jumps a few rocks, levels a bit, and then climbs as it reenters tree cover, which is welcome on hot, sunny days. It switchbacks downhill and ends up going northeast for at least 0.25 mile, traveling out into the open and more steeply down and then switchbacks on a steep slope where it is easy to end up off-trail—watch your feet closely to make sure you aren't hopping over rocks into closed trail sections. Also look out for poison ivy. The trail continues to switchback until it levels and intersects with the Well Gulch Nature Trail. The Timber Trail goes straight east and then turns north to the Timber Group Picnic Area. It will climb gradually to a viewpoint and then descend slowly for more than 1 mile.

Bear right and follow the Well Gulch Nature Trail that switchbacks west and then south before turning east. It winds its way east through a small, rock-lined arroyo for about 0.5 mile and then intersects the park road and the West Valley Trail. Turn right (south) on the West Valley Trail, go 1 mile, and climb back to where you started.

### Timber Trail

Another longer variation for climbing Arthur's Rock, with far fewer people, is to start at the Timber Group Picnic Area and take the Timber Trail south to the Well Gulch Nature and Westridge Trails. Be careful not to mistakenly take the West Valley Trail that goes east and then south from the picnic area. Once you climb the steep stretch from the picnic area onto the Timber Trail, it is a gently climbing trail with great views of the reservoir and hogback. Because it is completely exposed to the sun, it is better to enjoy the trail before the heat of midday. When you reach Well Gulch in about 1 mile, turn right (west) and take the Westridge Trail south to the summit. You enter tree cover a little less than 0.5 mile from the Well Gulch intersection, but the steep uphill warms you until you take a water and snack break.

The Well Gulch Trail is another possible starting point for a longer, less populous climb of Arthur's Rock or as a treat for a short family jaunt, especially in the spring and fall, to see wildflowers and changing colors, respectively. In the spring there are often a few frogs in the small stream that dries up later in the year. The beginning of the trail twists uphill through the rocky arroyo but the first 0.5 mile is an easy climb if you go slowly. The trail wanders over rocks, through tree cover, and across a small meadow. It eventually breaks into the open and goes more steeply uphill to the north to intersect with the Westridge and Timber Trails. The latter takes you to the Arthur's Rock summit. From the Well Gulch it is a steep climb to the ridgetop.

### 132  East & West Valley Trails

LORY STATE PARK

see map on p. 257

| | |
|---|---|
| **Distance** | 7 miles, loop |
| **Difficulty** | Easy |
| **Elevation Gain** | 300' (starting at 5,200') |
| **Trail Use** | Hiking, mountain biking, running, occasionally snowshoeing and cross-country skiing, leashed dogs OK |
| **Agency** | Lory State Park |
| **Map(s)** | *Lory State Park* |
| **Facilities** | Restrooms at both trailheads |

**HIGHLIGHTS** East and West Valley Trails are easy, rolling, gradually climbing trails on both sides of the pretty valley that is the eastern edge of Lory State Park. Enjoy the panorama of the hogback rocks on the east, the Arthur's Rock foothills ridgeline on the west, and all of the high-desert foothills flora and fauna in between. These trails can be enjoyed year-round with appropriate clothing.

**DIRECTIONS** From I-25 take the Prospect Road exit west. Take Prospect Road west, turn right (north) on Overland Trail Road to Bingham Hill Road, and turn west. Turn left at the next T intersection and right (west) at the next intersection, and follow the road to the turnoff for Lory State Park on the left where the paved road ends.

hese trails run parallel to each other on the east and west edges of the valley floor. They form a loop together or can be used independently for some side out-and-back treks. You can start your adventure from the north or south end of the park. If you want to drive less, take the first right just past the visitor center into the Timber Group Picnic Area and Park. The West Valley Trail starts with a short uphill section that goes south. Be careful not to accidentally end up on the Timber Trail that goes more steeply

uphill to the southwest. You also pass the Well Gulch Nature Trail as you travel south and a picnic area for a snack or water break.

When you reach the high point, you are at the south end of the park road and can take a restroom or water break, cross the parking lot to the east, and take the East Valley Trail back to your starting point. You will pass a picnic area and restrooms near the Well Gulch Nature Trail. You can also detour to the bay areas for picnic or snack breaks with water views.

## 133  Eagle's Nest Open Space
LARIMER COUNTY PARKS AND OPEN SPACES

see map on p. 262

| | |
|---|---|
| **Distance** | Up to 5 miles, figure eight |
| **Difficulty** | Easy |
| **Elevation Gain** | 200' (starting at 6,000') |
| **Trail Use** | Hiking, running, horseback riding, snowshoeing, skiing, option for kids, leashed dogs OK |
| **Agency** | Larimer County Parks and Open Spaces |
| **Map(s)** | Larimer County Parks and Open Spaces *Eagle's Nest Open Space* |
| **Facilities** | Restrooms at trailhead |

**HIGHLIGHTS** This area makes up in beauty what it lacks in size—towering rock formations, access to the north fork of the Poudre River, a pretty riparian bottomland, an easy rolling trail, and sweeping views almost all the way to Wyoming. The trail has no shade and so is best on cool days or with an early start on hot ones. The area features two loops (the Three-Bar and the OT Trails) connected in a figure eight. The trails are named after former ranching brands. The sweeping views of the soaring rock formations that hide the eagle's nest and the sparkling trickle that is the north fork of the Poudre River make this a worthwhile, hilly trek.

**DIRECTIONS** From the Denver or Fort Collins area, take CO 287 north to Livermore and turn left (west) past the Forks store; turn left (southwest) 0.25 mile from CO 287, and look for the sign on the right that points out the dirt road on the left. Drive 1 mile uphill to the parking area.

he only restroom is in the parking lot. Hiking both loops adds up to approximately 5 miles. The Three-Bar Trail loop, which you reach first, rolls away along the foothills and features sweeping views to the north and east. At the trailhead, either proceed straight downhill north on the road for the first loop, or bear left (west), which is what I recommend for somewhat better out-and-back scenery. You have outstanding 180-degree views from the outset. This lovely wildflower stroll roller-coasters along to a view of Eagle's Nest Rock. The trail then takes a bit of a plunge downhill, goes

through a livestock fence, and continues down to the bottom of the drainage.

At the intersection with a ranch road, approximately 1 mile out, you will see a sign saying that there is no public access to the road, either east or west. Cross the drainage and go north uphill to another road crossing; the west is not accessible, but the Three-Bar Trail loop continues to the right (east). Look south and enjoy the band of cliffs, several folds of rock climbing the ridge. In another 0.25 mile you reach the second road crossing. The trail descends past a metal trail marker and drops into a pretty

## Eagle's Nest Open Space

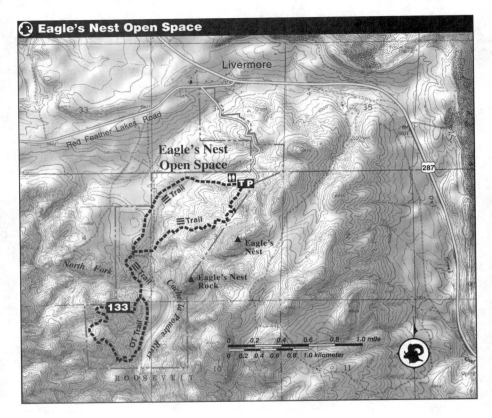

draw at around 1.5 miles. Pass through two more stock fences in the next 0.3 mile before reaching the river crossing and the OT Trail. When you reach the bottom of the hill, go left toward a small opening in the fence that leads into a grassy open meadow that can be used for picnics (but is usually closed February 1–July 15 because of the golden eagles' nesting area). If that's closed, veer to the right side of the bridge next to the river, and take a water or snack break while sitting on a friendly fallen tree.

If you don't want a break and want to walk another 2 miles before returning, continue straight past the metal OT Trail marker and cross the river bridge. Go uphill about 100 yards to reach the beginning of the OT Trail loop, next to another metal OT Trail post. I suggest bearing right (north) uphill, where the nonstop views begin in about 200 yards. The riparian river valley

opens to the west, cliffs soar on the south, and a tumble of foothills parapets to the north. After rounding a corner of the loop you see another cactus-speckled arroyo. The trail then rolls across the hills, with ever-changing, highly satisfying scenery as the beautiful riparian river valley opens up before you. You can see some fire-scorched trees in the distance. There is a 0.5-mile downhill section that ends with some short switchbacks.

At the bottom of the hill you intersect a ranch road inaccessible to the public; take a sharp left and begin your return trek. The next flat mile is surrounded by pastureland, and you might see some longhorn steers grazing; don't excite the bulls. Cross back over the river bridge and go back uphill to the Three-Bar Trail loop, the way you came. Approximately 0.25 mile uphill from the first livestock fence,

*Eagle's Nest*

you reach a ranch road. Turn left at the metal trail post to take the other side of the Three-Bar Trail loop back to the parking area if you want some variety. Somewhat less steep than the other side of the loop, it is a doubletrack dirt road. If you look carefully, you can see Red Mountain just over the top, doing its Monument Valley imitation. The 1-mile trek features a steeper section for the last 0.25 mile.

### GREAT FOR KIDS

The area where the trail crosses the Poudre River is a good turnaround point for people with small children or who are looking for an easier journey. You can picnic along the river, and enjoy the view of the cliffs.

---

## 134   Bobcat Ridge Natural Area: Ginny Trail
CITY OF FORT COLLINS

see map on p. 264

| | |
|---|---|
| **Distance** | Up to 6 miles, loop or out-and-back |
| **Difficulty** | Moderate hike, challenging mountain bike |
| **Elevation Gain** | 1,500' (starting at 5,500') |
| **Trail Use** | Hiking, mountain biking, option for kids |
| **Agency** | City of Fort Collins |
| **Map(s)** | City of Fort Collins *Bobcat Ridge Natural Area* |
| **Facilities** | Restrooms and picnic area at trailhead |
| **Note(s)** | Dogs are not permitted. Bikers can only travel uphill on the Power Line Trail segment, which means that mountain bikers wanting to complete the entire loop will need to do so in a counterclockwise direction. |

**HIGHLIGHTS** One of the most recent additions to the Fort Collins natural areas system, the Bobcat Ridge Natural Area is a superb slice of foothills southwest of Horsetooth Mountain Open Space near Masonville that almost makes you feel like you are in the red rock canyon country of Utah. The soaring cliffs and foothills, pretty rolling terrain, and quiet invite reverie. Arrive early if you want solitude. It is also sun drenched with little shade and so is not a good midday summer hike but is ideal for cooler spring and fall days. It offers easy mountain biking too—at least until you reach the eroded sections where the rocks protrude. Ginny Trail is a moderate hike and challenging mountain biking adventure that features steep switchbacks and lots of boulders. It could also be called the Bobcat Ridge Fire Trail because its journey onto the higher slopes is through the middle of the area scorched by an intense fire that burned 70 percent of the forested portion of Bobcat Ridge Natural Area in 2000. The stark scenery is dramatic and offers a transitional sort of beauty that reminds us that the natural world is one of constant change. The trail offers commanding views of the red rock cliffs, the west face of Horsetooth Rock, and the foothills and plains stretching out to the horizon.

**DIRECTIONS** Take County Road 38E to the southwest side of Horsetooth Reservoir; continue uphill past Horsetooth Mountain Open Space and then downhill to Masonville. Turn left on CR 27 in Masonville, and then right (west) on CR 32 in a little more than 0.5 mile. Go 1 mile west to Bobcat Ridge parking lot.

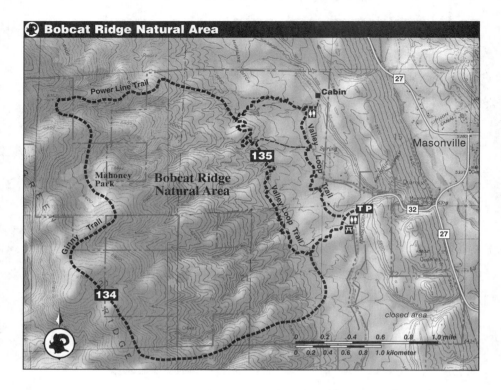

You can only access the Ginny Trail by using the Valley Loop Trail as a connector. For the shortest and most direct route, go straight (southwest) from the parking area, and then bear left past the picnic area, turning left where you see the horse sign. It's an easy climb for the first 0.7 mile, gaining 100 feet to the beginning of the Ginny Trail, which you will see uphill on the left. If you just want an out-and-back hike, you can venture as far and as high as you wish on the Ginny Trail before reversing course to the trailhead.

Once you reach the Ginny Trail the fun begins. You will climb steeply, going fairly straight up a small ridge for the first 0.25 mile and then switchbacking, gaining approximately 250 feet on the switchbacks in the first 0.6 mile. After 0.6 mile the trail levels for 0.25 mile. Enjoy the break because the next 0.6 mile is one of the steepest sections. The scenic, fire-ravaged scenery is unique and dramatic as you clamber over

ridge after ridge. You start climbing again around 0.8 mile from the start of the Ginny Trail. Over the next 0.7 mile you climb around 500 feet to reach near 1.5 miles (approximately 2.2 miles from the parking area). At that point you can catch your breath and savor an almost flat mile with spectacular views all around. As the crow flies, you will be approximately 1.5 miles from the beginning of the Ginny Trail, but you probably don't have wings to rely upon for the return, so plan on more than 3 miles back to the parking area. This is a good time to decide if you want to complete the loop, continuing north and descending to Power Line Trail and then the north end of the Valley Loop Trail. It is roughly equidistant, but Power Line Trail is a less challenging descent. You cannot, however, descend via Power Line Trail on a bike because only uphill biking is permitted on that trail.

It is much flatter for a longer distance if you go counterclockwise, but it is also much

*Abandoned cabin in Bobcat Ridge Natural Area*

farther to reach the Ginny Trail. The trail travels north, with views of the hogback formation and distant foothills, and rolls through a drainage on a small footbridge. After approximately 0.6 mile you reach the Power Line Trail "road," turn left, and go gradually uphill on the rolling trail for 0.5 mile. As the trail gets much steeper you will intersect the western side of the Valley Loop Trail. The Power Line Trail continues straight uphill, climbing west approximately 150 feet rather quickly, as you pass the Valley Loop Trail first on the left and then on the right. The trail flattens temporarily before starting its steady climb of more than a mile to the summit. As the trail climbs higher and higher you will, of course, have ever-improving views of the valley and the beautiful foothills surroundings.

### GREAT FOR KIDS

The first mile of this trail combination is an easy out-and-back for small children or short outings. You will reach the Ginny Trail after a gradual climb of 0.7 mile on the south portion of the Valley Loop Trail. Once you reach the Ginny Trail, slowly follow the switchbacks as they wend through the burn area. The charred trees provide a stark contrast to the usually blue sky and colorful surroundings. The first 0.3 mile climbs and steepens as you gain another 150 feet. You will be startled by the outstanding panorama to the south that this extra elevation affords. Have a water break and reverse your course, enjoying the great views all the way back to the picnic area, where you can have a snack or beverage break.

## 135    Bobcat Ridge Natural Area: Valley Loop Trail
CITY OF FORT COLLINS

| | |
|---|---|
| **Distance** | Up to 4.5 miles, loop |
| **Difficulty** | Easy |
| **Elevation Gain** | 200' (starting at 5,500') |
| **Trail Use** | Hiking, mountain biking, running, horseback riding, option for kids |
| **Agency** | City of Fort Collins |
| **Map(s)** | City of Fort Collins *Bobcat Ridge Natural Area* |
| **Facilities** | Restrooms and picnic area at trailhead |
| **Note(s)** | Dogs are not permitted. |

**HIGHLIGHTS** One of the most recent additions to the Fort Collins natural areas system, this superb slice of foothills southwest of Horsetooth Mountain Open Space near Masonville almost makes you feel like you are in the red rock canyon country of Utah. The soaring cliffs and foothills, pretty rolling terrain, and quiet invite reverie. Arrive early if you want solitude. It is also sun-drenched with little shade and so is not a good midday summer hike but is ideal for spring and fall. It offers easy mountain biking too, at least until you reach the eroded sections where the rocks pop out. The Ginny Trail loop is an advanced mountain biking adventure that is steep and rocky.

**DIRECTIONS** Take County Road 38E to the southwest side of Horsetooth Reservoir; continue uphill past Horsetooth Mountain Open Space and then downhill to Masonville. Turn left on CR 27 and then in a little more than 0.5 mile, go right (west) on CR 32. Go 1 mile west to Bobcat Ridge parking lot.

The 4.5-mile Valley Loop Trail is an easy, gently rolling trail that includes a possible side ramble to a historic cabin. It is much flatter for a longer distance if you go counterclockwise. If you want to start on the hilly section, turn left (south) for a clockwise loop after the picnic area at the sign that reads Horses. If you want an easy out-and-back trip good for small children or less ambitious adventures, head right (north) to go counterclockwise. The trail travels north with views of the hogback formation and distant foothills and rolls through a couple of drainages on small footbridges. After approximately 1 mile you reach the first significant hill. Go left uphill for the loop; go right (northeast) on a side trail to see the historic cabin that was probably a ranch bunkhouse.

Continuing on the loop, the trail goes into the hills section and then rolls along the west side of the valley. Stay on the trail and off the roads the trail crosses. The trail rolls as it climbs higher and higher and gives you ever better views of the valley and the beautiful foothills surroundings. After another 0.75 mile you can enjoy some shady spots for a water or snack break. There are also some excellent photo opportunities to the south. The trail plunges and climbs gently the entire

*An owl finds a shady spot for a nap in Bobcat Ridge Natural Area; photographed by John Bartholow.*

way until it reaches the south end of the valley and goes gradually downhill back to the picnic and parking area.

### GREAT FOR KIDS

The ranch ruins detour is only a 0.25-mile round-trip and worth it because the city has provided excellent signage for self-guided tours. An out-and-back to the cabin avoids any significant hills and is an easy 2-mile jaunt that could be followed by a picnic. The cabin is surrounded by old ranching equipment, the red rock and hogback views are excellent, and you'll even see an old well and a water pump.

**136** **Horsetooth Rock Trail**

LARIMER COUNTY PARKS AND OPEN SPACES

see
map on
p. 268

| | |
|---|---|
| **Distance** | 7 miles, out-and-back |
| **Difficulty** | Moderate |
| **Elevation Gain** | 1,500' (starting at 5,700') |
| **Trail Use** | Hiking, mountain biking, running, option for kids, leashed dogs OK |
| **Agency** | Larimer County Parks and Open Spaces |
| **Map(s)** | Larimer County Parks and Open Spaces *Horsetooth Mountain Open Space* |
| **Facilities** | Restrooms and picnic area at trailhead |
| **Note(s)** | Park fee required. |

**HIGHLIGHTS** Hiking any part of this trail is a treat, and summiting the rock requires a rocky scramble that adds to the thrill. Just hiking to the base of the rock gives you views of the plains and reservoir and the impressive east side of Horsetooth Rock. The Audra Culver Trail option offers a view of Longs Peak's snowy summit.

**DIRECTIONS** The park is 30 minutes from Fort Collins. From South Taft Hill Road turn west onto County Road 38E. It travels west and then switchbacks south up to Horsetooth Reservoir. Bear left and continue south and then west around the reservoir. The road climbs over a ridge, drops into the South Inlet Bay area, and then turns west and uphill again, where you see the parking lot on the right (north) side of the road.

When leaving the parking area, either go straight (north) on the Horsetooth Rock Trail or left (west) on the South Ridge Trail. The trail winds over and around the hills and provides more interesting scenery. The South Ridge Trail is as steep as but much wider than the Horsetooth Rock Trail. They meet back up at an intersection and continue north 100 yards. At that point you once again have the option of using either trail. South Ridge switchbacks up the hill to the left (southwest), and Horsetooth Rock continues straight. The South Ridge Trail is a much easier route for mountain bikers because of its width and offers peak views that you won't see on the narrower, rockier Horsetooth Rock Trail. For variety, you could go up the South Ridge and down the Horsetooth Rock Trail or vice versa; they intersect at the top of the ridge.

Go left (southwest) uphill on the service road, signed as the Audra Culver Trail, and switchback steeply for the first 0.25 mile, with views to the west and south. On a clear day you will see Longs Peak in the distance. The trail travels north along the top of a ridge, goes into a small arroyo, and then swings a little east. A route on the left—the actual, narrow Audra Culver Trail—goes straight up toward the south summit, edging along the west side of the ridgeline. If you go straight on the service road, it switchbacks once before intersecting with the Horsetooth Rock Trail.

If you stayed on the Horsetooth Rock Trail at the first intersection, it continues straight and comes to an intersection with the Horsetooth Falls Trail in about 0.25 mile. Turn sharply left (west) uphill to continue to the rock. Go straight if you want to take the short, easy jaunt to Horsetooth Falls (see the rest of the route description below). You can also continue past the turnoff for the falls and hike all the way north into Lory State Park. The Horsetooth Rock Trail narrows and becomes steep and rocky. The shade on this trail is welcome on hot, sunny days. It climbs approximately 0.5 mile to the top of the ridge, where you will see the Audra Culver Trail on the left coming in from the south. Bear right and go slightly downhill through the trees. The trail levels briefly before climbing again, scrambling over some rocks and veering

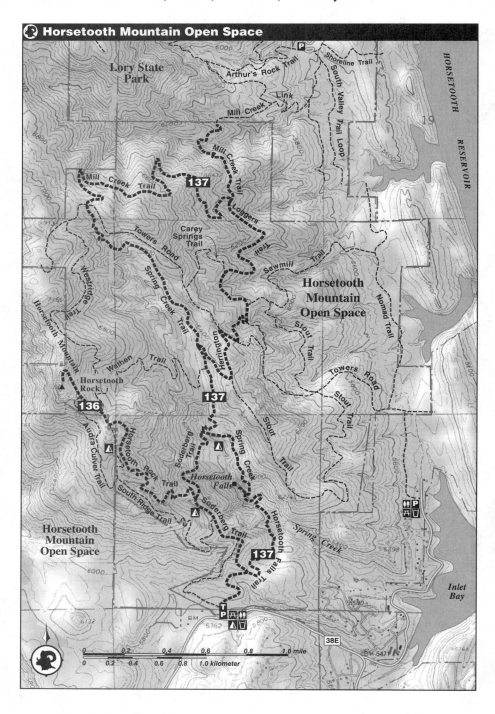

*Horsetooth Rock from the trail*

west as it does so. In a little more than a 0.25 mile you emerge from the trees to a good view of Horsetooth Rock.

At this point, the trail travels due west and you can either climb the south half or the north half of the rock. The south side, though shorter, is a bit trickier and not frequently climbed. Only try the south side if you are a creative, confident rock scrambler. For the north half of Horsetooth Rock, the most frequently climbed "standard" trail, continue straight (north) as the trail traverses and edges through rocks, descends slightly, and then climbs steeply over more rocks and dirt before leveling for 25 yards, traversing south to north at the base of Horsetooth Rock. The steep dirt trail then climbs into the trees and veers steeply due west between trees next to the summit route. When the dirt trail dead-ends, the final summit scramble is on the left (south) side of the trail. Carefully pick your route to the top. There are about three safe variations that avoid drop-offs along the edge. Enjoy your well-earned arrival on the small summit and the spectacular view that goes with it.

### GREAT FOR KIDS

If you aren't planning to climb the rock, the base of the rock is a good place to have a snack and water break and then turn around. The trail gets much steeper and rockier from here and requires intermittent rock scrambling that can be fun unless you have slippery shoes or aren't ready for the exertion and altitude gain. Most people are fine if they go at their own pace and aren't afraid of rock scrambling and heights. If anyone in your party has balance difficulties or a fear of heights, have them wait or turn around. Some people have fallen to their deaths or have been seriously injured on the standard, nontechnical route.

## 137   Horsetooth Falls & Connecting to Lory State Park
### LARIMER COUNTY PARKS AND OPEN SPACES

| | |
|---|---|
| **Distance** | 2 miles to Horsetooth Falls (out-and-back), 9 miles if continuing to Lory State Park (point to point) |
| **Difficulty** | Easy to Horsetooth Falls, moderate to Lory State Park |
| **Elevation Gain** | 300' (starting at 5,700'), another 300' if connecting to Lory State Park |
| **Trail Use** | Hiking, mountain biking, great for kids, leashed dogs OK |
| **Agency** | Larimer County Parks and Open Spaces |

|  |  |
|---|---|
| **Map(s)** | Larimer County Parks and Open Spaces *Horsetooth Mountain Open Space*; *Lory State Park* |
| **Facilities** | Restrooms at the primary trailhead |
| **Note(s)** | Horsetooth Mountain Open Space is a fee area. |

**HIGHLIGHTS** This is an easy trek for families with small children. The first 0.25 mile is steep, but the trail mellows and offers a stroll to a pretty little waterfall (that sometimes dries up during the summer or fall if there is a drought). The foothills ecosystem and views are worth the trek even if the falls are a trickle.

**DIRECTIONS** The park is 30 minutes from Fort Collins. From South Taft Hill Road turn west onto County Road 38E. It travels west and then switchbacks south up to Horsetooth Reservoir. Bear left and continue south and then west around the reservoir. The road climbs over a ridge, drops into the South Inlet Bay area, and then turns west and uphill again, where you will see the parking lot on the right (north) side of the road.

When leaving the parking area, either go straight (north) on the Horsetooth Rock/Soderberg Trail or left (west) to the service road. The trail winds over and around the hills and provides more interesting scenery. The service road is as steep as but much wider than the trail. They meet back up at an intersection and continue north for 100 yards. At that point you once again have the option of using either the road or the trail. The road switchbacks up the hill to the left (southwest) and has been named the Audra Culver Trail; the Horsetooth Rock/Soderberg Trail continues straight. The Audra Culver Trail is a much easier route for mountain bikers because of its width and offers peak views that you won't see on the narrower, rockier trail. For variety, you could go up the Culver Trail and down the Horsetooth Rock Trail or vice versa; they intersect at the top of the ridge.

Go left (southwest) uphill on the Audra Culver Trail and switchback steeply for the first 0.25 mile, with views to the west and south. On a clear day you see Longs Peak in the distance. The trail travels north along the top of a ridge, goes into a small arroyo, and then swings a little east. A route on the left goes straight up toward the south summit. If you go straight, it switchbacks once before intersecting with the Horsetooth Rock Trail.

The main trail continues straight and comes to an intersection with the Horsetooth Falls Trail in about 0.25 mile. When the Horsetooth Rock Trail turns left (west) uphill, go straight on the Soderberg/ Horsetooth Falls Trail. The trail goes gradually downhill for approximately 0.5 mile; enjoy the views of the foothills and plains and the unique foothills fauna and flora. After the trail winds through a clump of trees and rocks, look for the spur trail that breaks off to the left (west) for the falls. After soaking in the scene, savor the mostly downhill journey back to the parking lot.

## Connecting to Lory State Park

One of the most enjoyable jaunts in the area is a thru-hike with a car shuttle going from Horsetooth Mountain into Lory State Park or vice versa. It allows you to enjoy the "wilderness" in your backyard; you can make it a challenging day by including climbs of Horsetooth Rock and Arthur's Rock in Lory. You can easily mountain bike round-trip if you are an intermediate mountain biker and don't mind walking some steep advanced sections.

Where the spur trail to Horsetooth Falls branches off to the left (west), continue straight (north) uphill on the Soderberg Trail toward Lory State Park rather than turning left toward the falls, or enjoy the falls and then continue on this trail. The trail switchbacks and gradually climbs to the top of the ridge, intersecting the Spring Creek Trail (0.6 mile from the falls), with views to the east. The trail roller-coasters significantly as it travels north through comely meadows, and 0.8 mile from the falls passes the Wathen Trail that comes in from the left (west).

Approximately 1 mile north of the falls, you will see the Herrington Trail on the right (east) side of the trail. Use it to climb up on the ridgetop. You can either stay on the ridgetop on the Towers Trail 3 miles, until it intersects the Mill Creek Trail in Lory State Park, or descend to the valley floor fairly quickly on the Herrington Trail. The Herrington Trail descends steeply to

the Loggers Trail, which will also take you to the Mill Creek Trail in Lory State Park. The combination of the Herrington and Loggers Trails will save you at least 0.5 mile on your jaunt to Lory Park because they are more direct. Once you reach the Mill Creek Trail, it is then a gentle roller-coaster climb over hills to the closest parking lot at the south end of Lory.

---

## 138 Coyote Ridge Trail

see map on p. 272

CITY OF FORT COLLINS AND LARIMER COUNTY
PARKS AND OPEN SPACES

| | |
|---|---|
| **Distance** | 3–7 miles, out-and-back |
| **Difficulty** | Moderate |
| **Elevation Gain** | 500' (starting at 5,500') |
| **Trail Use** | Hiking, mountain biking, running, horseback riding, option for kids, leashed dogs OK |
| **Agency** | City of Fort Collins, Larimer County Parks and Open Spaces |
| **Map(s)** | Larimer County Parks and Open Spaces *Rimrock Open Space*; City of Fort Collins *Coyote Ridge* |
| **Facilities** | Restrooms 0.75 mile west of trailhead parking lot |

**HIGHLIGHTS** You will enjoy three geological walls of foothills rock formations stretching to the horizon and an enjoyable roller-coaster hike or bike up, along, and over the hogback ridgeline and into a hidden grassy valley. The trail is most often used as an out-and-back, but you can also connect to the Rimrock and Blue Sky Trails for longer adventures. It is a pretty hogback and foothills area worthy of moderate out-and-back trips for novice hiking or intermediate to expert mountain biking.

**DIRECTIONS** This access point is 1 mile south of the Larimer County Landfill on the west side of Fort Collins's Taft Hill Road and Loveland's Wilson Road (County Road 19).

From the parking area the trail gradually and then more steeply climbs due west up the wide doubletrack trail (former road) for 0.25 mile. It heads north along the first small ridge for 200 yards and then down steeply into the first valley interlude. From there the trail climbs 200 yards gradually up to a restroom (open year-round) and small visitor center (rarely open) that are 1 mile from the trailhead. It takes a sharp right, travels 0.25 mile north along the next foothill, sneaks to the left (west) around the hill, and then climbs more steeply for 0.25 mile southwest to an OVERLOOK WITH WILDLIFE sign. You are now in the second unique foothills habitat, with a variety of cacti and wildflowers.

Climb north 0.25 mile and then south 0.25 mile to reach the top of the ridge. The trail then continues to the south 200 yards on the ridge before descending on stairsteps at least 100 feet down into the hidden valley. After crossing the almost 0.5-mile meadow, the trail climbs through a notch in the next set of foothills to the top of its ridgeline, where it intersects the Rimrock Trail. You have the choice of continuing south to the end of the Devil's Backbone Trail, which terminates west of Loveland off CO 34; going north to Horsetooth Mountain Open Space or Inlet Bay; or simply crossing the valley, enjoying a loop in the next foothill "garden" and returning to the trailhead

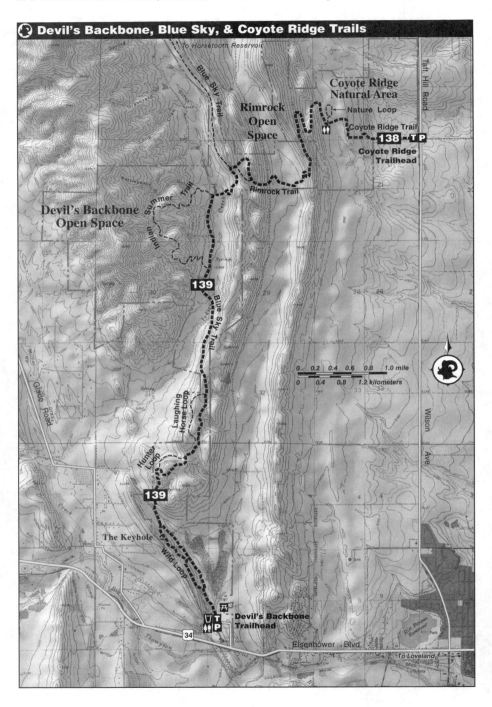

after a solid moderate hike or bike workout. It is less than 0.5 mile of gently climbing trail to cross the valley and enter the next enchanted area. When it leaves the open fields of short prairie grass, the trail sneaks around the corner and climbs sharply and more narrowly uphill. About 300 yards ahead surmount this small hill and enjoy another view of the seemingly endless series of foothills in both directions. Before the uplift of the Rocky Mountains, they were the bottom of a vast inland sea.

These rugged, land-based waves of foothills can be thousands of feet high, on par with the Appalachian Mountains, and are covered with foothills zone vegetation. Surmounting the hill you can either go south and east on a loop to return from whence you came or go downhill to the trail intersection, turn left, and continue downhill south toward the Devil's Backbone Trail. If you go uphill to the right (north), you can trek all the way to South Inlet Bay and Horsetooth Mountain Open Space. The route toward the South Inlet Trailhead is easy mountain biking or hiking. The route to Devil's Backbone is also easy until you reach a series of steep steps that surmount a ridge. At that point the route becomes more challenging for the next 0.5 mile, as the trail narrows and becomes steep at both ends of the ridge and many rocks appear. As you descend, you have excellent views of an arroyo and then the foothills to the west.

The steep section at the south end of the trail levels after your descent and offers some options. You can go straight up the slightly rolling valley or bear right (west) and climb up toward the hogback, where you can eventually enjoy a view through a rock window to the west. This loop is more hilly but also more scenically rewarding. The valley option is also pleasant and more mellow and wide, especially if you are on a bike.

### GREAT FOR KIDS

The stretch after the overlook is steeper and longer, so this might be a good turnaround point for groups with children. If they have the energy, it is well worth the view to negotiate the next two long switchbacks that end up on top of the highest ridge in another 0.25 mile or so. The view from the ridgetop is splendid in every direction, especially to the west. This is a good place for a snack and water break and makes a round-trip of 3 miles.

*View of Fort Collins from Coyote Ridge Trail*

## 139  Devil's Backbone, Blue Sky, & Coyote Ridge Trails
### LARIMER COUNTY PARKS AND OPEN SPACES

see map on p. 272

| | |
|---|---|
| **Distance** | Up to 16 miles, point to point |
| **Difficulty** | Easy–moderate |
| **Elevation Gain** | 400' (starting at 5,500') |
| **Trail Use** | Hiking, mountain biking, running, option for kids, leashed dogs OK |
| **Agency** | Larimer County Parks and Open Spaces |
| **Map(s)** | Larimer County Parks and Open Spaces *Devil's Backbone Open Space* |
| **Facilities** | Restrooms, water, and picnic area at trailhead |

**HIGHLIGHTS** This popular county trail west of the city of Loveland connects with the Coyote Ridge and Blue Sky Trails. This trail weaves through the dramatic rock formations in the foothills known as the hogback. A beautiful swath of land, Devil's Backbone Open Space was saved from development, and you can make your way north all the way to Horsetooth Mountain Open Space west of Fort Collins on it. You can set up a one-way car shuttle, with the Coyote Ridge access being the exit point short of South Inlet Bay and Horsetooth Mountain Open Space. That adventure is approximately 7 miles one-way and follows a pretty, moderate, roller-coaster trail. This trail can be used for out-and-back jaunts of any length; the eye candy makes it a treat regardless of your ambitions. Because there is virtually no shade on the trail, start early in the morning or early evening to avoid the blazing sun, or use it in the spring, fall, or even winter when temperatures are cool.

**DIRECTIONS** From Loveland take US 34 west of Loveland to just past mile marker 88. Turn right (north) onto Hidden Valley Drive just east of the old water tank. The trailhead is on your left. From Denver take I-25 north to Exit 257B for US 34 and Loveland. Drive west through Loveland and follow directions from above. From Fort Collins take Taft Hill Road south from Fort Collins to US 34 (Eisenhower) and turn right (west). Proceed west on US 34 and follow directions from Loveland above.

*View of Devil's Backbone Window Rock*

The trail goes north and then west across a drainage and uphill before climbing gradually in a northerly direction. After approximately 0.5 mile the trail splits, with a higher loop going left (west) up to the ridgeline for a view of the foothills through a rock window to the west. This loop is closed for part of each year because it is a nesting area for birds of prey. The trails join again in about 1 mile. You are then traveling in a broad valley, with rock formations on the east and west ridgelines framing the scene. The trail rolls gently for the first mile and then crosses the drainage and climbs more steeply.

The trail up to this point is easy for biking. Once it climbs onto the east ridge, however, it becomes an intermediate trail with some very rocky, steep, and narrow sections, which are great for hiking but more challenging for biking. Once you reach the top of the ridge, the trail levels and the views are a treat in every direction. Over the next 0.5 mile the trail descends gradually, evolving into steps, forcing most bikers to dismount. The trail rolls in the valley until it morphs into the Blue Sky Trail. As mentioned, the Blue Sky Trail will take you to South Inlet Bay at Horsetooth Reservoir, west of Fort Collins.

### GREAT FOR KIDS

The window rock view is worth the climb, and it is also a good turnaround point for families with small children; after this point the trail switchbacks downhill for 0.5 mile, narrows, and gets steep and rocky as it climbs uphill.

## 140  Crosier Mountain Trail
### ROOSEVELT NATIONAL FOREST

see map on p. 276

| | |
|---|---|
| **Distance** | Up to 10 miles, out-and-back |
| **Difficulty** | Moderate |
| **Elevation Gain** | 2,800' (starting at 6,500') |
| **Trail Use** | Hiking, horseback riding, snowshoeing, leashed dogs OK |
| **Agency** | Canyon Lakes Ranger District, Roosevelt National Forest |
| **Map(s)** | Trails Illustrated *Cache la Poudre & Big Thompson* |
| **Facilities** | None |

**HIGHLIGHTS** This beautiful foothills hike is in a montane transition zone between the lower foothills and the higher mountains. It offers great views of the Glen Haven Tributary of the Big Thompson Canyon, the destruction done by the 2000 Bobcat Fire, and the snowcapped peaks of Rocky Mountain National Park.

**DIRECTIONS** Take I-25 or CO 287 to Loveland (from the Denver/Boulder areas) and then CO 34/Big Thompson Canyon Road west 14 miles to Drake. Turn right at Drake and drive 2.4 miles, watching carefully for the small turnout on the left side of the road. There is a barbed wire fence, wooden gate, and U.S. Forest Service trailhead sign barely visible from the road about 100 feet uphill from the gate entrance. The two other accesses closer to Glen Haven require longer climbs to the summit. The one from Glen Haven is popular with equestrians.

The trail starts gradually uphill across an open field and then winds into the evergreens. The trail steepens as it enters the trees and begins to switchback. It gets very steep for the next 0.5 mile. Just when you begin to wonder if attempting this trail was a mistake, it levels out a bit in a forest primarily composed of tall fir trees. After you catch your breath for 0.25 mile, the trail starts to climb again steeply and rewards you with views of the canyon before reentering the trees. This is a good place for a few photos of the valley; the trail levels out as you mount a ridgeline and travel below

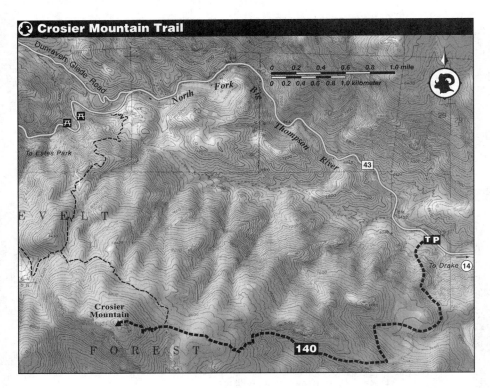

**Crosier Mountain Trail**

a large rock outcrop. As the trail goes back into the thicker trees, it steepens again but is less steep than before. Signs of the Bobcat forest fire are visible on the highest cliff. That fire affected approximately 50% of the trees you can see but stops at a beautiful mountain meadow that stretches in front of you and is a good place for a break. This part of the hike can be wet if you are early or late in the season.

After crossing the meadow, the trail is not well marked, but it runs southwest of the peak. The trail enters the trees again and climbs steadily toward the top of Crosier Mountain as it winds west and south next to a draw. The trail begins climbing steeply, turns west, switchbacks over a ridge, and then goes downhill into a gulch. You pass through a grove of aspen and around a ridge and into another more level open area. After winding around a ridge, you finally see Crosier's summit. When you

crest the top of Crosier Mountain, you have a panoramic treat with views of canyons, plains, and the snow-crested peaks of the Continental Divide.

*Looking into Estes Park from Crosier Mountain Trail; photographed by Jeff Eighmy*

## *NATURE'S DOMAIN*

It is clear that nature owns this canyon and humans are visitors. In summer 2000 the Bobcat Fire burned out of control for more than a week before being subdued. In 1976 a flash flood scoured Glen Haven and the Big Thompson Canyon. The flood was caused by a spectacular electrical storm and downpour of 11 inches of rain that fell over the canyon and its tributaries in about 4 hours. The river rose 20 feet in a matter of minutes. Almost 200 people were killed as the flood carried away houses and cars and completely destroyed US 34. The force of the water carried debris out to I-25. These chaotic ways of nature produce the dramatic scenery of cliffs and canyons you enjoy on this hike. If you do get caught in a sustained downpour and hear flash flood warnings, climb to the highest place you can in the canyon and stay there. Do not stay with your vehicle or try to outrun the flood.

## 141 North Fork Trail

ROOSEVELT NATIONAL FOREST,
ROCKY MOUNTAIN NATIONAL PARK

see map on p. 278

| | |
|---|---|
| **Distance** | Up to 14.8 miles, out-and-back |
| **Difficulty** | Easy–challenging, depending on distance |
| **Elevation Gain** | 1,800' (starting at 8,000') |
| **Trail Use** | Hiking, fishing, camping, snowshoeing, skiing, leashed dogs OK |
| **Agency** | Canyon Lakes Ranger District, Roosevelt National Forest; Rocky Mountain National Park |
| **Map(s)** | Trails Illustrated *Cache la Poudre & Big Thompson*; Trails Illustrated *Rocky Mountain National Park* |
| **Facilities** | Restrooms at trailhead, campsites |

**HIGHLIGHTS** This lesser-known trail features peaceful, varied topography in a riparian area. It winds through the forested broad canyon of the North Fork of the Big Thompson River, with striking rock outcrops and meadows, then climbs through a backcountry campground and more broad meadows and eventually ventures above treeline and into the stark beauty of the Lost Lake glacial cirque.

**DIRECTIONS** Take I-25 or CO 287 to Loveland (from the Denver/Boulder areas) and then CO 34/Big Thompson Canyon Road west 14 miles to Drake. This trail is at the end of Dunraven Glade Road, which is approximately 7 miles from Drake on the right side of County Road 43 if you are traveling west. It is another 2.4 miles down the well-maintained gravel road.

Also known as the Dunraven and Lost Lake Trail, this trail goes through a narrow portion of the Comanche Peak Wilderness before entering Rocky Mountain National Park (RMNP) and is a great way to spend a day in a pretty pine-and-aspen-forested valley. It is fairly level for a long time after an initial rapid descent, making it a good choice for family excursions or mellow outings. If you want a challenging all-day round-trip, make the lake your goal, and you won't be disappointed with a trek through a dazzling array of sights and sounds: sparkling water, golden meadows, and chaotic ridgelines.

The well-marked trailhead has a display with a trail description and map. From the parking lot, proceed past the toilet facilities and up a slight hill at the outset. The trail then descends about 0.5 mile down to the North Fork of the Big Thompson River, losing perhaps 150-plus feet of elevation. When you reach the bottom, you discover a wonderland of pretty brookside settings, tall pines, and a meandering babbling brook. The trail does have a few stream crossings on footbridges and there are a few very narrow, potentially wet spots in the first mile. The conditions can vary widely, depending on sun exposure; the first mile

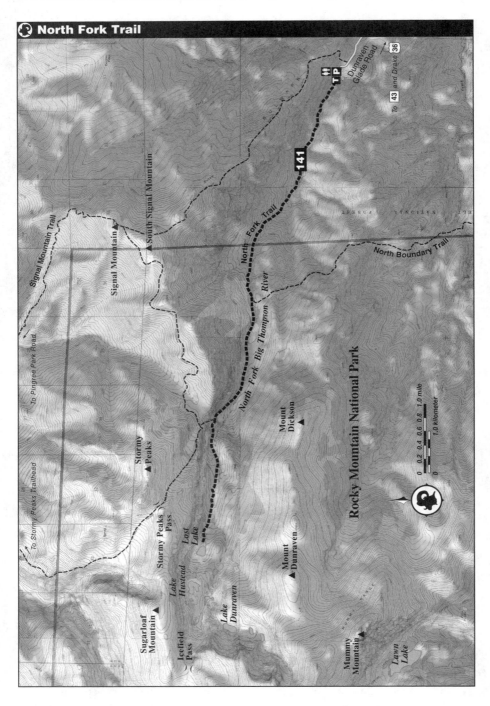

North Fork Trail

*North Fork Trail; photographed by Joe Grim*

is likely to be dry in late spring because it is open to southern exposure.

After about 0.5 mile, cross the stream on a footbridge, the first of many crossings. The trail then narrows and rolls as it parallels a horse camp across the stream from you. The trail then recrosses the stream and climbs uphill past a closed gate that notes the North Fork Trail and the horse camp. You then gradually climb and enter a high tree canopy, at which point you enjoy every variation of sunlight bouncing through the trees to dapple the trail at your feet. Though you are in a thick forest, the trees are tall and the branches high, so the ceiling is open and you have good views all the way.

Cross the stream a couple more times and leave the Comanche Peak Wilderness area to enter RMNP. Go through several golden meadows and then reach the backcountry campsites about 2 miles from the trailhead. There is a good bridge for a stream crossing to reach the sites. The trail climbs significantly before you enter RMNP but then levels again. You can decide when to turn around, depending on the conditions and your ambitions. Going all the way to Lost Lake means traveling below an impressive high ridge just beyond Lost Falls, almost 7.4 miles from the trailhead.

**Other Options**

This trailhead also offers access to the Signal Mountain Trail, which is at the top (north) side of the parking lot. This trail into the Comanche Peak Wilderness is a challenging, steep, rolling ridge trek to the top of Signal Mountain. The trail is above Dunraven Canyon and eventually allows hikers views of the Continental Divide, though there is fairly thick lodgepole pine tree cover for most of the route. It is a very long access route to the Pingree Park area mentioned in Chapter 10.

## 142  Red Mountain Open Space: Bent Rock Trail

LARIMER COUNTY PARKS AND OPEN SPACES

| | |
|---|---|
| **Distance** | 2 miles, loop |
| **Difficulty** | Easy |
| **Elevation Gain** | 200' (starting at 6,600') |
| **Trail Use** | Hiking, snowshoeing, great for kids |
| **Agency** | Larimer County Parks and Open Spaces |
| **Map(s)** | Larimer County Parks and Open Spaces *Red Mountain Open Space* |
| **Facilities** | Pit toilets |
| **Note(s)** | Dogs are not allowed in Red Mountain Open Space and Soapstone Prairie Natural Area. Closed December, January, and February. |

**HIGHLIGHTS** The scale of this open space is truly stunning. It is a magnificent ecosystem that has been saved. This is a beautiful route through a small arroyo, below a layer cake of red and white sedimentary rock. The grassland meadows and foothill mountain views after emerging from the small, short canyon are sweeping and gorgeous. This short, easy trail gives an impressive overview of this unique plains-foothills ecosystem.

**DIRECTIONS** From Fort Collins, take CO 1/Terry Lake Road to County Road 15 (also known as the Waverly turnoff). Go north (left) on CR 15, turn west (left) on CR 78, north (right) on CR 17, west (left) on CR 80, north (right) on CR 19 (pass gravel pit on left), and left on CR 21. Go over several cattle guards, traveling about 7 miles on CR 21, which will end at the trailhead parking area.

From I-25, take the Owl Canyon Road exit and head west. Owl Canyon Road is also CR 70. Go right (north) on CR 15, left (west) on CR 78, right (north) on CR 17, left (west) on CR 80, right (north) on CR 19 (pass gravel pit on left), and left on CR 21. Go over several cattle guards, traveling about 7 miles on CR 21, which will end at the trailhead parking area.

As you drive out to the open space, enjoy the expansive views of hay fields, grasslands and high, reddish foothills. Go left (west) out of the parking area, and you will see a sign for the Bent Rock Trail. It travels northwest to a stream crossing. Crossing can be a bit challenging during the height of spring runoff if the water is deeper than the rocks that have been placed to cross the stream. There is a small island to the right

*Bent Rock Trail*

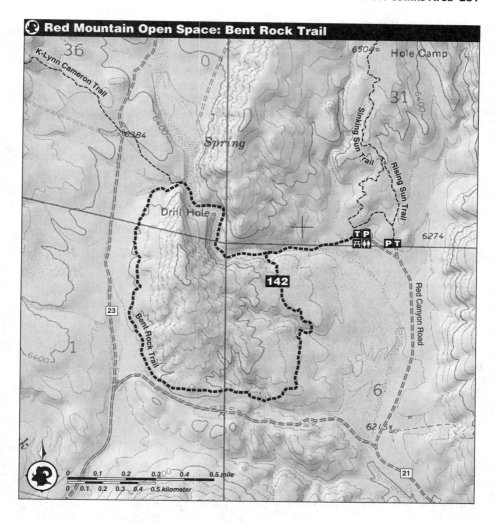

## Red Mountain Open Space: Bent Rock Trail

(north) that can be used to hop across if the rocks are submerged. As you walk up from the streambed you will be immediately struck by the curving, "bent," sweeping red cliffs, and namesake red hills. I prefer hiking this trail counterclockwise so you can immediately enjoy the small canyon. If you want to try that option, go straight at the first intersection rather than left. This loop hike will return you to the same place.

In the spring you will see the following flowers in the arroyo: evening primrose, gumweed, geraniums, blanket flowers, and yarrow. There is an excellent descriptive

plaque that gives you a geological overview of the dazzling sedimentary rock layers. Savor the colors of the millions of years of sediment that are exposed. At the west end of the canyon you will climb out and see another Bent Rock Trail sign. Go left (southwest) to complete the loop. Going straight will take you to the K-Lynn Cameron Trail. The views open up and you can enjoy beautiful meadows stretching to the horizons of more red and green foothills of every dimension. Go left (south) uphill to and through a gate. Look for the wavy leaf plant and flowers. In about 0.5 mile be careful not to lose the trail. It goes uphill left (southeast), while an intersecting drainage goes downhill right (southwest). This is the first of five small drainages that cross the trail. Some cairns mark the trail as it bears left, and you will see a large yucca plant. The trail rolls south and east, and you will see a closed road to the south.

The trail turns more sharply east as it climbs toward the top of the hill, becoming more faint and tracking northeast over the hill. At the next rock cairn, go west, not north or east. The trail winds its way west and north in this confusing section that is well marked with rock cairns in an ascending drainage. The northwest direction seems counterintuitive because you will be traveling away from the parking area to the northeast. It is a pretty section, worth the meander. You will see the canyon where you started, and then turn right (northeast), recross the stream, and go back to the parking area.

## 143    Soapstone Prairie Natural Area: Towhee–Overlook Trail
CITY OF FORT COLLINS

| | |
|---|---|
| **Distance** | 3 miles, loop |
| **Difficulty** | Easy–moderate |
| **Elevation Gain** | 300' (starting at 6,600') |
| **Trail Use** | Hiking, snowshoeing, great for kids |
| **Agency** | City of Fort Collins |
| **Map(s)** | City of Fort Collins *Soapstone Prairie Natural Area* |
| **Facilities** | Pit toilet |
| **Note(s)** | The first 0.25 mile to the Overlook is paved and wheelchair accessible. Dogs are not allowed in Red Mountain Open Space and Soapstone Prairie Natural Area. Hours are sunrise–sunset, March 1–November 30. Soapstone Prairie is closed December, January, and February. Hunting is not allowed at Soapstone Prairie. |

*Towhee–Overlook Trail*

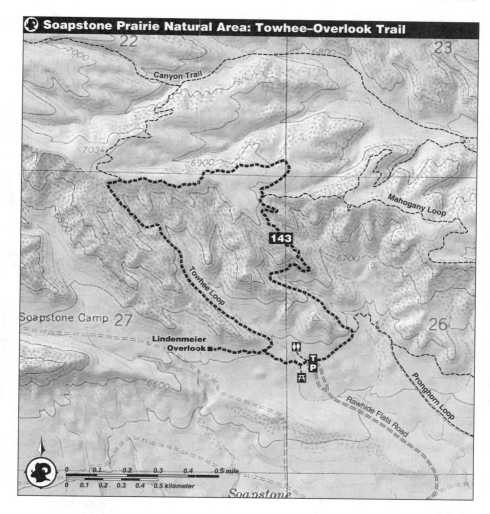

## Soapstone Prairie Natural Area: Towhee–Overlook Trail

**HIGHLIGHTS** The Overlook features several exhibit plaques that give an overview of the Lindenmeier archaeological site, where artifacts of 12,000 years of human habitation were discovered. There are also good views for pictures to the northwest from the covered site. You can start the loop trail and enjoy even more expansive views of the foothills, plains, and Wyoming border as the trail climbs up to the top of the ridge. The Towhee and Mahogany Trails are gateways to many other beautiful loop trails that will take you on great adventures in these foothills near the Wyoming border. You can easily extend your outing and add on 5–10 miles with the Canyon, Sand Wash, or Pronghorn Trails.

**DIRECTIONS** Soapstone Prairie is 25 miles north of Fort Collins. From Fort Collins, take CO 1/Terry Lake Road to County Road 15 north (toward Waverly). From CR 15, turn north onto Rawhide Flats Road and continue north to the entrance station. There are 9 miles of gravel road that can be dusty, rough, and bumpy. Please respect the neighbors and be safe by observing the speed limit.

From I-25, take Exit 288 (Buckeye Road) west to CR 15. Go north on CR 15 and turn north onto Rawhide Flats Road. Follow Rawhide Flats Road to the entrance station. Soapstone Prairie is not accessible via I-25 Exit 293 (CR 126/CR 5).

I suggest hiking this loop trail clockwise from the parking area, rather than taking the Towhee–Mahoney end first. Proceed toward the pit toilets, and look for the Towhee–Overlook sign. You will see the cement path traveling northwest that is great for wheelchairs and strollers. If you haven't visited the Overlook exhibit, it is well worth the short detour; bear left to see it. In addition to the historical and eco-system information, there is also a plaque honoring Kelly Ohlson and Linda Stanley for their tireless efforts to pass the sales taxes that made the purchase of the open space possible.

After looking at the exhibit, backtrack about 100 yards to the trail going uphill (northeast). It meanders and switchbacks about 0.9 mile to the top of the ridge. In the spring, you can enjoy green grass and wildflowers. If you want to stay on top of the ridge and cover the shortest loop, turn right (east) at the first intersection and go 0.8 mile to the connection with the Mahogany Loop. Continue another mile south downhill toward the parking area as the trail zigzags into a pretty arroyo. At the next intersection turn right (west) to get back to parking.

### LINDENMEIER ARCHAEOLOGICAL SITE

The Lindenmeier site, occupied as early as 11,000 years ago, is one of the largest known Folsom campsites. The site was excavated by Smithsonian archaeologists, led by Frank Roberts, in the 1930s. Roberts's team discovered thousands of artifacts—for camping, food processing, tool maintenance, and bison butchery—in distinct activity areas scattered over a 2-acre area. They also discovered remains of the now-extinct *Bison antiquus,* which were much larger than their modern descendants. The site prob-ably reflects the numerous camping episodes over several years or decades of occupancy. Furthermore, the Smithsonian archaeologists recovered evidence that later hunter-gatherers occupied the area.

The site was brought to the attention of profes-sional archaeologists by local amateur archaeologist Roy Coffin after his brother and nephew, Claude and A. Lynne Coffin, and C. K. Collins discovered it in the summer of 1924. Lindenmeier was the name of the landowner at the time of discovery. The site was declared a National Historic Landmark in 1961, and in 2004, the city of Fort Collins purchased the site and later made it part of the Soapstone Prairie Natural Area.

*Folsom point; illustration courtesy of the Smithsonian Institution*

RIMROCK OPEN SPACE TRAIL
Built in Partnership Between
Larimer County Parks and Open Lands
and Volunteers for Outdoor Colorado

LARIMER
COUNTY
COMMITTED TO EXCELLENCE

Volunteers
for Outdoor
Colorado

2002

*Take the Rimrock Trail from Coyote Ridge to the Devil's Backbone Trail (see page 271).*

*View of Thunder Pass and Rocky Mountain National Park from the bowls on Montgomery Pass*

# chapter 10

# Poudre Canyon & Cameron Pass Areas

## 1 HOUR OR LESS FROM FORT COLLINS
## 1.5–3 HOURS FROM DENVER-BOULDER

Colorado is graced with some of the most magnificent canyons in the world, and the Poudre Canyon is one of them. Long and spectacular, it offers some of the best hiking and biking trails. Some trails near the bottom of the canyon are very close to Fort Collins, and some are usable almost year-round. Its upper reaches will be wet from spring snowmelt in the late spring and early summer, but the trails are a treat after they dry out. In the winter the trails are nirvana for snowshoeing, backcountry skiing, and snowboarding.

Cameron Pass is over 10,000 feet, and most of the trails described start at elevations of 7,000–9,000 feet. At 9,000 feet you are in a Rocky Mountain climate zone roughly equivalent to the climate found at sea level 100 miles north of the Canadian border. Being in this climate zone generally translates to cool summer breezes on even the hottest days but almost daily afternoon thunderstorms in July and August in the higher elevations. Fortunately, these trails are generally well protected by stately evergreens that offer abundant shade on hot summer days and that break the not-uncommon winds when temperatures cool in the fall. There are a lot of ideal, warm, sunny days with welcome cool breezes moving down from the mountaintops.

Cameron Pass is bordered on the south by Rocky Mountain National Park's (RMNP) well-named Never Summer Range, which is crowned by the jagged Nokhu Crags, and on the south by the seldom-seen and little-known Rawah Range and its monarch, Clark Peak. West of the pass are the Colorado State Forest and the stark beauty of North Park.

To reach Poudre Canyon, take US 287 north from Fort Collins, and exit west onto CO 14 at Ted's Place. The high mountain trails are at least 1.25 hours from Fort Collins on this National Scenic Byway through the canyon. The trip features the largely unfettered Poudre River, winding through towering rock canyon walls, alternating with some of the most striking mountain meadows anywhere. The lower canyon trails are 20–30 minutes from Fort Collins. Cameron Pass and Pingree Park are at least 1.5 hours without motor home traffic.

### Pingree Park Area

A branch summer campus of Colorado State University and research and conference center, Pingree Park is not open to the public for visits, except for scheduled conferences or meetings. It enjoys a spectacular setting that features the majestic mountain backdrops of the Cache la Poudre Wilderness, Comanche Peak Wilderness, and RMNP. The surrounding area is Roosevelt National Forest and is open to the public with no permits required. This area also offers access to RMNP, which requires permits for camping. The Pingree Park area is approximately 27.5 miles from the entrance of the canyon at Ted's Place on US 287. The Pingree Park County Road (131) turnoff is on the left (south) side if you are driving west, and the road network accesses trails for the aforementioned wilderness areas, some of which start at 8,000 feet and offer less-busy access to some unique summits and lakes on the north side of RMNP.

**Long Draw Road**

Though Long Draw Road can be rough and is heavily used by vehicles on weekends, it offers good access to several nonmotorized routes through some exquisite old-growth forests of stately fir and spruce trees. It begins 60 miles west of Fort Collins on CO 14 across from the parking lot for Blue Lake. The trip is an enjoyable 19-mile drive to Long Draw Reservoir as the road rolls, climbing short hills at times. Fairly flat, it is a tree tunnel at times until it nears the edge of Long Draw Reservoir. Long Draw Campground has a dramatic setting in the Never Summer Range on the northern edge of RMNP and is a worthwhile destination. Long Draw Campground is located approximately 9 miles east of CO 14 on the Long Draw Road at an elevation of 10,030 feet. The campground's 25 sites enjoy the shade of many spruce and lodgepole pines. The campground offers excellent day-hike

access to RMNP and Thunder Pass via the Michigan Ditch Road and can be used for a car shuttle thru-hike to Trail Ridge Road destinations, via backpack or long day hike. For more information, see the descriptions for Little Yellowstone because that is where you can end up.

Mountain biking is possible on the road if you don't mind lots of weekend vehicle traffic or can use it during the week when traffic is lighter. The traffic is a fraction of what you see on CO 14 (Poudre Canyon Road). This road also accesses several great hiking or biking options—the Meadows Trail, Trap Park or Peterson Lake, RMNP at Corral Creek, Comanche Peak, Thunder Pass, and Never Summer Range summits.

**Other Areas of Interest: Gateway Park**

Between the Grey Rock and Hewlett Gulch Trails is the turnoff for this city recreation site—a wonderful place for a riverside picnic. It is at the confluence of the North Fork and main stem of the Poudre River. A fee area, it includes the very scenic, very short (1.5 miles) Black Powder walking trail and a picnic area and can be used as a launching point for paddlers.

## 144  Grey Rock

ROOSEVELT NATIONAL FOREST

| | |
|---|---|
| **Distance** | 7 miles, balloon |
| **Difficulty** | Moderate |
| **Elevation Gain** | 2,000' (starting at 5,500') |
| **Trail Use** | Hiking, rock climbing (off-trail), option for kids, leashed dogs OK |
| **Agency** | Canyon Lakes Ranger District, Roosevelt National Forest |
| **Map(s)** | Trails Illustrated *Cache la Poudre & Big Thompson* |
| **Facilities** | Restrooms next to the parking lot |

**HIGHLIGHTS** Grey Rock is one of the most popular trails in Poudre Canyon because of its proximity to Fort Collins and the spectacular scenery and varied terrain it offers. Starting at the river, you climb through a diverse mixed conifer forest and savor the ever-widening panorama of the canyon at your feet. Summiting buys you a stunning 360-degree view from the top.

**DIRECTIONS** Take US 287 north from Fort Collins, and exit west onto CO 14 at Ted's Place. Drive approximately 8.5 miles west on CO 14 from Ted's Place. The parking area is elevated from the roadway on the left (south) side of the highway and easy to miss.

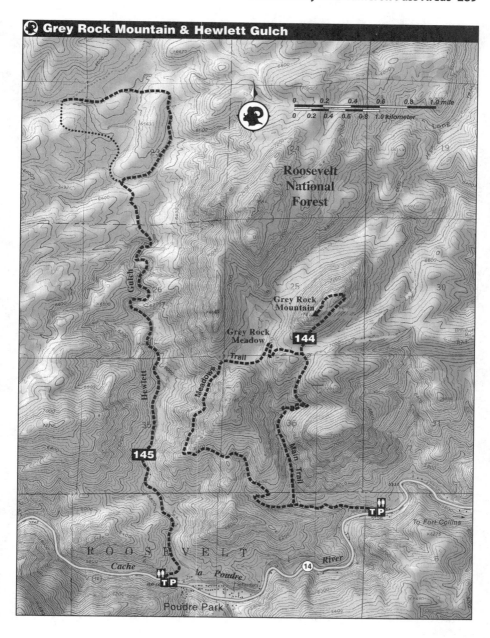

Grey Rock Mountain & Hewlett Gulch

*Grey Rock is a popular trail in the Fort Collins area.*

The trail is actually on the north side of the highway. Walk down the steps, cross the road carefully, and take the footbridge across the sparkling Poudre River. The trail goes west and veers away from the river into a creek drainage that is usually dry. It starts to climb immediately and crosses the creek. The trail is fairly rocky and bumpy before it recrosses the creek, smooths out, and climbs more steeply. After approximately 1 mile the trail comes to an intersection, where you can take either direction for a long, beautiful mountainside loop. If it is a warm day and you want to end the hike in more shade, go straight (bear left) to take the more open west loop first. If the heat and shade are not factors, then go right (east) and end up in the open on the return. The loop to the west is a bit longer because it travels through pretty Grey Rock Meadow. If you aren't planning to hike all the way to the summit and want

a moderate, less challenging hike, start on the west side and make the meadow your destination. If your goal is to summit and you want the shortest route, take the east route out and back.

### East Route

The trail traverses toward the drainage and parallels it for more than 0.5 mile. It then tracks west, away from the drainage and onto some broad switchbacks, breaking out of the thick tree cover and affording views across the canyon. After the switchbacks the trail goes northeast and then descends gradually to the level area that borders the meadow; this is the intersection with the meadow route. For a direct route to the summit, take the trail northeast (bear right), rather than taking the west loop down to the meadow.

The summit trail is better marked than ever, but it is still deceptive and it can be easy to get off-trail and become lost. A small child was lost several years ago and never found. Keep your children and hiking partners in view at all times. The trail levels for a little while after the intersection and then climbs through some steep sections. It traverses north for less than 0.5 mile and then takes sharp turns to the west and then south as it switchbacks and requires some rock scrambling. There is more than one route through this section, but try to take the marked trail if possible. You eventually emerge on a rocky ridge with a view of a small pond that dries up during very hot and dry summers. The summit rock is visible to the southwest and requires another hour round-trip from this point unless you are fast and don't stop and enjoy the view.

### West Route

The trail heads west and then northwest and follows an informal drainage as it steepens and emerges from the trees in about 0.5 mile. You enter sweeping switchbacks and reach an overlook for Hewlett Gulch. The switchbacks track north and east before leading you to a path that goes north, enters trees, narrows, and descends east toward the meadow. When you reach the meadow, a great place for a picnic, you'll have a terrific view of the Grey Rock summit and the technical climbing routes to the top.

Whether you want to complete the loop or reach the summit, continue east as the trail climbs gently to the intersection of the east trail. Turn right (south) to return to your starting point; go straight/ left (north) to start the rocky summit climb. As described previously, pick a route to the southwest around the water; then go west and find an easy scrambling route to the top. If you find that the climb has become technical, you have strayed off course—no technical skills are needed for the final short scramble to the summit.

### GREAT FOR KIDS

The meadow is a good turnaround point for families with small children. The rest of the trail to the top is steep and rocky and requires scrambling and route-finding.

---

**145**  ### Hewlett Gulch
ROOSEVELT NATIONAL FOREST

see map on p. 289

|  |  |
|---|---|
| **Distance** | 6 miles, out-and-back |
| **Difficulty** | Easy |
| **Elevation Gain** | 570' (starting at 5,670') |
| **Trail Use** | Hiking, mountain biking, horseback riding, snowshoeing, skiing, leashed dogs OK |
| **Agency** | Canyon Lakes Ranger District, Roosevelt National Forest |
| **Map(s)** | Trails Illustrated *Cache la Poudre & Big Thompson* |
| **Facilities** | Restrooms at trailhead |

**HIGHLIGHTS** Just west of the Grey Rock Trail, this trail is a rewarding, easy canyon/arroyo hike or bike through pretty meadows and lofty ridges, in a rocky environment that climbs to some viewpoints. An optional loop climbs to the open high point and sweeping views. The steep and rocky section of the loop can be avoided by taking the out-and-back route on the east (right) side of the loop.

**DIRECTIONS** Take US 287 north from Fort Collins, and exit west onto CO 14 at Ted's Place. Drive approximately 10.5 miles west on CO 14 from Ted's Place. The parking area is elevated from the roadway and hard to miss across the river on the right (north) side of the highway.

*Hewlett Gulch*

The trail goes north from the parking lot, and it rolls and climbs gradually through the gulch. After less than 0.5 mile, it descends and crosses the creek for the first of several crossings. Enjoy some tall cottonwoods, and after another 0.25 mile see the ridgetops and cliffs soaring above. The stream is much deeper, but passable, during the spring and dries to a trickle as summer progresses. After approximately 1.5 miles, if you look carefully at the top of the ridge on the east, you can see one of the routes up to Grey Rock high above.

After wandering through the narrowing gulch, the trail opens up into a broad meadow area that is a good spot for a picnic. Then it goes downhill to a trail intersection; bear right or plan to go straight uphill, very steeply, on a rocky, old four-wheel-drive road on the west side of the loop. Bear right for the east side of the loop

and travel through a small arroyo with pretty rock formations, with the generally dry streambed on the right. The trail winds and begins to climb in earnest over lots of rocks and through some trees. Then it goes much more steeply uphill, opens up considerably, and turns into a doubletrack trail. It tops out in a meadow area with a view of a rural subdivision to the north, an impressive rocky ridge to the east, and the jumbled canyon foothills to the south.

Turn around at any point along the way, especially if you have small children with you or if you are not an expert mountain biker. In early spring this is a good trail for wildflowers and has lots of places for snack and water breaks. If you turn around after topping out, you can avoid the unpleasant plunge on the narrow rocky road, though you will walk a bit farther on the return.

## 146 Mount McConnel

ROOSEVELT NATIONAL FOREST

see map on p. 294

| | |
|---|---|
| **Distance** | 4-plus miles, loop |
| **Difficulty** | Easy–moderate, depending on distance you hike |
| **Elevation Gain** | 1,240' (starting at 6,660') |
| **Trail Use** | Hiking, camping, leashed dogs OK |
| **Agency** | Canyon Lakes Ranger District, Roosevelt National Forest |
| **Map(s)** | Trails Illustrated *Cache la Poudre & Big Thompson* |
| **Facilities** | Restrooms at trailhead; campground nearby |

**HIGHLIGHTS** This is a short, relatively easy hike with spectacular views of the Poudre Canyon and distant peaks. Its location next to a campground and the river make a weekend river reverie tempting. The trail includes some steep sections.

**DIRECTIONS** Take US 287 north from Fort Collins and exit west onto CO 14 at Ted's Place. Take CO 14 approximately 5.5 miles west of Stove Prairie Road (County Road 27). Park where you see the sign for Mountain Park Campground on the left (south) side of the road.

The trailhead is near the restrooms at the end of the parking lot loop road on the south side. The route described here includes the William R. Kreutzer Nature Trail, which can be used for shorter, easier excursions. The nature trail has many interpretive signs along the way. The steepest, sketchiest section of the main trail is the east side of the loop. If you don't have good soles on your boots or a good sense of balance, you might want to avoid it because parts of it are a slippery chute.

If you want to see all of the sites and avoid the steep sections, go out and back to the summit on the west side, return to the trailhead, and then take a short jaunt on the east side of the loop and turn around after you have seen the view and enjoyed a few informational nature trail signs.

The west loop is wide, with frequent resting points and great views, one of which is a little more than 1 mile from the start. This is also a good turnaround point if you want to avoid steep climbing. The steep section is short and not that challenging and will take you just below the summit rocks. If you have a clear day, enjoy the distant Rawah Range peaks, as well as views of the canyon and river below. A side trail up to the summit is an easy rock hop. The loop

trail continues and plunges down the east side of the canyon slope, affording sweeping views of the canyon to the east. After you reach the summit, return to the trailhead the way you came, and enjoy a picnic lunch next to the whispering river.

*Stopping for a rest on the Mount McConnel Trail; photographed by Joe Grim*

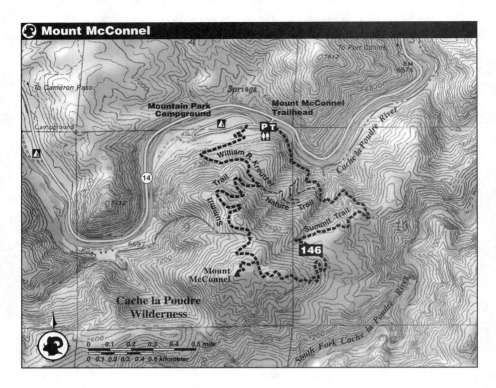

### 147  Lower Dadd Gulch

ROOSEVELT NATIONAL FOREST

|  |  |
|---|---|
| **Distance** | 7 miles, out-and-back |
| **Difficulty** | Easy–moderate, depending on distance you hike |
| **Elevation Gain** | 1,800' (starting at 7,030') |
| **Trail Use** | Hiking, mountain biking, horseback riding, leashed dogs OK |
| **Agency** | Canyon Lakes Ranger District, Roosevelt National Forest |
| **Map(s)** | Trails Illustrated *Cache la Poudre & Big Thompson* |
| **Facilities** | Restrooms and picnic area across the highway from the trailhead |

**HIGHLIGHTS** This is a shady, delightful trail near Rustic that rolls and gently climbs its way through some uniquely beautiful foothills terrain, crossing several streams and weaving through ponderosa pines, tall cottonwood trees, lodgepole pines, and aspens. The top end of the trail opens up for some great views of the high foothills that would be a major mountain range in most other states. On the return, you will enjoy views of the rock outcrops that top the Poudre Canyon. The trail tops out on a ridge and Dadd Gulch Road comes up the other side from Crown Point Road. You can picnic next to the Poudre River after your hike is over and cool your heels.

**DIRECTIONS** Drive approximately 2 miles east of Rustic (1.5 miles west of the Indian Meadows Picnic Area) on CO 14. Parking areas are available on both sides of the road. The one on the right (north) side is next to a pretty mountain meadow and has restrooms.

he trailhead is on the left (south) side of CO 14. Pass through two livestock gates and travel gently uphill though shade. After the first stream crossing, the trail begins to climb more steeply and then opens up and widens with views of rock formations. After the third stream crossing, you will have hiked 0.5 mile. You'll likely hear birds singing and see violet columbine blooms if you visit in the spring or early summer as you cross the stream for the fourth and fifth times. Cross a small meadow under a tangle of power lines and see charred terrain from a fire that swept through the area high on the ridgeline above. In season, you'll likely see many butterflies at each of the eight stream crossings.

At approximately the 1.3-mile mark, bear right as the main trail separates from

*Lower Dadd Gulch Trail rolls through lots of shade; photographed by Alan Stark*

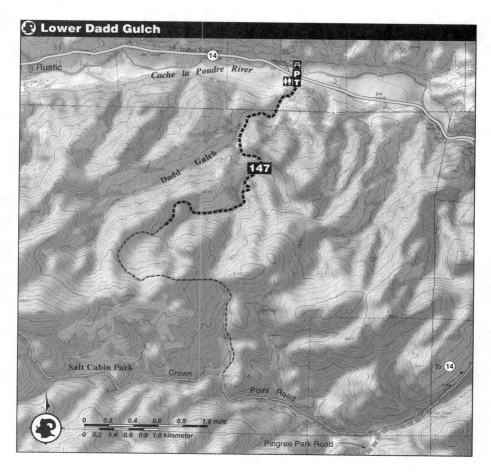

power lines, which follow a secondary trail, and you leave these signs of civilization behind. Enter an awesome ponderosa pine forest and climb, noticing a small ridge on the right. If you want a nice view, detour off-trail and enjoy, but please avoid trampling wildflowers, and you'll see the distant mountain range to the west. The rest of the trail is a long traverse that ends at Dadd Gulch, which is open to motorized travel and accessible from Crown Point Road. (If you're looking for a challenging mountain bike route, try the round-trip from the trailhead to Crown Point Road.) Turn around, retrace your steps, and dip your toes in the Poudre River before you drive back down the canyon or visit Rustic for a snack.

## 148 The Big South Trail

ROOSEVELT NATIONAL FOREST

|  |  |
|---|---|
| **Distance** | 6–16 miles, out-and-back |
| **Difficulty** | Easy–moderate |
| **Elevation Gain** | 960' (starting at 8,440') |
| **Trail Use** | Hiking, camping, snowshoeing, skiing, leashed dogs OK |
| **Agency** | Canyon Lakes Ranger District, Roosevelt National Forest |
| **Map(s)** | Trails Illustrated *Poudre River & Cameron Pass* |
| **Facilities** | Backcountry campsites |

**HIGHLIGHTS** The Big South is the sparkling south fork of the Cache la Poudre River that winds through a beautiful canyon as it rolls, tumbles, twists, and turns its way down from its origin in Rocky Mountain National Park. The trailhead is where CO 14 and the river part company, so you can hike along the wild and scenic river in the Comanche Peak Wilderness in peace away from the highway. This is a rolling, gradually climbing trail offering the cascading river, a mixed conifer and aspen forest, and the experience of trekking up the ever-changing canyon until it vanishes into deep forest green. Sections of the trail are very rocky because it skirts the edge of the compact arroyo, surrounded by richly stained colorful rock cliffs and rock falls. Three backcountry campsites a little more than 1 mile from the trailhead are nice for first-time backpacking experiences.

**DIRECTIONS** Take US 287 north from Fort Collins, and exit west onto CO 14 at Ted's Place. Drive approximately 48 miles west and south on CO 14 from Ted's Place. The parking lot is on the left side of the road 1 mile past Poudre Falls.

The trailhead is on the left or east side of the road just after the turnout for Poudre Falls. Poudre Falls can be dramatic during the spring runoff or in early winter, when portions of the waterfall freeze into unpredictable shapes and the sun glistens on the combination of ice and water. In its first 0.5 mile, the Big South Trail offers a similar spring torrent, as well as winter ice sculptures that often linger into early spring. The dazzling water is a treat in any season and is only a short stroll from the trailhead.

The beginning of the trail is rocky because it skirts the edges of rockfalls and the narrowest section of the arroyo, with small waterfalls and colorful rock outcrops. After 0.5 mile you enter the northeast corner of the Comanche Peak Wilderness; wilderness rules apply, which means biking is prohibited. The South Fork or Big South really isn't very big— more of a stream than a river but with a sweet melody. The trail stays on the east side of the river. It climbs slowly through the trees, over and around crumbling, picturesque rock walls, and quickly gains 100 feet. It then climbs a little more steeply over a narrow but short section of rocks that can be tricky early or late in the season if it's covered with snow or ice.

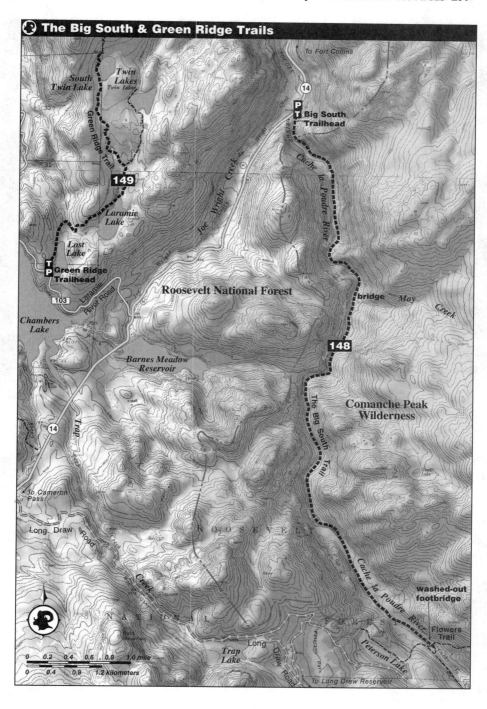

The Big South & Green Ridge Trails

To Fort Collins

South Twin Lake

Twin Lakes

14

Big South Trailhead

Green Ridge Trail

149

Joe Wright Creek

Cache la Poudre River

Laramie Lake

Lost Lake

**Roosevelt National Forest**

Green Ridge Trailhead

bridge

May Creek

103

Laramie River Road

Chambers Lake

148

*Barnes Meadow Reservoir*

**Comanche Peak Wilderness**

The Big South Trail

14

Trap

To Cameron Pass

Long Draw Road

Creek

R O O S E V E L T

Cache la Poudre River

**washed-out footbridge**

Flowers Trail

Peterson Lake

Bald Mountain

N A T I O N A L

Long Draw Road

Long Trap Lake

0   0.2   0.4   0.6   0.8   1.0 mile

0   0.4   0.8   1.2 kilometers

To Long Draw Reservoir

*Big South Trail; photographed by Joe Grim*

The trail drops down to the river for a flat stretch over the next mile that includes three backcountry campsites and then rolls back uphill through another rocky section. It breaks out of the trees for some great views of the soaring canyon foothills and then climbs another 100 feet to reach 8,700 feet in elevation. It descends back to the river temporarily before traversing a large rockfall near 8,800 feet in elevation.

At approximately 5 miles the canyon opens up and turns into a pleasing meadow that invites you to picnic. Relax and enjoy the view of the rock formations around you. In about another 2 miles, you will see Flowers Trail and a washed-out footbridge. After this point choose when to turn around and retrace your steps. If you continue to the end of the marked route, the trail ends at the edge of the forest.

# 1–2 HOURS FROM FORT COLLINS

**149** ## Green Ridge Trail
ROOSEVELT NATIONAL FOREST

see map on p. 297

| | |
|---|---|
| **Distance** | 200 yards to Lost Lake, 1 mile to Laramie Lake, 4.5 miles to North Twin Lakes; out-and-back |
| **Difficulty** | Easy |
| **Elevation Gain** | 495' (starting at 8,995') |
| **Trail Use** | Hiking, mountain biking, backpacking, fishing, motorized recreation, snowshoeing, skiing, option for kids, leashed dogs OK |
| **Agency** | Canyon Lakes Ranger District, Roosevelt National Forest |
| **Map(s)** | Trails Illustrated *Poudre River & Cameron Pass* |
| **Facilities** | None |

**HIGHLIGHTS** This easy hike on a gradually climbing, rolling trail that accesses four lovely lakes—Lost, Laramie, and the Twin Lakes. Take in one, some, or all of them for a nice jaunt. The lakes are pretty, and there are views of the surrounding mountains from them. The trail is usually closed to vehicles until July 4, so use it early to avoid off-highway vehicles, but be prepared for some wet spots. Bring insect repellent for early season adventures.

**DIRECTIONS** Take CO 14 approximately 50 miles west from Fort Collins. About 2.5 miles past the Big South Trailhead where the highway crosses the Poudre River, turn right (north) onto well-marked Laramie River Road. Closed in winter, this road goes by Chambers Lake Reservoir, is the access route for the Rawah Wilderness Area and lakes, and continues all the way to Laramie, Wyoming, via Glendevey and Wood's Landing. Take Laramie River Road approximately 1.5 miles north to reach the trailhead on the right (east) side of the road at the Lost Lake parking lot. You are getting close when you crest the hill next to Chambers Lake. The trailhead is well marked, and the trail has alternating blue and orange U.S. Forest Service diamonds; the orange ones indicate that it can also be used for motorized recreation.

The Green Ridge Trail, which is sometimes used by off-highway vehicles, is found off the Laramie River Road. The trail starts at Lost Lake and heads north through a thick lodgepole pine and fir forest along the lake's northwest shore for around 0.3 mile.

In 0.25 mile the trail forks, with the primary four-wheel-drive road going straight (north) and the trail to the lakes going downhill to the right. Follow the orange and blue diamonds. Views of the Rawah Wilderness are your reward from the north access to Lost Lake, where there is a small dam at around the 0.3-mile mark. Once you pass Lost Lake, the trail (former double-track four-wheel-drive road) meanders

through thick trees as it tracks northeast. The trail rolls and climbs steadily, and in another mile you can see part of Laramie Lake. Watch for a side trail down to the lake, which is virtually invisible from the trail. The side trail to the lake is unsigned.

From Laramie Lake it is another mile to South Twin Lake. The trail stays in the trees and heads north for 0.3 mile before taking the fainter side-loop trail over to South Twin Lake. North Twin Lake is a bit farther and somewhat anticlimactic after visiting the larger lakes but offers its own brand of serenity. It is directly north from Laramie Lake, or you can take the loop to visit South Twin Lake and then return more directly.

*View from South Twin Lake*

### GREAT FOR KIDS

If you're hiking Green Ridge Trail with small children or are looking for a small adventure, explore the south and north shores of Lost Lake and call it a day. If you go just a bit farther, you can also see Laramie Lake.

## 150  Sawmill Creek Trail to Clark Peak

### ROOSEVELT NATIONAL FOREST

| | |
|---|---|
| **Distance** | 3–10 miles, out-and-back |
| **Difficulty** | Moderate–challenging, depending on distance hiked and elevation gained |
| **Elevation Gain** | 3,500' (starting at 9,480') |
| **Trail Use** | Hiking, snowshoeing, skiing, leashed dogs OK |
| **Agency** | Canyon Lakes Ranger District, Roosevelt National Forest |
| **Map(s)** | Trails Illustrated *Poudre River & Cameron Pass* |
| **Facilities** | None |

**HIGHLIGHTS** This relatively lightly used trail offers access to a high mountain panorama of the soaring peaks in the Rawah Range, including its monarch Clark Peak. Summiting Clark Peak is a challenging day trip; it is more easily climbed from the west through the Colorado State Forest, or from the end of the Blue Lake Trail, but this is one of the challenging routes for climbing it. Alternatively, the trail works for out-and-back trips of any length with enthralling views. The trail ends up in the Rawah Wilderness Area, with an endless network of former logging roads to explore and try to get lost on. At least one goes over the ridge to the Blue Lake Trail. The possibilities are endless for the addicted backcountry rambler with compass and topographic map or a GPS unit in hand who wants to go beyond the described route or off-trail.

**DIRECTIONS** Drive 60 miles on CO 14 west from Fort Collins to the Blue Lake parking area on the right or west side of the road, across from Long Draw Road. It is well marked but doesn't have any facilities. If you reach Zimmerman Lake before seeing Blue Lake, turn around because you missed it. Park in the lot for Blue Lake and walk 200 yards west on CO 14; you will see the trailhead on the right (north) side of the road marked by a ROAD CLOSED gate. Do not park on the road or you might be ticketed or towed.

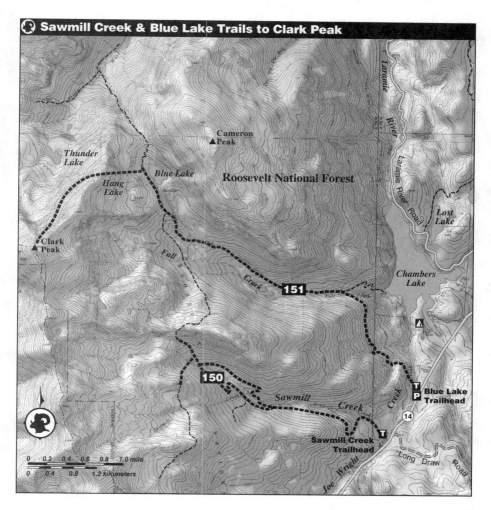

## Sawmill Creek & Blue Lake Trails to Clark Peak

The trail, an old logging road, starts off in the trees for the first mile or so and gradually steepens. You can sometimes see a blue diamond marker up fairly high on the trees, directing you away from dead ends and incorrect old logging roads. (The markers may not be in place after a windy stretch of weather.) The trail turns sharply to the left (west) after the first 0.5 mile, which can be easy to miss because a faint logging road continues straight ahead as well. On this sunny section of trail, you will warm up considerably. You can start to see views back to the southeast of the

mountains and cliffs above Zimmerman Lake all the way to the dappled ridgeline of Comanche Peak and its surrounding wilderness area. The trail then turns back to the Sawmill Creek drainage and travels primarily west-northwest.

After another mile of climbing, the trail levels somewhat and then goes slightly downhill to an intersection, which is a nice viewpoint for photos and a good place for a snack or lunch break. At this point the views of Clark Peak and its subpeak neighbors are nonstop and quite spectacular, but the wind can become a factor if it is a chilly

*Two skiers enjoy the view of the Comanche Peak Wilderness from the Sawmill Creek Trail.*

early spring or fall day. If clouds are gathering on the summits, plan wisely for a retreat when you hear the first peal of thunder.

For the last 2 miles to the headwalls and steeper treks up toward Clark Peak, choose between the north and south routes to reach the high mountain cirques. To journey beyond the end of these trails, you need good bushwhacking and route-finding skills; you will encounter multiple, sometimes confusing trails—a network of old logging roads that can suddenly disappear. If you keep traveling upslope southwest through the tall trees, you will eventually break through for a terrific sight. It is worth the extra effort to see the base of the Rawahs and the high bowls and peaks, even if you don't plan to climb

them. Either use a compass or carefully note the way back so you don't get lost. Aim for the drainage (downhill to the east) if you get turned around, and you'll get back to the highway.

If you want to climb Clark Peak, you'll need more than one topographic map, a compass, and perhaps a GPS unit and the skills to use them. After the trails peter out, the terrain becomes extremely steep. Go north and west when in doubt, and avoid climbing the dead-end ridges to the northeast as I did when I went with a friend. After going over a couple of ridges, you'll reach the cirque below the summit and follow the southwest ridge to the summit. Get an early start to avoid thunderstorms, and plan on a long but rewarding day.

## 151  Blue Lake Trail to Clark Peak

ROOSEVELT NATIONAL FOREST

see map on p. 301

| | |
|---|---|
| **Distance** | 2.5–12.4 miles, out-and-back |
| **Difficulty** | Easy–moderate/challenging, depending on distance hiked |
| **Elevation Gain** | Blue Lake: 1,300'; Clark Peak: 3,450' (starting at 9,500') |
| **Trail Use** | Hiking, backpacking, snowshoeing, option for kids, leashed dogs OK |
| **Agency** | Canyon Lakes Ranger District, Roosevelt National Forest |
| **Map(s)** | Trails Illustrated *Poudre River & Cameron Pass* |
| **Facilities** | None |

**HIGHLIGHTS** One of the most popular Cameron Pass area trails offers easy, short round-trip excursions; a challenging all-day adventure; or a backpack trip to a pristine mountain lake surrounded by towering mountains. This trail offers almost everything—stately trees, pretty riparian areas, meadows, stream crossings, and a winding, tree-covered path with striking views. It can be used for a relatively easy 5-mile out-and-back trip or a moderate to difficult 12.5-mile trip to the lake. Hiking all the way to the lake is an all-day adventure; don't attempt it if heavy weather is predicted unless you start early and are well prepared, or you may end up dodging lightning bolts. It is a popular overnight destination for backpackers but can also be a moderate to challenging and highly satisfying day hike if you are fit. If you start at the crack of dawn, you can summit Clark Peak.

**DIRECTIONS** Drive 60 miles on CO 14 west from Fort Collins to the parking area on the right or west side of the road, across from Long Draw Road. It is well marked but doesn't have any facilities. If you reach the Zimmerman Lake trailhead before seeing Blue Lake, you missed it.

The trail starts at the edge of the parking lot and travels right (north) and then veers gradually northwest. It descends gradually for about 0.25 mile, quickly enveloping you in the beautiful forest, and then gradually climbs about 300 feet in the first mile after crossing the drainage. At a viewpoint a little more than 1 mile from the trailhead on the right side, you can see Chambers Lake and across the valley behind you.

The next 0.5 mile to the creek crossing is a gentle climb; you can see the Rawahs in the distance before you descend. After descending to a stream crossing, the trail climbs again, this time more steeply, reaching the wilderness boundary in short order in less than 0.5 mile. The trail rolls quite a bit for most of the trip to the lake, but after crossing Fall Creek and viewing a meadow area, it climbs steadily to almost 11,000 feet. The last 0.5 mile is an almost 200-foot descent to the lake; save some energy for the return trip up. The sparkling lake is in a magnificent setting among some of the highest peaks of the Rawah Range, including its monarch 12,951-foot Clark Peak and 12,127-foot Cameron Peak. The summits are obscured by the steep shoulders of the mountains that surround the lake.

### Clark Peak via Blue Lake

You can summit Clark Peak from Blue Lake if you are very ambitious and start at the trailhead at dawn. It's easier to ascend the east slope of Clark Peak than the west slope from the Sawmill Creek route, but the former is also difficult because of the longer distance to Blue Lake. It is a great backpack and nontechnical climbing opportunity if you have the time. If you don't, prepare yourself for a long, challenging trek; start at dawn and expect to have an 8- to 12-hour day, depending on your fitness level, pace, and route-finding skills. Once you reach the lake, continue north and mount the ridge, or steep hill, to the northwest. From there take a sharp left (south) and proceed southwest up very steep slopes to the summit and its commanding 360-degree view.

*Blue Lake; photographed by Joe Grim*

### GREAT FOR KIDS

The first big viewpoint along Blue Lake Trail is a good turnaround point for small children. You might also consider continuing on the gentle climb to the creek crossing to enjoy a great view of the Rawah Mountains in the distance.

---

## 152  Trap Park Trail to Iron Mountain
ROOSEVELT NATIONAL FOREST

| | |
|---|---|
| **Distance** | 4.5 miles to end of Trap Park, 5.6 miles to Iron Mountain; out-and-back |
| **Difficulty** | Moderate–challenging |
| **Elevation Gain** | Trap Park: 1,300'; Iron Mountain: 2,745' (starting at 9,520') |
| **Trail Use** | Hiking, fishing, snowshoeing, skiing, option for kids, leashed dogs OK |
| **Agency** | Canyon Lakes Ranger District, Roosevelt National Forest |
| **Map(s)** | Trails Illustrated *Poudre River & Cameron Pass* |
| **Facilities** | None |

**HIGHLIGHTS**  This is a spectacular but little-known area off Long Draw Road. The trail edges uphill through a beautiful riparian area following the Trap Creek drainage on a narrow trail. Peterson Lake is a possible side-trail destination popular with fishermen. The park is a draw, or small canyon, and offers interesting, varied scenery and a rolling trail that climbs gently. After 1 mile, you reach the wide open, impressive "park" framed by a pretty mixed forest that opens into a series of high, tundralike meadows, topping out with a great view of the mountains. You can hike all the way to the top of Iron Mountain at the highest point. Be sure to wear bright colors in hunting season because the area is popular with hunters.

**DIRECTIONS**  Take CO 14 about 52 miles to Long Draw Road. The quickest access is to follow Long Draw Road. Turn left and drive 2.7 miles until you see the turnoff to the Trap Park parking area on the right.

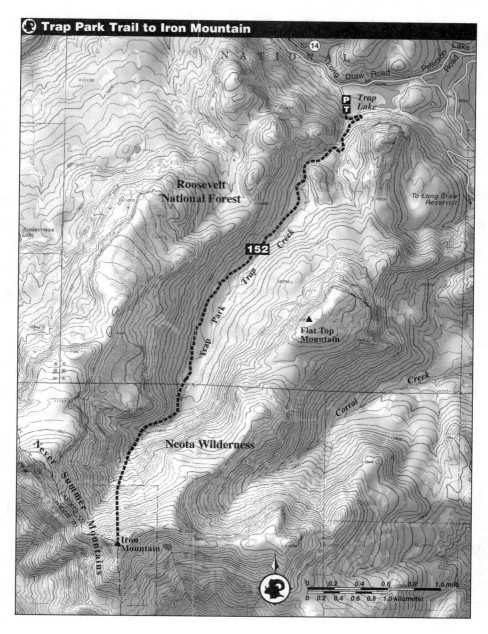

## Trap Park Trail to Iron Mountain

From the parking area, the trail goes west 0.25 mile to a fork where the Peterson Lake Trail goes left (south). Some informal game trails through the trees on the left meander to the lake. Please stay on the primary trails to avoid resource damage and help to preserve the semipristine environment. Like most of the canyon, this area is popular with hunters, especially during the elk and deer seasons, so be sure to wear bright colors. After approximately 200 yards, the Peterson Lake Trail is visible on the left

*Hiker on Trap Park Trail*

and the Trap Park Trail switchbacks somewhat steeply up a rocky hillside that offers a photo opportunity and view of the lake. The trail then climbs more slightly above Trap Creek toward the open park area.

When you crest the top of the small arroyo that frames the creek, the park opens up with a magnificent view of the mountain ridgeline, with Iron Mountain, on the north edge of the Never Summer Range, providing the dominant view to the southwest.

After a snack and water break, continue across the park to the 1.5-mile point, where a shortcut joins the main trail. From here, either descend to and follow a trail near the creek or stay high to climb the north-facing ridge for another mile to enjoy another natural spectacle. Climbing the slope southwest to the top of the ridge is a rewarding but challenging adventure, but don't proceed if thunderstorm clouds are looming. From the top of the pass, climb southeast to the top of Iron Mountain for spectacular views of the Rawahs and Michigan Reservoir. There is no trail on Iron Mountain, so route-finding skills are required.

## GREAT FOR KIDS

The top of this arroyo is a great place for a picnic and a turnaround spot for small children. You can see Iron Mountain and the beautiful park stretching out before you. There is a game trail across the drainage, which ends abruptly.

**153**  ## Zimmerman Lake Trail
ROOSEVELT NATIONAL FOREST

see map on p. 308

| | |
|---|---|
| **Distance** | 2.2–3 miles, loop or point to point |
| **Difficulty** | Easy |
| **Elevation Gain** | 475' (starting at 10,020') |
| **Trail Use** | Hiking, fishing, snowshoeing, skiing, option for kids, leashed dogs OK |
| **Agency** | Canyon Lakes Ranger District, Roosevelt National Forest |
| **Map(s)** | Trails Illustrated *Poudre River & Cameron Pass* |
| **Facilities** | Restrooms at trailhead |

**HIGHLIGHTS**  This is a short and steady climb to a small lake with great views of the surrounding remnants of the Never Summer Mountains. It is a popular trail, so expect company, but crowds thin out quickly when you reach the lake. The Rawah Wilderness and Never Summer Mountains that form the northwest border of Rocky Mountain National Park surround the lake. This can be the beginning of a mostly downhill hike with a car shuttle to the Meadows Trailhead. There is also a loop trail around the lake that features lots of trees and can be used to extend the short hike to the lake.

**DIRECTIONS**  Take CO 14 west from Fort Collins 58 miles, and park in the large parking lot, with restroom facilities, on the east (left) side of the road a few miles before reaching Cameron Pass, approximately 63 miles from Fort Collins. CO 14 generally travels east–west when it first enters the Poudre Canyon and then dips dramatically to the southwest at Kinnickinnick. By the time you stop for the Zimmerman Lake Trailhead, the road is actually more north–south than east–west.

The parking lot is usually almost full, and the trail can initially be busy. You can achieve off-trail solitude once you reach the lake. The trail goes southeast (right) out of the parking lot and then immediately east (left) into tall pine trees. It climbs gently for about 200 yards and then gradually steepens and narrows into switchbacks. The trail climbs almost 400 feet over the next 0.75 mile before exiting the trees and leveling somewhat next to a tree-rimmed meadow. The trail widens on the right edge of the meadow. You will see an expansive view of the Rawahs to the east from the top of the meadow. At this point, you'll also need to decide whether or not you want a longer jaunt to the lake because you've reached the intersection for the loop trail.

If you do, bear right (straight) and take the tree-lined loop to the far side of Zimmerman Lake. Otherwise, bear left for the main trail that climbs and then levels as it goes north back into the trees. In another 0.25 mile you will reach the west edge of the lake. Either stay on the trail to reach the northeast edge of the lake or climb a short hill to the right to the lake's surface. You can extend your hike on paths around the left (north) or right (south) edges of the lake.

Bushwhacking to the top of the ridgeline of Iron Mountain to the south is fun if you have good route-finding skills and like steep, challenging ascents. You can also survey the great scenery at the lake, have a snack, and reverse course if you've had enough. The trail continues north and then reaches a fork, where an easterly trail (right) heads to the north end of the lake and the northbound trail (straight or left) goes down to the Long Draw Road via the Meadows Trail. You can circle the lake in either direction late in the season, but you'll encounter bogs early in the season. To access more loop trails, take the almost flat right fork. Once you reach the northeast corner of the lake, you can bushwhack your way from there into the hills and onto the ridgeline above the lake if you have good mountaineering and route-finding skills and use a map and compass and perhaps a GPS unit.

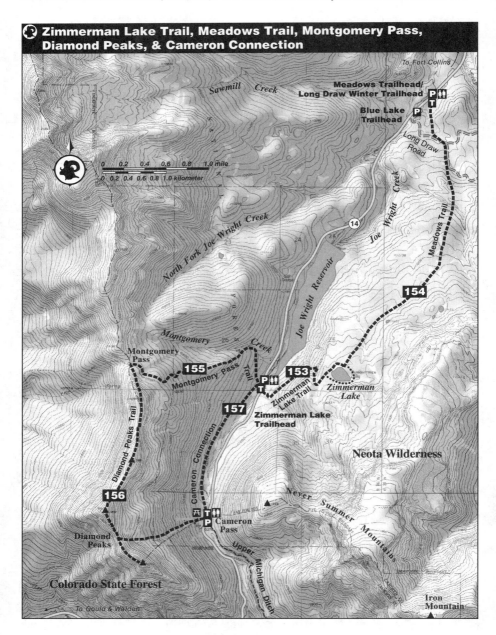

**Zimmerman Lake Trail, Meadows Trail, Montgomery Pass, Diamond Peaks, & Cameron Connection**

### GREAT FOR KIDS

Zimmerman Lake is a nice half-day activity for families with small children that can be extended with trails that lead north or east from the lake. Families with small children usually find making it to the lake enough fun and exercise for a day. Circumnavigating the lake, however, is an easy addition.

## 154  Meadows Trail
ROOSEVELT NATIONAL FOREST

| | |
|---|---|
| **Distance** | 10 miles, out-and-back |
| **Difficulty** | Moderate |
| **Elevation Gain/Loss** | From Meadows trailhead: 1,295' (starting at 9,200'); |
| | From Zimmerman Lake: 1,295' (starting at 10,490') |
| **Trail Use** | Hiking, snowshoeing, skiing, option for kids, leashed dogs OK |
| **Agency** | Canyon Lakes Ranger District, Roosevelt National Forest |
| **Map(s)** | Trails Illustrated *Poudre River & Cameron Pass* |
| **Facilities** | Restrooms at Meadows and Zimmerman Lake trailheads |
| **Note(s)** | Biking is prohibited. Dogs must be leashed in wilderness areas and under voice control on the rest of the trail. |

**HIGHLIGHTS** This trail winds through a superb old-growth forest of tall, stately fir and spruce trees. If you'd like a shorter trip, you can park a car shuttle at Zimmerman Lake Trailhead. If you start at Zimmerman Lake instead of at Meadows Trailhead, it is mostly downhill. It's a satisfying out-and-back from either end with viewpoints and picnic possibilities along the way. Visit in midsummer (after midsummer the wetlands have dried out). The trail enters the Neota Wilderness about halfway to Zimmerman Lake; from that point you can follow the markers for the cross-country ski/snowshoe trail.

**DIRECTIONS** Take CO 14 approximately 60 miles west from Fort Collins to the parking area on the left side of the road, across from Long Draw Road. Poorly marked, it is just before you reach Long Draw Road and the Blue Lake parking lot on the right.

If you want a major all-day adventure and challenging workout, try the Meadows Trail up to Zimmerman Lake and back. For a calmer adventure, leave a car at Long Draw Road or Meadows Trailhead and follow the Meadows Trail from the northwest side of the Zimmerman Lake loop. Look for red wooden arrows that mark the trail. From the Meadows Trailhead, go north to Long Draw Road, which will seem like it is east. A rolling trail with some moderate climbs and descents that is generally downhill from Zimmerman Lake, Meadows Trail requires at least a half-day commitment one-way or a full day for the round-trip, so you need an early start to make the trek without thunderstorms. The delightful trail winds through the stately spruce and fir trees of a dense forest. It then opens up into several namesake meadows and initially crests a ridgeline, with great views of the Rawahs as it winds through part of the Neota Wilderness.

When the wetlands have dried out for the year, you can park in the Meadows lot, southeast of the Blue Lake lot. The walk from the parking area adds about 0.5 mile to the hike but is a pretty, winding section of trail with a small brook that eventually retreats into its banks after inundating the trail during spring runoff.

When the wetlands are not dried out, it's easier to park on Long Draw Road about 0.25 mile from the Meadows Trailhead and hike from there. The trail is located on the right (northwest) side of the road on an uphill. You will see a white NO OHVS sign on the right side of the road where the trail—actually a wide former logging road—begins. After 100 yards it splits; take the right fork. The trail climbs gradually and then more steeply uphill northwest through a tree tunnel. When it levels temporarily, a break in the trees allows a great view of the Rawahs to the north and west. The trail bears left (south) past a meadow and then continues to climb, turning right (north) next to a large rock and then steepening. The trail continues to climb for the next 0.5 mile and then levels again, goes

*View from Meadows Trail*

downhill, reaches the wilderness boundary, and switchbacks more steeply to the top of a small ridge, where you get another view. It stays fairly level for the next 0.25 mile before starting to climb again.

When you reach another fork, look carefully for the brown marker with a black arrow, telling you to turn sharply right (north) to stay on the trail. It reenters thick trees and after about 100 yards winds through the trees, reaches a small meadow—a chief characteristic of this trail and suitable for a picnic—and then climbs again in earnest. It is still approximately 3.5 miles to Zimmerman Lake.

You climb through several switchbacks; it is easy to lose the trail in this section unless you watch carefully for the light-brown wood signs with black arrows that appear every 200 yards or less. After the sets of switchbacks, you reach an oblong hump where the trail turns sharply left and goes around a small hill. Be careful to avoid the false trail straight ahead. You will shortly see another arrow pointing the way. The trail then winds downhill to the first meadow, where it exits the trees and travels along the left (south) edge of the meadow. The trail reenters the thick tree cover at the other end of the meadow; watch carefully for the break in the trees where it reenters and starts to climb again. Though it is easy to lose the trail, if you watch carefully you will see that it is one of the best signed trails in the area.

The trail wanders through more turns, passes a small meadow, and climbs again. It descends to the second meadow and exits the trees again, following the left edge of the forest until it reenters and starts to climb again about 100 yards at the end of the second submeadow. Do not continue straight up the middle of the top of the meadow. As you enter the trees, the trail continues its serpentine swivel through and then down to the third meadow.

### GREAT FOR KIDS

The viewpoint after the wilderness boundary is a good family turnaround point; you won't see any great views again for some time, until you reach the first of the meadows, 0.5 mile ahead, beyond the fork in the trail. Though the trail itself is a great place for communion with the magnificent old-growth trees, when you reenter the thick tree cover the trail levels and rolls gently to some picnic spots before it gets steeper.

---

 **Montgomery Pass**

ROOSEVELT NATIONAL FOREST

see map on p. 308

| | |
|---|---|
| **Distance** | 3.5 miles, out-and-back |
| **Difficulty** | Moderate-plus |
| **Elevation Gain** | 1,000' (starting at 10,000') |
| **Trail Use** | Hiking, snowshoeing, skiing, leashed dogs OK |
| **Agency** | Canyon Lakes Ranger District, Roosevelt National Forest |
| **Map(s)** | Trails Illustrated *Poudre River & Cameron Pass* |
| **Facilities** | Restrooms at Zimmerman Lake parking lot |

**HIGHLIGHTS** The magnificent view from the top of the pass includes North Park, Clark Peak, the distant Zirkel Range, and the approach to Diamond Peaks, as well as the northern reaches of Rocky Mountain National Park. It is worth the steep but short 1,000-foot climb to the pass. You can descend the pass into the Colorado State Forest if you arrange a car shuttle or want a challenging out-and-back adventure. Or, once you have surmounted the pass, you can walk west into the ski bowls and enjoy a great view of the Nokhu Crags, Ute and Mahler Peaks, and Thunder Pass. Feel free to take a spectacular roller-coaster hike to the top of the Diamond Peaks if you have the time and energy in the summer; you don't have to worry about the avalanches that can make the peaks treacherous in the winter. You can also climb the pass from the west side through Colorado State Forest; check for details at the Moose Visitor Center. Unfortunately, the west side access also allows off-road, motorized vehicles that share the good hiking and biking route to the top.

**DIRECTIONS** Take CO 14 west from Fort Collins 58 miles to the Zimmerman Lake–Montgomery Pass Trailhead parking lot. Across from the Zimmerman Lake Trailhead, the trail is well marked but not easily visible from the road; it can be spotted in the trees down the road to the right from the Zimmerman Lake parking lot.

This intermediate trail gains 1,000 feet of elevation in the almost 2 miles it takes to reach the pass. You'll have to wait until early July to enjoy it, unless you like sloshing through icy water and mud, which isn't a good idea anyway because it causes severe trail erosion.

The trail starts out climbing west gradually and then gets steeper quickly through thick tree cover, paralleling the Montgomery Creek drainage. It tracks to the left (slightly northwest) after 0.25 mile. After another 0.25 mile you can momentarily relax before it gets steeper again in 100 yards. It essentially rolls steeply uphill—expect 200 feet of climbing per 0.25 mile with easy and difficult stretches. Because of its elevation change, the trail isn't for the poorly conditioned. After approximately 1 mile, you will come to a fork. The left takes you straight up to the bowls popular with skiers and snowboarders in winter, while the right takes you temporarily downhill and then gradually to the actual pass. The views from the bowls are just as good as or better than the pass and not to be missed.

Following the trail to the pass, you encounter broad switchbacks around 10,700 feet and see a meadow to the left (south). The next 200 feet to the top of the pass takes you out of the trees and affords spectacular views in all directions—Zimmerman Lake and Joe Wright Reservoirs to the east and north; the Rawah Range and its monarch, Clark Peak, to the northwest; and the cliffs and Nokhu Crags in the Never Summer Range of Routt National Forest to the southwest. It is usually fairly breezy on top year-round, so be prepared for a distinct temperature drop. Sunglasses or even goggles and a hat, cap, or hooded jacket are often necessary to hang onto your hair, and afternoon thunderstorms are always an issue during the summer climbing season. The worst you can face is an uncommon horizontal hurricane-force hailstorm.

From the top of the pass, you can climb to the top of the ridgeline to the left (southwest) and the Diamond Peaks or continue down the other side on a very steep four-wheel-drive road toward the Michigan Reservoir in the Colorado State Forest. Otherwise, have a snack and drink and enjoy your return trip down the trail.

## 156 Diamond Peaks

ROOSEVELT NATIONAL FOREST

see map on p. 308

| | |
|---|---|
| **Distance** | 4 miles, out-and-back and point to point options |
| **Difficulty** | Moderate-plus |
| **Elevation Gain** | 1,505' (starting at 10,275') |
| **Trail Use** | Hiking, leashed dogs OK |
| **Agency** | Canyon Lakes Ranger District, Roosevelt National Forest |
| **Map(s)** | Trails Illustrated *Poudre River & Cameron Pass* |
| **Facilities** | Restrooms at the parking lots for Zimmerman Lake and Montgomery Pass, as well as Cameron Pass |

**HIGHLIGHTS** The Diamonds are prominent peaks on Cameron Pass, with summits offering panoramic views of everything from North Park to the Never Summer Range. They can be climbed in a long, scenic traverse from Montgomery Pass or a more direct ascent from Cameron Pass. Summer and fall are much safer times to savor the summits because avalanches frequently scour them in the winter.

**DIRECTIONS** Take CO 14 west from Fort Collins 63 miles to the Zimmerman Lake parking lot. The Montgomery Pass Trailhead is across from the east end of the Zimmerman parking lot. Well marked but not easily visible from the road, it can be spotted in the trees down the road to the left from the Zimmerman Lake parking lot. Alternatively, drive to the summit of Cameron Pass and park in the lot on the north side of the road.

### From Montgomery Pass

Follow the directions to the Montgomery Pass Trailhead. From the summit of Montgomery Pass, turn west and traverse the right (northwest) side of the ridge. Stay below the top of the ridge to the right; it undulates, so you would have to do more up-and-down climbing if you hiked across the top. The traverse on the north (right) side of the ridge is somewhat vertical tundra and there is no trail to speak of. After rounding the ridge, aim for a saddle between the high point of the traversed ridge and the bottom of the peaks. An alternate but slower route with a faint trail is to go around the south (left) side of the ridge to the winter ski bowls and traverse much lower into the informal trail that then climbs up to the saddle. This route also rolls and descends as it approaches the peaks, making for more altitude to regain.

Once you reach the saddle just pick a route to the top of the first peak and create your own switchbacks to the top. Avoid hiking single file, preserving the tundra, and enjoy the wildflowers and nonstop views. You can return the way you came or go down and back to Montgomery Pass via the Cameron Pass and Cameron Connection Trails.

*Diamond Peak*

## Cameron Pass Route

You can do a car shuttle by going up Montgomery Pass and down to Cameron or vice versa, or just go round-trip from Cameron Pass. This is a shorter and more direct route than the Montgomery Pass route. More direct also means much steeper, as in short, sweet, and steep.

The trail begins at the back of the Cameron Pass parking lot. Bear left through the trees and generally follow the drainage. The trail is faint, and good bushwhacking skills are required. Once you are on top of the wettest part of the drainage, start climbing somewhat to the left (west). You will have to navigate through some marshy tundra if it is early in the season. Later in the summer it dries out. You will know if you are on track because veering too far to either the right or left takes you into the creek or onto terrain that is too steep. Once you are 1 mile from the trailhead and well above the drainage, it is easier to track toward the saddle that is more to the right (northwest)—the direct route to the left (west-southwest) is steep with a clump of trees. You don't have to veer very far northwest to hit the closest part of the saddle, and then you climb the peaks.

## 157 Cameron Connection

ROOSEVELT NATIONAL FOREST

see map on p. 308

| | |
|---|---|
| **Distance** | 3 miles, out-and-back |
| **Difficulty** | Easy |
| **Elevation Gain** | 200' (starting at 10,000') |
| **Trail Use** | Hiking, snowshoeing, skiing, leashed dogs OK |
| **Agency** | Canyon Lakes Ranger District, Roosevelt National Forest |
| **Map(s)** | Trails Illustrated *Poudre River & Cameron Pass* |
| **Facilities** | Restrooms at Zimmerman Lake Trailhead and the top of Cameron Pass |

**HIGHLIGHTS** This is a short, surprisingly scenic trail through an old-growth forest of spruce and fir. It shares its trailhead with the Montgomery Pass Trail and is often overlooked. It offers excellent shelter from prevailing winds and, though it parallels the highway, is far enough away to be completely buffered from its sound or sight. This trail is available only in the late summer and early fall because it crosses many streams and wetlands that don't dry out until the end of the summer hiking season.

**DIRECTIONS** Drive 58 miles on CO 14 from Fort Collins to reach the Zimmerman Lake parking lot on the left side of the road. You can park here or 1 mile farther down the highway on the right side of the road in the Cameron Pass parking lot.

This short, scenic trail shares one of its trailheads with the Montgomery Pass Trail. From there it journeys southwest to the summit of Cameron Pass, paralleling CO 14, but far enough from the highway to eliminate auto noise. It also features beautiful spruce and fir trees and three meadows with views near the pass. It is sheltered by trees most of the way to protect trail users on windy days. It climbs slowly and rolls gently, making it a good trail for beginners. Turn left (west) at the Montgomery Pass Trailhead.

If you start at the Cameron Pass parking lot, the trail goes downhill at first and then uphill on your return at the end. Blue diamonds mark the trailhead on the east (north) side of the Cameron Pass parking area and most of the trail, if they haven't been removed by weather.

## Cameron Pass

Just driving over Cameron Pass is a treat because you get to enjoy several peaks on the northern border of Rocky Mountain National Park. First you are greeted by the rugged splendor of the Nokhu Crags, with their rooster top rocks. You see Mount Richthofen peering over the Crags shoulder, daring you to try its scree slopes on another day. Then you see the tail end of the Never Summer Range, Seven Utes, Mahler Mountain, and the Diamond Peaks. The summit of CO 14 at 10,200 feet is one of the most popular destinations for hikers and bikers.

You might also encounter some overlap with off-highway vehicles approaching from the Lake Agnes or Colorado State Forest area when you take the Michigan Ditch Trail. From the parking lot you can also bushwhack northwest up the Diamond Peaks after the snow is gone, when there is no avalanche danger.

## 158  Brown's Lake

ROOSEVELT NATIONAL FOREST

see map on p. 316

| | |
|---|---|
| **Distance** | 8 miles, out-and-back |
| **Difficulty** | Moderate |
| **Elevation Gain** | 1,500' (starting at 10,500') |
| **Trail Use** | Hiking, snowshoeing, skiing, option for kids, leashed dogs OK |
| **Agency** | Canyon Lakes Ranger District, Roosevelt National Forest |
| **Map(s)** | Trails Illustrated *Poudre River & Cameron Pass* |
| **Facilities** | None |

**HIGHLIGHTS** This beautiful, rolling route has dramatic views of the Rawahs and Never Summer Mountains before it reaches two pristine mountain lakes surrounded by the rocky cliffs of a glacier-carved cirque.

**DIRECTIONS** Take US 287 north to CO 14. Then drive 26 miles west from Ted's Place to the Pingree Park Road. Drive 4 miles south; turn right (west) for Crown Point Road. Drive 12 miles to the Brown's Lake Trailhead; the parking area is on the right (north) side of the road and the trailhead on the left (south).

*The trail to Brown's Lake*

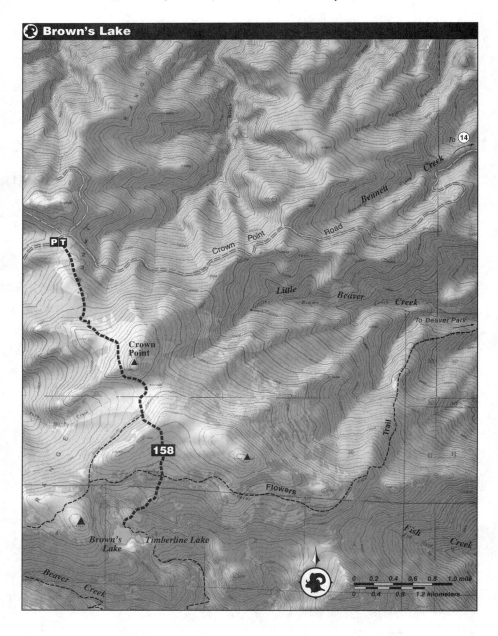

Brown's Lake

The Brown's Lake Trail goes gradually uphill from the trailhead and weaves through the trees. After around 0.25 mile it steepens considerably. After 200 feet of elevation gain, it gets much rockier and climbs approximately 500 feet more over 1 mile to almost the height of 11,462-foot Crown Point, which is next to the trail. You will have great panoramic views from this point onward. Hike up to the left (east) toward the small, rocky summit and find a spot to enjoy the view and declare victory.

Continuing toward Timberline Lake, the trail veers downhill to the right (west), crosses a valley, and then climbs another long hill ahead, regaining the 150 feet it lost and a bit more to reach the top of the next ridge at 11,400 feet. From there the trail descends again and doubles back on itself as it switchbacks through the trees. If you look carefully, you will glimpse the cliffs above the lakes. The long switchbacks take you down 200 feet to a high point overlooking the two adjoining lakes that make up this body of water captured in the cirque. From this point, continue your descent another 600 feet to the lakeshore at 10,600 feet. Timberline Lake is the smaller of the two adjoining lakes; Brown's Lake is the larger one.

### GREAT FOR KIDS

If you have small children, the rocky summit near Crown Point is a good turnaround point after you enjoy a picnic spot. That gives you a 360-degree spectacular view, without the rest of the roller-coaster hike to the lake. The downside is that you don't see the lake.

---

**159**  ## Mineral Springs Gulch to Prospect Mountain
ROOSEVELT NATIONAL FOREST

see map on p. 318

| | |
|---|---|
| **Distance** | 4 miles, out-and-back |
| **Difficulty** | Easy |
| **Elevation Gain** | 500' (starting at 9,300') |
| **Trail Use** | Hiking, snowshoeing, skiing, great for kids, leashed dogs OK |
| **Agency** | Canyon Lakes Ranger District, Roosevelt National Forest |
| **Map(s)** | Trails Illustrated *Poudre River & Cameron Pass* |
| **Facilities** | None |

**HIGHLIGHTS** This pretty woodland meadow has beautiful aspen and pine trees and views of Poudre Canyon and the distant Rawah and Medicine Bow Mountains from the top of Prospect Mountain. A low-key adventure, it is a short, easy jaunt and could include a picnic on the summit.

**DIRECTIONS** Take US 287 north to CO 14. Then drive 26 miles west from Ted's Place to Pingree Park Road. Drive 4 miles south; turn right (west) for Crown Point Road. Approximately 4.5 miles from Pingree Park Road on the right (north) side of the road, the access road is after the two turnoffs for Salt Cabin Park.

Take the closed road uphill and ignore the first side road with a locked gate that you come to around 0.25 mile. Stay left and eventually crest the hill after a little less than 1 mile. The trail meanders downhill through the trees. At the bottom of the hill, you reach the foot of a pretty meadow with the top of Prospect Mountain and the ridgeline visible to the right (north). Go left (west) and look for a faint road or trail on the right that heads to the top of the mountain at around 1.5 miles. The trail is in thick trees at the outset but breaks out into southern exposure on the 0.5-mile gradual uphill trek to the top. As you near the top, you see great views of the plains to the east and the top of Poudre Canyon to the north. The top affords views of the Rawah and Mummy Ranges to the west.

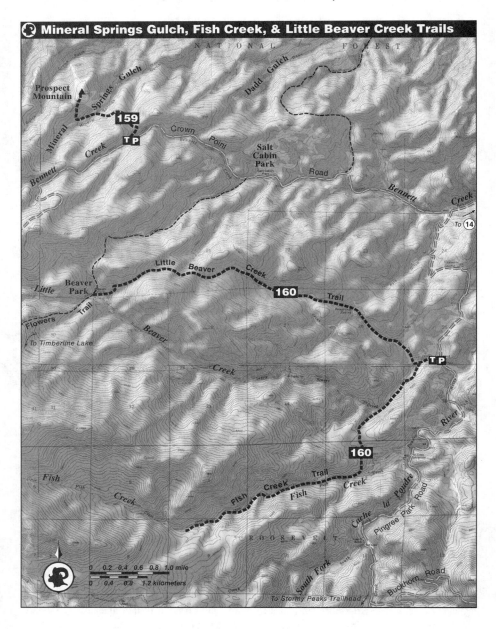

Mineral Springs Gulch, Fish Creek, & Little Beaver Creek Trails

*The trail to Prospect Mountain*

## 160   Fish Creek & Little Beaver Creek Trails

ROOSEVELT NATIONAL FOREST

| | |
|---|---|
| **Distance** | 4–10 miles, out-and-back |
| **Difficulty** | Easy–moderate |
| **Elevation Gain** | 600' (starting at 8,010') |
| **Trail Use** | Hiking, horseback riding, snowshoeing, great for kids, leashed dogs OK |
| **Agency** | Canyon Lakes Ranger District, Roosevelt National Forest |
| **Map(s)** | Trails Illustrated *Poudre River & Cameron Pass* |
| **Facilities** | None |
| **Note(s)** | Biking is prohibited because this trail is in a wilderness area. |

**HIGHLIGHTS** These lightly used trails are graced by the beauty of the Comanche Peak Wilderness towering magically above, with the often snowcapped peak for which it's named highlighting the view. This trail requires some route-finding skills because it is not well marked. It rolls up and over a large hill and then descends into the glade on the other side, with peekaboo views along the way. You can choose from two very different options if you want to hike to the end of one of the trails.

**DIRECTIONS** Take US 287 north to CO 14. Then drive 26 miles west from Ted's Place to the Pingree Park Road. Take Pingree Park Road 8 miles from its intersection with CO 14 to the trailhead. Pass Crown Point Road and the Jack Gulch Campground. The well-marked trailhead is on the right (west) well beyond the campground. Cross the cattle guard and park near the largest trailhead sign, making sure you don't block the cattle guard gate. To get to the trailhead, walk back through the cattle guard and look for a sign to the right of the fence that indicates that the Comanche Peak Wilderness is 1 mile and the Beaver Creek intersection is 2 miles. The trail goes up the hill to the left at a sharp angle.

This double trailhead starts off as Fish Creek Trail and then intersects Beaver Creek Trail. Both trails go into the Comanche Peak Wilderness Area. According to the U.S. Forest Service trailhead sign, they intersect and part company after 2 miles. According to the map, however, they intersect and part company only 1.5 miles or so from the trailhead, which seems more accurate.

Choose between two options: the Little Beaver Creek Trail to Beaver Park where it intersects with Flowers Road, or the Fish Creek Trail that ends at the Beaver Creek Trailhead on Beaver Road near Hourglass Reservoir. The trail is faint. If you keep in mind that it goes west and then northwest and that you should end up on top of the ridge to your right, it doesn't matter if you lose the trail. You will see a great view of Fall Mountain (12,258 feet), Comanche Peak (12,702 feet), and other mountains in the Mummy Range after 0.5 mile or less. Keep the drainage and peaks on your left and make your way slowly to the top of the ridge,

watching for tree blazes (where bark has been removed). The ridgeline levels out around 8,400 feet for a much more gradual climb. Then you enter the wilderness and turn right (north) and eventually go back west.

Stay on top of the ridge and you are en route; enjoy the thick lodgepole pine and spruce forest. You come to a power pole and telephone line for Pingree Park at around 8,600 feet—not typical wilderness landmarks. As the trail swings back around west, you can see Comanche Peak and the Mummies.

If you want a short excursion, turn around there and retrace your route. Except for climbing back up the last hill, it's downhill to the trailhead. If you choose to go farther, the Fish Creek branch offers better views over the next mile or two. The Little Beaver Creek Trail stays in the trees for the most part and offers views of the heavily forested valley, while Fish Creek continues to have good views of the Comanche Peak summits.

*GREAT FOR KIDS*

Because you have easily exceeded 1 mile when you reach 8,600 feet and see the views of the Comanche Peak and the Mummies, you might want a break. Also, this is the last sunny viewpoint for a while; the trail goes downhill about 0.25 mile to the intersection with the Little Beaver Creek Trail.

---

### 161  Stormy Peaks Trail

ROOSEVELT NATIONAL FOREST

| | |
|---|---|
| **Distance** | Up to 10 miles, out-and-back |
| **Difficulty** | Easy for first 2 miles, challenging if you climb a peak |
| **Elevation Gain** | 3,120' (starting at 9,030') |
| **Trail Use** | Hiking, snowshoeing, skiing, option for kids, leashed dogs OK |
| **Agency** | Canyon Lakes Ranger District, Roosevelt National Forest |
| **Map(s)** | Trails Illustrated *Poudre River & Cameron Pass* |
| **Facilities** | None |

**HIGHLIGHTS** Enjoy the impressive mountain backdrop of Comanche Peak and Fall Mountain as you traverse and then climb above the valley, gradually making your way above treeline. The trail has very rocky sections and can be wet in the early spring. The stark beauty of the burn area dominates the start, but then healthy lodgepole pine, fir, and spruce trees grace the trail.

**DIRECTIONS** Take US 287 north to CO 14. Drive 26 miles west from Ted's Place to the Pingree Park Road. Drive 18 miles to the end of the Pingree Park Road, and park in the last parking area on the left.

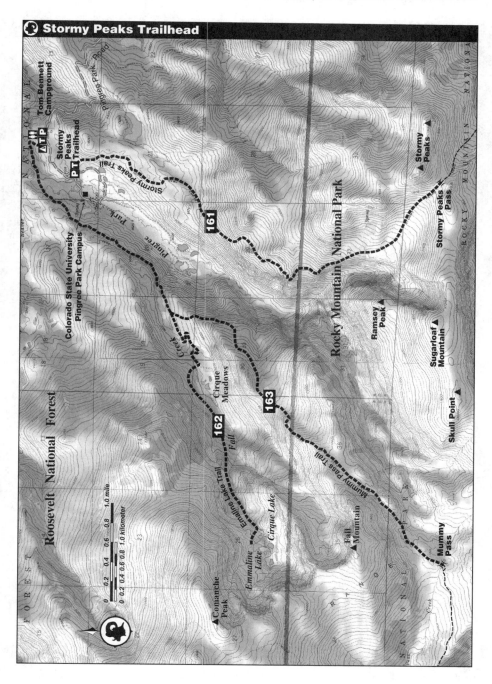

Stormy Peaks Trailhead

*Hiking among the clouds on Stormy Peaks Trail*

The Pingree Park fire swept through the area in 1994, destroying the Colorado State University (CSU) area facilities. The beginning of the trail has the stark beauty of the darkened timber and remnants of the fire. The trail starts off in tree cover and then takes a short set of switchbacks toward the top of the low ridgeline. The CSU campus and most of the Pingree Park area are visible from the ridgeline. Though you cannot see Emmaline Lake, you can see the top of the rocky cirque above the valley to the northwest. Watch for tree blazes that mark the trail because it can be hard to follow, especially in the burned area; stay on the west side of the ridge.

As you travel southwest, the 12,000-foot Fall Mountain and Comanche Peak massif is a constant and impressive backdrop. After the first mile, you enter a tree tunnel that obscures the view but allows you to relish the flora for more than 0.5 mile, until you reach the Comanche Peak Wilderness boundary. A series of steep switchbacks and several rocky sections require you, in early

spring, to negotiate wet or muddy spots. The boundary is approximately 2 miles from the trailhead, and you enjoy a view as the trees thin, with your best view yet of Comanche Peak, Emmaline Lake, Mummy Pass, and Wyoming to the north. This is a good place for a snack, water, and photos before you start climbing again.

Once you enter the wilderness area, the trail gets considerably steeper, with lots of large rocks and several small stream crossings. Hopefully, most of the rocks will be tame and all of the streams will be dry; they should be unless you are attempting an early-season trek. Look for tree blazes (slashes in the tree bark), keeping in mind that wilderness trails are not well marked. Good route-finding skills are necessary once you reach the boundary, but once you reach the major drainage and drop-off, there is only one way to go: sharply left (southeast) and uphill whether or not you are on a trail.

It is well worth the minor aggravation of negotiating a few wet spots and rocks because in about 0.5 mile you are treated to a superb view of the U-shaped glacier-carved "park" of Pingree in the canyon below Ramsey Peak (11,582 feet) and Sugarloaf Mountain (12,101 feet). You pay for this view, however, by gaining another 200 feet of elevation. At 3 miles the trail crosses into Rocky Mountain National Park (RMNP), and you enjoy more views of the glacier-carved box canyon below and get a good view of the Stormy Peaks above for the first time. This is another good break spot for water, snacks, or photos.

From here the trail veers due south and continues uphill poorly marked because of disuse. Stay parallel to the Stormy Peaks drainage, and frequently check the landscape against your map and compass to orient yourself. After 0.25 mile from the RMNP boundary you should see a sign for one of the RMNP Stormy Peaks campsites.

Just when you think you'll never reach treeline, you emerge into a wonderland of high mountain tundra, windswept meadows festooned with wildflowers, and dramatic rock outcrops of the Stormy Peaks at 11,500 feet. If you feel up to it, mounting the pass or even climbing the Stormy Peaks is worthwhile, but keep watch for the namesake storm clouds so that you don't have to do a lightning dance on the way out.

## 162  Emmaline Lake Trail
### ROOSEVELT NATIONAL FOREST

see map on p. 321

| | |
|---|---|
| **Distance** | Up to 10 miles, out-and-back |
| **Difficulty** | Easy to Cirque Meadows, moderate-plus to Emmaline Lake |
| **Elevation Gain** | 2,100' (starting at 8,900') |
| **Trail Use** | Hiking, mountain biking to wilderness or Rocky Mountain National Park boundary only, backpacking, snowshoeing, skiing, option for kids, leashed dogs OK |
| **Agency** | Canyon Lakes Ranger District, Roosevelt National Forest |
| **Map(s)** | Trails Illustrated *Poudre River & Cameron Pass* |
| **Facilities** | Restrooms at Tom Bennett Campground |

**HIGHLIGHTS** Think pristine high mountain lake and dramatic glacier-carved cirque, and your mind's eye will have the vision you are trekking toward. This is a trail that offers views of the Stormy Peaks and then the dramatic backdrop of Fall Mountain and the Comanche Peak massif framing the high mountain lake surrounded by the rocky, craggy cirque. After an open, sunny, and warm beginning, the cool shade of the thickly forested trail will protect you from sun and wind until just before you emerge onto the tundra and rock for the final steep ascent to enjoy the beauty of the lake.

**DIRECTIONS** Take CO 14 about 27 miles west to the Pingree Park Road turnoff. Take the road most of the way to the Pingree campus, and look for the right turn for Tom Bennett Campground. Go another 0.25 mile beyond that turnoff, around a sharp left hairpin turn, staying straight when the road turns right uphill toward Sky Ranch. Park where you see a sign for Cirque Meadows; it's actually the Emmaline Lake/Cirque Meadows Trailhead.

This interesting trail is rewarding regardless of the distance you travel on it. The first mile of the trail makes a good family out-and-back trip, while going all the way to Emmaline Lake makes for a moderate almost all-day hike for an acclimated hiker. Cirque Meadows is a magnificent intermediate stop along the way. One possible variation, because the road can be a bit tiresome on the way out, is to bike to the wilderness boundary and then hike the rest of the way to the lake. You then have a pleasant downhill ride to look forward to rather than slogging along the road at the end of a 10-mile trek.

The first 1.5 miles of the trail is out in the open on an old logging road, Cirque Meadows Road, and travels through the

*Emmaline Lake Trail*

burn area. It is exposed to sun and wind and can be very warm or very chilly, depending on the season. Once you reach the thick tree cover, you are protected from the wind and sun. Cross Fall Creek on a footbridge.

At the intersection with Mummy Pass Trail, continue right (southwest) to Emmaline Lake. The trail enters the trees, which should provide good sun protection and cooler temperatures. The trail winds, rolls, and switchbacks through a long tree tunnel, with occasional glimpses of the valley below. Pass the backcountry campground nestled in the trees, and then the trail climbs steeply until you break free at Cirque Meadows. Cirque Meadows is a superb setting, with the

backdrop of Fall Mountain's glacier-carved cirque and the vibrant colors of the vegetation swaying out of the wetlands.

After the wet meadows, cross a footbridge and follow the old logging road until it becomes a trail, reentering the trees and paralleling the stream. The trail zigzags through a lovely, tree-sheltered, undeveloped camping area with an active mosquito population and then climbs steeply until it breaks out of the trees. The final scrambling switchbacks take you over rocks and through tundra to the magic of Emmaline Lake and its surroundings, with the Comanche Peak and Fall Mountain massif towering above.

## 163  Mummy Pass Trail
ROOSEVELT NATIONAL FOREST

see map on p. 321

| | |
|---|---|
| **Distance** | Up to 14 miles, out-and-back |
| **Difficulty** | Moderate-plus |
| **Elevation Gain** | 2,500' (starting at 8,900') |
| **Trail Use** | Hiking, mountain biking to wilderness or Rocky Mountain National Park boundary only, snowshoeing, skiing, option for kids, leashed dogs OK |
| **Agency** | Canyon Lakes Ranger District, Roosevelt National Forest |
| **Map(s)** | Trails Illustrated *Poudre River & Cameron Pass* |
| **Facilities** | Restrooms at Tom Bennett Campground |

**HIGHLIGHTS** This is the most spectacular option in the area other than climbing Comanche Peak. It evolves into an open climb above treeline on tundra up a mountainside, offering splendid views of Pingree Park's superb surroundings of summits, rivers, trees, and wetlands. This awe-inspiring perch lets you see the soaring granite cirque that is part of the Comanche Peak massif and that cradles Emmaline Lake. The access point for this trail that goes into Rocky Mountain National Park is the same as the Emmaline Lake Trail. In terms of difficulty, it is longer and involves slightly more elevation gain.

**DIRECTIONS** Take US 287 north to CO 14. Take CO 14 about 27 miles west to the Pingree Park Road turnoff. Take the road most of the way to the Pingree campus, and look for the right turn for Tom Bennett Campground. Go another 0.25 mile beyond that turnoff, around a sharp left hairpin turn, staying straight when the road turns right uphill toward Sky Ranch. Park where you see a sign for Cirque Meadows; it's actually the Emmaline Lake/Cirque Meadows Trailhead.

The first 1.5 miles of the trail is out in the open on an old logging road, Cirque Meadows Road, and travels through the burn area. It is exposed to sun and wind and can be very warm or very chilly, depending on the season. Once you reach the thick tree cover, you are protected from the wind and sun. Cross Fall Creek on a footbridge.

As you are walking down closed Cirque Meadows Road, you have a good view of the Pingree Park campus and its beautiful high-mountain setting. In about 0.5 mile a side trail on the right heads 1.25 miles to Surprise Pond and Beaver Falls. The trail then parallels Bennett Creek, with small waterfalls and the sounds of the stream below. After approximately 1.25 miles cross Bennett Creek on a small footbridge, and disregard a side trail on the left. In another 0.25 mile (about 2 miles from the trailhead), turn left at signed Mummy Pass Trail. The signs at the intersection list distances of 5 miles to Mummy Pass and 3 miles to the Rocky Mountain National Park boundary.

After the intersection, the trail goes steeply uphill on one of the rockiest sections of trail. In 0.25 mile you reach the wilderness boundary, beyond which mountain biking is prohibited. The trail mellows and the rocks thin after 0.75 mile. You emerge

from the trees in another 0.25 mile and enter a spectacular panorama.

The switchbacks begin and are steady, well marked, and broad as you gain another 1,000 feet; pace yourself if you aren't especially fit. The view of Pingree Park is 180 degrees of wow, with the Stormy Peaks to the east, the Comanche Peak and Fall Mountain massif to the west, and the top of the cirque that frames Emmaline Lake coming into sight. After you reach a pile of shapely rocks that are a good place for an even better view (see "Great for Kids" below) the next 0.3 mile of uphill is worth the even better view of Comanche Peak. The trail levels somewhat as it goes up and over the ridgeline, where you will finally top out around 11,400 feet. This area has some low willow bushes to protect you from the wind and is a good spot for a snack or lunch break. From there the trail descends 200 feet and then rolls up and over another high spot, regaining and then losing a bit of the altitude. The Mummy Range comes into view and looks like a scene out of Patagonia if there is any snowcap left when you're hiking. You will descend once again before the final ascent, circumventing the Mummy's head and finally arriving at Mummy Pass.

---

### GREAT FOR KIDS

If you have weary people after 3.25 miles, stop and have a snack and enjoy the great panorama when you reach treeline, and then wander back to the trailhead. If you want to go just a bit farther (0.3 mile), you will arrive at some prominent rock outcrops after the next set of switchbacks. It is an even better rest stop, with superb views of the Fall Mountain and Comanche Peak massif and rocks to clamber around on.

## 164   Signal Mountain Trail

ROOSEVELT NATIONAL FOREST

| | |
|---|---|
| **Distance** | Up to 10 miles, out-and-back |
| **Difficulty** | Moderate-plus |
| **Elevation Gain** | 2,700' (starting at 8,560') |
| **Trail Use** | Hiking, fishing, backpacking, snowshoeing, skiing, leashed dogs OK |
| **Agency** | Canyon Lakes Ranger District, Roosevelt National Forest |
| **Map(s)** | Trails Illustrated *Poudre River & Cameron Pass* |
| **Facilities** | Restrooms at trailhead |

**HIGHLIGHTS** This little-used trail offers protection from wind and heat, along with a tour of a magical river arroyo. It starts off gently, following the enchanting streambed for 2 miles. Signal Mountain is a steep climb from there as you accomplish most of the gain in the last 3 miles and climb above treeline and onto the tundra to enjoy the spectacular view. It offers a trip through a beautiful riparian area that features a mixed old-growth forest of aspen, pine, fir, and spruce and striking rock outcrops. It makes a nice out-and-back trip of any length; climbing Signal Mountain, however, would be a serious all-day adventure.

Another access to Signal Mountain, via the Bulwark Ridge, is at the North Fork/Dunraven Trailhead parking lot. It is 4 steep miles one-way to the summit on a ridge of Signal Mountain, with views of the Dunraven Creek valley below.

**DIRECTIONS** Take US 287 north to CO 14. Then drive 26 miles west from Ted's Place to Pingree Park Road. This trailhead is a bit closer to CO 14, making for a somewhat shorter drive. There are actually two access points to this trail and mountain: one in Pingree Park and one on the south end of the trail near Glen Haven. For this one take CO 14 to Pingree Park Road. The trail is on the left (east) side of the road approximately 10 miles from the entrance and 2 miles from the Pingree Park Campus. It is approximately 0.5 mile beyond the turnoff for Pennock Pass. Park alongside the road.

The trail runs along Pennock Creek, dropping down to the stream and then winding through the thick forest. The path is fairly level with views across the stream. At approximately 1 mile into the trek you cross Pennock Creek on a footbridge. The trail begins to climb steadily and gains another 200 feet to reach 9,000 feet in the next mile or so as it parallels the stream. Bear right when the trail meets an old road.

The beaver ponds mark the halfway point; the trail leaves the main Pennock Creek drainage, crosses a smaller stream, and begins to climb more steeply as it leaves the streambed. A striking rock spire makes a good lunch or turnaround point, depending on your ambitions. After you enjoy that area, continue on the trail as it climbs to a tree-obscured saddle where you might see an old road. Pick up the faint trail on the right and continue to climb toward treeline and the North Signal Mountain summit. The South Signal Mountain summit is a short ridge walk away and is 14 feet lower than the northern summit. The view from the summit ridge is superb, with a panorama of the canyons, foothills, and plains below. You can even see Longs Peak in the distance.

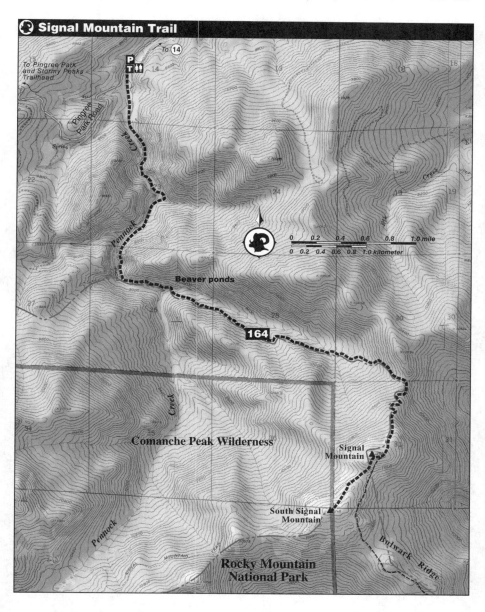

Signal Mountain Trail

*Dowdy Lake at sunset; photographed by John Bartholow*

# chapter 11

# Red Feather Lakes Area

## 1 HOUR FROM FORT COLLINS

## 2 HOURS OR MORE FROM DENVER-BOULDER

The Red Feather Lakes Area is bordered on the northwest by the beautiful Medicine Bow Mountains that grace this part of northern Colorado and southern Wyoming and by the majestic Rawah Range that looms to the southwest. It offers unique vistas that ease the soul. Rolling foothills and low mountains are transformed into the limitless horizons of the high plains of southern Wyoming. The lakes are petite but comely, and festooned by the rocks left behind when the glaciers retreated at the end of the last glaciation of the most recent ice age.

The region is approximately 45 miles northwest of Fort Collins, close to the Wyoming–Colorado border, and the trails are not as heavily used as those in the Poudre Canyon. The lakes region features unique and striking terrain, combining the rolling characteristics of the foothills and hogbacks with the conifer forests of the high mountains. The vistas are crowned with interesting rock formations, and the picturesque valleys and canyons are as varied as they are beautiful. Popular for camping, fishing, and horseback riding, the area isn't overwhelmed with throngs of hikers and mountain bikers.

## Beaver Meadows Resort

If you want a good place for beginners or families with easy-to-use, difficult-to-lose trails and the convenience of a low-key rustic lodge and restaurant, check out Beaver Meadows Resort. The day-use fee is charged only in the winter. The resort offers a variety of overnight accommodations. If you complete all of the hiking routes outlined on the resort map, you will have a satisfying day with a wide variety of views and trails that climb, roll, ascend, and descend through an aspen and pine forest and cross some beautiful, sunny meadows.

### 165  Mount Margaret Trail

ROOSEVELT NATIONAL FOREST

| | |
|---|---|
| **Distance** | 8 miles from the Red Feather Road trailhead, 7 miles from the Dowdy Lake trailhead; figure eight |
| **Difficulty** | Easy |
| **Elevation Gain** | 255' (starting at 7,700') |
| **Trail Use** | Hiking, mountain biking, horseback riding, snowshoeing, skiing, leashed dogs OK |
| **Agency** | Canyon Lakes Ranger District, Roosevelt National Forest |
| **Map(s)** | Trails Illustrated *Red Feather Lakes & Glendevey* |
| **Facilities** | Campground, restrooms, and picnic areas at Dowdy Lake |

*View from Mount Margaret Trail*

## Mount Margaret & Dowdy Lake Trails

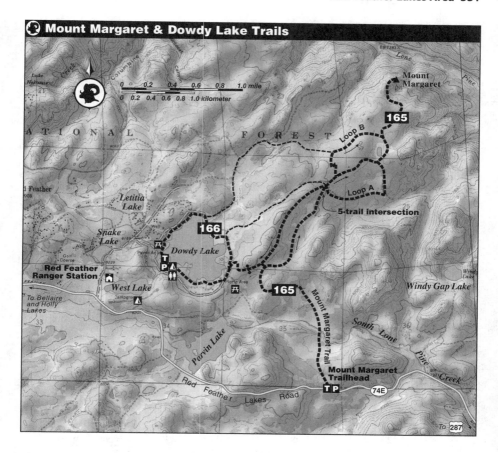

**HIGHLIGHTS** The round-trip to the summit can be a pleasant half-day-plus adventure, but it is worthwhile to hike or bike even a small section of this scenic trail to enjoy the high mountain meadows and rock formations. You don't have to bag the anticlimactic Mount Margaret summit that was recently "relocated" when its previous location was found to be incorrect. This popular summer hiking route has a relatively low altitude of 7,700 feet and limited shade, so it can be very warm in midsummer. It is ideal for hiking in spring, early summer, or early fall, unless you get an early start and beat the heat. If you do arrive in early spring, be prepared for the marshy area at the beginning of the trail and a slightly wider stream crossing.

**DIRECTIONS** From Fort Collins drive north on US 287 toward Laramie. After 10 miles, you pass the turnoff for Poudre Canyon (CO 14); keep going north another 10 miles until you reach the junction with Red Feather Lakes Road (County Road 74E), known as The Forks near Livermore, which many maps show as Livermore. At the bottom of a long hill where US 287 veers to the right, turn left (west) onto paved CR 74E. It's another 23 miles to the Red Feather and Dowdy Lakes area on a road with lots of curves and climbs and a speed limit of generally 45 miles per hour. Allow at least 30 minutes from Livermore or 1 hour or more for a leisurely, low-stress drive from Fort Collins. The trailhead is approximately 20 miles from Livermore on the right (north) side of the road.

To reach an alternate route, take Red Feather Lakes Road to the trailhead 1 mile before the Dowdy Lakes area on the north (right) side of the road. It is easy to miss if there aren't any cars in the small parking lot, and there is a fence because the area is sometimes used for grazing.

The trail has some stands of aspens and a variety of evergreens but is mostly open. It features vistas of the foothills, rock outcrops good for minor scrambles (or bouldering), peaceful mountain meadows guarded by stately conifers, and the smaller but scenic canyons and valleys of North Larimer County.

The trail first goes gently uphill and then gently downhill into the Lone Pine Creek drainage. It crosses Lone Pine Creek in 0.5 mile. The trail travels right to a footbridge. After crossing the narrow bridge, look left for the continuation of the trail. The recent rerouting of the trail to the west avoids the marsh.

After crossing the creek, the trail passes the first of the dramatic rock formations and one of many pretty meadows often covered with wildflowers in the spring. The trail travels north about 1 mile, where you go through a gate. When you reach the fork in the trail, bear right. You will come to a tricky intersection at about 2.5 miles. There are trails on the left from Dowdy Lake, and a loop trail on the right. Bear right, without taking the hard right, and then look for a sign that points to Mount Margaret for confirmation of your route.

After you see the sign for Mount Margaret, the trail broadens and the trees thin, passing more dramatic rock formations on a gentle roller coaster to the base of the summit. If you make it all the way to Mount Margaret, you are treated to views of canyons and valleys that surround the rocky summit. The actual summit rock requires a nontechnical rock scramble. Be wary if the rock is wet or icy, and forgo the underwhelming summit.

## 166 Dowdy Lake Trail
### ROOSEVELT NATIONAL FOREST

see map on p. 331

| | |
|---|---|
| **Distance** | 1.5 miles, loop |
| **Difficulty** | Easy |
| **Elevation Gain** | Negligible (starting at 7,700') |
| **Trail Use** | Hiking, camping, paddling, fishing, great for kids, leashed dogs OK |
| **Agency** | Canyon Lakes Ranger District, Roosevelt National Forest |
| **Map(s)** | Trails Illustrated *Red Feather Lakes & Glendevey* |
| **Facilities** | Campground, restrooms, and picnic areas |
| **Note(s)** | This is a fee area. |

**HIGHLIGHTS** A pleasant, easy, and scenic stroll heads around a most comely mountain lake punctuated by striking rock outcrops dating from the last glaciation of the most recent ice age. I imagine the lake was a favorite watering hole for the Ute Indians, who inhabited the area from about 4,000 years ago until the 1860s, when they were forced to leave. The campground is popular, so reservations are necessary.

**DIRECTIONS** From Fort Collins, drive north on US 287 toward Laramie. After 10 miles, you will pass the turnoff for Poudre Canyon (CO 14); keep going north another 10 miles until you reach the junction with Red Feather Lakes Road (County Road 74E), known as The Forks near Livermore, which many maps show as Livermore. At the bottom of a long hill where US 287 veers to the right, turn left (west) onto paved CR 74E. It's another 23 miles to the Red Feather and Dowdy Lakes area on a road with lots of curves and climbs and a speed limit of generally 45 miles per hour. Allow at least 30 minutes from Livermore or an hour or more for a leisurely, low-stress drive from Fort Collins. The trailhead is approximately 20 miles from Livermore on the right (north) side of the road. Then continue on the Red Feather Lakes Road (CR 74E) to the Dowdy Lake turnoff. Turn right toward the campground, and look for a place to park at an unused campsite.

alk through the campground to the edge of the lake, and circumnavigate in either direction. I prefer clockwise because you are likely to encounter fewer people. The trail crosses one or two streams, but they are generally trickles. As the trail rounds the lake, the view is ever changing, with some of the best views from the far side of the lake. You can get a peek at the Rawah Peaks from the far side if you want to circumnavigate.

You might also walk along a beautiful, less-visited trail across the road from the Dowdy Lake Trailhead that wanders through some gorgeous meadows while rolling over hill and dale before joining the Mount Margaret Trail, described previously.

## 167 North Lone Pine Trail to Mount Baldy Overlook
ROOSEVELT NATIONAL FOREST

see map on p. 334

| | |
|---|---|
| **Distance** | 5–12 miles, out-and-back |
| **Difficulty** | Moderate |
| **Elevation Gain** | 400' (starting at 9,300') |
| **Trail Use** | Hiking, snowshoeing, skiing, leashed dogs OK |
| **Agency** | Canyon Lakes Ranger District, Roosevelt National Forest |
| **Map(s)** | Trails Illustrated *Red Feather Lakes & Glendevey* |
| **Facilities** | Picnic area at trailhead |

**HIGHLIGHTS** This lightly used trail passes through 20-foot-tall fir trees and 2-foot-tall pines in a part of Roosevelt National Forest that has recovered from forest fires and logging. Its topography is similar to that of Beaver Meadows and Mount Margaret, but it climbs higher and provides views of the high plains and canyons as they climb steeply into the stark terrain of southern Wyoming in the distance. The North Lone Pine Trailhead is well marked, but the trail is not and requires good route-finding skills to be navigated successfully.

*North Lone Pine Trail climbs high.*

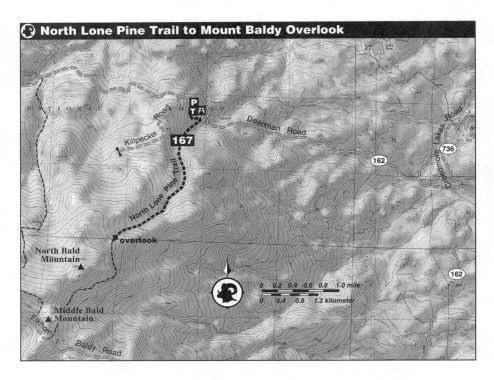

**North Lone Pine Trail to Mount Baldy Overlook**

**DIRECTIONS** From Fort Collins, drive north on US 287 toward Laramie. After 10 miles, you pass the turnoff for Poudre Canyon (CO 14). Then go north another 10 miles until you reach the junction with Red Feather Lakes Road (County Road 74E) in Livermore. At the bottom of a long hill where US 287 veers to the right, turn left (west) onto paved CR 74E. Follow CR 74E another 24 miles (on a road with curves and climbs and a speed limit of 45 miles per hour), and pass the Creedmore Lakes Road (CR 180) turnoff. The road becomes gravel Deadman Road (CR 162). The trailhead and the picnic area are on the right (north) side of the road. It is an ideal place, weather and wind permitting, for photos or a lunch or snack break before beginning to hike the trail.

You are fairly high up on the mountain when you reach the trailhead. Well marked and impossible to miss on the south (left) side of the road, the trailhead is fairly obvious from the trail marker and information board, but the trail is unmarked after that. Follow the trail by tracing the small tree tunnel it forms. It climbs steadily and roller-coasters some as it meanders through the thick tree cover and goes from 9,300 feet to 10,400 feet. As you travel to the higher reaches of the trail, some breaks in the trees offer views.

After approximately 2 miles on the trail, you cross an old logging road. You'll cross the road again about 0.75 mile later. Assume it will take you at least 2 hours round-trip to reach and return from the Mount Baldy overlook from the trailhead.

The trail levels somewhat and has a view of one of the Baldy Mountains on the left, staying high on the ridge. Leave the trail when you reach a rock outcrop on the left, and climb the rock carefully for the best view of the Baldys. The trail continues and eventually dead-ends at the Elkhorn-Baldy four-wheel-drive road, but I suggest turning around at this point and finding your way back to the trailhead.

*Listen to the frog pond near Mount Margaret (see page 330).*

*Nokhu Crags*

# chapter 12

# Colorado State Forest

## 2 HOURS OR MORE FROM FORT COLLINS

## 3.5–4 HOURS FROM DENVER-BOULDER

This spectacular and lesser-known Colorado state park is a wonderful weekend destination with an abundance of hiking and biking trails, as well as lake and stream fishing and good camping and backpacking. It takes a minimum of 2 hours to reach the forest from Fort Collins (probably more like 2.5 hours with summer traffic) and about 1.5 hours from Granby.

### Seven Utes Mountain & Mount Mahler

If you want panoramic views of Mount Richthofen, the Diamond Peaks, as well as a unique view of the Never Summer Range, the Zirkels, and the Medicine Bow mountain ranges, then Seven Utes and Mahler peaks are a must. Attempt this duo if you have good route-finding skills, as there are few formal trails once you reach Seven Utes. A lot of the informal trails are old logging roads that can be used for mountain biking. The trail to the peaks beyond the first overlook is too narrow and covered by fallen timber to be biked, but there are lots of alternatives for intermediate to advanced bikers. The many roads can cause confusion on the way up too.

Families with young children can enjoy the great views of the peaks by following the first mile of the route and turning around. The only downside is that you might encounter all-terrain vehicles on the approach. Neither of these nontechnical peaks should be attempted without good raingear and other equipment because the summits are far from the road.

### Camping on the Pass

There is good overnight, rustic backpacking off of the Thunder Pass/American Lakes

Trail, even if you are a beginner. A state park daily pass is required, but there is no camping fee. It is important that you let someone know exactly where you are going and when you plan to return. I recommend picking a cozy site in some healthy trees in case the wind kicks up, which often happens. The area is good for beginners because when the sun goes down you feel like you are in the wilderness even though you are only a couple of miles from the road, giving you a margin of safety. Needless to say, a major weather event can erase that margin in a very short period of time. The Nokhu Hut and the Colorado State Forest Yurt System, or Michigan Reservoir cabins, are less demanding alternatives for overnights in this high mountain paradise.

### Colorado State Forest Cabins & Never Summer Yurts

There are two good, inexpensive options for staying overnight in the Colorado State Forest. The Colorado State Park system rents several rustic cabins in the Gould area on North Michigan Lake, while Never Summer Yurts has a system of yurts available. The Lake Agnes Nokhu Hut is the latest addition to the Never Summer Yurt system. The settings for the yurts and cabins are dramatic, with the Medicine Bow Mountains Rawah Range forming an enormous and majestic backdrop to the east and north, and there are easy trails in and around the huts, with nonstop views in every direction. The North Michigan Reservoir cabins are heated by either wood-burning stoves or propane. Water is available nearby. The cabins have vault toilets within walking distance, sleep 6–10 people in bunk beds, and are no more than 400 feet from parking places. The yurts also vary in size and sleep 6–10 people. They are heated with wood-burning stoves and have a variety of bunks and beds. Dancing

Moose and Grassy Hut are 0.25 and 0.6 mile from the road, respectively, while the others are farther. Two websites (**cpw.state .co.us/placestogo/parks/stateforest** and **neversummernordic.com**) include complete descriptions, pictures, and prices.

## 168  Michigan Ditch Trail to Thunder Pass Trail
COLORADO STATE FOREST

| | |
|---|---|
| **Distance** | 2–12 miles, out-and-back and point to point options |
| **Difficulty** | Michigan Ditch Trail out-and-back: Easy; Top of Thunder Pass: Difficult |
| **Elevation Gain** | Michigan Ditch Trail out-and-back: 100'; Top of Thunder Pass: 1,060' (starting at 10,275') |
| **Trail Use** | Hiking, mountain biking, backpacking, snowshoeing, skiing, option for kids, leashed dogs OK |
| **Agency** | Colorado State Forest |
| **Map(s)** | Trails Illustrated *Poudre River & Cameron Pass* |
| **Facilities** | Toilets and picnic area on the northwest side of the highway |
| **Note(s)** | This fee area has parking on the northwest side of the highway. |

**HIGHLIGHTS** One of the most popular trails in the Cameron Pass area, Michigan Ditch Trail has something for everyone. It is an almost level trail at the outset and is an excellent entrance to Thunder Pass and the Never Summer Mountains of Rocky Mountain National Park. It offers spectacular views of the Never Summer Range and Nokhu Crags across the Michigan River drainage, Diamond Peaks, and North Park in the distance. It also features a gentle roll at the start and can be used for either hiking or biking because it is a wide service road for the Michigan Ditch, part of the Transmountain/Transcontinental Divide water storage system that funnels water from the western slope of the Continental Divide to the thirsty eastern-slope cities. It can be used for short and easy family jaunts or backcountry adventure for those who want to spend the night and surmount Thunder Pass and sneak in the back door of Rocky Mountain National Park.

**DIRECTIONS** Take CO 14 to the top of Cameron Pass. Parking and toilet facilities are on the right (west) side of the highway. The well-marked, gated trail is on the left (east) side of CO 14. The trail is actually a closed four-wheel-drive road used to maintain the Michigan Ditch.

The first 1.5 miles is a flat, highly scenic trail. It is an ideal family out-and-back trip. For more adventure, continue on the winding road for another 0.5 mile until the trail intersects the Thunder Pass and American Lakes Trail. At that point, either continue to follow the road around the bottom of the ridgeline and cross to the other side of the drainage south (if there is no snow or avalanche danger), or take the Thunder Pass and American Lakes Trail left and climb steadily toward the rocky panorama above treeline at 11,000 feet. The former is an easy, short trek on a flat

trail; the latter a more challenging, longer route above treeline. If you decide to take the latter, you find a constantly climbing but rolling trail. There are some very steep stretches but also some moderate to easy sections. Go as far as you wish; any length is a treat.

The upper reaches of this trail offer impressive views of the northern edge of the Never Summer Range, including the summit of Richthofen, LuLu, and Mahler peaks and the Nokhu Crags. If you make it to the top of Thunder Pass, you can see down into the Colorado River drainage of

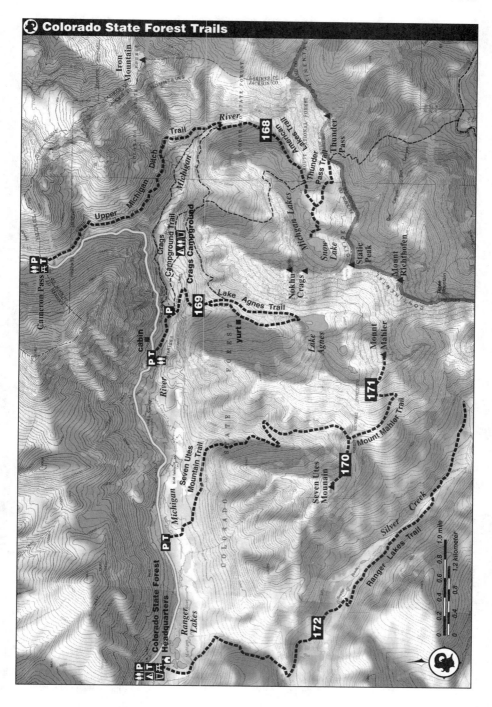

## Colorado State Forest Trails

*American Lakes from Thunder Pass; photographed by Joe Grim*

Rocky Mountain National Park (RMNP). Continue down the west side of the pass, over the ditch road, and into Box Canyon in RMNP. You could even plan to backpack this or take a very long and challenging day hike and arrange a car shuttle to pick you up after you emerge on the west side of Trail Ridge Road near Grand Lake.

How long it takes to reach the summit of Thunder Pass very much depends on the individual. It should only be attempted as an all-day adventure by the fit and well prepared. It is a moderate-to-challenging day hike or easy backpack on an easy-to-find trail at high altitude with striking scenery.

### GREAT FOR KIDS

If you want an easy out-and-back for small children, this is it. The first 1.5 miles follow the road. If you are taking a novice or family expedition, this is an almost flat trek, and you can turn around at the group of cabins that is about 1 mile one-way.

 **169**  **Lake Agnes Trail**

COLORADO STATE FOREST

see map on p. 339

| | |
|---|---|
| **Distance** | 1.6 miles, balloon |
| **Difficulty** | Easy |
| **Elevation Gain** | 500' (starting at 10,000') |
| **Trail Use** | Hiking, fishing, snowshoeing, skiing, great for kids, leashed dogs OK |
| **Agency** | Colorado State Forest |
| **Map(s)** | Trails Illustrated *Poudre River & Cameron Pass*; Trails Illustrated *Rocky Mountain National Park* |
| **Facilities** | Restrooms, campground, and a yurt and cabin (yurt and cabin available for winter use only) |

**HIGHLIGHTS** This popular and very scenic trail heads to a high mountain lake surrounded by a cirque of the Never Summer Range. The scenic drama is high, with the soaring summits and ridgelines of the Diamond Peaks, Nokhu Crags, and Mount Richthofen in view as you climb to and circumnavigate the lake. It is a much shorter and easier route in the summer than in the winter, so take advantage of it.

**DIRECTIONS** The trailhead is 2.5 miles west of the summit of Cameron Pass on the left or south side of the road if you are driving west. Follow the, at first, smooth road to the bottom of the hill and turn right; Crags Campground is straight. Drive 1 mile uphill on the steep, rough, but passable road to the small parking lot.

You immediately enjoy panoramic views of the Nokhu Crags and the west side of Cameron Pass. The summer parking lot is next to the cabin used by skiers and snowshoers in the winter (it's closed in the summer). Take the trail right of the restrooms uphill into the trees. The trail starts out steep but flattens on top of the short hill. The view of the Nokhu Crags is worth the price of admission. After 0.3 mile you come to an intersection. Left goes across the drainage to the American Lakes and Crags Campground Trail. Bear right and uphill for Lake Agnes. At the next intersection are short, roughly equal trails to the lake: one in the treeless drainage, the other through trees.

When you reach the lake, there are trails going around both sides. If you want to circumnavigate the lake, you can alternate your routes out and back for variety. Go left to walk on the edge of a drainage and then along scree to get to the other side. Go right to wander through trees and then emerge onto the narrow trail around the edge. After 0.25 mile the trail goes back uphill into the trees and winds back to a pretty corner. From there it goes downhill and around to the other side. Once you trek around to the far side of the lake, you can access the trail to the top of the scree heap known as Mount Richthofen. (Mount Mahler and Seven Utes Mountain are much more enjoyable climbs.)

*Lake Agnes*

## 170  Seven Utes Mountain Trail
COLORADO STATE FOREST

see map on p. 339

| | |
|---|---|
| **Distance** | 2–8 miles, out-and-back |
| **Difficulty** | Moderate |
| **Elevation Gain** | 2,000' (starting at 9,400') |
| **Trail Use** | Hiking, snowshoeing, skiing, option for kids, leashed dogs OK |
| **Agency** | Colorado State Forest |
| **Map(s)** | Trails Illustrated *Poudre River & Cameron Pass*; Trails Illustrated *Rocky Mountain National Park* |
| **Facilities** | None |

**HIGHLIGHTS** The easier, much lower summit of neighboring peaks, Seven Utes Mountain is probably considered to be a barely significant subpeak of Mount Mahler by grumpy geographers, but it is a truly enjoyable climb in a somewhat lesser but still magnificent panorama that includes the Diamonds and Crags.

**DIRECTIONS** When you are approximately 3.8 miles past the summit of Cameron Pass driving west on CO 14 and almost at the bottom of the incline, look for a partially paved drive with a green gate on the left (south) side of the road angling to the southeast. It is the former Seven Utes Lodge entrance. Park either at the partially paved closed road or about another 0.25 mile down in the turnout on the same side, and hike back on the other side of the fence lining the road. The State Forest Moose Visitor Center, which opens at 9 a.m., is 2 miles west of the trailhead on CO 14; the staff there can help you with advice and directions. If you reach the Ranger Lakes Campground, you have gone too far west on CO 14 and are about 1 mile west of the trailhead.

As with most of the trails described in this book, a good time can be had by hikers of all skill levels: Attempt the entire round-trip if you are a fit hiker, and a much smaller segment if you are less ambitious. From the summit of Mahler, you can see Mount Richthofen, the Crags shoulder, and the tail end of the Never Summer Range, including Static Peak and Teepee Mountain. You can also glimpse the edge of North Park. Even 1 or 2 miles uphill on this gradually steepening trail gives you views, and the closer you get to Seven Utes, the more impressive they are.

Graced with stately, tall pine trees, the trailhead is at the old Seven Utes Lodge site driveway; the lodge is long gone and there are no longer any signs or markers for it. Just beyond the green gate, take either of the trails you see on the right. When you are at the trailhead, orient yourself by looking at your topographic map and then at the ridge of Seven Utes and the drainage to the southeast where you want to end up. Once you are in the trees and encountering

lots of logging roads, it is easy to get disoriented. Go downhill gradually, and then go steeply uphill east and southeast on an old road. Don't take the trail going left (east) before the road steepens. There are no trail markers, but it is easier if you keep in mind the general direction you are traveling toward the drainage.

When the trail gets steeper, it merges with another wide, old logging road used by all-terrain vehicles and that can be mountain biked. Go to the left, or east, uphill on the road, and follow the trail on the left as you round the first hard right turn—it is not well marked, so look carefully for it, remembering which drainage you want to reach. Mountain bikers can stay on the road, which will take them steeply uphill to Michigan Ditch in a roundabout way. The trail up Seven Utes is too narrow and steep and features lots of fallen trees that make biking impossible; it is not an old road and has thick vegetation and a 30- to 40-foot drop-off on your left. Behind you to the northeast is a spectacular view of the Diamond Peaks.

The trail goes downhill and to the other side of the drainage, crossing a stream that can be difficult in early spring. Uphill back into the trees, east and south, you go as the trail steepens considerably. Dodge trees as you climb to treeline next to the drainage. Dead ahead you see the ridge that goes right (west) toward the base of Seven Utes. Keep to the right at intersecting trails. As you traverse the short ridge, you see Seven Utes to the southwest (right) and Mount Mahler to the northeast (left). You must decide which peak to climb—Seven Utes or Mahler. Add 2 hours if you choose Mahler. The trail going to the right (west) across the top of the drainage cirque is your route over to Seven Utes. Cross the top of the cirque and pick your route up to the summit. A panoramic view of the northern edge of the Never Summer Range and the southern tip of the Rawah Range of the Medicine Bow Mountains greets you.

*View of Seven Utes Mountain from the Ranger Lakes Trailhead*

`171`  **Mount Mahler Trail**
COLORADO STATE FOREST

see
map on
p. 339

| | |
|---|---|
| **Distance** | 10 miles, out-and-back |
| **Difficulty** | Moderate–challenging |
| **Elevation Gain** | 3,000' (starting at 9,400') |
| **Trail Use** | Hiking, snowshoeing, skiing, leashed dogs OK |
| **Agency** | Colorado State Forest |
| **Map(s)** | Trails Illustrated *Poudre River & Cameron Pass*; Trails Illustrated *Rocky Mountain National Park* |
| **Facilities** | None |

**HIGHLIGHTS** Though higher and more challenging than Seven Utes, Mount Mahler affords you panoramic views of Mount Richthofen and the Diamond Peaks, as well as a unique view of the Never Summer Range, the Zirkels, and the Medicine Bow mountain ranges. It is a real mountain, while Seven Utes is just an impressive subpeak—the additional panorama is worth the extra effort.

**DIRECTIONS** When you are approximately 3.8 miles past the summit of Cameron Pass driving west on CO 14 and almost at the bottom of the incline, look for a partially paved drive with a green gate on the left (south) side of the road angling to the southeast. It is the former Seven Utes Lodge entrance. Park either at the partially paved closed road, or park about another 0.25 mile down in the turnout on the same side and hike back on the other side of the fence lining the road. The State Forest Moose Visitor Center, which opens at 9 a.m., is 2 miles west of the trailhead on CO 14; they can help you with advice and directions. If you reach the Ranger Lakes Campground, you have gone too far west on CO 14 and are about 1 mile west of the trailhead.

From the summit of Mahler, you can see Mount Richthofen, the Crags shoulder, and the end of the Never Summer Range, including Static Peak and Teepee Mountain, and can glimpse the edge of North Park. Graced with stately, tall pine trees, the trailhead is at the old Seven Utes Lodge site driveway; the lodge is long gone and there are no longer any signs or markers for it. Just beyond the green gate, take either of the trails you see on the right. When you are at the trailhead, orient yourself by looking at your topographic map and then at the ridge of Seven Utes and the drainage to the southeast where you want to end up. Once you are in the trees and encountering lots of logging roads, it is easy to get disoriented. Go downhill gradually, and then go steeply uphill east and southeast on an old road. Don't take the trail going left (east) before the road steepens. There are no trail markers, but it is easier if you keep in mind the general direction you are traveling toward the drainage.

When the trail gets steeper, it merges with another wide, old logging road that's used by all-terrain vehicles and can be mountain biked. Go to the left (east) uphill on the road, and follow the trail on the left as you round the first hard right turn—it is not well marked, so look carefully for it, remembering which drainage you want to reach. Mountain bikers can stay on the road, which will take them steeply uphill to Michigan Ditch in a roundabout way. The trail up Seven Utes is too narrow and steep and features lots of fallen trees that make biking impossible; it is not an old road, and it has thick vegetation and a 30- to 40-foot drop-off on your left. Behind you to the northeast is a spectacular view of the Diamond Peaks.

The trail goes downhill and to the other side of the drainage, crossing a stream that can be difficult in early spring. You go uphill back into the trees, east and south, as the trail steepens considerably. Dodge trees as you climb to treeline next to the drainage. Dead ahead you see the ridge that goes right (west) toward the base of Seven Utes. Keep right at intersecting trails. As you traverse the short ridge, you see Seven Utes to the southwest (right) and Mount Mahler to the northeast (left). You must decide which peak to climb—Seven Utes Mountain or Mount Mahler. Add 2 hours if you choose Mahler.

For Mount Mahler bear northeast (left), and don't take the trail across the top of the cirque to your right. Instead continue uphill, but bear straight and then left, making your way toward the right (southwest) side of the mountain. Avoid the steep climbs on the west-facing slopes. Make your way around to the southwest side of the mountain for a more gradual, enjoyable climb. The southwest ridge is a steady, less direct ascent. Make your way to the southwest flank of the mountain, and carefully pick your way up to the top of the ridge saddle and then right (south) to the summit. It is a terrific view in all directions on top.

## 172 Ranger Lakes Trail
### COLORADO STATE FOREST

see map on p. 339

| | |
|---|---|
| **Distance** | Up to 10 miles (8.8 miles to the first crossing of Silver Creek), out-and-back |
| **Difficulty** | Easy |
| **Elevation Gain** | 610' (starting at 9,280') |
| **Trail Use** | Hiking, mountain biking, motorized recreation, snowshoeing, skiing, leashed dogs OK |
| **Agency** | Colorado State Forest |
| **Map(s)** | Trails Illustrated *Poudre River & Cameron Pass*; Trails Illustrated *Rocky Mountain National Park* |
| **Facilities** | Restrooms at campground |

**HIGHLIGHTS** This trail starts behind the Ranger Lakes Campground and is easy to find. Enjoy a 2-mile round-trip jaunt to see the views in the next valley, and continue if you want more of a workout. The parking lot at the trailhead offers great views of the riparian area and Seven Utes Mountain. The first mile is a moderate climb in a tree tunnel until you make it over the top of the hill and things open up into a beautiful high-mountain valley.

**DIRECTIONS** It is approximately 5.8–6 miles from the summit of Cameron Pass to the campground on the left (south) side of the road. There is a recreational area parking lot another 0.8 mile west of the Ranger Lakes Campground.

To find the trailhead, drive past the campground loop road to a dead end in the day-use parking area. The trails on the left head to the lakes if you want a short side trip. The trail covered here goes straight ahead and slightly downhill from the parking lot and emerges from the trees to give you a view of the ridgeline of the Never Summer Mountains—Seven Utes and Mahler in particular. Cross the Michigan River on a small bridge. The trail then reenters the trees and climbs uphill for more than 1 mile before cresting and then descending into the Silver Creek drainage.

Though the trail is a tree tunnel except for a few glimpses at the hillcrest and on the descent, it is indeed a beautiful and peaceful forest.

At approximately 1.5 miles you see a trail labeled Silver Creek (which is also still Ranger Lakes Trail); bear right and stay on the main trail toward Illinois Pass. In another 0.25 mile you reach the high point of the trail with limited views. You might encounter an occasional off-highway vehicle, though I neither saw nor heard any the day I was on this trail. In fact, I saw no one on the trail the entire time—a rare experience. If you want to enjoy the Silver Creek Meadows, add another 2 miles to your round-trip distance; it is well worth it. At around the 2-mile mark, go left at the trail intersection. Reach the Silver Creek drainage at just under 2.5 miles and either have a snack and reverse course or roll over more meadows and ascend higher into the foothills of the Never Summer Range.

## 173  Grass Creek Yurt Trail
COLORADO STATE FOREST

| | |
|---|---|
| **Distance** | 5.3 miles, loop; 10 miles, out-and-back |
| **Difficulty** | Easy–moderate |
| **Elevation Gain** | 400' (starting at 9,000') |
| **Trail Use** | Hiking, mountain biking, yurting, snowshoeing, skiing, leashed dogs OK |
| **Agency** | Colorado State Forest |
| **Map(s)** | Trails Illustrated *Poudre River & Cameron Pass* |
| **Facilities** | None, other than the yurt |

**HIGHLIGHTS** The backdrop of the Rawah Range of the Medicine Bow Mountains is the highlight of this rolling trail through a pretty valley. You can take a short, easy loop hike or a much longer trek as high and far as your heart desires.

**DIRECTIONS** Take CO 14 over Cameron Pass west 10 miles to Gould. Watch for signs on the left (north) side of the highway for the state forest campground and the KOA, and turn right and then left to enter the campground. The entrance station includes a map. Follow the dirt road approximately 4 miles until you see the parking area for Grass Creek Yurt on the left side of the road. After you pass North Michigan Reservoir, cross the road to find the trailhead.

*Pretty valley below the Rawah Range*

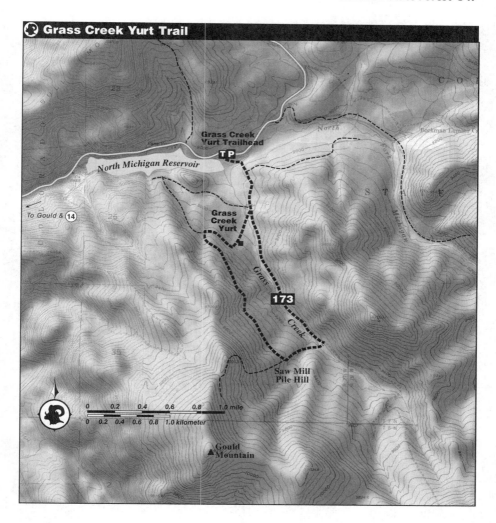

From the trailhead you travel south toward the yurt. When you come to the trail junction, bear right to go directly past the yurt or left to travel the doubletrack, and then singletrack, trail that affords a view of the yurt without passing too closely. If you take the left branch, you gradually climb up the drainage. You can then either turn back on the loop to the right about 2.25 miles from the trailhead or continue straight ahead up Saw Mill Pile Hill and beyond to the end of the trail.

The right branch goes past the hut and climbs more steeply up on top of a small ridge. After approximately 2.5 miles the two branches meet again to complete the loop.

*Trails through the magical rock formations of the Garden of the Gods; photographed by Joe Grim*

# chapter 13

# Colorado Springs Area

## 1 HOUR OR LESS FROM COLORADO SPRINGS
## 2 HOURS OR MORE FROM DENVER

The Colorado Springs area offers many recreational options, from hiking and climbing on Pikes Peak to rambling through the easy but busy trails at Garden of the Gods and many other parks and open spaces closer to and a bit farther from the city lights.

### Fox Run Regional Park

Below 7,000 feet in elevation, this park is just outside Monument and very close to Colorado Springs but offers shade and cooler temperatures on hot days. It features some of the thick tree cover of the Black Forest area. Fox Run is next to the infamous Monument Hill that closes I-25 during many snowstorms, so keep your forecast up-to-date in the early spring and late fall.

Most of the park's almost 400 acres is part of the Fallen Timber Wilderness Area. The three trails are all short and easy. You can enjoy views of Pikes Peak from some areas, though most of the trails are thickly wooded. The tree cover blocks the wind but also limits the views.

### Garden of the Gods

This soaring rock garden is not to be missed. Sculpted by the gods, the glowing sandstone and dizzying cliffs stand as monuments to humankind's relatively short stroll on the planet. A variety of short, easy trails wind among the striking red rocks, often with snowcapped Pikes Peak looking over their shoulder. There is a small mountain biking area, and there are bike lanes on all paved roads.

### Pikes Peak

No trip to the Colorado Springs area would be complete without exploring some of the trails on Pikes Peak, even if you don't want to summit. You can always drive to the top after your hike if you don't want to climb at least 3,000 feet to make it an official summit. You can hike any round-trip distance on the Barr Trail or do the same thing from the top.

### Mueller State Park & Wildlife Area

This state park is a treat, with the western slopes of the Pikes Peak Massif on the east and the distant and enticing backdrop of the Sangre de Cristo Mountains on the west. The park is on top of a plateau almost 10,000 feet high, with trails going downhill from the top. You can savor a colorful tapestry of aspen, pine, fir, and spruce trees, and most of the trails feature good views.

The park is open year-round, as is one of the campgrounds, and it is a delightful place to spend a night or two, though facilities are limited to pit toilets in the winter. The park trail map can be a little confusing because it shows so many trail options, but the trails are well marked and are clearly designated for use by hikers, cyclists, or equestrians. The visitor center is closed during the week in the winter but is always open on weekends, and there is a self-service entry station near the campgrounds. I like using the campgrounds as a starting point because they are the highest point along the access road.

## 174 Garden of the Gods

CITY OF COLORADO SPRINGS

| | |
|---|---|
| **Distance** | Up to 5 miles, loop |
| **Difficulty** | Easy |
| **Elevation Gain** | 300' (starting at 6,200') |
| **Trail Use** | Hiking, mountain biking, great for kids, wheelchair-accessible, leashed dogs OK |
| **Agency** | Garden of the Gods Park, City of Colorado Springs |
| **Map(s)** | City of Colorado Springs *Garden of the Gods Park* |
| **Facilities** | Restrooms at trailhead |

**HIGHLIGHTS** Circumnavigate one of Colorado's easily accessible scenic wonders—magical massive red rock sculpted by wind, water, and the sands of infinite geologic time. This short, easy route gives you a 360-degree view of this spectacular foothills rock garden. There are also wheelchair-accessible trails.

**DIRECTIONS** Take the Garden of the Gods exit west from I-25 onto Garden of the Gods Road. Bear left on Mesa Road to 30th Street, and follow signs to the visitor center. From the visitor center, drive west on Gateway Road to Juniper Way Loop Road and turn right (north) to the main parking area on the north end of the park.

There are many short trail options within the park. This route links together the Palmer, Siamese Twins, Cabin Canyon, Scotsman, and Central Garden Trails. From the main parking lot, walk north, and cross Juniper Way Loop Road to intersect the Palmer Trail. Turn west and follow the trail as it rolls first northwest, then west, and finally south, paralleling Juniper Loop Road but far enough away to avoid the vehicles and noise. Walk slowly and enjoy the ever-changing views of the Tower of Babel rock face. The trail climbs very slowly for the first 0.5 mile before topping out on a narrow ridgeline with nonstop views of the rock formations. As you stroll south through fragrant pinyon pine trees, the Kissing Camels and Pulpit Rocks come into view to the east. The trail descends slowly to intersect a trail that goes east to the Central Garden Trails. If this is good enough for you, exit to the left and stroll around the paved garden trails.

Otherwise, continue south. The trail levels and travels next to the road for a short distance before veering sharply to the west and climbing gradually uphill. At an intersection, go right (northwest) on the Siamese Twins Trail, a short tour around the toothsome twin rocks, to get farther from the road. Climb the gentle hill behind the rocks and feel like you have escaped to Utah's red rock canyons. After the short climb, you go gently downhill to intersect the Cabin Canyon Trail. Turn right (northwest) and descend into the shallow canyon that is more like a small arroyo, decorated with rock outcrops, through rolling terrain to where the trail turns left (south). After 0.3 mile the trail intersects with a trail that would cross the road to the Balanced Rock Trail. Turn left (northeast) for your return route, toward the Spring Canyon Trailhead. At the next intersection, turn right, avoiding the Spring Canyon Trailhead and completing the rest of the Siamese Twins Loop, unless you wish to lengthen your hike and repeat the loop.

In 0.1 mile you reach a second intersection and turn left to cover the part of the Siamese Loop you haven't hiked and return to the Palmer Trail in 0.2 mile. Turn right at the next trail intersection, and walk on a fairly level part of the trail toward the road and the Scotsman Picnic Area. In 0.2 mile you can cross the road and enjoy a rest and

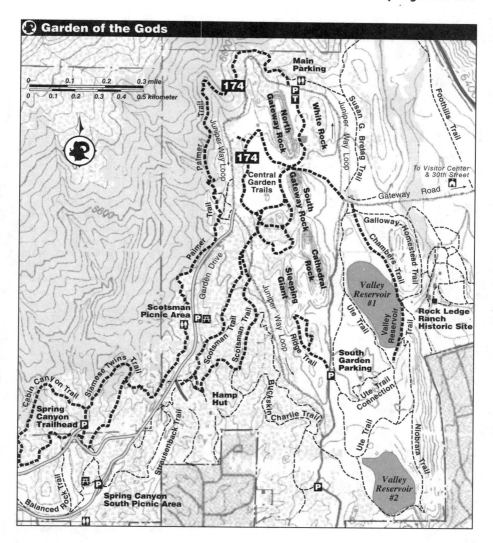

**Garden of the Gods**

snack at the Scotsman. Take the Scotsman Trail north back to the Central Garden Area. It is a gradual uphill with great views of the Keyhole Window and Sleeping Giant formations. You also see Gray/Cathedral Rock peeking through—it is worth a short side trip to take it in. Once back in the Central Area you are up close and personal with the South Gateway Rock. Cut between the two major formations to make your way back to the Main Parking area, enjoying White Rock along the way.

### MOUNTAIN BIKING AT THE GARDEN

If you are a mountain biker, visit the Ute Trail bike loop, which is accessible from the South Garden parking lot. It is an easy, approximately 4- to 5-mile loop, depending on how many side trails you include.

**175**  ## Devil's Head Lookout
PIKE NATIONAL FOREST

|  |  |
|---|---|
| **Distance** | 1.5 miles, out-and-back |
| **Difficulty** | Moderate |
| **Elevation Gain** | 940' (starting at 8,810') |
| **Trail Use** | Hiking, leashed dogs OK |
| **Agency** | Pikes Peak Ranger District, Pike National Forest |
| **Map(s)** | *Pike National Forest* |
| **Facilities** | Restrooms and campground at trailhead; picnic area, restrooms, and many benches along the trail |

**HIGHLIGHTS** This spectacular viewpoint provides a commanding panorama from Pikes Peak to Mount Evans from a historic fire lookout tower built in 1912. The first woman fire lookout ranger in the U.S. Forest Service, Helen Dowe, worked there from 1919 to 1921 and reported 16 fires in her first year alone. The tower was in a state of disrepair until it was reconstructed in 1951 with the help of 100 men and 72 mules. Devil's Head is the last remaining Front Range lookout tower and is on the National Register of Historic Places.

The challenge is getting to the trailhead over the very rough, gravel Rampart Range Road. It doesn't require four-wheel drive, except during downpours, but you'll need good shock absorbers and sound teeth for the sections of deep washboard. There is a campground that makes the long round-trip drive in one day unnecessary. Rampart Range Road is an off-road-vehicle mecca, with

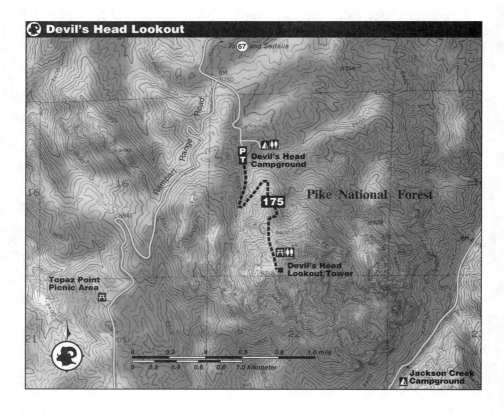

trails paralleling almost the entire length of the road, so keep that in mind when you consider visiting. Love 'em or leave 'em, you cannot avoid them. The Devil's Head Lookout Trail is nonmotorized.

**DIRECTIONS** There is no easy way, but from Woodland Park you can drive north approximately 23 miles on Rampart Range Road. Woodland Park is approximately 15 miles west of Colorado Springs on CO 24. From Indian Creek Campground from the north, the trailhead is 16 miles round-trip. Avoiding the 7 miles of rough road is well worth the backtracking. Indian Creek is southwest of Sedalia on CO 67. Assume at least 1.5 hours from Colorado Springs with dry roads.

From the parking area, the wide, well-maintained trail employs long, sweeping switchbacks to reach the meadow and picnic area that is just short of the top. Wooden benches and some signs found frequently along the trail allow for rest stops. The picnic area features restrooms; a pretty, well-shaded meadow; and a historic cabin still used by rangers. From there it is straight up on metal and wooden steps that surmount the impressive rock that is the base of the tower's lofty perch. You will enjoy great views of Pikes Peak from the top.

## 176 Pikes Peak
### PIKE NATIONAL FOREST

see map on p. 354

| | |
|---|---|
| **Distance** | 10.7 miles (point to point) to 21.4 miles (out-and-back) from summit, 12 miles for Barr Camp (out-and-back) |
| **Difficulty** | Challenging |
| **Elevation Gain** | Summit: 7,500'; Barr Camp: 3,400' (starting at 6,600') |
| **Trail Use** | Hiking, snowshoeing, leashed dogs OK |
| **Agency** | Pikes Peak Ranger District, Pike National Forest |
| **Map(s)** | *Pike National Forest* |
| **Facilities** | Restrooms at the trailhead, Barr Camp at midpoint, and a restaurant and visitor center on top. Cog Railway can be used in season for return trip. |

**HIGHLIGHTS** No trip to the Colorado Springs area is complete without exploring some of the trails on Pikes Peak, even if you don't want to summit. You can always drive to the top after your hike if you don't want to climb at least 3,000 feet to make it an official summit (the minimum requirement of the Colorado Mountain Club). You can hike any round-trip distance on the Barr Trail or from the top. Barr Camp offers four types of overnight accommodations.

**DIRECTIONS** From Colorado Springs, drive west on CO 24 to Manitou Springs. Take Ruxton to the Cog Railway Depot, and park. Follow signs to the Barr Trail.

Because there are several fine fourteener books that describe, in glorious detail, the various routes up 14,110-foot Pikes Peak, you can use this broad-brush overview for minor excursions or peak climbs. Buy a detailed book or check **14ers.com** for detailed route descriptions if you plan to climb to the summit. This description does not have a detailed ascent route. The primary route for the hale and hearty is the Barr Trail. There is even a Pikes Peak Marathon and Half Marathon that wild-and-crazy fitness "fools" (OK, I'm jealous) use to run up and down the mountain. It is 13 miles one-way, with a gain of 7,500 feet. You can, however, take the Cog Railway back down if it's running, take the railway up and hike down, or have someone take the toll (fee) road to pick you up from or drop you off at the top. Another option is to start at the top for an out-and-back, first down and then back up.

Your decision depends on the altitude you want to experience and enjoy on your

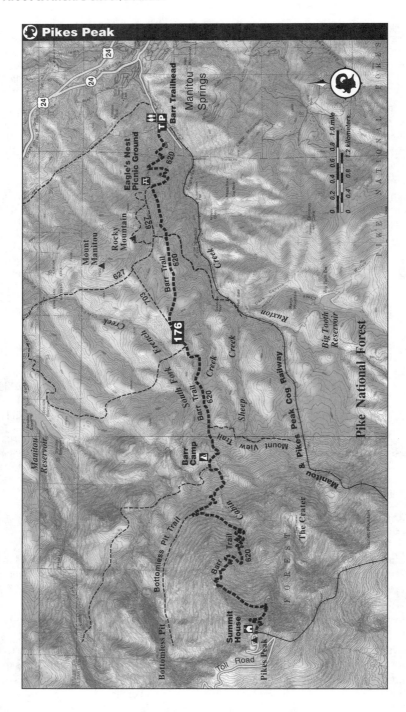

hike. If you want to experience the slow-motion impact of immediate high altitude, from 14,000 to 13,000 feet, start on top and enjoy the spectacular panorama without the obstruction of trees on the rocky, sometimes icy and snowy, switchback path at your feet. Keep in mind that you will be climbing back up what you go down, and it will be at least twice as difficult. If you start at the bottom, you are encased in the beauty of the forest, with peekaboo views all the way to Barr Camp, a challenging day-hike destination. I have enjoyed many briefer, satisfying jaunts up and back on the Barr Trail.

The first 3 miles of the Barr Trail is steep but has wide, sweeping switchbacks and a beautiful towering tree cover of ponderosa pine, white fir, and blue spruce, keeping it fairly cool on hot days. The elevation gain is around 2,200 feet in that first section and might convince you that that is quite enough. You will have some intermittent views, back over your shoulder, of the city below.

When you reach the enormous rocks that frame the rock tunnel, you enjoy a much more gradual angle of ascent. The next 3 miles to Barr Camp climbs a mere 1,200 feet, making for a much more breathable climb. As you climb you get rewarding glimpses of the mountain's shoulder while savoring the ponderosa pine, aspens, and granite rock formations that frame the trail. Unless you can reach Barr Camp (10,200 feet) early in the morning, consider spending the night or turning around. You still have almost 4,000 feet and around 5 miles and likely at least another 4 hours of high-altitude exertion to reach the summit, and you want to be there before noon to avoid thunderstorms. In another 900 feet, you reach the treeline and tundra and are completely exposed to the whims of the weather. The steep switchbacks begin, and you might encounter snow on the trail early or late in the season, so bring hiking sticks or an ice ax during the late spring or late fall. You will likely need extra layers of clothing, as the temperature typically drops and the wind increases as you get closer to the clouds. As compensation, you will have

*View from the top of Pikes Peak; photographed by Joe Grim*

the panoramic views only eagles enjoy, which seem to sweep across the mountains and plains all the way to Colorado's eastern border.

Mere mortals can summit an easier way (7 miles and 4,100 feet) from the back (west) side of the mountain, near the Crags area, though it involves crossing and paralleling the road for short stretches. If you are less ambitious but still want to enjoy the vistas above treeline and retain some

bragging rights for the couch potatoes back home, have someone drop you off along the road, and shave off part of that trail.

With any mountain climb, an early start is wise, as afternoon thunderstorms can start early in these cloud-top environments. Be prepared for very cold weather at any time of the year when you venture above 9,000 feet; imagine a stiff breeze in a sleet storm if you will be far from shelter, and prepare accordingly.

### ACCOMMODATIONS AT BARR CAMP

Barr Camp offers four overnight accommodations for a fee by reservation, with a limited amount of bottled spring water available each day:

- A bunkhouse-style main cabin that sleeps 15 people
- Lean-to shelters, each of which sleeps 3 people
- Upper private cabins, each of which has three double beds, sleeps up to 12 people, and can be rented as a whole unit
- Tent sites within the Barr Camp perimeter

### 177 The Crags

PIKE NATIONAL FOREST

| | |
|---|---|
| **Distance** | 1–3.5 miles, out-and-back or loop |
| **Difficulty** | Easy–moderate |
| **Elevation Gain** | 800' (starting at 10,100') |
| **Trail Use** | Hiking, snowshoeing, option for kids, leashed dogs OK |
| **Agency** | Pikes Peak Ranger District, Pike National Forest |
| **Map(s)** | Trails Illustrated *Pikes Peak & Canon City* |
| **Facilities** | Restrooms |
| **Note(s)** | This is a fee area. |

**HIGHLIGHTS** The Crags are dramatic pinnacles, and the area—across from Mueller State Park—is ideal for hiking or scrambling on the back side of Pikes Peak. Hiking through the valley is worth the price of admission, and the view from atop one of the pinnacles is breathtaking in more ways than one. You can see the Sangre de Cristo Mountains in the distance, as well as the back side of Pikes Peak and the interesting landscape of Mueller State Park and Wildlife Area. You can choose a short, easy jaunt up the valley to the base of the rocks or a steep scramble to the summit. The trail rolls and climbs gradually to the base of the Crags. It is straight uphill steeply from there to summit a crag. The area often stays snowy, wet, or marshy until mid- to late July in normal snow years because of the elevation.

**DIRECTIONS** To reach the Crags Trailhead, take US 24 from Colorado Springs to Divide. From Divide turn south on CO 67 and drive 4 miles. Turn left on Forest Service Road 383, at a sign for the Crags Campground and Rocky Mountain Camp. The dirt road through the campground to the trailhead parking lot is narrow and deeply rutted. You can park at the old trailhead or the new one, which is another 0.5 mile.

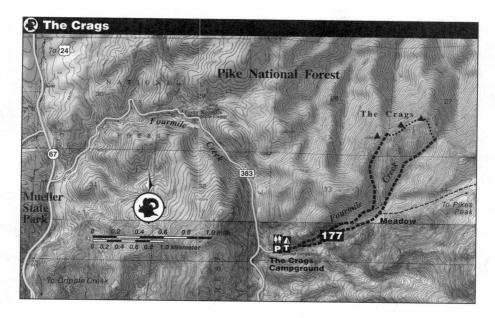

**The Crags**

Remember which trailhead you start from; on the way back you will need this information to know which fork to take in the trail, though if you make a mistake you can simply walk on the road back to the correct parking area. This description starts from the old (first) trailhead. The well-marked trail goes up a few steps out of the parking lot. Follow it about 100 yards and you will come to a fork with two options. You can go straight up the valley, enjoying views and warm sun all the way, or cross the creek and stay in the cool tree cover until you reach the base of the Crags. The left (straight) branch is more open with excellent views after the first 0.25 mile. The right branch is a little more direct for climbing a pinnacle but has fewer views. You could go up on one branch and return on the other for variety.

If it's hot and sunny and you want a tree-sheltered route, the latter choice is better, but the views are obscured. It has a short stretch of boulders that the trail circumvents. If you prefer the cool, deep forest green, look for a small footbridge and cross the creek on the right. Enjoy the streamside sounds and quaking aspens.

If you choose the left (straight) branch, you will have your first view of the Crags in just 0.25 mile. The trail then rolls and climbs and comes to a beautiful meadow area at approximately the 0.75-mile mark. From there the trail makes its way to the base of the Crags, an adequate destination for many. If you want to do a bit of climbing, reaching the top of the first ridgeline is rewarding because you get some views there. Use your judgment to determine whether to go all the way to a summit, based on how wet or dry the rock is and whether you feel like climbing straight uphill for a total of 3.5 miles.

*GREAT FOR KIDS*

If you want a casual excursion at The Crags or have kids along, bear left up the valley on the main trail. You will have excellent views of the Crags rock outcrops in 0.25 mile and be at the foot of beautiful meadows in 0.75 mile or so. There are many options for picnics, as long as it isn't too early in the summer, when it can still be wet or marshy.

## 178 What in a Name Trail

EL PASO COUNTY

| | |
|---|---|
| **Distance** | 0.25 mile, out-and-back |
| **Difficulty** | Easy |
| **Elevation Gain** | Negligible (starting at 9,600') |
| **Trail Use** | Hiking, snowshoeing, skiing, great for kids |
| **Agency** | Fox Run Regional Park, El Paso County |
| **Map(s)** | El Paso County *Fox Run Regional Park* |
| **Facilities** | The Roller Coaster Road trailhead at the north end of the park and the Fallen Timbers trailhead at the main entrance provide restrooms, parking, potable water, picnic units, and interpretive displays. |
| **Note(s)** | Dogs, horses, and bikes are prohibited because the trail is too short and heavily used. |

**HIGHLIGHTS**  Fox Run Regional Park is an easy outing. This heavily used, family-excursion trail is perfect for photography because of its view of Pikes Peak. Circle petite Spruce and Aspen Lakes for waterfowl and additional picnic options.

**DIRECTIONS**  From Colorado Springs drive north on I-25 and take the Monument exit. Take CO 105 east about 5 miles. Turn right onto Roller Coaster Road and take it south. You will pass signs for the park. Turn east (left) in Higby and then south back onto Roller Coaster Road. You reach the north trailhead on the west side of the road after about 2 miles. Though there's no prominent sign for the park, it is an obvious parking area.

To reach the main entrance and the Fallen Timbers trailhead, take I-25 to Exit 156A for Northgate Road. Turn east on Northgate Road and proceed 3.5 miles. Turn north on Roller Coaster Road and continue 1.5 miles to Stella Drive. From CO 83, go west on Northgate Road 0.5 mile and then north on Roller Coaster Road 1.5 miles to Stella Drive.

This trail is essentially an easy family outing, more of a stroll than a hike, and is probably the most heavily used trail in the park due to its easy access to parking. You can circle Spruce and Aspen Lakes, which are small but pretty. The trail features lots of interpretative signs discussing flora, fauna, geology, and history. Definitely plan to find a shady spot for a picnic, or use the tables in the picnic areas. On a clear day, you even enjoy a distant view of Pikes Peak.

*What in a Name Trail is great for kids.*

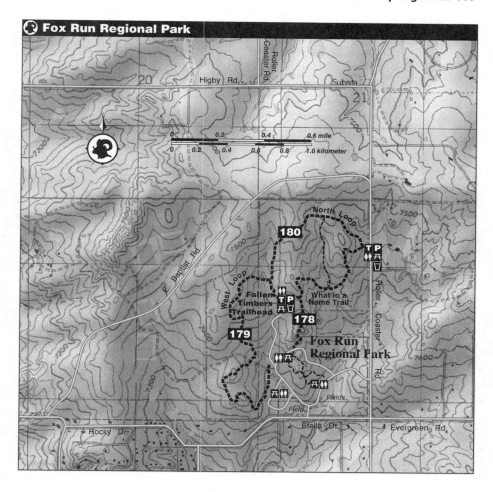

**Fox Run Regional Park**

---

**179**  **West Loop**

EL PASO COUNTY

|  |  |
|---|---|
| **Distance** | 2 miles, loop |
| **Difficulty** | Easy |
| **Elevation Gain** | 100'–200' (starting at 7,000') |
| **Trail Use** | Hiking, snowshoeing, skiing, great for kids, leashed dogs OK |
| **Agency** | Fox Run Regional Park, El Paso County |
| **Map(s)** | El Paso County *Fox Run Regional Park* |
| **Facilities** | The Roller Coaster Road trailhead at the north end of peaceful Fox Run Park and the Fallen Timbers trailhead at the main entrance provide restrooms, parking, potable water, picnic units, and interpretive displays. |

**HIGHLIGHTS** If you want an easy mountain biking or walking option with lots of shade in the thick "black" forest, this is a good one. You will enjoy rolling hills, thick fragrant ponderosa pines, and a view or two of Pikes Peak to the south. It is also possible, if you look carefully, to see red foxes, mule deer, Steller's jays, mountain chickadees, and nuthatches.

**DIRECTIONS** From Colorado Springs, drive north on I-25 and take the Monument exit. Take CO 105 east about 5 miles. Turn right onto Roller Coaster Road and take it south. You will pass signs for the park. Turn east (left) in Higby and then south back onto Roller Coaster Road. You reach the north trailhead on the west side of the road after about 2 miles. Though there's no prominent sign for the park, it is an obvious parking area.

To reach the main entrance and the Fallen Timbers trailhead, take I-25 to Exit 156A for Northgate Road. Turn east on Northgate Road and proceed 3.5 miles. Turn north on Roller Coaster Road and continue 1.5 miles to Stella Drive. From CO 83, go west on Northgate Road 0.5 mile and then north on Roller Coaster Road 1.5 miles to Stella Drive.

The West Loop trail rolls significantly but not steeply on its 2-mile circuit. It rolls in and out of the forested hills and provides a surface and terrain that is easy for beginner mountain bikers. You will enjoy a few glimpses of Pikes Peak along the way, and the forest is a real treat.

## 180   North Loop
### EL PASO COUNTY

see map on p. 359

| | |
|---|---|
| **Distance** | 2.3 miles, loop |
| **Difficulty** | Easy |
| **Elevation Gain** | Negligible (starting at 7,000') |
| **Trail Use** | Hiking, snowshoeing, skiing, great for kids, leashed dogs OK |
| **Agency** | Fox Run Regional Park, El Paso County |
| **Map(s)** | El Paso County *Fox Run Regional Park* |
| **Facilities** | The Roller Coaster Road trailhead at the north end of pretty Fox Run Park and the Fallen Timbers trailhead at the main entrance provide restrooms, parking, potable water, picnic units, and interpretive displays. |

**HIGHLIGHTS** Enjoy the ponderosa pines and tassel-eared squirrels, red foxes, mule deer, Steller's jays, mountain chickadees, and nuthatches that are residents of Fox Run Regional Park. This virtually flat trail is less intensely used than those on the south end of the park, so you are more likely to see wildlife and enjoy a bit of solitude.

**DIRECTIONS** From Colorado Springs, drive north on I-25 and take the Monument exit. Take CO 105 east about 5 miles. Turn right onto Roller Coaster Road and take it south. You will pass signs for the park. Turn east (left) in Higby and then south back onto Roller Coaster Road. You reach the north trailhead on the west side of the road after about 2 miles. Though there's no prominent sign for the park, it is an obvious parking area.

To reach the main entrance and the Fallen Timbers trailhead, take I-25 to Exit 156A for Northgate Road. Turn east on Northgate Road and proceed 3.5 miles. Turn north on Roller Coaster Road and continue 1.5 miles to Stella Drive. From CO 83, go west on Northgate Road 0.5 mile and then north on Roller Coaster Road 1.5 miles to Stella Drive.

This heavily forested trail offers stately ponderosa pines and is great for a family excursion with little kids or people not used to exertion and altitude. It features two adjoining, somewhat overlapping loops, each approximately 1 mile long, that you can cover in either order. You can cut the distance in half by using only one of the two adjoining loops. There is excellent shade on this trail.

## 181  Peak View, Elk Meadow, & Livery Loop

MUELLER STATE PARK

| | |
|---|---|
| **Distance** | 4 miles, loop |
| **Difficulty** | Moderate |
| **Elevation Gain** | 400' (starting at 9,600') |
| **Trail Use** | Hiking, snowshoeing, skiing, option for kids, leashed dogs OK |
| **Agency** | Mueller State Park |
| **Map(s)** | *Mueller State Park* |
| **Facilities** | Restrooms in campground |

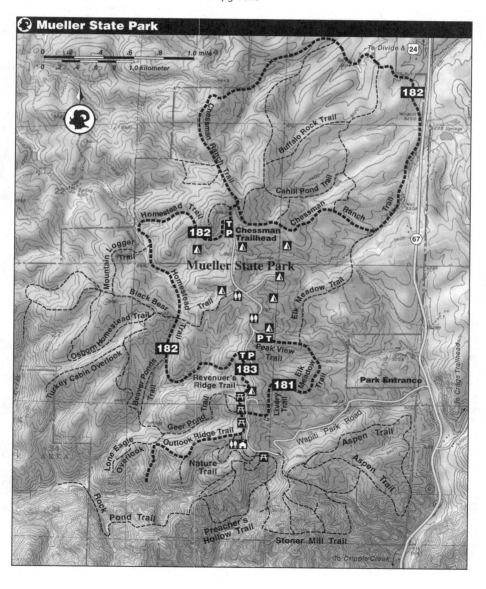

**HIGHLIGHTS** This trail (19) is near a campground popular for its great views of the western slopes of Pikes Peak. The easy-to-locate, well-marked trailhead features an open out-and-back trail that heads downhill (east) outbound and uphill (west) on the return, as do most of the trails in Mueller State Park.

**DIRECTIONS** Take CO 24 from Colorado Springs to Divide (25 miles). From Divide turn south onto CO 67 and drive approximately 4 miles. The park will be on the right.

Peak View Pond is visible on the right as you descend through the colorful mixture of aspen and pine trees. It is worth a short detour to get some close-up shots of the pond. The easiest and shortest route is to take the ridge down the gentle slope about 0.25 mile to the intersection with the Elk Meadow Trail.

If you are looking for a longer adventure, continue either north or south on the Elk Meadow Trail. If you take it south, it rolls gently and eventually climbs back uphill to the road, intersecting with the Livery Trail (20) and then meandering across the ridge to the Livery Trailhead. If you complete that loop, you go approximately 1.6 miles one-way. You are then about 0.5 mile from the Peak View Trailhead via the road.

*GREAT FOR KIDS*

This trail is good for short outings with kids. Just turn around at the intersection with Elk Meadow Trail, and then return to the trailhead. It's a pleasant 2-mile stroll.

---

**182   Homestead Trail**

MUELLER STATE PARK

see map on p. 361

| | |
|---|---|
| **Distance** | 2.5 miles, loop |
| **Difficulty** | Easy–moderate |
| **Elevation Gain** | 300' (starting at 9,600') |
| **Trail Use** | Hiking, snowshoeing, skiing, leashed dogs OK |
| **Agency** | Mueller State Park |
| **Map(s)** | *Mueller State Park* |
| **Facilities** | Restrooms in campground |

**HIGHLIGHTS** This aspen-lined trail can be covered as a loop or an out-and-back. Either way, you enjoy a fairly hilly trail that rolls, heading mostly downhill on the way out and uphill on the return, and you have good views of the Sangre de Cristo Mountains.

**DIRECTIONS** Take CO 24 from Colorado Springs to Divide (25 miles). From Divide turn south onto CO 67 and drive approximately 4 miles; the park will be on the right. There are three trailheads from Wapiti Park Road for this trail—two in the campground area and a third downhill from the campground entry station. When I scouted it, I started at the one near the entry station.

At the trailhead you see several options, with statistics listed for each. When you start from the campground entry area, go gradually downhill and immediately see the Revenuer's Ridge Trail traversing the ridge off to the left. It looks like a hiking trail, while the Homestead Trail is so wide that it looks more like a service road. If it is a clear day, the Sangre de Cristo Mountains are visible in the distance peeking through the trees. Descend fairly steeply to the wetland valley through a mixed aspen forest, cross the wetlands, and then climb up to the short ridge. The trail then rolls and intersects with Beaver Ponds Trail. When you top out, you are in a pretty grove of aspens—a good place for a snack or lunch. You then descend into another aspen-lined valley and intersect the Mount Logger Trail. The Grouse Mountain section is a great area to enjoy pine trees. An uphill climb brings you to the end of the campground road and the Chessman Trailhead.

## 183  Revenuer's Ridge

MUELLER STATE PARK

see map on p. 361

| | |
|---|---|
| **Distance** | 2.3 miles, out-and-back |
| **Difficulty** | Easy |
| **Elevation Gain** | 100' (starting at 9,600') |
| **Trail Use** | Hiking, snowshoeing, skiing, great for kids, leashed dogs OK |
| **Agency** | Mueller State Park |
| **Map(s)** | *Mueller State Park* |
| **Facilities** | Restrooms in campground |

**HIGHLIGHTS** Though this trail stays high for the most part, it descends into some beautiful meadows along the way. You will enjoy views in all directions. This is one of few trails in Mueller State Park that isn't a significant uphill on the way back, so it is ideal for families with small children or group members who are less ambitious. The trail has multiple easy-access points, making it possible to hike as much or as little of the trail as you wish.

**DIRECTIONS** Take CO 24 from Colorado Springs to Divide (25 miles). From Divide turn south onto CO 67 and drive approximately 4 miles. The park will be on the right.

Pick one of the trailheads along the road to access this trail: Black Bear is at Pisgah Point at the north end, near the camper services building; the Homestead Trail can be accessed 0.5 mile south; Geer Pond can be accessed 0.25 mile farther south; and the Outlook Ridge Trail, just south of the visitor center, is the southernmost access point.

If you start at the south end, near the visitor center, the trail stays high for 0.7 mile, paralleling the primary campground road, though the road is not visible. It then descends and crosses beautiful meadows and wetlands fringed by aspens. As it climbs gently out of the valley, it passes a striking rock formation and ends up near the camper services building.

## 184　Rainbow Gulch Trail to Rampart Reservoir

PIKE NATIONAL FOREST

| | |
|---|---|
| **Distance** | 3 miles to Rainbow Gulch, out-and-back; 11 miles to Rampart Reservoir, loop |
| **Difficulty** | Easy |
| **Elevation Gain** | 200' (starting at 9,000') |
| **Trail Use** | Hiking, mountain biking, fishing, camping, swimming, snowshoeing, option for kids, leashed dogs OK |
| **Agency** | Pikes Peak Ranger District, Pike National Forest |
| **Map(s)** | Trails Illustrated *Pikes Peak & Canon City* |
| **Facilities** | Restrooms, campgrounds, and picnic areas |

**HIGHLIGHTS** Easy access from Colorado Springs is the primary benefit of this recreational area. The reservoir is also in a beautiful foothills and mountain setting, with giant granite boulders; aspen, fir, and spruce trees; sun-drenched hillsides; and good views of Pikes Peak in the distance. The trail is great for children and novice mountain bikers because it rolls gently and has no challenging terrain. You will find that there are sections where you'll have to walk your bike to get around the picturesque boulders.

**DIRECTIONS** From Colorado Springs take CO 24 west 17 miles to Woodland Park. Stay on the highway 3 miles; when you see the sign for Rampart Reservoir, turn right at McDonald's onto Loy Creek Road (Forest Service Road 393). Follow the reservoir signs to Rampart Range Road and turn right. Take it 2.5 miles south to Rainbow Gulch Road.

The Rainbow Gulch Trail is a gently sloping trail that takes you to the shoreline of the reservoir. The trail starts in a ponderosa pine forest and then opens up into a meadow before joining the trail around the lake. You can take the Rampart Reservoir Trail either due east on the south side of the reservoir or northeast to the north side of the reservoir. In either direction, the trail is essentially the same—gently rolling with some rocky sections. You will come to trail intersections at times for side trails to picnic areas, campgrounds, or parking lots. When these options arise, turn toward the reservoir to stay on the main trail.

### GREAT FOR KIDS

The beauty of visiting this reservoir is the variety of short family hike options. Take a look at the map available at the reservoir, and pick a section that has a picnic area. Decide on a short out-and-back that includes a place to have a snack or lunch in a picnic area. Then bring along a snack, and use the picnic area as your turnaround point.

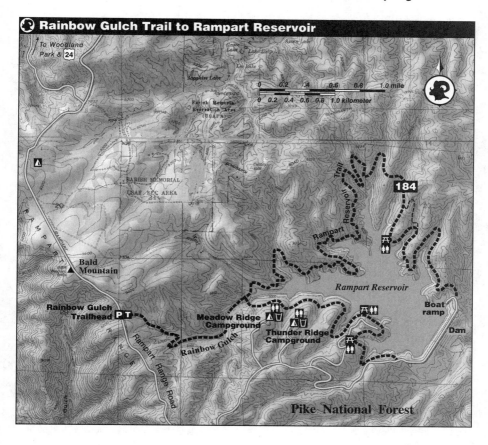

Rainbow Gulch Trail to Rampart Reservoir

# Best Trails for . . .

## Mountain Biking

## Mountain Summits

# Recommended Reading

Abbey, Edward. *Desert Solitaire: A Season in the Wilderness.* New York: Ballantine Books, 1990 (reprint).

Apt, Alan R. *Snowshoe Routes: Colorado's Front Range, 2nd Ed.* Golden, CO: Colorado Mountain Club Press, 2011.

The Colorado Trail Foundation. *The Colorado Trail, 8th Ed.* Golden, CO: Colorado Mountain Club Press, 2010.

Dziezynski, James. *Best Summit Hikes in Colorado, 2nd Ed.* Birmingham, AL: Wilderness Press, 2012.

Ells, James. *Rocky Mountain Flora, 2nd Ed.* Golden, CO: Colorado Mountain Club Press, 2011.

Foster, Lisa. *Rocky Mountain National Park: The Complete Hiking Guide.* Estes Park, CO: Renaissance Mountaineering, 2013.

Grim, Joe, and Frédérique Grim. *Comanche Peak Wilderness Area: Hiking & Snowshoeing Guide.* Golden, CO: Colorado Mountain Club Press, 2010.

Jacobs, Randy, ed., with Robert M. Ormes. *Guide to the Colorado Mountains, 10th Ed.* Golden, CO: Colorado Mountain Club Press, 2000.

*Mountaineering: The Freedom of the Hills, 8th Ed.* Seattle: Mountaineers Books, 2010.

Roach, Gerry. *Colorado's Fourteeners: From Hikes to Climbs, 3rd Ed.* Golden, CO: Fulcrum Publishing, 2011.

Turnbaugh, Kay. *Around Nederland.* Charleston, SC: Arcadia Publishing, 2011.

Turnbaugh, Kay, and Brooks, David (illustrator). *The Mountain Pine Beetle—Tiny but Mighty.* Boulder, CO: Westwinds Press, 2011.

Work, James C. *Windmills, the River & Dust: One Man's West.* Boulder, CO: Johnson Books, 2005.

# Agencies & Information Sources

## COLORADO STATE PARKS

Individual park websites can be accessed at **cpw.state.co.us**.

### COLORADO STATE FOREST
**cpw.state.co.us/placestogo/parks/stateforest**
56750 CO 14
Walden, CO 80480
970-723-8366

### ELDORADO CANYON STATE PARK
**cpw.state.co.us/placestogo/parks/eldoradocanyon**
9 Kneale Road, Box B
Eldorado Springs, CO 80025
303-494-3943

### GOLDEN GATE CANYON STATE PARK
**cpw.state.co.us/placestogo/parks/goldengatecanyon**
92 Crawford Gulch Road
Golden, CO 80403
303-582-3707

### LORY STATE PARK
**cpw.state.co.us/placestogo/parks/lory**
708 Lodgepole Drive
Bellvue, CO 80512
970-493-1623

### MUELLER STATE PARK
**cpw.state.co.us/placestogo/parks/mueller**
21045 CO 67 S.
Divide, CO 80814
719-687-2366

### ROXBOROUGH STATE PARK
**cpw.state.co.us/placestogo/parks/roxborough**
4751 N. Roxborough Drive
Littleton, CO 80125
303-973-3959

## NATIONAL FORESTS & PARKS

For general information about the Rocky Mountain region of the U.S. Forest Service, visit **www.fs.fed.us/r2**.

### ARAPAHO AND ROOSEVELT NATIONAL FORESTS
**www.fs.usda.gov/arp;** 970-295-6600

- *Boulder Ranger District*
  2140 Yarmouth Ave.
  Boulder, CO 80301
  303-541-2500

- *Canyon Lakes Ranger District*
  2150 Centre Ave., Bldg. E
  Fort Collins, CO 80526
  970-295-6700

- *Clear Creek Ranger District*
  101 CO 103/Chicago Creek Road
  Idaho Springs, CO 80452
  303-567-3000

- *Sulphur Ranger District*
  9 Ten Mile Drive
  Granby, CO 80446
  970-887-4100

### PIKE AND SAN ISABEL NATIONAL FORESTS
**www.fs.usda.gov/psicc**
2840 Kachina Drive
Pueblo, CO 81008
719-553-1400

- *Pikes Peak Ranger District*
  601 S. Weber St.
  Colorado Springs, CO 80903
  719-636-1602

- *South Park Ranger District*
  320 US 285
  Fairplay, CO 80440
  719-836-2031

WHITE RIVER NATIONAL FOREST
www.fs.fed.us/r2/whiteriver
900 Grand Ave.
Glenwood Springs, CO 81602
970-319-2670

- *Dillon Ranger District*
  680 Blue River Parkway
  Silverthorne, CO 80498
  970-468-5400

ROCKY MOUNTAIN NATIONAL PARK
nps.gov/romo
1000 US 36
Estes Park, CO 80517
**Visitor Information:** 970-586-1206
**Visitor Information Recorded Message:** 970-586-1333
**Visitor Information for the Hearing Impaired (TTY):**
970-586-1319
**Backcountry Office:** 970-586-1242
**Campground Reservations:** 877-444-6777

## WEATHER FORECASTS

As mentioned elsewhere, mountain weather is volatile and highly variable. For up-to-date forecasts and warnings, visit **weather.gov.**

## HUTS & YURTS

NEVER SUMMER NORDIC, INC.
neversummernordic.com
247 County Road 41
Walden, CO 80480
970-723-4070

**10TH MOUNTAIN DIVISION HUTS**
huts.org
1280 Ute Ave., Ste. 21
Aspen, CO 81611
970-925-5775

APPENDIX 3

# Conservation & Hiking Groups

## THE BACKCOUNTRY SNOWSPORTS ALLIANCE

The Backcountry Snowsports Alliance represents winter backcountry users and advocates the preservation of nonmotorized areas on public lands. For more information, visit **backcountryinitiative.blogspot.com.**

## THE COLORADO FOURTEENERS INITIATIVE

The 54 mountains that comprise the 14,000-foot summits in Colorado have been affected by the millions of people who climb them. The Colorado Fourteeners Initiative helps protect and preserve the trails and natural beauty of Colorado's fourteeners. You can volunteer by visiting **14ers.org.**

## COLORADO MOUNTAIN CLUB

The club sponsors outings, conservation, and education year-round throughout the state, all of which are open to members and nonmembers. For local chapter and statewide activities, visit **cmc.org.**

## COLORADO SPECIAL OLYMPICS

Special Olympics volunteers in Colorado assist with hiking, camping, cycling, skiing, and snowshoeing. For more information, visit the group online at **specialolympicsco.org** or at 410 17th St., Ste. 200, Denver, CO 80202. You can also call the group at 303-592-1361.

## COLORADO TRAIL FOUNDATION

The Colorado Trail stretches almost 500 miles from Denver to Durango. The Colorado Trail Foundation (CTF) organized the volunteers who built the Colorado Trail and continues to improve and maintain it. Enjoy the trail through the Adopt-A-Trail program, and help with maintenance. To volunteer, visit **coloradotrail.org.**

## DIAMOND PEAKS SKI PATROL

The patrol is affiliated with the National Ski Patrol, and volunteers patrol trails in the upper Poudre Canyon. For more information, visit **diamondpeaks.org.**

## EDUCO

EDUCO offers outdoor experiences for children of all ages. For more information, visit **educoadventures.org.**

## THE NATURE CONSERVANCY

The Nature Conservancy has preserved 600,000 acres in Colorado. Guided tours of some of the areas are offered. To find out more about the group's work in Colorado, visit **nature.org/ourinitiatives/regions /northamerica/unitedstates/colorado.**

## POUDRE WILDERNESS VOLUNTEERS

Trail volunteers with this group patrol the upper Poudre Canyon for the U.S. Forest Service. For more information, visit **pwv.org.**

## ROCKY MOUNTAIN CONSERVANCY

The Rocky Mountain Conservancy (RMC) supports the wilderness character of Rocky Mountain National Park (RMNP). RMC sponsors a variety of nature seminars and field trips, which are listed at **rmconservancy.org.** Donations to RMC help RMNP with resource protection, capital construction, historical preservation, and education. Gifts are 100% tax deductible. Call the group at 970-586-0108, or visit it at 48 Alpine Cir. in Estes Park.

## ROCKY MOUNTAIN SIERRA CLUB

The Sierra Club sponsors a wide variety of outings and presentations year-round, open to members and nonmembers. There are local chapters throughout Colorado. Visit the Rocky Mountain Chapter online at **sierraclub.org/rocky-mountain-chapter,** or contact it at 1536 Wynkoop St., Fourth Floor, Denver, CO 80202 or at 303-861-8819.

## SAVE THE POUDRE

This organization has been fighting to protect and preserve the Poudre River for years. It is currently opposing the destructive Glade Reservoir project. Visit **savethepoudre.org.**

## WILDLANDS RESTORATION
## VOLUNTEERS

Wildlands Restoration Volunteers is a nonprofit organization that provides an opportunity for people to come together, learn about their natural environment, and take direct action to restore and care for the land. For more information, visit **wlrv.org.**

## WOMEN'S WILDERNESS INSTITUTE

The Women's Wilderness Institute offers wilderness courses, ranging from backpacking to rock climbing, for women and girls age 12 and up. For more information about the courses and the institute, visit **womenswilderness.org.**

# Index

INDEX

# About the Authors

Photographed by Nancy Martin

**A**lan Apt has been roaming Colorado's hills and dales for more than 30 years. He is the author of the best-selling guidebook *Snowshoe Routes: Colorado's Front Range*. He is a somewhat reformed peak bagger who has climbed many of the state's highest summits but also thoroughly enjoys the lakes, vales, and rivers. Alan is an avid hiker, biker, snowshoer, backcountry skier, kayaker, and backpacker and has trekked in the Andes, Alps, Himalayas, and Sierra Nevada.

Alan is a member of the Colorado Mountain Club and a Sierra Club trip leader, as well as a member of Friends of the Poudre. He is a former Fort Collins city council member and worked to create the city's Wind Power Program. He also served on the city's Natural Resources Board. He is a National Ski Patrol volunteer member with the Bryan Mountain Nordic Ski Patrol. Formerly a technical book publisher, he is now a freelance writer and editor living in Nederland, Colorado.

**K**ay Turnbaugh, an avid hiker, mountain biker, road biker, snowshoer, and skier, has lived in the small mountain town of Nederland, Colorado, for almost all of her adult life. She was the editor and publisher of *The Mountain-Ear*, an award-winning weekly newspaper in Nederland, for 27 years. She has written three books: *The Mountain Pine Beetle—Tiny but Mighty*, a book for 8- to 12-year-olds that is also enjoyed by many adults; *Around Nederland*, a book about Nederland's history; and *The Last of the Wild West Cowgirls*, a biography of Goldie Griffith, who rode bucking broncos for Buffalo Bill, trained war dogs, ranched near Nederland, ran restaurants, and reinvented herself whenever necessary. *The Last of the Wild West Cowgirls* won a Willa Literary Award in 2010 for creative nonfiction.

Photographed by Bill Ikler

Visit the book's Facebook page at **facebook.com/coloradofrontrangetrails**.